Eckard's Principles of Civil Procedure in the Magistrates' Courts

Eckard's Principles of Civil Procedure in the Magistrates' Courts

Dr Theo Broodryk
BA LLB LLD (Stell)

JUTA

First Edition 1984
Second Edition 1990
Third Edition 1996
Fourth Edition 2001
Reprinted 2003
Fifth Edition 2005
Reprinted April 2007
Reprinted December 2009
Reprinted July 2010
Reprinted December 2011
Reprinted August 2012
Second Impression 2012
Third Impression 2012
Reprinted May 2015
Reprinted June 2016
Sixth Edition 2019

© Juta and Company (Pty) Ltd
First Floor,
Sunclare Building,
21 Dreyer Street,
Claremont 7708

The author and the publisher believe on the strength of due diligence exercised that this work does not contain any material that is the subject of copyright held by another person. In the alternative, they believe that any protected preexisting material that may be comprised in it has been used with the appropriate authority or has been used in circumstances that made such use permissible by law.

Although every care is taken to ensure the accuracy of this publication, supplements, updates and replacement material, the authors, editors, publishers and printers do not accept responsibility for any act, omission, loss, damage or the consequences thereof occasioned by a reliance by any person upon the contents hereof.

ISBN 978 1 48513 363 6

SET IN 11 ON 12 POINT TIMES ROMAN BY HELANNA TYPESETTERS

PREFACE TO THE SIXTH EDITION

The First Edition of this work was published in 1984. This is the Sixth Edition since then. In the Preface to the First Edition Eckard stated the purpose of the work:

> . . . I have again come to realize that articled clerks, advocates serving pupillage and senior students frequently require a work which explains in substance how the principles of civil procedure are applied in practice.

That the work has lived for so long is testimony to the value of the original conception. More practical training is now given to junior students than in 1984. In the result, the work is perhaps most useful to university students making their first encounter with civil procedure in the lower courts.

Since the previous edition numerous changes to the Act and Rules have been effected. In fact, there have been changes over the entire spectrum of civil litigation in the lower courts, most recently brought about by the Courts of Law Amendment Act 7 of 2017. This edition attempts to present the law as at 1 November 2018.

ACKNOWLEDGEMENTS

The size of the project necessitated that I rely on the input and support of various individuals.

I am grateful:

Marlene, for your unconditional love and support.

David, for your encouragement and reinforcement.

My family, for always being there.

Steve, for your extremely efficient and capable handling of the project.

Marlinee, for entrusting me with this esteemed work.

Stephan, for being a sounding board.

SU Law Faculty, for enabling me.

CONTENTS

TABLE OF CASES

N

ALPHABETICAL LIST OF SUBJECTS AND SECTIONS

(Adapted from arrangements of sections of the Magistrates' Courts Act 32 of 1944 as amended. References are to the sections of the Act.)

NUMERICAL LIST OF RELEVANT SECTIONS OF THE MAGISTRATES' COURTS ACT 32 OF 1944

NUMERICAL LIST OF RELEVANT RULES
OF THE MAGISTRATES' COURTS

Numerical List of Relevant Forms Appearing in Annexure 1 to the Rules

ALPHABETICAL LIST OF SUBJECTS AND RULES

(Adapted from the schedule to the rules promulgated in terms of the Magistrates' Courts Act 32 of 1944 in RGN 740, Government Gazette No. 33487 of 23 August 2010. References are to the rules.)

ALPHABETICAL LIST OF EXAMPLES

References are to page numbers.

Chapter 1

HISTORICAL REVIEW

The first traces of magistrates' courts in South Africa are to be found in the dim and distant past. As early as 1682, ie barely 30 years after the first Dutch settlers arrived at the Cape, a court known as the *Commissarissen van Kleinen Zaken* was established. Little is known about this court, however, and it has clearly not had much influence upon the later development of our court hierarchy.[1]

The development of the lower courts began really with the establishment of local management boards known as *Landdrost en Heemraden* which acted also as courts of law, hearing minor civil and criminal cases.[2] The procedure before these courts was informal and the parties conducted their cases in person unless prevented by sickness or other sufficient cause from doing so.

Appeals lay from the courts of *Landdrost en Heemraden* to the *Raad van Justitie* in Cape Town. This *Raad van Justitie* sat as a court of law as early as 1656, but in reality was more a branch of the governing body in the early Cape, the *Raad van Politie*, than a court of law.

In 1795 the Cape was occupied by Britain for the first time. The English introduced a Court of Justice to deal with the administration of justice, but the existing court procedures were retained and the system of administration of justice as it stood under the Dutch authorities remained almost entirely unchanged during this period.

In 1803 the first British Occupation came to an end and the Cape was again handed over to the Netherlands, known then as the Batavian Republic. At this time Commissioner-General De Mist visited the Cape to investigate the administration in the colony and decided, as part of his reform plans, inter alia to have new rules of court drawn up for the *Landdrost en Heemraden*.

In 1806, however, Britain again occupied the Cape and few of De Mist's proposed reforms came to pass. From this time onward the existing courts fell increasingly under the influence of English procedural rules and in 1825–6 English became the language medium used in the courts.

In 1827 the Charter of Justice was adopted which set the final pattern for the development of all the subsequent South African courts. The whole idea was to organise the courts and court procedure along typically English lines.

English influence became prevalent from this period onward and in 1830 Ordinance 72 was enacted, stipulating that the English rules of civil procedure were to apply in the courts. The courts of *Landdrost en Heemraden* were replaced by a system of 'residential magistrates'. The jurisdiction of these magistrates' courts was limited in regard to both the amount and the nature of the matter that

---

[1] It is interesting to note that 300 years later, on 19 April 1984, the Small Claims Courts Act 61 of 1984 was assented to.

[2] C Graham Botha 'The Early Inferior Courts of Justice at the Cape' (1921) 38 *SALJ* 406.

could be tried. The first vestiges of the present system of lower courts in the Republic became more clearly discernible at this time—both the title 'magistrate' and the fact that limitations as to amounts and causes of action were placed upon the jurisdiction of these 'magistrates' courts'.

The law of procedure of the magistrates' courts in the Cape served for a very long time as the model for the civil procedure used in the lower courts that were in existence in the other regions of southern Africa at the end of the last century.

In Natal the first magistrate's court came into being in 1846. The originally restricted civil jurisdiction of the lower courts in Natal was gradually expanded but, in line with the typical pattern of the lower courts, limitations were always placed upon their jurisdiction.

Further north, in the Voortrekker republics, the lower courts were originally modelled on different lines to the court of *Landdrost en Heemraden* that existed under the Dutch administration in the Cape. In this regard the code proposed by De Mist in 1805 exercised considerable influence. But English influence was still discernible in the fact that limitations upon jurisdiction (which played a large role in the English legal system) were found in the court of *Landdrost en Heemraden* of those republics in certain cases.

After the British annexation of the Orange Free State in 1848, that colony's courts of *Landdrost en Heemraden* bore a considerable similarity to the magistrates' courts already in existence at that time in Natal.

During the years of independence of the Orange Free State Republic, the lower court structure consisted of courts on two tiers. On the lower tier there was a *landdrost* with limited jurisdiction and above him a court consisting of the *landdrost* and two of the six *heemraden* of the district.

As was the case in the South African Republic, the *landdroste* had no formal legal education and functioned as both judicial and administrative officials.

The law of civil procedure in the lower courts of the Orange Free State was strongly influenced by the law of civil procedure applicable in the magistrates' courts of the Cape.

In the Transvaal (the South African Republic), a court of *Landdrost en Heemraden* was established by the constitution of 1858. In some instances the jurisdiction of this court (depending upon the number of *heemraden* sitting as members) is strongly reminiscent of the jurisdiction of the present-day South African High Court. In other ways the court fulfilled the same functions as the magistrates' courts of the Cape and Natal.

In 1874, rules of civil procedure modelled on the law of civil procedure applicable in the Cape were adopted.

During the British annexation of the Transvaal (1877–81) the court procedure followed under the South African Republic was left intact.

After the battle of Amajuba and the termination of the British Occupation in 1881, changes were made to the constitution of the superior courts. The existing structure of *landdroste* was, however, retained, though the jurisdiction of the lower courts was increased.

In both independent Boer republics the law of civil procedure in the lower courts bore strong similarities to the English law of procedure applied in the magistrates' courts of the Cape and Natal.

After the Second Anglo-Boer War, the British in 1902 introduced a large number of changes in the conquered Boer republics.

A new supreme court was established in the Transvaal and the old structure of the lower courts with their *landdroste* was replaced by magistrates' courts similar to those already in existence in the Cape and Natal. The language medium employed in the courts was originally English, but in a number of specially proclaimed magistrates' courts the use of Dutch as a language medium was permitted from 1908. The law of civil procedure was, however, structured entirely along English lines.[3]

Between the Treaty of Vereeniging in 1902 and the establishment of the Union in 1910 each colony had its own system of magistrates' courts. This state of affairs persisted after Union, until the first Magistrates' Courts Act 32 of 1917 introduced a uniform lower court structure and a concomitant law of civil procedure.

The present Magistrates' Courts Act 32 of 1944 was signed in Afrikaans on 16 May 1944 by the Officer Administering the Government and came into operation on 2 July 1945. Although the Act has been amended many times since, its basic principles have remained unchanged.

Magistrates' courts are divided into district and regional courts.[4] In terms of the provisions of s 2 of the Act, the Minister of Justice and Correctional Services has the power, inter alia, to create magisterial districts and regional divisions, to determine the limits of each district and regional division, to establish courts for those districts and regional divisions, and to appoint seats of magistracy within them.[5]

District courts exercise civil and criminal jurisdiction. Previously, the regional magistrates' courts only possessed jurisdiction over criminal matters. However, since 15 October 2010, regional divisions also possess jurisdiction over certain civil disputes.[6]

The Magistrates' Courts Rules[7] embody the procedure that should be followed in the magistrates' courts. Whereas the Magistrates' Courts Act may only be amended by Parliament, the rules may be amended or repealed by a statutory body

---

[3] On 31 March 2017, the Heads of Courts Forum resolved that English must be the official language of record in both criminal and civil cases in all courts in the Republic of South Africa. To date, no national directive has been issued by the Office of the Chief Justice to this effect.

[4] Section 1 of the Magistrates' Courts Act defines 'court' to mean 'a magistrate's court for any district or for any regional division'.

[5] Magisterial districts are in the process of being rationalised to ensure alignment with municipal boundaries and to increase access to justice. Regarding Gauteng and North West, see GN 43 in *GG* 37258 of 24 January 2014, and regarding Mpumalanga and Limpopo, see GN 32 and 33 in *GG* 39601 of 15 January 2016. See also, regarding KwaZulu-Natal, GN 407 in *GG* 41552 of 29 March 2018, and regarding Eastern Cape, GN 406 in *GG* 41552 of 29 March 2018. Regarding the areas of jurisdiction of offices of sheriffs in the lower courts, see GN 959 in *GG* 41092 of 4 September 2017. See also GN 670 in *GG* 33418 of 29 July 2010 regarding the establishment of certain regional courts.

[6] Jurisdiction of Regional Courts Amendment Act 31 of 2008. See also the Magistrates' Courts Amendment Act 19 of 2010 which, inter alia, regulates the inclusion of magistrates of regional divisions on the list of magistrates who may adjudicate civil disputes.

[7] The Rules Regulating the Conduct of the Proceedings of the Magistrates' Courts of South Africa are published under GN R740 in *GG* 33487 of 23 August 2010 (with effect from 15 October 2010), as amended.

called the Rules Board for Courts of Law, established by the Rules Board for Courts of Law Act 107 of 1985, which came into operation on 20 February 1987. In terms of s 3 of that Act, the Rules Board consists of the following members appointed by the Minister:

(1) a current or former judge of the High Court, the Supreme Court of Appeal or the Constitutional Court as chairman;

(2) a current or former judge of the High Court, the Supreme Court of Appeal or the Constitutional Court as vice-chairman;

(3) a regional and a district magistrate;

(4) two practising advocates selected in consultation with the General Council of the Bar;

(5) two practising attorneys selected in consultation with the Association of Law Societies;[8]

(6) a lecturer in law at a university in the Republic;

(7) an officer of the Department of Justice;

(8) not more than two persons who, in the opinion of the Minister, have the necessary expertise to serve as members of the Rules Board; and

(9) a sheriff appointed in terms of the Sheriffs Act 90 of 1986 who is nominated by the South African Board for Sheriffs.

In terms of s 6, the Rules Board is empowered to review the existing rules of court on a regular basis and, subject to the approval of the Minister, to make, amend or repeal rules of court regulating a wide range of matters, including the practice of and procedure for litigation; the form, contents and use of process; the execution of process; writs and warrants; the procedure for the giving of security and the tariff of fees chargeable by legal practitioners.

No new rule or amendment or repeal of a rule may come into operation unless it has been published in the *Gazette* at least one month before the day upon which the rule, amendment or repeal is expressed to take effect.[9]

It must always be borne in mind, however, that the amendments are usually only of a technical nature and do not modify the clearly established principles of the law of civil procedure in the magistrates' courts.

It is these principles with which this book deals.

---

[8] See the brief discussion in chapter 3 below regarding the introduction of a Legal Practice Council as the new singular regulatory body of the South African legal profession.

[9] Section 6(4).

Chapter 2

GENERAL COMMENTS ON PROCEDURAL LAW

The law can be divided into substantive and procedural or adjectival law.

Substantive law is the body of generally accepted, binding legal norms which apply to society and which regulate it. This body of law defines the content of the legal rights and duties which exist between legal subjects, and their relationship to things.

Procedural law, on the other hand, is that body of legal rules which determines how such rights and duties are protected and enforced within the community. The courts are the chief means of such protection and enforcement. It is of vital importance to society that disputes are resolved peacefully, and without citizens' taking the law into their own hands. Procedural law is therefore fundamental to the well-being of society. Aggrieved persons need to feel assured of speedy access to the dispute-resolution processes set up by society, and, once access has been gained, that they will be given a proper hearing. Only in this way will all involved in the dispute accept the decision and feel that their substantive rights are being upheld by the courts. It is, of course, a truism that a substantive right is worthless without the ability to protect or enforce it. Indeed, the aggrieved person who has no remedy is doubly aggrieved, because his substantive and procedural rights are both rendered nugatory. Seen in this light, the division between substantive and procedural law is somewhat artificial, and it is not surprising that the revision of our procedural law is just as political a question as the revision of other branches of the law.

The purpose of procedural law is to do justice between the parties.[1] Every decision in civil procedure revolves around this principle. Where strict compliance with a procedural rule is required, it is because anything less will potentially disadvantage the other party, and, where an indulgence is asked for, it will be granted only if there is no prejudice to the other side. It is always possible for practitioners to attempt to use the rules to gain a procedural advantage over their adversaries, and within certain limits there can be no objection to this. But the court will be loath to allow a litigant to use the procedure to thwart the proper ventilation of the issues between the parties.[2]

Procedural law sets up the bodies which offer official adjudication of disputes. Persons with disputes may turn to other avenues of dispute resolution. For instance, the legislature provides the means by which parties may submit disputes

---

[1] See *Whittaker v Roos & another* 1911 TS 1092 at 1102.

[2] As to whether the magistrate's court has the power to prevent an abuse of its process, see Jones & Buckle Rules 1–9.

to arbitration.[3] This present work, however, is concerned only with how disputes are resolved in the lower courts.

There are certain common procedural principles at work in the lower courts. They are creatures of statute, and, unlike the High Court, have no inherent jurisdiction.[4] In each instance the law establishes the court and its officers, and provides for its jurisdiction. The jurisdiction is limited with respect to the cause of action, the type of remedy being sought and, if an order for the payment of money is sought, its quantum. The procedure for placing a dispute before the court is defined, as is the process whereby the court adjudicates upon the dispute.

Because of the similarity between the civil procedure of the magistrates' courts and that of the High Court, authorities on the procedure of the High Court can be binding on the interpretation of the rules governing the magistrates' courts. At every stage of this work such authorities will be referred to, and students and practitioners are warned and encouraged always to look beyond the rules of the magistrates' courts to the practice in the High Court.

Especially because of the increased jurisdiction of the magistrates' courts, many cases previously heard in the High Court only are heard in the lower courts. This provides a challenge to all practitioners and presiding officers to ensure that the same standards that are currently in existence in the High Court are maintained in the lower courts.

The rules of the magistrate's court have the authority of subordinate legislation. The purpose of the rules is 'to secure the inexpensive and expeditious completion of litigation between the parties'.[5] Although the rules have to be complied with, the court has power to condone certain departures from the rules by virtue of rule 60. The court will also be generous in its interpretation of the rules.

---

[3] See the Arbitration Act 42 of 1965 and the International Arbitration Act 15 of 2017.
[4] Jones & Buckle Act 77.
[5] See Jones & Buckle Rules 1–9 and cases cited there.

Chapter 3

COURT PERSONNEL, MEDIATION, AND LEGISLATIVE DEVELOPMENTS

The country is divided into many magisterial districts, each of which is served by a particular magistrate's court (commonly referred to as district courts). A number of magistrates' courts for regional divisions (commonly referred to as regional courts) have also been established to deal with civil matters.

In this chapter the staff which are common to the magistrates' courts are discussed. Thereafter, the small claims court and court-annexed mediation are considered. Recent legislative developments will also be mentioned in so far as they may be relevant to civil procedure in the magistrates' courts.

1 THE REGISTRAR AND CLERK OF THE COURT

No court can function without efficient administration. The official responsible for this administration in the district court is the registrar or clerk of the court. He or she, and as many assistants as are necessary, is appointed by the magistrate of the district.[1] The equivalent official in the regional court is the registrar.[2] The Director-General of the Department of Justice and Constitutional Development appoints for each regional division a registrar and so many assistant registrars as may be necessary. Rule 13A(4) provides that '[a]ny reference in any law to a "clerk of the court" is, in so far as that law relates to a court of a regional division, deemed to be a reference to the registrar or assistant registrar of that regional division'. These officials are the equivalent of the registrar of the High Court.

Civil procedure is dependent on the processing of many documents, and the registrar and clerk's chief functions are the receiving and recording of these documents and the issuing of processes of the court. In so doing, there are occasions in which he or she has to exercise an administrative discretion which has

---

[1] Section 13(1).
[2] Section 13A.

to be exercised in accordance with the powers vested in him or her. A refusal by the registrar or clerk of the court to perform his or her duties is subject to review by the court.[3] The rules applicable to the review of administrative acts in general will apply.

The chief duties of the registrar and clerk include the following:

(1) the issuing of summonses[4] and of other processes such as subpoenas and warrants of arrest and execution, all of which have to be signed by the registrar or clerk;[5]

(2) receiving all pleadings and notices in connection with cases and filing them of record;[6]

(3) the safekeeping of the records, the supervising of public access to the records and the making of copies of the court records;[7]

(4) notifying the plaintiff forthwith in writing:
    (a) of the defendant's consent to judgment before entry of appearance to defend;
    (b) of a defective entry of appearance to defend entered by a defendant who is not represented by an attorney, and in what respect such entry of appearance is defective; and
    (c) of the refusal of an application for a judgment by default;[8]

(5) noting on a certified copy of a judgment at the request of the party to whom such copy is issued:
    (a) particulars of any other judgment by the court in that matter; and
    (b) any costs incurred after judgment and payable by the judgment debtor;[9]

(6) receiving any fines payable in terms of an order of the court;[10]

(7) taxing bills of costs;[11] and

(8) compiling the court roll.[12]

2 THE SHERIFF

The Sheriffs Act 90 of 1986, which became operative on 1 March 1990, renamed the previous messengers of the court sheriffs.[13] Anything in any law which refers to a messenger now refers to the sheriff appointed for the magistrate's court.[14] The

---

[3] Sections 13(2) and 13A(3).

[4] Rule 3(2), (3) and (4) provides that the first document in a case is given a case number, under which all subsequent documents are filed. This first document may not be a summons in the case of the particular debt-collecting procedure established by ss 57 and 58 of the Act. See in this connection rule 4.

[5] Rule 3(1).

[6] Rule 3(3) and (4).

[7] Section 7(1) and rule 3(5).

[8] Rule 3(6).

[9] Rule 3(7)(a).

[10] Rule 3(11).

[11] Rule 34(3)(a).

[12] There are other duties as well; for example, the duties of the clerk in the context of court-annexed mediation (discussed below).

[13] Section 64(2).

[14] Section 65.

Minister of Justice, after considering the report of an advisory committee, appoints sheriffs or deputy sheriffs.[15] In certain circumstances, the Minister may appoint sheriffs only after consultation with the advisory committee and the Board of Sheriffs.[16] Sheriffs may be appointed for either the lower or superior courts, or for both.[17] The sheriff has jurisdiction only within the area for which he or she is appointed.[18] Any act performed outside that area would therefore be void. A High Court may authorise a sheriff to attach property found outside his or her area of jurisdiction.[19] If there is no sheriff appointed in any area, the sheriff's duties may be performed by the police.[20] A sheriff may not perform, or engage himself or herself to perform, remunerative work outside his or her office as sheriff without the approval of the Minister.[21]

The Sheriffs Act requires every sheriff to open and keep a separate trust account. The Act provides details regarding the management of such trust accounts.[22]

The State is not liable for any loss or damage arising out of any act of omission by a sheriff or his or her deputy.[23] Instead, a Fidelity Fund is established by the Act.[24] This fund is liable for any loss or damage which is the result of the failure of a sheriff to pay out monies, or as a result of an act or omission in connection with the service or execution of any process or the arrest of any person.[25]

When a charge of improper conduct is laid against a sheriff, he or she may be suspended by the Minister pending the institution of the inquiry laid out in the Sheriffs Act.[26]

The duties of the sheriff are set out in the Acts governing the courts to which he or she is appointed.

The sheriff is the executive officer of the court. He or she executes the orders and carries out the instructions of the court. The duties relate mainly to the service of documents, the execution of writs and arrests. The sheriff is obliged to serve documents and execute on writs sued out by practitioners, unless a practitioner is in arears for services performed more than three months previously and the practitioner has not paid notwithstanding a request for payment. When this happens, the sheriff may refer the process to a judicial officer of the court, who may in writing under his or her hand authorise the sheriff to refuse to serve or execute the process until the outstanding amount has been paid.[27]

---

[15] Section 2(1).

[16] Section 2(3)

[17] Section 2(2).

[18] Section 3(3). Regarding the areas of jurisdiction of offices of sheriffs in the lower courts, see GN 959 in *GG* 41092 of 4 September 2017.

[19] *PMB Hardware Wholesalers CC v Yusuf* 2003 (2) SA 73 (N).

[20] Section 15(1)(*a*) of Act 32 of 1944. Fees are still due and are payable into the Consolidated Revenue Fund (s 15(1)(*b*)).

[21] Section 53.

[22] Chapter III s 22 *et seq.*

[23] Section 54.

[24] Section 26.

[25] Section 35.

[26] Chapter IV s 43 *et seq.*

[27] Sections 14(7) and (8) of Act 32 of 1944.

Service of documents on a litigant by the sheriff is the means by which the court is assured that the litigant is aware of the proposed legal steps to be taken. This is a most responsible task. The sheriff, once he or she has delivered and explained the contents of a document to a litigant, sends back to the registrar or clerk of the court a 'return' in which he or she explains what he or she has done. This return constitutes *prima facie* evidence of the matters stated in it.[28] Sheriffs should therefore be very careful in drawing up these returns.

Further rules relating to service, execution and arrest are dealt with in connection with the relevant procedure.

3　LEGAL REPRESENTATIVES AND THE LEGAL PRACTICE ACT

The Right of Appearance in Courts Act 62 of 1995 provides that any attorney possesses right of appearance in any South African court, except the superior courts.[29] Section 8 of the Attorneys Act 53 of 1979 provides that candidate attorneys may appear in any court, other than the High Court, the Supreme Court of Appeal or the Constitutional Court, and before any board, tribunal or similar institution in or before which his or her principal is entitled to appear, instead of and on behalf of such principal. However, a candidate attorney may not appear in a regional court unless he or she has previously practised as an advocate for at least half a year or has served for at least one year under his or her articles or contract of service or has at least one year's experience as a state advocate, state prosecutor or magistrate.

The Legal Practice Act 28 of 2014 (LPA)[30] will in future regulate legal practitioners' right of appearance in South African courts. The LPA aims to provide a legislative framework for the transformation and restructuring of the South African legal provision. The LPA establishes, for the first time in South Africa's history, a single Legal Practice Council in order to regulate the South African legal profession. The LPA will be implemented in transitional phases. Chapter 10, Parts 1 and 2, came into effect on 1 February 2015. This brings into effect the National Forum on the Legal Profession, the transitional body which laid the platform for the Legal Practice Council.[31] It was initially envisaged that Chapter 2 would come into operation three years after the date of commencement of Chapter 10 or at an earlier date fixed by the President by proclamation in the *Gazette*. Said chapter came into effect on 31 October 2018.[32] The remaining

---

[28] Section 17 of Act 32 of 1944.
[29] Section 3. To acquire right of appearance in the superior courts, the procedure in s 4 should be followed.
[30] GN 740 in *GG* 38022 of 22 September 2014.
[31] GN 10351 in *GG* 38412 of 23 January 2015.
[32] Proclamation No R 31 of 2018. See also the Legal Practice Amendment Act 16 of 2017 in GN 41389 in *GG* 41389 of 18 January 2018.

provisions of the LPA, some of which came into effect on 1 November 2018,[33] will come into effect after the commencement of Chapter 2.[34]

The LPA provides that a person may only practise as a legal practitioner if he or she is admitted and enrolled to practise as such in terms of the LPA. Section 25 of the LPA regulates right of appearance of 'legal practitioners' and 'candidate legal practitioners'. Any person who has been admitted and enrolled to practise as a legal practitioner in terms of the LPA is entitled to practise throughout South Africa unless his or her name has been ordered to be struck off the Roll or he or she is subject to an order suspending him or her from practising. A legal practitioner, whether practising as an advocate or an attorney, has right of appearance in any South African court or before any board, tribunal or similar institution. However, an attorney who wishes to appear in the High Court, the Supreme Court of Appeal or the Constitutional Court must apply to the registrar of the Division of the High Court in which he or she was admitted and enrolled as an attorney for a prescribed certificate to the effect that he or she has the right of appearance in said courts.

A candidate attorney may appear in any court, other than the High Court, the Supreme Court of Appeal or the Constitutional Court and before any board, tribunal or similar institution. A candidate attorney may only appear in a regional division if he or she has previously practised as an advocate for at least one year or has undergone at least one year of practical vocational training.[35]

4 MAGISTRATES

Prior to the commencement of the Magistrates Act 90 of 1993 on 1 October 1993, magistrates were appointed and supervised by the Minister of Justice. This Act created a measure of independence for magistrates by establishing a Magistrates Commission which has the task of overseeing the entire work of magistrates. This independence has been constitutionally entrenched.[36] Since 11 March 1994 magistrates have been appointed by the Minister after consultation with the Commission.[37]

The Commission draws up recommendations regarding conditions of service, which are then promulgated as Regulations under s 16 of the Act. The independence of the magistrates is safeguarded by their remuneration being fixed and tabled in Parliament:[38] any reduction in the salary paid to a magistrate has to

---

[33] Proclamation No R 31 of 2018. The following sections came into operation on 1 November 2018: Chapter 1; Chapter 3, with the exclusion of s 35(1), (2), (3) and (7) up to and including (12); Chapter 4 with the exclusion of ss 37(5)(*e*)(ii), 40(1)(*b*)(ii) and (7)(*b*), 41 and 42; Chapters 6 and 7; Chapter 8, with the exclusion of s 93(5); Chapter 9, with the exclusion of s 95(2); and Parts 3 and 4 of Chapter 10.

[34] Section 120 of the Legal Practice Act 28 of 2014.

[35] Section 25(5).

[36] *Van Rooyen & others v The State & others* 2002 (5) SA 246 (CC) and also *De Kock & others v Van Rooyen* 2005 (1) SA 1 (SCA).

[37] Section 10.

[38] Section 12.

be by Act of Parliament.[39] Further independence is provided for by the disciplinary procedure established by s 13 of the Act. The Minister may suspend a magistrate on the recommendation of the Commission, and remove him or her from office for misconduct, continued ill-health and incapacity to carry out his or her duties of office efficiently. Such removal from office has to be tabled in Parliament.[40] No magistrate shall, without the consent of the Minister, perform any paid work outside his or her duties of office.[41] Such measures add to the dignity of the office.

Magistrates perform a variety of tasks, some of which are administrative. They are appointed at various levels. For instance, the magistrate may be allowed to hear only simple criminal cases, or, at the other end of the spectrum, may hear only complicated civil matters.

Certain practitioners may also be appointed for a period, or even for a specific case, as magistrates. In this case, the person is regarded as a full magistrate for that particular period.[42]

Where the Magistrates' Courts Act refers to 'judicial officer' this means a magistrate, an additional magistrate or an assistant magistrate; however, where it refers to a magistrate, this does not include an assistant magistrate.[43]

The magistrate normally sits alone as presiding officer in civil cases, but in terms of s 34 he or she may summon assessors to advise him or her. The assessors are not part of the court and do not take part in making the actual decision. Either party can request, but not compel, the magistrate to appoint assessors. The application form for so doing is provided in Form 21 of the Act; the summons to an assessor is Form 22.

5 THE SMALL CLAIMS COURT

This court was established when the Small Claims Courts Act 61 of 1984 came into operation on 24 August 1985. The idea was to establish a type of court in which a plaintiff could obtain legal relief both quickly and cheaply. In particular, the procedure of the court was to be as simple as possible. The court appears to be a success.[44]

The courts are presided over by commissioners, who are relatively senior practitioners, that is, advocates, attorneys or magistrates with over five years' experience but who are not in the employ of the State.[45] The court is established either by the Minister or the local magistrate, and these persons appoint the commissioner.

The magistrate of the district has to appoint a clerk of the court.[46] In most places the clerk of the magistrate's court acts in this capacity. The sheriff of the

---

[39] Section 12(6).
[40] Section 13.
[41] Section 15.
[42] Section 9*quat*.
[43] Section 1. Section 1 of Act 120 of 1993 also excludes temporary magistrates from the definition.
[44] A useful practical guide is S A S Strauss *You in the Small Claims Court* 2 ed (Juta, 1990).
[45] Section 9.
[46] Section 11(1).

magistrate's court acts for the small claims court.[47] A special provision exempts the State, a clerk of the court, an assistant clerk of the court or a legal assistant from any liability as a result of damage or loss arising out of advice given to litigants in good faith.[48]

Only a natural person may institute proceedings,[49] but juristic persons, excluding the State, may be sued.[50] The defendant must reside or carry on business or be employed within the area of jurisdiction of the court; or the cause of action must have arisen in that area; or, where the action is in respect of immovable property in that area, owned by the defendant.[51] The court will not have jurisdiction to hear any action which otherwise exceeds its jurisdiction, by virtue of the consent of the parties.[52] A court may transfer an action to another on grounds of convenience.[53]

Parties must appear in person and they may not be represented in court. A juristic person must be represented by a duly appointed director or other officer.[54]

The present monetary jurisdiction of the court stands at R20 000;[55] this can be amended by the Minister by proclamation in the *Gazette*. The court has jurisdiction to hear actions for the delivery of movable or immovable property, for ejectment, and those based on liquid documents, credit agreements and other non-specified actions. The court will allow counterclaims.[56] The court may not hear matrimonial disputes, matters involving the interpretation of wills, or the status of a person in respect of his mental capacity. Further, the court may not award an order for specific performance without the alternative of damages, except where the rendering of an account or the delivery or transfer of property is claimed. The court may not hear an action in which a decree of perpetual silence or an interdict is sought, nor cases in which damages are sought for defamation, malicious prosecution, wrongful imprisonment, wrongful arrest, seduction, or breach of promise to marry.[57] The plaintiff may not rely upon a cession for his or her right to sue.[58] Also, if the court decides that the matter contains difficult issues of fact or law which cannot be adequately or fairly decided by it, or should not be decided by it, it will stop the proceedings and the plaintiff will have to institute fresh proceedings in another court.[59]

A simplified procedure is adopted. A defendant must receive a letter of demand from the plaintiff at least 14 days prior to the issue of the summons. Summons will

---

[47] Section 11(2).
[48] Section 11(3).
[49] Section 7(1).
[50] Section 14(2).
[51] Section 14.
[52] Section 22.
[53] Section 13.
[54] Sections 7(2) and 7(4).
[55] GN 296 in *GG* 42282 of 5 March 2019.
[56] Section 15.
[57] Section 16.
[58] Section 14(4).
[59] Section 23.

be issued only upon proof that the defendant received the letter.[60] No further pleadings are necessary, but the defendant may file a written statement setting out his or her defence.[61] The clerk sets down the case and at the hearing evidence is adduced under oath, but the court is empowered to proceed inquisitorially to ascertain the relevant facts.[62]

Judgment is given, from which there is no appeal.[63] The usual grounds of review of actions of other courts also apply here.[64] Certain judgments may be rescinded if it can be shown that they were obtained without the defendant's knowledge, or by fraud or mistake.[65] Patent errors can also be corrected. The court may order costs only to cover court fees, the issue of summons and the expenses of the sheriff.[66]

If a party fails to pay the amount due in terms of a judgment, the judgment creditor must apply to the clerk of the small claims court to have the matter transferred to the clerk of the magistrate's court. Once this is done, a writ of execution may be sued out in the magistrate's court.[67]

6 MEDIATION

Commercial legislation now often makes provision for alternative dispute resolution (ADR) mechanisms and alternative forums to deal with disputes that may arise from the relevant legislation.[68] The most important recent development from a civil procedural context in magistrate's court practice is the introduction of court-annexed mediation.

The Access to Justice Conference of July 2011 was aimed at discussing means to achieving the delivery of accessible and quality justice for all. At the conference it was resolved that steps be taken to introduce ADR mechanisms, preferably court-annexed mediation, into the court system.[69] Accordingly, during December 2014, court-annexed mediation was introduced in certain magistrates' courts through an amendment of the rules.[70] The rules provide the procedure for the voluntary submission of civil disputes to mediation in selected courts.[71] The

---

[60] Section 29.
[61] Section 29(3).
[62] Section 26.
[63] Section 45.
[64] Section 46.
[65] Section 36.
[66] Section 37.
[67] Section 41.
[68] Chapter 7 of National Credit Act 34 of 2005; Chapter 7, Parts C and F, of the Companies Act 71 of 2008; and ss 70 and 75 of the Consumer Protection Act 68 of 2008.
[69] Rule 70 of the Rules Regulating the Conduct of Proceedings of Magistrates' Courts of South Africa.
[70] Rules Board for Courts of Law Act 107 of 1985: Fees payable to mediators, qualification, standards and levels of mediators, GN 854 in *GG* 38163 of 31 October 2014. Amended rules were published in *GG* 37448 of 18 March 2014, effective 1 August 2014. However, the commencement date of 1 August 2014 was amended to 1 December 2014 by GN 571 in *GG* 37848 of 18 July 2014.
[71] Rule 72.

court-annexed mediation process is accordingly not available in all South African district and regional courts.[72]

'Mediation' is defined in the rules as 'the process by which a mediator assists the parties in actual or potential litigation to resolve the dispute between them by facilitating discussions between the parties, assisting them in identifying issues, clarifying priorities, exploring areas of compromise and generating options in an attempt to solve the dispute'.[73] The rules define a 'mediator' as 'a person selected by parties or by the clerk of the court or registrar of the court from the schedule referred to in rule 86(2), to mediate a dispute between the parties'.[74]

The mediation rules apply to the voluntary submission by parties to mediation of disputes prior to commencement of litigation and disputes in litigation which has already commenced and as contemplated in rules 78 and 79.[75] The parties may refer a dispute to mediation prior to the commencement of litigation or after commencement of litigation but prior to judgment, provided that where the trial has commenced the parties must obtain the authorisation of the court. A judicial officer may at any time after the commencement of litigation, but before judgment, enquire into the possibility of mediation of a dispute and accord the parties an opportunity to refer the dispute to mediation.[76]

The Minister determines the qualifications, standards and levels of mediators who may mediate under the rules, and he or she publishes a schedule of accredited mediators from which mediators must be selected.[77]

If a settlement is not reached at mediation in a dispute which is not the subject of litigation, the clerk or registrar of the court must, upon receipt of the report from the mediator, file a report. If a settlement is not reached at mediation in a dispute which is the subject of litigation, the clerk or registrar of the court must, upon receipt of the report from the mediator, file a report to enable the litigation to continue, from which time all suspended time periods will resume.[78]

If the parties reach a settlement, the mediator must assist the parties to draft the settlement agreement, which must be transmitted by the mediator to the clerk or registrar of the court. If a settlement is reached at mediation in a dispute which is not the subject of litigation, the clerk or registrar of the court must, upon receipt of the settlement agreement from the mediator, file the settlement agreement. If a

---

[72] The mediation pilot project was launched at pilot project sites in Gauteng and the North-West Province. GN 150 in *GG* 4146828 of 28 February 2018 (with effect from 1 April 2018) declares certain regional divisions listed in the schedule attached to the aforesaid notice as places in respect of which Chapter 2 of the Rules Regulating the Conduct of Proceedings of Magistrates' Courts of South Africa, published under GN R183 in *GG* 37448 of 18 March 2014, shall apply. See also W De Vos & T Broodryk 'Managerial judging and alternative dispute resolution in Australia: An example for South Africa to emulate?' (part 2) (2018) *TSAR* 18.

[73] Rule 73.

[74] Ibid.

[75] Rule 74.

[76] Rule 75.

[77] Rule 86. Fees payable to mediators, qualification, standards and levels of mediators have been published (GN 854 in *GG* 38163 of 31 October 2014). A list of accredited mediators is maintained on the website of the Department of Justice and Constitutional Development.

[78] Rule 82.

settlement is reached at mediation in a dispute which is the subject of litigation, the clerk or registrar of the court must, at the request of the parties and upon receipt of the settlement agreement from the mediator, place the settlement agreement before a judicial officer in chambers for noting that the dispute has been resolved or to make the agreement an order of court, upon the agreement of the parties. Settlement agreements must be reduced to writing and signed by the parties.[79]

Parties participating in mediation are liable for the fees of the mediator, except where the services of a mediator are provided free of charge. Liability for the fees of a mediator must be borne equally between opposing parties participating in the mediation, provided that any party may offer or undertake to pay in full the fees of a mediator. The tariffs of fees chargeable by mediators have been published by the Minister.[80]

As alluded to above, the rules provide that the time periods prescribed for the delivery of pleadings and notices and the filing of affidavits, or the taking of any step by a litigant, are suspended from the time that an agreement to mediate has been concluded until the termination of mediation proceedings.[81]

7 NATIONAL CREDIT ACT

The introduction of the National Credit Act 34 of 2005 (NCA) has impacted on civil procedure in the magistrates' courts in a number of respects. Although detailed consideration of the NCA falls outside the scope of this book, it may be prudent to briefly refer to its impact on civil procedure in the magistrates' courts.

The NCA applies to 'every credit agreement between parties dealing at arm's length and made within, or having an effect within, the Republic'.[82] It does not apply to a credit agreement in terms of which the consumer is a juristic person whose asset value or annual turnover equals or exceeds a certain threshold value determined by the Minister in terms of s 7(1), the State or an organ of State.[83]

A 'credit agreement' is defined as an agreement that meets all the criteria set out in s 8.[84] In terms of s 8, an agreement constitutes a credit agreement for the purposes of the NCA if it is a credit facility, a credit transaction, a credit guarantee or any combination of the above. An agreement, irrespective of its form, is not a credit agreement if it is an insurance policy or credit policy extended by an insurer solely to maintain the payment of premiums on a policy of insurance, a lease of immovable property or a transaction between a stokvel and a member of that stokvel in accordance with the rules of that stokvel. 'Credit', when used as a noun, is defined as 'a deferral of payment of money owed to a person, or a promise to defer such a payment' or 'a promise to advance or pay money to or at the direction of another person'.

---

[79] Ibid.

[80] Rule 84. Fees payable to mediators, qualification, standards and levels of mediators have been published (GN 854 in *GG* 38163 of 31 October 2014).

[81] Rule 81.

[82] Section 4.

[83] Ibid.

[84] Section 1.

With the above in mind, the following issues are worth mentioning in so far as civil practice in magistrates' courts is concerned:

(1)   The magistrates' courts now possess jurisdiction in respect of actions on or arising out of any credit agreement.[85] Importantly, there is no monetary limitation on the magistrates' courts' jurisdiction to hear such matters.[86]

(2)   A clause in a credit agreement aimed at providing consent to the jurisdiction of a court seated outside the jurisdiction of the court where the consumer resides or works, is unlawful.[87]

(3)   Where a credit agreement is enforced in an action procedure, the particulars of claim would need to contain averments alleging compliance with the relevant provisions of the NCA. The relevant provisions in this regard are:

   (a)   Section 127, which deals with the surrender of goods by a consumer under an instalment agreement, secured loan or lease.

   (b)   Section 129, which stipulates certain required procedures that should be complied with before debt enforcement.[88] If a consumer is in default under a credit agreement, the credit provider may not commence legal proceedings before issuing a written notice. The notice must draw the default to the consumer's attention and propose that the consumer refer the credit agreement to a debt counsellor, ADR agent, consumer court or ombud with jurisdiction. The purpose of the notice is for the parties to resolve any dispute under the agreement or develop and agree on a plan to bring the payments under the agreement up to date.

   (c)   In addition to s 129, the credit provider must comply with s 130 before commencing legal proceedings.[89] Section 130 provides, inter alia, that a credit provider may seek to enforce a credit agreement at court if:

      (i)   the consumer remains and has been in default for at least 20 business days;

      (ii) at least 10 business days have lapsed since the credit provider delivered the s 129 notice;

      (iii) the consumer has not responded to the s 129 notice or has responded by rejecting the credit provider's proposals; and

      (iv) the matter is not pending before the National Consumer Tribunal.

The relevant documentation must be attached to the particulars of claim to ensure compliance with s 129(7), including a copy of the s 129 notice and proof of transmission via registered post. Complying with the specific requirements of the different divisions of the High Court is also important.[90]

---

[85] Section 29(1)*(e)* of the Magistrates' Courts Act.

[86] *Nedbank Ltd v Mateman & others; Nedbank Ltd v Stringer & another* 2008 (4) SA 276 (T).

[87] Section 90(2)*(k)*(vi)*(bb)*. See also *University of Stellenbosch Legal Aid Clinic & others v Minister of Justice and Correctional Services & others* 2015 (5) SA 221 (WCC) para 51.

[88] Regarding the s 129 notice, see *Sebola & another v Standard Bank of South Africa Ltd & another* 2012 (5) SA 142 (CC) and *Kubyana v Standard Bank of South Africa Ltd* 2014 (3) SA 56 (CC). Section 129 was amended in 2014 by the National Credit Act Amendment Act 19 of 2014 (with effect from 13 March 2015).

[89] Section 129.

[90] Proposed amendments to the function and requirements of the simple and combined summons in terms of the Magistrates' Courts Rules with regard to matters where the National Credit Act 34 of

(4)   Where summary judgment is sought, failure to comply with the provisions of the NCA will result in the court refusing judgment.

(5)   Section 58[91] of the Magistrates' Courts Act applies where the application for judgment is based on a credit agreement under the NCA. Complying with ss 129 and 130 of the NCA is also important.[92]

(6)   In terms of s 85 of the NCA, in any court proceedings in which a credit agreement is being considered, if it is alleged that the consumer under a credit agreement is over-indebted, the court may:

    (a)   refer the matter directly to a debt counsellor with a request that the debt counsellor evaluate the consumer's circumstances and make a recommendation; or

    (b)   declare that the consumer is over-indebted and make an order to relieve the consumer's over-indebtedness.

The order may declare the credit agreement to be reckless, it may re-arrange the consumer's obligations or it may be a combination of both.[93] A consumer is deemed to be over-indebted if it appears that he or she is or will be unable to satisfy, in a timely manner, all the obligations under all the credit agreements to which he or she is a party, having regard to his or her financial means, prospects and obligations and his or her probable propensity to satisfy, in a timely manner, all the obligations under all the credit agreements to which he or she is a party, as evidenced by the consumer's history of debt repayment.[94]

Importantly, a consumer may not apply for debt review in respect of a credit agreement at a stage where the credit provider has acted in terms of s 130 to enforce the agreement.[95] In other words, the consumer must apply for debt review before the summons of the credit provider is served upon him or her.

8 CONSUMER PROTECTION ACT AND COMPANIES ACT

The Consumer Protection Act 68 of 2008 (CPA) and Companies Act 71 of 2008 have also impacted upon civil procedure in the magistrates' courts, albeit to a lesser extent compared to the NCA.

The CPA, in certain circumstances, ousts the jurisdiction of the magistrate's courts.[96] Furthermore, civil courts may only be approached to enforce a right conferred by the CPA or in terms of a transaction or agreement if the consumer has exhausted all other remedies available to him or her in terms of national

---

2005 is applicable is currently being considered with a view to bringing the process in the magistrates' courts in line with the provisions of the NCA. The reason for the proposed amendment appears to be that the current stipulations for the rule on the simple summons, as an instrument to initiate claims based on the NCA, fail to adequately address the requirements stated in ss 129 and 130 of the NCA.

[91] The section deals with consent to judgment or to judgment and an order for payment of judgment debt in instalments.

[92] *African Bank Ltd v Myambo NO & others* 2010 (6) SA 298 (GNP).

[93] Section 87.

[94] Section 79.

[95] Section 86(2) read with s 129.

[96] Section 115. Also see s 69*(d)* which requires parties to first exhaust available remedies before approaching a court.

legislation.[97] The CPA also deals with the powers of a court to ensure fair and just conduct, terms and conditions.[98]

An example of the impact of the Companies Act on civil procedure in the lower courts can be found in the requirement in the Companies Act that a company must register the address of its office or principal office where it has more than one office.[99] In *Sibakhulu Construction (Pty) Ltd v Wedgewood Village Golf Country Estate (Pty) Ltd*[100] the court held that a company resides for purposes of jurisdiction only at its registered office. Therefore, from a jurisdictional perspective, under the new Companies Act the registered office is the same as its principal place of business.

---

[97] Section 69.
[98] Section 52.
[99] Section 23(3)*(b)*.
[100] 2013 (1) SA 191 (WCC).

JURISDICTION

1 CONSTITUTIONAL ISSUES

The procedure to be adopted in the magistrates' courts when a constitutional issue is raised was set out in terms of s 103 of the Constitution of the Republic of South Africa Act 200 of 1993 (the Interim Constitution). The scheme of the Interim Constitution was that the lower courts did not have the power to enquire into or adjudicate on the constitutionality of any Act of Parliament. Section 103(2) provided that where a lower court did not have the competency to enquire into the validity of a law or provision, it should decide the matter on the assumption that the law or provision is valid. Thereafter, if the presiding officer was of the opinion that it was in the interest of justice to do so, he or she could in terms of s 103(3) postpone the case and refer the matter to the appropriate High Court which had jurisdiction.

The power of the magistrate's court was only limited to the enquiry into the constitutionality of an Act of Parliament. This did not mean that the lower courts were not obliged to apply the constitution; for instance, it was necessary to apply the fair trial provisions in the criminal jurisdiction. No such clear procedural provisions are to be found in the Constitution of the Republic of South Africa,1996 (the Constitution). Section 170 of the Constitution provides that magistrates' courts may decide any matter determined by an Act of Parliament, but a court of a status lower than a High Court may not enquire into or rule on the constitutionality of any legislation or any conduct of the President.

The first part of this section appears to be a general enabling provision. The second part is clear in its prohibition. However, the procedural issue is left untouched.

In order to cure the difficulty, Act 80 of 1997 introduced a new s 110 into the Magistrates' Courts Act. It provides in sub-s (1) that a court shall not be competent to pronounce on the validity of any law or conduct of the President. This is a mere repetition of s 170 of the Constitution. Section 110(2) then provides:

'If in any proceedings before a court it is alleged that–
(a) any law or any conduct of the President is invalid on the grounds of its inconsistency with a provision of the Constitution; or
(b) any law is invalid on any ground other than its constitutionality,
the court shall decide the matter on the assumption that a law or conduct is valid: Provided that the party which alleges that a law or conduct of the President is invalid, may adduce evidence regarding the invalidity of the law or conduct in question.'

The result is that any evidence required to the adjudication of the constitutional point should be led in the magistrate's court, but the magistrate will decide the case on the assumption that the impugned provision is valid.[1] Thereafter it will be up to the party advancing the constitutional point to take the matter on appeal to the appropriate forum to decide the constitutional issue.

There is considerable debate amongst commentators as to whether the magistrates' courts have the power to develop the common law. Jones & Buckle, for instance, suggest that the magistrate's court does not have the jurisdiction to enquire into or rule on the validity of rules of common law.[2] It is respectfully submitted that this approach is incorrect. It is submitted that where s 110 refers to 'any law' it means a statute and not the common law. There is only one law in South Africa. There is not a common law which remains untouched by the Constitution. The Constitutional Court has stated that the development of the common law lies outside its function. It is submitted that this function is given to all the common-law courts, including the magistrate's court. It may well happen that courts are called upon to decide issues in relation to the common law taking into account the Constitution.[3]

---

[1] Care should also be taken that the correct parties are joined in the action.

[2] Jones & Buckle Act 678, where reference is made to the opinion of Wouter de Vos 'Civil Procedural Law and the Constitution of 1996: An Appraisal of Procedural Guarantees in Civil Proceedings' 1997 *TSAR* 444 at 446, which is adopted here.

[3] The debate in the cases began with *Qozeleni v Minister of Law and Order & another* 1995 (3) SA 625 (E), which was commented on by a Full Bench in *Port Elizabeth Municipality v Prut NO & another* 1996 (4) SA 318 (E). See also the *obiter* comment of Langa DP in *Pretoria City Council v Walker* 1998 (3) SA 363 (CC) at 374B. The matter is discussed in Chaskalson et al *Constitutional Law* at 6–7 to 6–10, and at 6–34.

As was the case before the Constitution, the lower courts are bound by the system of precedent. They are bound by decisions of the Supreme Court of Appeal and, where there is no definitive decision from that source, they are bound by the division of the High Court within which they are situated.[4]

2 WHICH COURT?

Various factors have to be taken into account in order to determine which court will have the necessary jurisdiction to hear the matter. These are the residence of the parties, the type of dispute (ie the cause of action and the relief sought), the place where the dispute arose, and the amount claimed. The rules governing jurisdiction are set out in the Act, but it is useful to have an understanding of the common law relating to jurisdiction. Once this is understood, the statutory provisions are more easily followed.

The underlying principle which permeates the many rules relating to jurisdiction is that the court to have jurisdiction must be empowered to see that its orders are carried out. This is the 'doctrine of effectiveness'.[5] The court will be able to give effect to its judgment by seizing the defendant's property and selling it in order to pay the plaintiff. This is the process of execution, and it is the court that has this power that will normally be the proper court in which to proceed.

The doctrine of effectiveness has become a legal fiction in relation to jurisdiction, because 'a court which has jurisdiction to try an action shall have jurisdiction to issue against any party thereto any form of process in execution of its judgment in such action'.[6] The doctrine of effectiveness now exists in the form of the primary principle that the court in which the defendant is resident has jurisdiction, because that court has power over the defendant's person and property.

A plaintiff enquiring about from which court to issue summons against a defendant will, therefore, first ask where the defendant is resident and will then proceed to that court. This principle is expressed in the maxim *actor sequitur forum rei*.

There are, however, other competing principles, namely, that a court may have jurisdiction by virtue of the consent of the defendant, or because the cause of action arose within the area of jurisdiction of the court. These common-law principles are all codified in the Act.

It happens, therefore, that a plaintiff may have a choice of courts in which he or she may proceed against a defendant. In this event the plaintiff, because he or she is *dominus litis*, is free to choose which court is going to be more convenient. This choice arises, for instance, where the defendant is not resident where a motor

---

[4] See H R Hahlo & Ellison Kahn *The South African Legal System and its Background* (Juta, 1968) 257.

[5] *Minister of the Interior v Cowley NO* 1955 (1) SA 307 (N) at 311H. See also *Thermo Radiant Oven Sales (Pty) Ltd v Nelspruit Bakeries (Pty) Ltd* 1969 (2) SA 295 (A). According to Harms, it is questionable whether the doctrine remains important in light of the judgment in *Bid Industrial Holdings v Strang & another* 2008 (3) SA 355 (SCA). In this regard, see D Harms *Civil Procedure in the Superior Courts* Vol 1 (Service Issue 61, 2018) A4.7–A4.8.

[6] Section 62(1). See s 42 of the Superior Courts Act 10 of 2013.

collision took place. The court of residence of the defendant and the court in whose district the collision took place will have jurisdiction. The plaintiff may choose whichever is more convenient. The availability of witnesses, the costs of transporting them, and the necessity for an inspection *in loco,* would be relevant considerations.

The various facts which have to be present to provide the basis for jurisdiction have to exist at the time of service of the summons upon the defendant.[7]

2.1 Jurisdiction in respect of persons

In general s 28 provides that a court will have jurisdiction over the defendant if the defendant is resident in the area of the court, or he has immovable property in that area, or the whole cause of action arose in that area. This section also provides other bases upon which the court may have jurisdiction. Each section is dealt with in turn:

> **Section 28(1)(a):** 'any person who resides, carries on business or is employed within the district or regional division'.

Section 2 of the Interpretation Act 33 of 1957 defines 'person' to include any divisional council, municipal council, village management board, or like authority; any company incorporated or registered as such under any law; and any body of persons corporate or unincorporated. It also includes the State.[8]

'[A]ny person who resides': whether a natural person is resident in a particular place is answered by reference to three principles:[9]

(1) A distinction is drawn between a place of residence and a person's domicile. Domicile is acquired by establishing residence at a particular place with the intention of remaining there permanently.[10]

(2) A person may have more than one place of residence. In such a case he or she must be summonsed to appear in the court of the area in which he or she is resident at the time the summons is served.[11]

(3) A person does not reside at a place which he or she is visiting only temporarily. Should a person who has his domicile in Cape Town be sent for a week to Tshwane on a course, he or she does not reside in Tshwane. What length of residence in a place is required before that place becomes a place of residence will depend on the facts of each case. The person would have to consider that place to be one of his or her homes at least for the time being.[12]

If the juristic person is a company or a close corporation, it must have a registered office. Previously, under the Companies Act 61 of 1973, a company's jurisdiction was determined by the location of its registered address and its

---

[7] *Mills v Starwell Finance (Pty) Ltd* 1981 (3) SA 84 (N); *Jasat v Interim National Medical and Dental Council* 1999 (1) SA 156 (N) at 1591.

[8] Section 28(2).

[9] See *Ex parte Minister of Native Affairs* 1941 AD 53.

[10] See B van Heerden et al *Law of Persons and the Family* 2 ed (Juta, 1999) chapter 6.

[11] *Barens en 'n ander v Lottering* 2000 (3) SA 305 (C) at 309F–G.

[12] *Robinson v Commissioner of Taxes* 1917 TPD 542 at 548. See also *Mayne v Main* 2001 (2) SA 1239 (SCA).

principal place of business.[13] However, as mentioned in chapter 3, following the case of *Sibakhulu Construction (Pty) Ltd v Wedgewood Village Golf Country Estate (Pty) Ltd*,[14] adjudicated under the auspices of the new Companies Act, it appears that a company resides only at the place of its registered office.[15] The position regarding close corporations seems to remain unchanged.[16] Such entities may well have their administrative control in a different area to their registered office. When this happens, the close corporation is said to be resident at both places, and the plaintiff is free to issue summons from either court.[17]

It could be argued that the residence of the State is Tshwane.[18]

'[C]arries on business': what constitutes carrying on business is not defined. The voluminous case law indicates that there should be some regularity in conducting affairs at a particular place, usually but not necessarily for profit.[19]

Where a firm or sole proprietorship is being sued and jurisdiction is sought on this ground, the business must be owned by the person who is the real defendant. In this instance the defendant is cited as, for example, John Smith t/a John's Cafe.[20] John Smith may, therefore, be sued where he or she is resident as well as where he or she carries on business. If the plaintiff does not know who the proprietor is, the defendant may be cited in its business title and the proprietors may be established by means of requiring the information in terms of rule 54(1). It is necessary to do this because, unless the proper defendant is before the court, it will not be possible to execute against his or her personal property, but only against the business property.[21]

'[I]s employed within': a measure of permanence is required in the employment. A defendant may not be sued when he or she is employed only temporarily within the jurisdiction of the court, as when he or she is seconded for only a short period to a particular branch of a business. The date of service of the summons is the critical date for determination of the issue, rather than the date of issue of summons.[22]

---

[13] *Bisonboard Ltd v K Braun Woodworking Machinery (Pty) Ltd* 1991 (1) SA 482 (A) at 496C–D; *Leibowitz t/a Lee Finance v Mhlana & others* 2006 (6) SA 180 (SCA) at 183–184.

[14] 2013 (1) SA 191 (WCC).

[15] This decision was criticised in *Lonsdale Commercial Corporation v Kimberly West Diamonds Mining Corporation* (unreported, Northern Cape High Court, case no 312/2012, 17 May 2013); *Phillippus Johannes De Bruyn v Grandselect 101 & another* (unreported, Northern Cape High Court, case no 1961/2013, 5 March 2014); and *Lanarco Home Owner Association v Prospect SA Investments 42 (Pty) Ltd* 2014 JDR 2273 (KZP).

[16] See Jones & Buckle Act 96–96A.

[17] See *Bisonboard v K Braun Woodworking Machinery* (supra).

[18] See *Minister of Law and Order v Patterson* 1984 (2) SA 739 (A). However, this case was based on s 23 of the Republic of South Africa Constitution 32 of 1961, which designated Pretoria as the 'seat of the Government of the Republic'. This is no longer the case under the Constitution of the Republic of South Africa, 1996.

[19] See *Cape Town Municipality v Clarensville (Pty) Ltd* 1974 (2) SA 138 (C) at 248B *et seq*, and the cases cited there. See also Jones & Buckle Act 96B–98.

[20] This is an abbreviation for 'trading as'.

[21] Rule 54(1) cannot be used to bring a party who is not a member of the firm before the court. *DF Scott (EP) (Pty) Ltd v Golden Valley Supermarket* 2002 (6) SA 297 (SCA).

[22] *Mills v Starwell Finance (Pty) Ltd* 1981 (3) SA 84 (N).

Section 28(1)(b): 'any partnership which has business premises situated or any member whereof resides within the district or regional division'.

At common law a partnership is not a juristic entity and all partners have to be sued jointly. This section revises this position.[23] One may now sue the partnership in the partnership name provided it has business premises within the jurisdiction of the court, or one of the partners is resident in that area. In *Metlika Trading Ltd & others v Commissioner, South African Revenue Service*[24] it was held that if the principal place of business of the partnership is located within the jurisdiction of a specific court, it is likely to be sufficient to confer jurisdiction on that court. A notice may then be served on the partnership requiring it to divulge who all the partners were at the time the cause of action accrued.[25] The reason for the necessity of doing this is the same as set out above in connection with firms.

Section 28(1)(c): 'any person whatever, in respect of any proceedings incidental to any action or proceeding instituted in the court by such person himself or herself'.

It is necessary to decide what incidental proceedings are. Many proceedings are obviously incidental to an action or proceeding, such as an application to set aside a judgment, or an application for leave to sue.

What is not so obvious is the situation of a counterclaim. A defendant may, as a general rule, sue the plaintiff in the same action by means of a counterclaim. The situation may arise in which the plaintiff has jurisdiction over the defendant but the defendant, in his or her counterclaim, does not have jurisdiction over the plaintiff. For instance, suppose that A, who is not resident in the area of a court, sues B, who is resident in that area, for payment for goods sold and delivered. When B files his or her plea, he or she launches a counterclaim against A for damages arising out of an assault committed against him or her by A when he or she went to discuss the overdue account with A. The assault happened outside the jurisdiction of the court. The court will have jurisdiction to hear the counterclaim only if the counterclaim is incidental to the claim of A against B.

In common law a plaintiff is presumed to have submitted to the jurisdiction of the court out of which he or she sues process.[26] A defendant may therefore bring a counterclaim against a plaintiff even when the defendant would not ordinarily be able to sue the plaintiff in that court.[27] However, the jurisdiction of the lower courts is provided for by statute and not by the common law.[28]

Statute requires that the counterclaim should be incidental to the main claim if the defendant is to have jurisdiction on that basis over the plaintiff. Old cases

---

[23] For the High Court equivalent see rule 14 of the Uniform Rules.

[24] 2005 (3) SA 1 (SCA) at 13C–G.

[25] Rule 54(1). The procedure to follow where the defendant refuses to disclose who the partners are is dealt with in Jones & Buckle Rule 54-3.

[26] D Pistorius *Pollak on Jurisdiction* 2 ed (Juta, 1993) 65 *et seq.*

[27] For convenience the naming of the parties as for the claim in convention is retained. The two claims are, however, entirely distinct actions. For detailed discussion, see chapter 14 below.

[28] There is no room for attempting to bring the statute into conformity with the common law through rules of statutory interpretation as was incorrectly done in *Innes-Grant v Kelsey* (1924) 45 NLR 268. See *Van Heerden v Muir* 1955 (2) SA 376 (A) at 379.

followed the common law.[29] But it is now settled that the word 'incidental' means 'arising out of the same facts'. It is especially s 28(1)(*f*) which leads to the result that the Act departs from the common law. This section provides the possibility that a defendant in reconvention, that is, the plaintiff in convention, may object to the jurisdiction of the court. This provision would be wholly redundant if such a party were automatically subject to the jurisdiction of the court.

The position is, therefore, that a plaintiff who is not resident within the jurisdiction of the court in which he or she sues the defendant and where the whole cause of action of the counterclaim is not within the area of the court, may only be met by a counterclaim which is incidental to the main claim. This means that the counterclaim must arise out of the same facts as the claim in convention. Typical instances would be where the dispute concerns a breach of contract and both parties claim the other is in breach, or, where there is a claim for damages and the defendant in convention wishes to plead contributory negligence on the part of the plaintiff. What the defendant may not do is to sue such a plaintiff in reconvention with a claim wholly unrelated to the main claim. If he or she wishes to do this, a new summons will have to be sued out of the proper court.

Section 28(1)(*d*): 'any person, whether or not he or she resides, carries on business or is employed within the district or regional division, if the cause of action arose wholly within the district or regional division'.

This section creates another ground upon which a court may have jurisdiction besides those based upon the residence or employment of the defendant. The court acquires jurisdiction purely on the basis of the fact that the cause of action arose wholly within its area of jurisdiction. It is necessary to determine what the phrase 'cause of action arose wholly within the area of jurisdiction of the court' means.

Suppose that A (a resident of Tshwane) and B (a resident of Cape Town) are both on the road to the Kruger National Park. Their cars are involved in a collision with each other within the area of jurisdiction of the magistrate's court of Middelburg, Mpumalanga. As *dominus litis* A is not obliged to summons B in Cape Town on the basis of the provisions relating to residence, but he may issue summons against B in Middelburg.

The term 'cause of action' is defined by means of reference to a distinction between the *facta probanda* and the *facta probantia* of the case.[30] The *facta probanda* (facts which have to be proved) are the facts which form the basis of the cause of action. These are the facts that the plaintiff must prove in order to succeed in his action. The *facta probantia* (facts which prove) are the facts which are used in order to prove the facts in dispute. As Watermeyer J put it in *Abrahamse & Sons v SAR&H*:[31]

'The proper legal meaning of the expression "cause of action" is the entire set of facts which gives rise to an enforceable claim and includes every fact which is

---

[29] See *Stoffels v James* 24 SC 701 and *Salkinder v Van Zyl & Buissinne* 1922 CPD 59.

[30] *McKenzie v Farmers' Co-operative Meat Industries Ltd* 1922 AD 16 at 23. See also *Dusheiko v Milburn* 1964 (4) SA 648 (A).

[31] 1933 CPD 626 at 637, quoted in *King's Transport v Viljoen* 1954 (1) SA 133 (C) at 135 and in *Evins v Shield Insurance Co Ltd* 1980 (2) SA 814 (A) at 838G. See also *Cape Town Municipality & another v Allianz Insurance Co Ltd* 1990 (1) All SA 30 (C).

material to be proved to entitle a plaintiff to succeed in his claim. It includes all that a plaintiff must set out in his declaration in order to disclose a cause of action. Such cause of action does not "arise" or "accrue" until the occurrence of the last of such facts and consequently the last of such facts is sometimes loosely spoken of as the cause of action.'

In the case of the collision referred to, the plaintiff would have to prove that his motor vehicle was damaged through the negligence of the defendant and that the damages amounted to a certain sum. That proof of some of these facts might require evidence of events outside the jurisdiction of the court does not mean that all the *facta probanda* did not occur within the jurisdiction of the court. For instance, the fact that one of the drivers is an employee and acting in his capacity as an employee of the defendant does not alter the position with regard to jurisdiction. The proof of the employment contract would be a *facta probantia*.[32]

The distinction *between facta probanda* and *facta probantia* is often a matter of substantive law. For instance, in cases in which the plaintiff relies on a contract, both the offer and acceptance must occur in the same district. Where plaintiff sues on a contract of sale, the contract and delivery of the goods must be in the same district. Payment of a cheque takes place where the cheque is drawn.[33]

Section 28(1)(e): any party to interpleader proceedings, if–
(1) the execution creditor and every claimant to the subject matter of the proceedings reside, carry on business, or are employed within the district or regional division; or
(2) the subject matter of the proceedings has been attached by process of the court; or
(3) such proceedings are taken under s 69(2) and the person therein referred to as the 'third party' resides, carries on business, or is employed within the district or regional division; or
(4) all the parties consent to the jurisdiction of the court.

Interpleader proceedings arise either where a sheriff has attached goods and more than one person lays claim to such goods, or where competing claims are made to goods which are in the possession of someone who is not a sheriff. The procedure is discussed below when dealing with the relevant rule.

Where the goods in dispute have been attached by the sheriff, a court within whose area of jurisdiction all the parties are resident, carry on business or are employed will have jurisdiction. This may not be the court in whose area the goods have been attached, or even the court authorising the attachment. The second ground relates to the court issuing the process by which the goods are attached. Since processes run throughout the Republic, the court giving judgment and the court within whose jurisdiction the goods are attached will probably not be the same. The interpleader summons may be issued from either court. This subsection must be read together with s 35(2), which provides that '[a]n interpleader summons, if issued out of the court of the district in which the

---

[32] See *King's Transport v Viljoen* (supra) and *Dusheiko v Milburn* (supra).
[33] For an example in which the requirements set out above were not met, see *Buys v Roodt (nou Otto)* 2000 (1) SA 535 (O).

property was attached, may at the discretion of the court, be remitted for trial to the court in which the judgment was given'.

There is thus concurrent jurisdiction. The court by whose order the goods were attached has interpleader jurisdiction over goods attached elsewhere. Reciprocally, the court in whose jurisdiction the goods were attached may hear the interpleader proceedings or it may remit the matter to the judgment court.

The remaining provisions of the section are either self-explanatory or dealt with below.

Section 28(1)(*f*): 'any defendant (whether in convention or reconvention) who appears and takes no objection to the jurisdiction of the court'.

The mere entering of appearance to defend does not mean that the defendant consents to the jurisdiction of the court. A defendant gives notice of his or her intention to defend only in order to prevent a plaintiff from taking default judgment against him or her.

The reference to not taking an objection is a reference to an obsolete procedure. The proper procedure now is to incorporate the objection into a plea.

The rules provide time limits after appearance to defend has been entered within which the defendant's plea has to be filed. In the High Court a plea of lack of jurisdiction is raised by way of a special plea. Although no provision is made for this procedure in the magistrates' courts, there is no reason why such a procedure should not be followed.[34] Rule 17(7) provides that such a point can be set down for a separate hearing at 10 days' notice to the other side.

The common law is that, should the defendant not raise the plea of the lack of jurisdiction of the court in his or her plea, he or she is regarded as having submitted to the court's jurisdiction.[35] The plea of lack of jurisdiction should therefore be included with the plea on the merits. In *William Spilhaus & Co (MB) (Pty) Ltd v Marx*[36] Van Winsen J held that circumstances could exist in which a court should allow the plea of lack of jurisdiction to be raised at a later stage through amendment of the pleadings. This would be permissible only when the defendant was not aware of the true facts at the time of pleading. In the same case Theron J was not prepared to consider this exception. In *Muller v Möller & another*[37] the court did not have to choose between the two alternatives. The matter thus remains undecided, but it is submitted that only the most exceptional circumstances would justify the exception allowed by Van Winsen J. Not only the knowledge of the defendant should be considered but also the equity of allowing the amendment of the plea. Such an amendment of the plea should not be allowed

---

[34] On the special plea, see chapter 14 below at para 1.4 *et seq*.

[35] See Pistorius *Pollak on Jurisdiction* 2 ed 11 *et seq*. See also *Minister of Safety and Security v Xhego* [2003] 2 All SA 269 (Ck) para 12.

[36] 1963 (4) SA 994 (C).

[37] 1965 (1) SA 872 (C). In *Presto Parcels v Lalla* 1990 (3) SA 287 (E) a plaintiff, who had not objected to an amendment which introduced a plea of lack of jurisdiction, was not allowed to argue that the defendant had submitted to the jurisdiction of the court by pleading to the merits. See also *Purser & another v Sales & another* 2001 (3) SA 445 (SCA) and *Silhouette Investments Ltd v Virgin Hotels Group Ltd* [2009] 3 All SA 172 (SCA) para 40.

when it will only lead to the case being heard in another forum with the resultant escalation of costs and prolonged delay.

A defendant who fails to object to the court's jurisdiction may be taken to have consented to the jurisdiction of the court only in respect of his or her *person*. The defendant may never in this way consent to the jurisdiction of the court in cases in which the court in any event lacks jurisdiction in respect of the size of the claim or the type of order sought.[38]

> **Section 28(1)(g):** 'any person who owns immovable property within the district or regional division in actions in respect of such property or in respect of mortgage bonds thereon'.

Rule 5(6)(b) provides that if a plaintiff wishes to rely on this section to establish the jurisdiction of the court, an averment to this effect must be contained in the summons.

In *Kleynhans v Wessels NO*[39] Hoexter JA reaffirmed the principle previously established that the action does not have to relate to a real right in respect of the property but it may also refer to personal rights.

2.1.1 *Foreign defendants*

> **Section 30*bis*:** '[t]he court may order attachment of property to found or confirm jurisdiction against any person who does not reside in the Republic, in respect of an action within its jurisdiction, where the claim or the value of the matter in dispute amounts to at least R2 500, exclusive of any costs in respect of the recovery thereof, and may grant an order allowing service of any process in such action to be effected in such manner as may be stated in such order.'

Attachment to found jurisdiction is necessary when the defendant is foreign and no other jurisdictional basis exists. Confirmation of jurisdiction is necessary when there is another basis for the court's jurisdiction but the defendant is resident outside the Republic. In both instances the purpose of the attachment of goods is to give effect to the order of the court.

This section does no more than bring the magistrates' courts within the ambit of the common law. The section must therefore be interpreted in the light of the situation which exists in the High Court, and those authorities should be followed.[40]

Various situations need to be considered in connection with claims sounding in money.[41] For instance, where the plaintiff is resident within the area of the jurisdiction of the court, he or she may attach the foreign *peregrinus* defendant's property in order to found jurisdiction, ie without there being another basis for the court's jurisdiction. This means that the cause of action may have no connection with that area other than the attachment.[42] Where the plaintiff is not resident within

---

[38] *Hydromar (Pty) Ltd v Pearl Oyster Shell Industries (Pty) Ltd* 1976 (2) SA 384 (C) at 388G–H.

[39] 1998 (4) SA 1060 (SCA). See Jones & Buckle Act 61.

[40] See Jones & Buckle Act 113–114, and contra H N Pretorius *Burgerlike Prosesreg in Die Landdroshowe* (Butterworths, 1986) 135 *et seq.*

[41] See *Ewing McDonald & Co Ltd v M&M Products Co* 1991 (1) SA 252 (A) at 258D *et seq.*

[42] *Thermo Radiant Oven Sales (Pty) Ltd v Nelspruit Bakeries (Pty) Ltd* 1969 (2) SA 295 (A) at 300C–D. See also *Bid Industrial Holdings v Strang & another* 2008 (3) SA 355 (SCA). In the latter

the area of the jurisdiction of the court and the defendant is foreign, then both a recognised basis for jurisdiction and an attachment are essential, ie to confirm jurisdiction. This could be done, for example, where the cause of action arose.[43]

2.2 The amount and nature of the claim

The magistrates' courts may hear cases only where the quantum of the claim is within certain limits. If the claim exceeds these limits the plaintiff may either proceed in the High Court, where there are no such limits, or he or she may abandon a portion of the claim in order to bring the claim within the jurisdictional limit of the court. Recently, the Full Bench of the Gauteng Division in *Nedbank Ltd v Thobejane and Similar Matters*[44] held that the High Court may transfer a matter *mero motu* to a magistrate's court with jurisdiction if it is in the interest of justice to do so.

The precise monetary limits are proclaimed from time to time by the Minister in the *Gazette*. The Minister may determine different amounts contemplated in s 29(1)*(a)*, *(b)*, *(d)*, *(f)* and *(g)* in respect of courts for districts and courts for regional divisions.[45] Currently, the amount in respect of district courts is R200 000 and the amount for regional courts is R400 000.

Because of the form of s 29, it has the effect not only of limiting the amount of the claim but also of defining the nature of various claims.

In *Nedbank v Thobejane*,[46] the Full Bench of the Gauteng Division held that, with effect from 2 February 2019, where the monetary value of a civil action and/or application falls within the monetary jurisdiction of the magistrate's court, it should be instituted in such court unless the High Court has granted leave to hear the matter. In other words, all civil matters falling within the monetary jurisdiction of the magistrate's court may not be enrolled in the High Court, unless the High Court has granted leave to hear such matter. The decision is aimed at promoting access to justice.

> **Section 29(1):** '[s]ubject to the provisions of this Act and the National Credit Act, 2005 (Act 34 of 2005), a court in respect of causes of action, shall have jurisdiction in–'.

---

case, the Supreme Court of Appeal developed the common law by allowing the practice according to which a division of the High Court will have jurisdiction if the summons is served on the defendant while he or she is within South African borders and if there is a sufficient connection between the suit and the area of jurisdiction of the court concerned so that the disposal of the case by the court is appropriate and convenient. In this regard, see D E Van Loggerenberg *Erasmus Superior Court Practice* 2 ed (Service 6, 2018) A2-106 *et seq.*

[43] For further details, see *Erasmus Superior Court Practice* A2-106 *et seq.* Although the Supreme Court Act 59 of 1959 has been repealed and replaced by the Superior Courts Act 10 of 2013, the commentary of *Erasmus* on this issue remains relevant.

[44] 2019 (1) SA 594 (GP). The decision is currently pending appeal before the Supreme Court of Appeal and therefore, in terms of s 18(1) of the Superior Courts Act 10 of 2013, execution of the decision is suspended.

[45] Section 29(1A); GN 216 and GN 217 in *GG* 37477 of 27 March 2014.

[46] Supra. The decision is currently pending appeal before the Supreme Court of Appeal and therefore, in terms of s 18(1) of the Superior Courts Act, execution of the decision is suspended.

The structure of the section is important in its interpretation. The section sets out eight causes of action which may found an action.[47]

Proceedings in terms of s 30 (interdicts, attachments and *mandamenten van spolie*) are also subject to the limitations placed by s 29 upon the value of causes of action.[48]

Section 29(1)(a): 'actions in which is claimed the delivery or transfer of any property, movable or immovable, not exceeding in value the amount determined by the Minister from time to time by notice in the *Gazette*'.

The 'value' referred to is the actual market value of the property at the time when the action[49] is instituted.[50] It is not necessary for the plaintiff to state the value of the property in his or her particulars of claim in order to indicate that the matter falls within the jurisdiction of the lower court.[51] The defendant may, however, raise the special plea that the court lacks jurisdiction.[52]

The action may be vindicatory or may be a claim for specific performance of a contract. This section needs to be read with s 46(2)(*c*)(ii).[53]

Section 29(1)(b): 'actions of ejectment against the occupier of any premises or land within the district or regional division: Provided that, where the right of occupation of any such premises or land is in dispute between the parties, such right does not exceed the amount determined by the Minister from time to time by notice in the *Gazette* in clear value to the occupier'.

An action for ejectment is not based upon a contract and is therefore not affected by s 46(2), which prohibits a magistrate issuing an order of specific performance without an alternative claim for damages.

If the value of the right of occupation is disputed by the defendant so as to oust the jurisdiction of the court, the *onus* rests on him or her to prove what he or she alleges.[54] The magistrate will not enter into the merits of the dispute but will determine simply whether there is a *bona fide* dispute and then attempt to determine the value of the right of occupation.[55]

An objective test is applied in assessing the value of the right of occupation, but the personal circumstances of the occupier are taken into consideration.[56] The

---

[47] See *In re Pennington Health Committee* 1980 (4) SA 243 (N) and *Jordan & another v Penmill Investments CC & another* 1991 (2) SA 430 (E).

[48] *Sellars NO v Grobler NO en andere* 1961 (3) SA 583 (T).

[49] *In re Pennington Health Committee* (supra) at 247 the court held that '[p]rocedure by way of application is recognised, but the intention appears to have been to confer jurisdiction generally in actions (in the narrow sense) while authorising application proceedings only in specific cases'.

[50] *Van der Merwe NO v Van der Merwe* 1973 (1) SA 436 (C).

[51] *Illustrious (Pty) Ltd v Deutz* 1948 (3) SA 65 (W) at 69–70; *Smith v Coetzee* 1945 TPD 359 at 362 and 363.

[52] *Garda v Bonato* 1913 TPD 810.

[53] For a discussion of s 46 see below at p 32 *et seq.*

[54] *Klerksdorp & District Muslim Merchants Association v Mahomed & another* 1948 (4) SA 731 (T) at 739; *Jordaan v De Beer Scheepers & another* 1975 (3) SA 845 (T).

[55] *Durban City Council v Kadir* 1971 (1) SA 364 (N) at 367–8. See also *Gallman v Dombrowsky* 1973 (2) SA 261 (C) at 263.

[56] *Van der Westhuizen v Petersen* 1922 TPD 412; *Gallman v Dombrowsky* (supra); *Smith v Coetzee* (supra) at 362.

rental paid by the occupier does not necessarily provide a basis for the calculation of the value of the right to him or her, because the rental really represents the value of the right to the lessor and not to the lessee. The rental may nevertheless serve as a guide in the determination of the value of his or her right of occupation to the lessee if the rental of the premises is compared to the rental of comparable premises elsewhere over the period of occupation.[57] A general method of calculating the value of the right of occupation is to assess the rental for two months, for a monthly contract of lease may usually be terminated on one month's notice and it thus gives no greater security of tenure than two months.

Should the premises be occupied for business purposes, either the costs of hiring other business premises or the profit that the occupier could reasonably have expected to make may serve as a basis for the calculation.

The market value of the premises is irrelevant unless the title to the premises is in dispute.[58]

The jurisdiction of this court has been limited by the Land Reform (Labour Tenants) Act 3 of 1996, the Extension of Security of Tenure Act 62 of 1997 and the Prevention of Illegal Eviction from and Unlawful Occupation of Land Act 19 of 1998. The terms of these Acts lie outside the scope of the present work.[59]

Section 29(1)(c): 'actions for the determination of a right of way notwithstanding the provisions of s 46'.

The qualification means that it is not necessary to consider whether or not the determination amounts to an order for specific performance. Nor is it necessary to determine the value of the right of way, since the court is given absolute jurisdiction. The Appellate Division in *Van Rensburg v Coetzee*[60] has confirmed that this anomalous situation is in fact our law. In *Cloete v Karee-Aar Landgoed Bpk*[61] it was held that this section, read with s 30(1) and (2), confers jurisdiction on the court to grant an interdict pending the finalisation of a dispute regarding a right of way.

Section 29(1)(d): 'actions on or arising out of a liquid document or a mortgage bond, where the claim does not exceed the amount determined by the Minister from time to time by notice in the *Gazette*'.

A liquid document is a document in which the debtor, above his or her signature or that of his or her authorised representative, admits or is in law deemed to admit that he or she is liable in a fixed or ascertainable monetary amount.[62]

The essence of a liquid document is thus that the obligation to make payment appears *ex facie* the liquid document.

---

[57] *Langham Court (Pty) Ltd v Mavromaty* 1954 (3) SA 742 (T).
[58] *Agambaram v Nimdhari* 1939 NPD 28 at 44–6; *Klerksdorp & District Muslim Merchants* (supra) at 740.
[59] See Jones & Buckle Act 136–136A. See *Nduna v Absa Bank Ltd & others* 2004 (4) SA 453 (C).
[60] 1977 (3) SA 130 (T).
[61] 1997 (3) SA 30 (NC).
[62] *Rich & others v Lagerwey* 1974 (4) SA 748 (A) at 754H; *Western Bank Ltd v Pretorius* 1976 (2) SA 481 (T); *Harrowsmith v Ceres Flats* 1979 (2) SA 722 (T).

In order to determine whether or not a lower court must regard a document as liquid, one asks whether the High Court would grant provisional sentence on that document. If so, the lower court must regard the document as liquid.[63]

The jurisdictional limits of R200 000 and R400 000 refer to the claim based upon the liquid document and not to the amount shown to be owing on the liquid document. Consequently, a plaintiff will be entitled to base a claim of R200 000 on a mortgage bond demonstrating indebtedness to the amount of R280 000 in the district court.

The interest and costs of the action are not taken into consideration in determining the amount of the claim.[64]

The procedure for summary judgment set out in rule 14 may be relevant, as is rule 14A relating to provisional sentence.

Section 29(1)*(e)***:** 'actions on or arising out of any credit agreement as defined in section 1 of the National Credit Act, 2005 (Act 34 of 2005)'.

The National Credit Act (NCA) generally applies to all credit agreements between parties dealing at arm's length and made or having an effect in South Africa.[65] A credit agreement is defined in s 1 as 'an agreement that meets all the criteria set out in s 8'. Where a matter is covered by the Act, the magistrates' courts have unlimited monetary jurisdiction as a result of the provisions of s 29(1)*(e)* of the Magistrates' Courts Act and s 172(2) of the NCA.[66]

Section 29(1)*(f)***:** 'actions in terms of section 16(1) of the Matrimonial Property Act, 1984, where the claim or the value of the property in dispute does not exceed the amount determined by the Minister from time to time by notice in the *Gazette*'.

Section 15 of the Matrimonial Property Act provides that, for marriages in community of property, spouses require the consent of the other spouse in order to perform various juristic acts with regard to the joint estate. Section 16 allows the spouse who cannot obtain the consent of the other spouse to apply to the court for leave to enter into the transaction. Section 16 provides that the procedure is by means of application.

Section 29(1)*(fA)***:** 'actions, including an application for liquidation, in terms of the Close Corporations Act, 1984 (Act 69 of 1984)'.

This section was included in order to settle a disputed point. There was a difference between the Witwatersrand Local Division and other divisions as to whether the jurisdiction of the lower courts to grant a liquidation order of a close corporation is exclusive, or whether the High Court has concurrent jurisdiction. The better view was that the High Court may order such a liquidation.[67] The

---

[63] *Chequers Outfitters (Bloemfontein) (Pty) Ltd v Sussman* 1959 (3) SA 55 (O) at 57; *Tuckers Land & Development Corporation (Pty) Ltd v Viljoen* 1979 (1) SA 677 (T) at 680. See *Erasmus Superior Court Practice* Bl–65 *et seq.*

[64] Section 37(3); *Van Coppenhagen v Van Coppenhagen* 1947 (1) SA 576 (T).

[65] The Act was amended in important respects by the National Credit Amendment Act 19 of 2014. The Amendment Act came into operation on 13 March 2015.

[66] See the discussion of the impact of the NCA on civil procedure in the magistrates' courts in chapter 3 above.

[67] See *Sams Voedsel (Edms) Bpk v Bethlehem Koelkamers Bpk* 1989 (2) SA 595 (O).

matter has now been resolved by an amendment to the Close Corporations Act providing for concurrent jurisdiction. This is the only insolvency application competent in the magistrates' courts.

> **Section 29(1)(g):** 'actions other than those already mentioned in this section, where the claim or the value of the matter in dispute does not exceed the amount determined by the Minister from time to time by notice in the *Gazette*'.

The following are instances falling within this section:
(1) The enforcement of an arbitrator's award. The court may not, however, make the award an order of court. This procedure is reserved for the High Court.
(2) The granting of a perpetual interdict.
(3) The enforcement of a foreign judgment.[68]

> **Section 29(1B)(a):** '[a] court for a regional division, in respect of causes of action, shall, subject to section 28(1A), have jurisdiction to hear and determine suits relating to the nullity of a marriage or a civil union and relating to divorce between persons and to decide upon any question arising therefrom, and to hear any matter and grant any order provided for in terms of the Recognition of Customary Marriages Act, 1998 (Act 120 of 1998)'.

Section 29(1B) was inserted into the Magistrates' Courts Act by the Jurisdiction of Regional Courts Amendment Act 31 of 2008.[69] Regional magistrates' courts now have the same jurisdiction as the High Court to determine suits on the nullity of a marriage or civil union and regarding divorce and issue arising therefrom, irrespective of the monetary value associated with the claim.[70]

2.3 Extension of the jurisdiction in respect of amounts claimed

The previous section deals with the usual upper limit of an amount which can be claimed in the magistrates' courts. The Act, however, provides for three ways in which the jurisdiction of the court can be extended so that claims involving higher amounts may also be adjudicated upon. These are:
(1) by consent of the parties in terms of s 45;
(2) by abandonment by the plaintiff of part of his claim in terms of s 38; and
(3) by deduction in terms of s 39 by the plaintiff of a debt which he admits owing to the defendant.

2.3.1 *Consent of the parties in terms of s 45*
Section 45:

> '(1) Subject to the provisions of section 46, the parties may consent in writing to the jurisdiction of either the court for the district or the court for the regional division to determine any action or proceedings otherwise beyond its jurisdiction in terms of section 29(1).
> (2) Any provision in a contract existing at the commencement of the Act or thereafter entered into, whereby a person undertakes that, when proceedings

---

[68] See Jones & Buckle Act 142–146.
[69] GN 41 in *GG* 33448 of 6 August 2010.
[70] See also the Civil Practice Directives for the Regional Courts in South Africa (2013 Revision). A fourth revision was recently published (2017).

have been or are about to be instituted, he will give such consent to jurisdiction as is contemplated in the proviso to subsection (1), shall be null and void.

(3) Any consent given in proceedings instituted in terms of section 57, 58, 65 or 65J by a defendant or a judgment debtor to the jurisdiction of a court which does not have jurisdiction over that defendant or judgment debtor in terms of section 28, is of no force and effect.'

This section previously created two situations which depended upon whether or not the court had jurisdiction over the defendant in terms of s 28. If the court did so have jurisdiction, the defendant could consent in writing to an increase of the jurisdictional limit at any time.[71] But if the court lacked this jurisdiction, then the only consent to an increase in the jurisdictional limit which will be valid will be that given once those proceedings have been or are about to be instituted. Thus, if the defendant neither lived nor worked within the jurisdictional area of the court but he or she entered into a hire-purchase contract which contained a clause by which he or she consented to the jurisdiction of the court, that clause will be null and void.[72]

The position changed with the introduction of the Courts of Law Amendment Act 7 of 2017.[73] The amended s 45 makes no reference to s 28 other than in relation to those sections listed in s 45(3). Thus, if a matter is not excluded from the jurisdiction of the magistrate's court by virtue of s 46, regardless of whether or not the court has jurisdiction over the defendant in terms of s 28, it is possible to consent to the jurisdiction of a district or regional court. Jurisdiction over the defendant in terms of s 28 is, however, required for proceedings instituted in terms of ss 57, 58, 65 and 65J.[74]

The consent must be in writing, but no formalities are required. Such consent may, therefore, be contained in correspondence.[75]

2.3.2 *Abandonment by the plaintiff of a portion of his or her claim in terms of s 38*

Section 38:

'(1) In order to bring a claim within the jurisdiction, a plaintiff may in his summons or at any time thereafter explicitly abandon part of such claim.

(2) If any part of a claim be so abandoned it shall thereby be finally extinguished: Provided that, if the claim be upheld in part only, the abandonment shall be deemed first to take effect upon that part of the claim which is not upheld.'

Abandonment is used when the plaintiff wishes to save the costs of a High Court action by litigating in the magistrate's court, but his or her claim exceeds the

---

[71] *Truck & Car Co (Pty) Ltd v Ewart* 1949 (4) SA 295 (T); *Skead v Swanepoel* 1949 (4) SA 763 (T).

[72] *Van Heerden v Muir* 1955 (2) SA 376 (A).

[73] With effect from 1 August 2018.

[74] Regrettably, sub-s (1) is worded in such a way that it could also be interpreted to mean that it is only possible to consent to matters that are 'otherwise beyond its jurisdiction in terms of section 29(1)' and that jurisdiction in terms of s 28 remains a prerequisite. It is submitted that, especially when considering the section upon a conspectus, such an interpretation would not be correct.

[75] *David v Naggyah & another* 1961 (3) SA 4 (N), which was approved in *Neale v Edenvale Plastic Products (Pty) Ltd* 1971 (3) SA 860 (T) and in *Hydromar v Pearl Oyster* (supra) 387E *et seq.*

jurisdictional limit of the lower court. The plaintiff must still claim the full amount, but he or she must abandon the part in excess of the jurisdiction of the court.

The court must adjudicate on the full amount claimed and cannot merely hold that it exceeds the jurisdictional limit. If the amount found to be owing exceeds the limit of the court but is not the full amount claimed, then the shortfall is set-off first against the amount abandoned.

Thus, if the plaintiff claims damages of R412 000 and abandons R12 000 to bring it within the jurisdiction of the regional court, but is able to prove damages of only R405 000, the shortfall of R7 000 is deducted from the R12 000 abandoned. The result is that the plaintiff will be awarded R400 000.[76]

The abandonment should properly be incorporated into the summons so as to avoid the probability of a special plea, but the abandonment can take place at any stage prior to judgment by amendment of the pleadings.[77] An example is the following:

> 'In consequence of the above the defendant is indebted to the plaintiff in the sum of R412 000. In order to bring his claim within the jurisdiction of the magistrate's court, the plaintiff in terms of s 38 of the Magistrates' Courts Act 32 of 1944 hereby abandons the amount of R12 000.
> Wherefore plaintiff claims:
> (1) Judgment against the defendant in the amount of R400 000 ....'

The result of such abandonment is that the claim is extinguished. The amount abandoned can thus not be used for any purpose such as set-off.

If the defendant institutes a counterclaim, the total due to the party with the higher claim is calculated with regard to the amount which the court may award. In other words, the counterclaim does not operate on the amount prior to abandonment to bring the result within the jurisdiction of the court. The reason for this is that each claim is separate and the amount abandoned is extinguished.

2.3.3 *Deduction in terms of s 39 by the plaintiff of a debt which he or she admits owing to the defendant*

Section 39:

> 'In order to bring a claim within the jurisdiction a plaintiff may, in his summons or at any time after the issue thereof, deduct from his claim, whether liquidated or unliquidated, any amount admitted by him to be due by himself to the defendant.'

Just as in the case of abandonment, the plaintiff must set out expressly in his or her particulars of claim all the details of the deduction.

The admission of a debt which is owing amounts to set-off, and the admission of the debt automatically renders the debt liquid. There is no need, however, for the plaintiff's claim to be liquidated.

A deduction may be accompanied by an abandonment, if the deduction by itself will not bring the claim within the jurisdiction of the court.

---

[76] *Santam Versekeringsmaatskappy Bpk v Brown* 1973 (2) SA 326 (C).
[77] In *General Carpets v De Villiers* 1990 (4) SA 411 (W) the abandonment took place on appeal.

There is no question of the debt, which is being set-off, being deducted from the amount abandoned, as happens in terms of s 38. The amount which the plaintiff admits and deducts from his or her gross claim is for all practical purposes conclusively proved as being owed to the defendant. Should the plaintiff's claim thus be upheld in part only, the amount of the admitted debt is deducted from that portion of the plaintiff's claim upheld by the court.

3   CASES IN WHICH THE MAGISTRATES' COURTS LACK JURISDICTION

In contrast with the High Court, which, on account of its inherent jurisdiction, may try virtually any type of case, there are numerous matters which are expressly excluded from the jurisdiction of the lower courts. In these cases, the lower courts, as creatures of statute, will not possess jurisdiction, not even by means of the consent of all the parties. In other words, such cases must be pursued in the High Court even if the claim value is less than R400 000. In this regard, s 46(2) provides as follows:

Section 46(2):

'A court shall have no jurisdiction in matters–
(a) in which the validity or interpretation of a will or other testamentary document is in question;
(b) in which the status of a person in respect of mental capacity is sought to be affected;
(c) in which is sought specific performance without an alternative of payment of damages, except in–
  (i) the rendering of an account in respect of which the claim does not exceed the amount determined by the Minister from time to time by notice in the *Gazette;*
  (ii) the delivery or transfer of property, movable or immovable, not exceeding in value the amount determined by the Minister from time to time by notice in the *Gazette;* and
  (iii) the delivery or transfer of property, movable or immovable, exceeding in value the amount determined by the Minister from time to time by notice in the *Gazette,* where the consent of the parties has been obtained in terms of section 45.
(d) in which is sought a decree of perpetual silence.'

It is important to note that s 46 does not include divorce-related matters. Section 29(1B) affords jurisdiction in such matters to regional magistrates' courts.

The purpose of s 46(2) is to limit the power of the court to impose orders of specific performance.[78] Considerable case law has dealt with what constitutes specific performance. There are two main issues. First, whether the performance relates only to specific performance on a contract or whether it relates to performances generally. Secondly, whether the performance relates to the payment of a debt *(ad pecuniam solvendam)* or to the performance of some other kind of action *(ad factum praestandum)*. The matter is not free of difficulty because a claim for payment of the purchase price on a contract of sale is in fact a claim for

---

[78] For a summary see Jones & Buckle Act 301 *et seq.*

specific performance, and to speak of an alternative claim for damages under such circumstances is nonsense. The better view is that orders sounding in money, regardless of the cause of action, are not, for the purposes of this section, orders for specific performance.[79]

The section is applied where there is a claim for specific performance of a contract, that is, where the defendant has to do some particular act.[80] This is the technical meaning of the term 'specific performance' in the law of contract.[81] Other claims for performance, which are not based upon contract, will need to be reconciled with s 30(1), which gives the court the power to grant, amongst other things, an interdict and a *mandament van spolie*. In *Zinman v Miller*[82] it was held that a *mandament van spolie* is not an order for specific performance and that s 30 is not to be qualified by s 46(2)*(c)*.

However, the court is not empowered to grant an interdict which has the effect of granting a claim for specific performance.[83]

The various exceptions in the section are self-explanatory and overlap with the provisions of s 29.

4 MISCELLANEOUS PROVISIONS CONCERNING JURISDICTION

4.1 Incidental jurisdiction
Section 37:

'(1) In actions wherein the sum claimed, being within the jurisdiction, is the balance of an account, the court may enquire into and take evidence if necessary upon the whole account, even though such account contains items and transactions exceeding the amount of the jurisdiction.

(2) Where the amount claimed or other relief sought is within the jurisdiction, such jurisdiction shall not be ousted merely because it is necessary for the court, in order to arrive at a decision, to give a finding upon a matter beyond the jurisdiction.

(3) In considering whether a claim is or is not within the jurisdiction, no prayer for interest on the principal sum claimed or for costs or for general or alternative relief shall be taken into account.'

Section 37(1) is self-explanatory and should be read together with s 46(2)*(c)*(i).

Section 37(2) provides for the situation in which the claim is within the jurisdiction, but, in order to come to a decision on the claim, the court must make a finding on another issue outside its jurisdiction. For instance, in *De Villiers & another v De Villiers*[84] the plaintiff claimed the eviction of the defendant in a claim within the jurisdiction, but the defence depended upon a plea of prescription that

---

[79] *Tuckers Land and Development Corporation (Edms) Bpk v Van Zyl* 1977 (3) SA 1041 (T). See also *Otto en 'n ander v Basson* 1994 (2) SA 744 (C).
[80] *Maisel v Camberleigh Court (Pty) Ltd* 1953 (4) SA 371 (C); *Olivier v Stoop* 1978 (1) SA 196 (T).
[81] *Malkiewicz v Van Niekerk and Fourouclas Investments CC* [2008] 1 All SA 57 (T). See also *Wannenburg v Madamu Technologies (Pty) Ltd* [2012] ZAKZPHC 35 (13 June 2012) para 18 and *Van der Walt v Road Accident Fund* 2015 JOL 34916 (GJ).
[82] 1956 (3) SA 8 (T).
[83] *Badenhorst v Theophanous* 1988 (1) SA 793 (C) 793 at 801G.
[84] 1949 (2) SA 173 (C).

fell outside the jurisdiction. The court held that the magistrate had to make a finding on the defence of prescription, which fell outside its jurisdiction, in order to adjudicate on the claim for eviction.[85]

Section 37(3) is self-explanatory.

4.2 Cumulative jurisdiction and splitting of claims
Section 43:

'(1) If two or more claims, each based upon a different cause of action, are combined in one summons, the court shall have the same jurisdiction to decide each such claim as it would have had if each claim had formed the sole subject of a separate action.

(2) If a claim for the confirmation of an interdict or arrest granted *pendente lite* be joined in the same summons with a claim for relief or any other character, the court shall have the same jurisdiction to decide each such claim as it would have had if each claim had formed the sole subject of a separate action, even though all the claims arise from the same cause of action.'

There is no limit to the number of claims which a plaintiff may include in one summons, provided he or she abides by the rules relating to joinder, which are set out below. Whether or not a claim is based upon the same or a different cause of action is usually self-evident. However, care should be taken with regard to the distinction between claiming payment of instalments on a credit agreement, where each outstanding payment gives rise to a new cause of action,[86] and claiming payment of a debt where the debt has been split up merely to bring the claim within the jurisdiction.[87] The splitting of claims is prohibited by s 40:

Section 40:

'A substantive claim exceeding the jurisdiction may not be split with the object of recovering the same in more than one action if the parties to all such actions would be the same and the point at issue in all such actions would also be the same.'

5 JOINDER OF PARTIES

The common law with regard to joinder is not set out in the Act or the Rules but still applies. In general, the court will insist that every person who has a direct and substantial interest in any order which the court might make is a necessary party and should be joined.[88]

One must, therefore, distinguish between *necessary joinder* and *discretionary joinder*.

---

[85] See, for example, *Tshisa v Premier of the Free State & another* 2010 (2) SA 153 (FB) and *Ntshingila & others v Minister of Police* 2012 (1) SA 392 (WCC).

[86] *Lochrenberg v Sululu* 1960 (2) SA 502 (E).

[87] *Cohen v Sherman & Co* 1941 TPD 134 at 137–8; *Marais v Du Preez* 1966 (4) SA 456 (E); *Badenhorst v Alum Konstruksie en 'n ander* 1986 (2) SA 225 (T) at 228B–C.

[88] *Amalgamated Engineering Union v Minister of Labour* 1949 (3) SA 637 (A) at 659; *Erasmus Superior Court Practice* D1-124 notes 4 and 5 and the cases cited there. Also Jones & Buckle Act 271 *et seq.* The matter is also discussed in chapter 14 below in connection with the special plea of non-joinder or misjoinder.

5.1 Joinder of plaintiffs
Section 41:

'(1) Any number of persons, each of whom has a separate claim against the same defendant, may join as plaintiffs in one action if their right to relief depends upon the determination of some question of law or fact which if separate actions were instituted would arise in each action: Provided that if such joint action be instituted the defendant may apply to court for an order directing that separate trials be held and the court in its discretion may make such order as it deems just and expedient.

(2) In any joint action instituted as aforesaid judgment may be given for such one or more of the plaintiffs as may be found entitled to relief.

(3) If all the plaintiffs fail in any such action, the court may make such order as to costs as to it may seem just; in particular, it may order that the plaintiffs pay the costs of the defendant jointly and severally, the one paying the other to be absolved, and that if one plaintiff pays more than his pro rata share of the costs of the defendant, he shall be entitled to recover from the other plaintiffs their pro rata share of such excess.

(4) If some of the plaintiffs succeed and others fail, the court may make such order as to costs as it may deem just.'

It is thus possible for plaintiffs to join under the common law if it is convenient to do so and even if there are no common questions of law or fact which, if separate actions were instituted, would arise in each action.[89]

A common instance of the application of this section is where a number of plaintiffs are injured in a motor accident. Each may sue separately, but for convenience it is possible to sue as co-plaintiffs in one action. A defendant may not compel such plaintiffs to proceed in one action.[90]

The critical factor is the question whether the issues between the parties 'depend upon the determination of some question of law or fact which if separate actions were instituted would arise in each action'. It is submitted that the word 'some' should be interpreted through reference to rule 10(1) of the Uniform Rules, where the term employed is 'substantially the same'. It should not be sufficient to justify joinder if there is only a tangential overlap between the actions. The purpose of the section is to vary the common law so as to expedite resolution of the disputes and to minimise costs and inconvenience.[91]

5.2 Joinder of defendants
Section 42:

'(1) Several defendants may be sued in the alternative or both in the alternative and jointly in one action, whenever it is alleged by the plaintiff that he has suffered damages and that it is uncertain which of the defendants is in law responsible for such damages; Provided that on the application of any of the defendants the court may in its discretion order that separate trials be held, or make such other order as it may deem just and expedient.'

---

[89] Jones & Buckle Act 271.
[90] *Licences and General Insurance Co Ltd v Van Zyl* 1961 (3) SA 101 (D).
[91] As to the continued effect of the common law, see *Erasmus Superior Court Practice* B1–96.

Similarly, s 42 is not intended to restrict common-law joinder of defendants.[92]

It is not permissible to raise mutually contradictory claims unless they are alternatives.

The discretion referred to will be exercised with the following in mind: 'convenience, equity, the saving of costs and the avoidance of multiplicity of actions'.[93]

Section 42 contains substantially the same provisions for the payment of costs as those set out in s 41.

Should a plaintiff neglect to join a necessary party in his summons, or should he or she wish to join another defendant after service of the summons, the plaintiff is required in terms of rule 28 to make an application to the court for such a joinder. Such application would follow the requirements of rule 55.[94]

6 COUNTERCLAIMS EXCEEDING THE JURISDICTION

For jurisdictional purposes, counterclaims are, in general, treated as claims in convention.[95] However, where the counterclaim exceeds the monetary jurisdiction of the court, a special provision applies. Note that the defendant cannot acquire personal jurisdiction over a plaintiff merely because the plaintiff has instituted an action in the defendant's court.[96]

Section 47:

'(1) When in answer to a claim within the jurisdiction the defendant sets up a counterclaim exceeding the jurisdiction, the claim shall not on that account be dismissed; but the court may, if satisfied that the defendant has *prima facie* a reasonable prospect on his counterclaim of obtaining a judgment in excess of its jurisdiction, stay the action for a reasonable period in order to enable him to institute an action in a competent court. The plaintiff in the magistrate's court may (notwithstanding his action therein) counterclaim in such competent court and in that event all questions as to the costs incurred in the magistrate's court shall be decided by that competent court.

(2) If the period for which such action has been stayed has expired and the defendant has failed to issue and serve a summons in a competent court in relation to the matters and the subject of such counterclaim the magistrate's court shall on application either–
   (a) stay the action for a further reasonable period; or
   (b) dismiss the counterclaim (whether the defendant does or does not reduce such counterclaim to an amount within the jurisdiction of the court).'

This section should be read together with rule 20. When a defendant wishes to counterclaim with a claim which exceeds the jurisdiction of the court, he or she has two alternatives. First, the defendant may abandon that part of the counterclaim which exceeds the jurisdiction of the court, or, secondly, he or she may apply to have the counterclaim adjudicated in another court prior to the

---

[92] Jones & Buckle *Act* 275.
[93] *Gemeenskapontwikkelingsraad v Williams & others* (2) 1977 (3) SA 955 (W) at 971H.
[94] *Khumalo v Wilkins* 1972 (4) SA 470 (N).
[95] See s 44.
[96] See above.

adjudication of the plaintiff's claim. When the defendant wishes to follow the second alternative, rule 20(5) provides that an application must be made to the court within five days of filing the counterclaim for the court to decide whether or not the counterclaim exceeds its jurisdiction and to stay the plaintiff's action. There is a duplication between rules 20(5) and 20(6), but it would appear that if the application in terms of rule 20(5) does not also ask for a stay in the plaintiff's action, then the defendant has a further five days in which to make application for such a stay in terms of rule 20(6).

Such a defendant may then institute an action in the competent court, which will usually be the High Court. This must be done by issue and service of summons within the period for which the magistrate's court has stayed the action. If it is not so done, s 47(2) applies. The defendant may not at this stage abandon part of his or her counterclaim but faces the dismissal of the whole counterclaim.

Section 47(3) merely provides that if the defendant's counterclaim, now an action in another court, comes to nought, then the counterclaim is dismissed in the magistrate's court and the court proceeds to adjudicate on the plaintiff's claim.

7 REMOVAL OF ACTIONS FROM THE LOWER COURTS TO THE HIGH COURT

Section 50 regulates the removal of actions from the lower courts to the High Court. Where a defendant feels that the case is too complex for it to be adjudicated in the lower court, he or she may apply for the case to be transferred to the High Court.

The claim to be transferred has to exceed an amount determined by the Minister.[97] Notice of intention to apply for the transfer of the action must be given to the plaintiff before the date on which the matter is set down for hearing. Such a notice must object to the hearing taking place in any magistrate's court, and must tender such security for costs as the court may decide and payment of an amount for costs already incurred and which may be incurred, not exceeding a sum determined by the Minister.[98]

As soon as the defendant satisfies all of these requirements, the magistrate's court is obliged to stay the action in that court and to remove it to a competent provincial or local division of the High Court.

Upon the removal, the summons in the lower court stands as the summons in the division to which the action is removed, provided that the plaintiff does not object to it. Alternatively, the plaintiff may issue fresh summons in the High Court.

The only check on the defendant's right to force the plaintiff into the High Court is the discretion that court has in awarding costs. The defendant must show that there were good grounds for the removal to the High Court, otherwise he or she will not be granted costs on the High Court scale.[99]

Should a plaintiff be successful after his or her case has been removed to the High Court, he or she may be awarded costs on an attorney-and-client basis, and

---

[97] Section 50(1). The amount at present is R3 000 (GN 217 in *GG* 37477 of 27 March 2014).
[98] Section 50(1)*(c)*. The amount at present is R3 000 (GN 217 in *GG* 37477 of 27 March 2014).
[99] *Rheeder v Frank* 1939 CPD 446.

not on the usual party-and-party basis. It is only where the High Court expresses its displeasure at the plaintiff's conduct that attorney-and-client costs will *not* be awarded.[100]

This rule as to costs does not apply where a plaintiff, as is his or her right, decides from the outset to proceed in the High Court in a matter in which a lower court has jurisdiction. Should the High Court consider this an abuse of its process, it will hear the case and make an order for appropriate costs.[101]

It is submitted that these rules require revision and that there should be much easier access to the High Court in matters which depend upon difficult points of law or fact.

---

[100] *Da Mota v Jourdan* 1949 (4) SA 348 (W).
[101] *Standard Credit Corporation v Bester & others* 1987 (1) SA 812 (W).

Chapter 5

THE FORMS THAT PROCEEDINGS MAY TAKE

There are two forms that proceedings in the magistrates' courts may take: *action* (or trial) and *application* (or motion) proceedings.

The action proceeding begins with the service of a summons to which may be attached the first pleading, being the particulars of plaintiff's claim, if the cause of action is not set out in the summons itself. The form of the summons is set out in Forms 2, 2A, 2B, 2C and 3.[1] The proceeding continues with the exchange of documents and leads to a trial at which oral evidence is heard. The parties are called 'plaintiff' and 'defendant'.

The application proceeding begins with the service of a notice of motion to which is annexed an affidavit. The application is set out in terms of Forms 1, 1A, 1B and 1C.[2] The facts relied upon by the other party may also be presented to the court by way of affidavit, to which the applicant has the opportunity to reply. The matter is then set down for hearing, usually during a weekly motion court, and it is argued on the basis of the facts set out in the affidavit. Only in exceptional circumstances will the matter be referred to the hearing of oral evidence. The parties are called 'applicant' and 'respondent'.

When one may use application proceedings is one of the differences between High Court practice and that of the lower courts. In the High Court the general rules are that one may use application proceedings only if there is no anticipated dispute of fact,[3] or if urgency demands it,[4] or if a statute compels one to do so. Certain types of relief, such as divorce, can be obtained only by way of action. In terms of the common law a litigant may often, therefore, have a discretion whether to proceed by way of application or by way of action.

The situation in the lower courts is rather different. Because the courts are governed by their statutes and do not have inherent jurisdiction, the governing statutes determine what kind of proceeding has to be followed.[5] The Magistrates'

---

[1] Form 2 (simple summons); Form 2A (provisional sentence summons); Form 2B (combined summons); Form 2C (combined summons: divorce action) and Form 3 (summons (in which is included an automatic rent interdict)).

[2] Form 1 (short form notice of motion); Form 1A (long form notice of motion); Form 1B (notice of application to declare immovable property executable in terms of rule 43A) and Form 1C (notice of motion (short form, for Interlocutory or other applications incidental to pending proceedings)).

[3] See Room Hire Co (Pty) Ltd v Jeppe Mansions (Pty) Ltd 1949 (3) SA 1155 (T).

[4] See *Luna Meubel Vervaardigers (Edms) Bpk v Makin (t/a Makin's Furniture Manufacturers)* 1977 (4) SA 135 (W).

[5] *Wolman v Block (2) 1928 OPD 119; E Castignani (Pty) Ltd v Claude Neon Lights (SA) Ltd* 1969 (4) SA 462 (O) at 465; *In re Pennington Health Committee* 1980 (4) SA 243 (N); *Van der Schyff v Taylor* 1984 (2) SA 688 (C).

Courts Act refers generally to actions, as in s 29(1), and this has been interpreted to mean that the general form of proceeding will be the action proceeding. Application proceedings are allowed only when the Act or the rules provide that application may be made or that a matter may be decided on application. Certain statutes also provide that application may be made in the lower courts, as for instance for the winding-up of a close corporation.

This means that there is not the same discretion in the magistrates' courts as exists in the High Court, and many types of relief which are granted in the High Court by way of application have to be dealt with in the magistrates' courts either by way of action or not at all.

Applications fall into two categories: they may either commence a proceeding and see it through to its conclusion, or they may be part of another proceeding. The second kind of application is called an *interlocutory application*. For instance, in an action it may be necessary for one of the parties to apply to court for an order to compel the other to conform to one or other of the rules relating to the filing of documents. Such an interlocutory application conforms generally to the rules applicable to applications, except in so far as the requirements for service and notice are required.

It happens that action and application proceedings can be interwoven in a different way. A creditor could, for example, issue summons for payment of an amount of money still due to him or her on the ground of an instalment sale transaction in respect of a car, and at the same time by way of application seek an interdict to prevent the defendant from making further use of the car; or a lessor may issue summons for arrear rent, and at the same time make application for the attachment of the lessee's furniture by the sheriff in order to secure the lessor's hypothec over such furniture.

The following chapters deal first with application proceedings in more detail, and then move on to describe the action proceeding.

Both action and application proceedings lead to a judgment by the court. The process by which the person in whose favour judgment is given (referred to as the *judgment creditor*) enforces judgment is known as *execution*. This is discussed in chapter 17.

Although the procedure instituted by the issue of summons comes to an end with the handing down of judgment and its subsequent execution, there is naturally always the possibility that one of the parties feels aggrieved by the judgment and wishes to take the matter on appeal or review. These subjects are treated in chapter 18.

Chapters 19 and 20 each deal with a distinct area of the law of civil procedure. In chapter 19 the debt-collecting procedure is considered. This procedure today occupies a special place in lower court practice and is used by practitioners for the collection of debts on behalf of their clients.

Chapter 20 deals with the administration order. An administration order may be made by a civil court and may be regarded as a type of insolvency proceeding. Although the estate of a debtor in respect of whom an administration order has been granted is not sequestrated by the order, the order serves as a type of halfway house to insolvency. In terms of the administration order, the debtor must pay over a stipulated amount to his administrator at periodic intervals, and the administrator in turn makes pro rata payments to the debtor's various creditors.

Chapter 6

THE APPLICATION PROCEDURE

1   TYPES OF APPLICATION

A general outline of application proceedings has already been given in the previous chapter. There it was stated that only those applications specifically provided for in the Act may be brought, and they include:

- setting aside an automatic rent interdict (s 31(4));
- attaching property in security of rent (s 32(1));
- setting aside an order attaching property in security of rent (s 32(2));
- appointing an assessor (Form 21) (s 34);
- for transfer of an action or proceeding to another lower court (s 35);
- for rescission of judgment (s 36);
- for separation of trials where plaintiffs have joined (s 41);
- for separation of trials where defendants are sued jointly (s 42);
- for dismissal of a counterclaim exceeding the jurisdiction where the defendant has failed to institute an action in the High Court under s 47 (s 47(3));
- for removal of the case to the High Court (s 50);
- for the approval of interrogatories (s 52);
- for revival of a superannuated judgment (s 63);
- paying debts by instalments (s 73);
- for an administration order (s 74);
- for amendment of proceedings (s 111);
- for summary judgment (Form 7) (rule 14(1));
- for stay of action under s 47 (rule 20(5));
- costs for withdrawal of an action (rule 27(3));
- recording a settlement (rule 27(6), (7) and (8));
- entering a judgment in terms of a settlement (rule 27(9));
- amending the record (rule 30(11));
- for adjournment of an action (rule 31);
- for stay of action when previous costs are unpaid (rule 32(3));

- for a garnishee order (Form 39) (rule 47);
- for review of judgment (rule 49);
- for leave to sue or defend as a *pro Deo* litigant (rule 53);
- for leave to amend pleadings (rules 55 and 55A);
- attachments;
- interdicts and spoliation orders (rules 56, 57 and 55(9));
- securing compliance with the rules (rule 60).

All applications must be brought on notice of motion, supported by an affidavit as to the facts upon which the applicant relies for relief.[1] Interlocutory and other applications incidental to pending proceedings must be brought on notice, supported by affidavits if facts need to be placed before the court.[2]

Where the matter is urgent, the court may make an order dispensing with the forms and service provided for in the rules and may dispose of the matter at such time and place and in accordance with such procedure as the court deems appropriate. Such an application must be supported by an affidavit which expressly states the circumstances which the applicant avers render the matter urgent and the reasons why the applicant claims that he or she could not be accorded substantial redress at a hearing in due course.[3]

2 PROCEEDINGS IN THE MOTION COURT

The motion court normally sits in one of the existing courtrooms of the lower court. A certain day or days will be allocated for motion court hearings. It is important for practitioners to know these dates because the notice of motion has to set out the day on which the application will be made, and various steps have to occur and time periods have to be complied with prior to that date. In general, 10 days must elapse between the date on which the respondent or other interested party is given notice of the application and the day on which the application is heard in court, but where the State is the respondent it has to be given 15 days' notice.[4] These days are calculated excluding Saturdays, Sundays and public holidays, and are often referred to as 'court days'.[5]

All papers in each application are filed with the registrar or clerk of the court, who arranges the files in order and draws up a roll. The applications are then dealt with by the magistrate in the order of the roll. When the case is called, the applicant, or his or her legal representative, stands and addresses the court. The magistrate may ask questions or require argument about some aspect of the papers or the law. The application will be granted if it is unopposed and the necessary averments are in the papers.

If the application is opposed, it will either have been set down for the end of the roll or it will stand down to the end, so that the unopposed applications may be disposed of first. In some centres opposed applications are set down on a separate

---

[1] Rule 55(1).
[2] Rule 55(4).
[3] Rule 55(5).
[4] Rule 55(1)(*e*) and (6).
[5] Rule 2(2), which states: 'A Saturday, Sunday or public holiday shall not, unless the contrary appears, be reckoned as part of any period calculated in terms of these rules.'

roll. The opposed applications must be heard in open court, but it is possible for unopposed applications to be heard in a magistrate's chambers.[6]

The court has a discretion whether to hear *viva voce* evidence to clarify a disputed point, but it will not so order merely to fill gaps in affidavits. Where a dispute of fact arises which was not anticipated originally by the applicant, the magistrate may order that the application be transformed into an action and go to trial.[7] If the dispute of facts should have been anticipated and the applicant should not have proceeded by way of application, the application will be dismissed.

The notice of motion launching an application may take either of two forms:

(1)   the *ex parte* notice of motion; or

(2)   the notice of motion addressed to a respondent, ie on notice.

2.1   The *ex parte* application

2.1.1   *Cases in which the* ex parte *application may be used*

An *ex parte* application is one of which notice is not given to the person against whom legal relief is sought prior to the initial hearing.[8]

The following applications are examples of *ex parte* applications:

*   garnishee orders;
*   attachments;
*   interdicts;
*   spoliation orders.

Ex parte applications may be brought where the giving of notice to the party against whom the order is claimed would defeat the purpose of the application or where the degree of urgency is so great that it justifies dispensing with notice.[9] The notice of motion prescribed in Form 1 of Annexure 1 to the rules may be used.[10] *Ex parte* orders are of an interim nature and must call upon the party against whom they are made to appear before the court on a specified return date to explain why the order should not be confirmed.[11] Any person against whom an *ex parte* order is granted may anticipate the return day upon delivery of not less than 24 hours' notice.[12]

A legal representative may sign the notice of motion, but only the party with personal knowledge of the facts may attest to an affidavit.[13] An *ex parte* application in the magistrates' courts will usually ask for an order against someone; that person, or persons, is cited as 'respondent'.[14] Strictly speaking, an *ex parte* application involves no respondent at all, but such applications are almost

---

[6] Rule 55(3)*(h)* provides that *ex parte* applications may be heard in chambers.

[7] Rule 55(3)*(k)*.

[8] *Simross Vintners (Pty) Ltd v Vermeulen & two other cases* 1978 (1) SA 779 (T) at 783A–B.

[9] Rule 55(3)*(a)*.

[10] It may be varied as circumstances require. In this regard, see Jones & Buckle Rule 55-26B.

[11] Rule 55(3)*(c)*.

[12] Rule 55(3)*(d)*.

[13] *Raphael & Co v Standard Produce Co (Pty) Ltd* 1951 (4) SA 244 (C); *Wright v McGuinness* 1956 (3) SA 184 (C) at 186.

[14] Rule 55(3)*(e)*.

unknown in lower court practice. Examples in High Court practice are applications for admissions as legal practitioners and various insolvency applications.

Rule 56(1) expressly provides that applications for interdicts, attachments to secure claims and *mandamenten van spolie* may be made *ex parte*. The authorisation for this provision is to be found in s 30 of the Act. The rule is enabling and not peremptory.

The reason why the *ex parte* application is used in these cases is self-evident and logical. Where it is necessary to obtain immediate relief because any delay would result in the relief sought being unenforceable later, it would be senseless to warn the person concerned (the respondent) in advance that the application will be brought.[15]

Suppose that some conduct on the part of the respondent could bring about irreparable damage to the applicant. If the party threatened by such action must first issue summons to obtain an interdict or even bring an application in the ordinary way (in which latter event the case may be heard by the court two weeks later at the earliest) then it may be too late to prevent the harm threatened, and the party harmed would then have to be content with a claim for compensation for the harm sustained by him or her. With the *ex parte* application, however, an interdict to prevent the harm threatened may be obtained within an hour or two.

Although no form is prescribed for the *ex parte* notice of motion,[16] the following may serve as an example in the context of district court litigation:[17]

IN THE MAGISTRATE'S COURT FOR THE DISTRICT OF .... held at ....   ***For use in the District Court**   Case No .... of 20..............   In the matter between   .... Applicant   and   .... Respondent
NOTICE OF MOTION
TAKE NOTICE that application will be made on behalf of the above-named applicant on the .... day of .... at 9:00 or as soon thereafter as the parties may be heard for an order in the following terms: (a)   (b)   (c)   And that the affidavit of .... annexed hereto will be used in support hereof.

---

[15] See chapter 7 below.

[16] Rule 55(3)(*b*) simply provides that the notice of motion in an *ex parte* application shall be similar to Form 1 of Annexure 1.

[17] Also see Form 1 of Annexure 1 to the rules regarding the form of notice of motion to be used in the regional court.

Kindly place the matter on the roll for hearing accordingly.

DATED at .... on this .... day of .... 20.........

....

APPLICANT'S ATTORNEY

Address: ....

....

TO:

THE CLERK OF THE COURT

The most important requirement that the applicant must satisfy in bringing an *ex parte* application is that he or she must show it is really necessary to bring the application without notice to the respondent. There must be the requisite urgency or some other good reason why no notice should be given to the respondent.[18] Should the *ex parte* application be brought with undue haste and without good reason, the court will not grant the application and the applicant will consequently have to bear the costs of the failed application.

In the applicant's reasons for his or her application, or his or her affidavit, which is called a *founding affidavit*, he or she should set out the facts upon which his or her cause of action is based and why notice has not been given to the respondent.

Good faith on the part of the applicant is required in applications brought *ex parte*.[19] An applicant is therefore duty bound to place all possible facts before the court, even if some are adverse to his or her case. This duty has been expressed as follows:

> 'It cannot, I think, be too strongly insisted upon that in *ex parte* applications it is the duty of the applicant to lay all the relevant facts before the Court, so that it may have full knowledge of the circumstances of the case before making its order.'[20]

Where the applicant is unable to place all the relevant facts before the court by means of his or her own affidavit or by further affidavits deposed to by others, he or she may state that certain facts exist to the best of his or her knowledge. He or she must then, however, always explain the source of the information and it must be apparent to the court that it has to proceed on the basis of these averments on account of the urgency of the matter. Even prior to s 3(1) of the Law of Evidence Amendment Act 45 of 1988 this constituted an exception to the bar on the admission of hearsay evidence. This Act relaxes the position still further.[21]

---

[18] *Office Automaton Specialists CC & another v Lotter* 1997 (3) SA 443 (E).

[19] *Spilg v Walker* 1947 (3) SA 495 (E) at 499; *Shaw & Bosman v Tatham* 1912 WLD 75. See also: *Schlesinger v Schlesinger* 1979 (4) SA 342 (W) at 348E–349B; *Commissioner for the South African Revenue Services v Bachir & others* [2016] ZAGPPHC 251 (22 April 2016); *Pretoria Portland Cement Co Ltd & another v Competition Commission & others* 2003 (2) SA 385 (SCA) at 45; *Thint (Pty) Ltd v National Director of Public Prosecutions & others; Zuma v National Director of Public Prosecutions & others* 2009 (1) SA 1 (CC) at 115A–E; and *Ex parte Arntzen (Nedbank Ltd as intervening creditor)* 2013 (1) SA 49 (KZP) at 5.

[20] *Estate Logie v Priest* 1926 AD 312 at 323.

[21] For example, see *Mnyama v Gxalaba & another* 1990 (1) SA 650 (C) at 652J *et seq.*

2.1.2 *Powers of the court on hearing the* ex parte *application*

The *ex parte* application constitutes an exception to the principle *audi et alteram partem,*[22] which principle underlies the entire law of civil procedure.[23] For this reason, the court will not issue a final order without the person concerned (usually the person against whom the order is made) being afforded an opportunity of putting his or her case.

In the *ex parte* application the court therefore issues an interim order, and a date (called the *return day)* is set upon which the person against whom the order has been issued must be able to give reasons why the order should not be made final. The court therefore issues only an interim order and the applicant is granted only provisional relief.

This type of order is called a rule *nisi.*

In this way, the applicant immediately obtains the legal relief he or she desires, but the opponent also obtains an opportunity to put his or her case. The applicant is under a duty to have a copy of the court's order together with the founding affidavit served upon the respondent (and upon any other interested party who should have been joined as a respondent).[24] Further, the minutes of any order required for service or execution shall be drawn up by the party entitled thereto and shall be approved and signed by the registrar or clerk of the court.[25]

The following example of an order for an interdict obtained *ex parte* in the regional court may serve as an illustration:[26]

No. 16
Order for Interdict Obtained *Ex Parte*
* For use in the Regional Court
In the Regional Court for the Regional Division of ....
held at ....
Case No .... of 20 ....
In the matter between
.... Applicant
and
.... Respondent
It is ordered:

---

[22] Literally means: hear also the other side.

[23] *Skeyi v Ordemann* 1910 EDL 60 at 62: 'It is true that litigation must have an end, and the rules of court must be observed, but there is also a sound maxim, *audi alteram partem.* Courts should always afford both parties every assistance in laying their cases before them.' See also *Central News Agency Ltd v Publications Control Board* 1970 (2) SA 290 (C); *Sachs v Minister of Justice* 1934 AD 11 at 38; *Van Aswegen v Administrator, Orange Free State & others* 1955 (3) SA 60 (O); *Shagan Bros v Lewis & another* 1911 TPD 417.

[24] Rule 55(3)*(e)* and *(g).* Service is to be effected in accordance with rule 9. See also *Schoeman v Acting Assistant Magistrate of Harrismith* 1933 OPD 47 where it was held that a magistrate is not entitled to issue a final order upon an *ex parte* application without the respondent being afforded an opportunity of putting his or her case.

[25] Rule 55(8)*(a).*

[26] Annexure 1 Form 16.

(1) That a rule nisi be and is hereby granted calling upon .... (respondent) of .... (address) to show cause to this court on the .... day of ...., 20 ...... at .... (time), or so soon thereafter as the matter can be heard, why .... shall not be interdicted from .... (set out the acts from which respondent or any other person is restrained) pending the decision of an action by the applicant against the said .... (respondent) for .... (set out the nature of the claim).

(2) That this rule nisi operates as an interim interdict.

The aforesaid date may be anticipated by the respondent upon 12 hours' notice[27] to the applicant.

By Order of the Court,

....

Registrar

....

Applicant/Applicant's Attorney

Address:

....

....

....

The magistrate may also require the applicant to give security for any damage which may be caused by an interim order and the court may also require such additional evidence as it may think fit.[28]

2.1.3 *Discharge of the order granted* ex parte *on application by the respondent*

The respondent or any person affected by the *ex parte* application is free to oppose the court's order and request that it be discharged. He or she may anticipate the return day upon delivery of the order on not less than 24 hours' notice.[29] This notice has to be in writing.

When application is made to discharge the order granted *ex parte,* the magistrate may (whether the application is opposed or not):

(1) confirm, discharge or vary the order on good cause shown by any person affected thereby and on such terms as to costs as the court may deem fit;[30] or

---

[27] This is the notice period provided for under rule 56(6) of the former rules. This notice period is in conflict with the 24-hour notice period provided for in the current rule 55(3)(*d*). The notice period provided for in rule 55(3)(*d*) enjoys precedence and should be given effect to.

[28] Rule 56(3).

[29] Rule 55(3)(*d*).

[30] Rule 55(3)(*g*). The rule is aligned with s 36(1)(*d*) which provides that a magistrate may, on application, rescind or vary any judgment in respect of which no appeal lies. A 'judgment' is defined in s 1 to include a 'decree', 'rule' or 'order'. No appeal lies against interim orders. Final orders, such as an interdict or *mandament*, could be rescinded in terms of rule 49 on the ground that the order was granted in the absence of the respondent, or that it was void *ab origine* or was obtained by fraud or common mistake (see s 36(1)(*b*)). Section 18(2) of the Superior Courts Act 10 of 2013 provides that, unless there are exceptional circumstances, the operation and execution of a decision which is an interlocutory order and which does not have the effect of a final judgment is not suspended when an appeal is filed. See *Incumbeta Holdings (Pty) Ltd & another v Ellis & another* 2014 (3) SA 189 (GJ). The order as to costs normally follows the success of the *ex parte* order, ie if the applicant's order

(2) direct the applicant or respondent or any person who deposed to the affidavit to appear before him or her to be examined or cross-examined.[31]

2.2 The application procedure where a respondent appears

Rule 55(1)*(a)* requires every application to be brought on notice of motion supported by affidavit as to the facts upon which the applicant relies for relief. These applications include those in which an order is sought in terms of s 30, viz an order for attachment, an interdict or a *mandament van spolie*.

There are also applications for which a special form is prescribed. There are three such types of applications, viz:

(1) applications for summary judgment (Annexure 1 Form 7);
(2) applications for a trial with assessors (Annexure 1 Form 21); and
(3) applications for administration orders in terms of s 74(1) (Annexure 1 Form 44).

The notice of motion in every application other than one brought *ex parte* must be similar to Form 1A of Annexure 1.[32] The gist of rule 1(4)*(a)* is that the forms in Annexure 1 may be used with such variations as the circumstances require.

It is customary to insert on the standard form of notice of application, as a final paragraph, immediately prior to the words 'Dated at': 'Take notice further that the affidavit of .... attached hereto will be used in support of this application.'

The standard form of notice of motion for district court litigation reads as follows:

No. 1A
Notice of Motion (Long Form)
* For use in the District Court

In the Magistrate's Court for the District of ....

held at ....

Case No .... of 20...........

In the matter between

....Applicant

and

.... Respondent

TAKE NOTICE that .... (hereinafter called the applicant) intends to make application to this Court for an order *(a)* .... *(b)* .... *(c)* ....
(here set forth the form of order prayed) and that the accompanying affidavit of .... will be used in support thereof.

TAKE NOTICE FURTHER that the applicant has appointed .... (here set forth an address referred to in rule 55(1)*(e)*) at which applicant will accept notice and service of all process in these proceedings.

---

obtained *ex parte* is not discharged, the respondent is obliged to pay the costs; if the respondent succeeds in obtaining the discharge of the order, then the applicant must pay the costs.

[31] Rule 55(3)*(f)*.
[32] Rule 55(1)*(d)*.

TAKE NOTICE FURTHER that if you intend opposing this application you are required
(a) to notify applicant or applicant's attorney in writing on or before the ....
(b) and within 10 days after you have so given notice of your intention to oppose the application, to file your answering affidavits, if any; and further that you are required to appoint in such notification an address referred to in rule 55(1)*(g)* at which you will accept notice and service of all documents in these proceedings.
If no such notice of intention to oppose be given, the application will be made on the .... at .... (time)
DATED at ....this .... day of .... 20 ......
....
Applicant or applicant's Attorney
(Physical address)
To:
    (1) C.D.
       (Physical Address)
       RESPONDENT
    (2) The Clerk of the above Court
       ....

A respondent who wishes to oppose the relief sought against him or her must:
(1) give written notice to the applicant, within the time stated in the notice of motion, that he or she intends to oppose the application (ie notice of intention to oppose);
(2) in the above written notice, appoint an address generally within 15 kilometres of the office of the registrar or clerk of the court, at which he or she will accept notice and service of all documents;
(3) indicate in the notice his or her postal, facsimile or electronic mail addresses where available; and
(4) within 10 days of notifying the applicant of his or her intention to oppose the application, deliver his or her answering affidavit, if any, together with any relevant documents.[33]

If the respondent does not timeously deliver the notice of intention to oppose, the applicant may place the matter on the roll for hearing by the court on a stipulated day, giving at least five days' notice.[34]

Where the respondent delivers a notice of intention to oppose and an answering affidavit, the applicant may deliver a replying affidavit within 10 days after the answering affidavit was served on him or her.[35]

---

[33] Rule 55(1)*(g)*. There is no prescribed form in Annexure 1 that the notice of intention to oppose should take.
[34] Rule 55(1)*(f)*.
[35] Rule 55(1)*(h)*.

Chapter 7

ARRESTS, ATTACHMENTS, INTERDICTS AND *MANDAMENTEN VAN SPOLIE*

1 GENERAL

Section 30 of the Magistrates' Courts Act 32 of 1944 expressly confers upon a court the power to issue orders for attachments, interdicts and *mandamenten van spolie* against person and property.

These orders may, however, be made only within the general limits of jurisdiction laid down in the Act. A magistrate may thus not issue an order in terms of s 30 if the court lacks jurisdiction in respect of the respondent's person under s 28, in respect of the size of the cause of action under s 29 or in respect of the nature of the cause of action under s 46.[1]

In terms of s 46(2)*(c)* a magistrate's court shall have no jurisdiction in matters in which is sought specific performance without an alternative of payment of damages, except in:

---

[1] In *Sellars NO v Grobler NO en andere* 1961 (3) SA 583 (T) the court found that the words '[s]ubject to the limits of jurisdiction' in s 30(1) of Act 32 of 1944 referred to s 29 and that a lower court usually lacked jurisdiction to issue a spoliation order in connection with cattle that had been removed where their value exceeded £200 (the jurisdictional limit at that time). Cf also *Le Roux v Le Roux & others* 1980 (2) SA 632 (C).

(1) the rendering of an account in respect of which the claim does not exceed the amount determined by the Minister from time to time by notice in the *Gazette*;[2]

(2) the delivery or transfer of property, movable or immovable, not exceeding the amount determined by the Minister from time to time by notice in the *Gazette;* and

(3) the delivery or transfer of property, movable or immovable, exceeding the amount determined by the Minister from time to time by notice in the *Gazette* in value where the consent of the parties has been obtained in terms of s 45.

The question arises whether the extraordinary legal remedies for which s 30 makes provision are not perhaps affected by the provisions of s 46(2)*(c)*. The courts have, however, determined that a magistrate has the power to make an order for specific performance in terms of s 30 without complying with the provisions of s 46(2)*(c)*.[3]

These attachments, interdicts and *mandamenten van spolie* are discussed below.

2 ARRESTS *TANQUAM SUSPECTUS DE FUGA*

Previously, if a debtor attempted to leave the Republic in order to prevent a court from giving judgment against him or her, a creditor could apply for an order for his or her arrest to compel him or her to give security for the expected judgment in a case which the creditor intends to institute.

The creditor could therefore obtain an order for arrest *tanquam suspectus de fuga*,[4] which is an order to abide the judgment of the court and not an order to satisfy the court's judgment. If a judgment had already been granted against a debtor and he or she thereafter flees to another country, the judgment creditor could follow him or her and attempt to enforce the judgment against him or her in the foreign country.

The common law required that the fleeing debtor had to physically be within the jurisdiction of the court issuing the order at the time of the issue of the warrant. It was not sufficient that the court should have jurisdiction over his or her person by virtue of his or her residence, when at the time of the issue of the warrant he or she is elsewhere.[5]

In *Malachi v Cape Dance Academy International (Pty) Ltd*,[6] the Western Cape High Court declared the common law and s 30 of the Magistrates' Courts Act, which made provision for an order for arrest *tanquam suspectus de fuga*, to be invalid and unconstitutional. The constitutional invalidity of s 30 was subse-

---

[2] The amount in each instance is R200 000 (district courts) and R400 000 (regional courts). See GN 216 and GN 217 in *GG* 37477 of 27 March 2014.

[3] *Zinman v Miller* 1956 (3) SA 8 (T); *Sellars NO v Grobler NO* (supra); *Weepner v Kriel* 1977 (4) SA 212 (C).

[4] Literally means: 'an arrest as if being suspected of being a fugitive'.

[5] *Ex parte Boshoff* 1972 (1) SA 521 (E); *Tedecom Electrical Engineering Services (Pty) Ltd v Berriman* 1982 (1) SA 520 (W).

[6] 2010 (7) BCLR 678 (WCC).

quently confirmed by the Constitutional Court.[7] The Act and the rules have been amended in so far as they no longer authorise *arrest tanquam suspectus de fuga*.[8]

3 ATTACHMENTS IN SECURITY OF CLAIMS

3.1 General

In actions for the payment of a sum of money or actions in which relief in regard to property is sought, the plaintiff may have the property in the defendant's possession attached in order to obtain security for his or her claim. This would be proper when the debtor is about to abscond or is about to dispose of his property so as to frustrate his or her creditors, or when money, which is the fruit of a theft, is sought to be attached. The usual requirements for the granting of an interdict apply.

3.2 Procedure for attachment

Rule 56(1) provides that an application for an interdict or attachment or for a *mandament van spolie* must be made in terms of rule 55. Every application must be accompanied by an affidavit stating the facts upon which the application is made and relief is sought.[9] The affidavit will have to lay the basis for the relief claimed.

The property is taken into custody by the sheriff in terms of the court order. He or she draws up an inventory of the goods and keeps it in safe custody until judgment in the case has been given. The order is *ipso facto* discharged upon security being given by the respondent for the amount to which the order relates together with costs.[10] The court may require the applicant to give security for any damage which may be caused by the attachment order.[11]

3.3 Attachments of property in security of rent

The Magistrates' Courts Act contains special rules which enable a lessor of premises to attach the lessee's movable property in security of the lessor's claim for rent due. This procedure enforces the common-law rule that a landlord has a hypothec over the immovable property of a lessee who fails to pay the rent.

In terms of s 32(1) the court may on application:

> '[u]pon an affidavit by or on behalf of the landlord of any premises situate within the district, that an amount of rent not exceeding the jurisdiction of the court is due and in arrear in regard to the said premises, and that the said rent has been demanded in writing for the space of seven days and upwards, or, if not so demanded, that the deponent believes that the tenant is about to remove the movable property upon the said premises, in order to avoid the payment of such rent . . . issue an order to the

---

[7] *Malachi v Cape Dance Academy International (Pty) Ltd & others* 2010 (6) SA 1 (CC).

[8] The words '*arrest tanquam suspectus de fuga*' in s 30(1) and (3) were deleted. See ss 2(a) and 2(b) of the Judicial Matters Amendment Act 42 of 2013. Rule 56, which dealt with the procedure for the arrest, was amended by GN 611 in *GG* 34479 of 29 July 2011.

[9] Rule 56(2).

[10] Rule 56(4).

[11] Rule 56(3).

messenger requiring him to attach so much of the movable property upon the premises in question and subject to the landlord's hypothec for rent as may be sufficient to satisfy the amount of such rent, together with the costs of such application and of any action for the said rent.'

The court will issue such an order only if security is given to the satisfaction of the clerk of the court for all damage, costs and charges which the lessee of such premises, or any other person, may sustain or incur by reason of the attachment if it should thereafter be set aside.

The lessor's (applicant's) founding affidavit reads as follows:

No. 9
Affidavit under Section 32 of the Act

* For use in the District Court

In the Magistrate's Court for the District of ....

held at ....

Case No .... of 20 ....

In the matter between

.... Applicant

and

.... Respondent

I, ... of .... (address), make oath and say:

(a) I am the landlord (or the agent of the landlord ....) of premises situate (describe the premises).

(b) .... (tenant) is justly indebted to me (or to my said principal) in the sum of R .... for rent of the said premises from the .... day of ...., 20.... to the .... day of ...., 20...

(c) The said sum of R .... became due and recoverable upon the .... day of ...., 20....

(d) The said rent was demanded from the said .... on the .... day of ...., 20..... but has not yet been paid.

or

(e) I believe that the said .... is about to remove certain movables, now upon the said premises, from such premises in order to avoid payment of the said rent.

....

Signature

The deponent has acknowledged that he/she knows and understands the contents of this affidavit.

Signed and sworn to before me at .... on this .... day of ...., 20 ......

....

Commissioner of Oaths

....

Area

....

Office held if appointment is held *ex officio*

The security that must be given by the applicant for damage, costs and charges that might arise in consequence of the attachment reads, according to Annexure 1 Form 10, as follows:

No. 10

Security under Section 32 of the Act

* For use in the District Court

In the Magistrate's Court for the District of ....

held at ....

Case No .... of 20 ....

In the matter between

.... Applicant

and

.... Respondent

Whereas .... (landlord) has applied for the issue of an order to attach the movable property upon .... (describe the leased premises) for the sum of R .... for rent due by .... of .... (name tenant) and R .... for costs;

Now therefore the said .... and .... of .... hereby bind themselves jointly and severally as sureties and co-principal debtors together with the above-named Applicant to pay the above-named Respondent or whom else may lawfully claim against the Applicant as a consequence of this application all damages, costs and charges which he or she or they may sustain by reason of the attachment of the said movable property in case the said attachment is set aside.

Signed and dated at .... this .... day of ...., 20.......
in the presence of the undersigned witnesses.

....

Landlord

Witnesses:

1. ....

Signature and address

....

Surety and Co-principal Debtor

2. ....

Signature and address

....

The order that will be issued by the court should it grant the application reads, according to Annexure 1 Form 11, as follows:

No. 11
Order under Section 32 of the Act

* For use in the District Court

In the Magistrate's Court for the District of ....

held at ....

                                                  Case No .... of 20 ....

In the matter between

.... Applicant

and

.... Respondent

It is ordered:

That the sheriff of the court attaches so much of the .... (describe the movables) in the .... (house, store, as the case may be) situate at .... (describe the premises) as shall be sufficient to satisfy the sum of R .... rent and R .... costs.

Further, should the respondent wish to show cause why the order of attachment should not be confirmed, he shall appear before this court on the .... day of .... 20.........., at .... (time) for that purpose.

The aforesaid date may be anticipated by the respondent upon 12 hours' notice to the applicant.

Upon security being given to the satisfaction of the sheriff of the aforesaid court for the amount of the applicant's claim and the costs of the application for attachment, the aforesaid property shall be released from attachment and upon such security being given the order for attachment shall *ipso facto* be discharged.

Dated at .... this .... day of ...., 20.........

....

Clerk of the Court

....

Applicant/Applicant's attorney

Address ....

....

Rule 42(3) provides that the method of attachment of property under s 32 of the Act shall *mutatis mutandis* be the same as that of attachment in execution.[12]

The lessee whose property is attached may in terms of s 32(3) by notice in writing to the clerk of the court admit that such property is subject to the lessor's hypothec and may in such notice consent that such property (other than property protected from seizure by the provisions of s 67) be sold in satisfaction of the amount of the arrear rent and costs, and such notice has the same effect as a consent to judgment for the amount specified.

According to Annexure 1 Form 12, the consent to the sale of the goods reads as follows:

---

[12] *Letsoho Developers (Pty) Ltd v Messenger of the Magistrate's Court, Alberton & another* 1993 (2) SA 634 (W).

No. 12
Consent to Sale of Goods Attached under Section 32 of the Act
* **For use in the District Court**

In the Magistrate's Court for the District of ....

held at ....

                                                                        Case No .... of 20 ....

In the matter between

                       .... Applicant

                             and

                       .... Respondent

To the Clerk of the Court

I, ..., of ...., the above-mentioned respondent, hereby admit that the property attached in the above matter is subject to a hypothec to the above applicant to the extent of R .... and I consent to the sale of the said property in satisfaction of the said amount of R .... plus costs and Sheriff's charges.

Dated at .... this .... day of ...., 20.........

....

Respondent

Witnesses:

1   ....

   Signature and address

   ....

2   ....

   Signature and address

   ....

---

4 INTERDICTS

4.1 General

An interdict is a court order in terms of which a person is ordered either to refrain from performing a stipulated act or to perform a stipulated act.[13]

    The interdict is a remedy that is granted by the court in cases in which there is an actual or a threatened invasion of the rights of the applicant.[14]

    The magistrates' courts have no jurisdiction to grant an interdict which amounts to an order for the specific performance of a contractual obligation.[15]

    This prohibition covers such relief as the enforcement of a negative covenant such as a restraint of trade agreement. Generally, interdicts are granted to prohibit the commission of a delict or a crime, to prevent infringements of rights to property, whether this be physical or intellectual property or trade secrets. The

---

[13] See D E Van Loggerenberg *Erasmus Superior Court Practice* 2 ed (Service 6, 2018) D6–1 *et seq.*
[14] According to Jones & Buckle Act 165, an interdict is 'a remedy of a summary and extraordinary nature, allowed in cases where a person requires protection against an unlawful interference, or threatened interference, with his rights'. An authoritative discussion on the nature of the interdict may be found in the judgment of the Appellate Division in *Setlogelo v Setlogelo* 1914 AD 221.
[15] *Badenhorst v Theophanous* 1988 (1) SA 793 (C) at 797. See also *Malkiewicz v Van Niekerk and Fourouclas Investments CC* [2008] 1 All SA 57 (T) at 60f–i.

substantive relief sought will have to fall within the general requirements of the jurisdiction of the particular court in which the application or action is brought.

Traditionally, interdicts are classified into different groups, viz:

(1) prohibitory interdicts;
(2) mandatory interdicts; and
(3) restitutory interdicts.

A *prohibitory interdict* is an order in terms of which a person is prohibited from performing a certain act or from continuing to perform such an act.

A *mandatory interdict* is an order in terms of which a person is directed or ordered to perform some or other positive act in order thereby to rectify an unlawful state of affairs brought about by him or her, or to perform some act that he or she is legally obliged to perform. Where, for example, a respondent makes it impossible for a home owner to gain access to his or her premises by dumping a heap of rubbish in his or her driveway, the court may order the respondent by way of a mandatory interdict to remove the rubbish.

A *restitutory interdict* is in issue where a person has taken the law into his or her own hands and deprived another of the possession of movable or immovable property or even of some other right. This deprivation of possession is known as spoliation.

Because it is a basic principle of our law that no one may take the law into his or her own hands, the law grants a remedy known as the *mandament van spolie* to the victim of the extrajudicial appropriation of property in his possession.[16] This *mandament van spolie* is another name for the restitutory interdict.

Apart from the division into prohibitory, mandatory and restitutory interdicts, interdicts may be further classified as final or interim.

A *final interdict* is an order whose operation is not curtailed by the passage of time.

An *interim* or *temporary interdict* is a provisional order that is granted either:

(1) pending the *outcome of a case* to determine the rights of the parties (this is known as an interdict *pendente lite* and its effect is that the status quo is frozen until the court decides the action or confirms the rights of the parties); or

(2) pending *confirmation of the order* on a return date.

A temporary interdict is usually granted when the court is approached for relief by way of an *ex parte* application. Because an *ex parte* application has been brought, the court must still give the person against whom the relief in question has been sought (the respondent) the opportunity to present his or her side of the case. For this reason, the court usually grants an interim interdict and orders the respondent to give reasons within a stipulated time why the interim interdict should not be made final—in other words, a rule *nisi* is granted.

---

[16] 'It is a fundamental principle that no man is allowed to take the law into his own hands; no one is permitted to dispossess another forcibly or wrongfully and against his consent of the possession of property, whether movable or immovable. If he does so, the Court will summarily restore the *status quo ante*, and will do that as a preliminary to any inquiry or investigation into the merits of the dispute' (*Nino Bonino v De Lange* 1906 TS 120 at 122).

When the applicant decides to obtain an interdict by way of application, he or she may either give notice of the application to the respondent in accordance with the normal procedure or he or she may make use of the *ex parte* application procedure.[17]

The applicant will proceed *ex parte* only if the matter is one requiring expedition and he or she does not wish to notify the respondent that he or she intends bringing the application. In matters of urgency an *ex parte* order is requested and thereafter the respondent is given the opportunity to object to the interdict that was granted *ex parte*.

Both the prohibitory and the mandatory interdict may be either temporary or final.

A restitutory interdict can only be a final interdict. Here a person is directed to restore property to someone who was in possession of it before the spoliation took place.[18] Where the matter is heard *ex parte* because of urgency and a rule *nisi* is issued, the rule will generally not order immediate return of the property, but will call upon the respondent to present his or her case on the return day why he or she should not be ordered to return the property.

It is sometimes stated that an interdict is an exceptional remedy, which will be granted in the lower courts only in exceptional circumstances. The Act itself provides for certain kinds of interdict and there should be no talk of exceptional circumstances in these cases. The question is simply whether the relief sought falls within the jurisdictional limits of the court.

4.2   Procedure for obtaining an interdict

In order to obtain an interdict, the applicant must persuade the court that the requirements for the granting of an interdict have been satisfied.

These requirements are briefly as follows:[19]

4.2.1   *A clear right*

To obtain a final interdict, the applicant must be able to show that he or she has a clear, ie a certain and established, right.[20] He or she must prove the existence of such a right on a balance of probabilities.

---

[17] See chapter 6 above.

[18] Cf *Nienaber v Stuckey* 1946 AD 1049 at 1053–4, where Greenberg JA explains: 'Although a spoliation order does not decide what, apart from possession, the rights of the parties to the property spoliated were before the act of spoliation and merely orders that the *status quo* be restored, it is to that extent a final order and the same amount of proof is required as for the granting of a final interdict, and not of a temporary interdict . . . .'

[19] These requirements are firmly rooted in our law. See Van der Linden *Regtsgeleerd, Practicaal, en Koopmans Handboek* 3.1.4.7; Van der Linden *Verhandeling over de Judicieele Practijcq of Form van Procedeeren* 2.19.1; *Setlogelo v Setlogelo* 1914 AD 221 at 227; *Meyer v Administrateur, Transvaal* 1961 (4) SA 55 (T); *Free State Gold Areas Ltd v Merriespruit (Orange Free State) Gold Mining Co Ltd & another* 1961 (2) SA 505 (W). For recent authority, see *Van Deventer v Ivory Sun Trading 77 (Pty) Ltd* 2015 (3) SA 532 (SCA) at 540C; *Hotz & others v University of Cape Town* 2017 (2) SA 485 (SCA) at 496G–H, 496I and 497G–H.

[20] According to Jones & Buckle Act 173, a clear right means 'a right clearly established'. See also *Motswagae & others v Rustenburg Local Municipality & another* 2013 (2) SA 613 (CC); *Pilane & another v Pilane & another* 2013 (4) BCLR 431 (CC) paras 40–45.

For the granting of an interim interdict, it is not required that a clear right be proven on a balance of probabilities.[21] The test for the granting of an interim interdict was expounded as follows in *Webster v Mitchell*:[22]

'From the Appellate Division cases to which I have referred I consider that the law which I must apply is that the right to be set up by an applicant for a temporary interdict need not be shown by a balance of probabilities. If it is *"prima facie* established though open to some doubt" that is enough ...

    ... The proper manner of approach I consider is to take the facts as set out by the applicant, together with any facts set out by the respondent which the applicant cannot dispute, and to consider whether, having regard to the inherent probabilities, the applicant *could on those facts obtain final relief at a trial.* The facts set up in contradiction by the respondent should then be considered. If serious doubt is thrown on the case of the applicant he could not succeed in obtaining temporary relief, for his right, *prima facie* established, may only be open to "some doubt" ' (my italics).[23]

Should an applicant for an interim interdict be able to prove the right that he or she seeks to protect only *prima facie*[24]—and not on a balance of probabilities—he or she must also, over and above the *prima facie* proof of his or her right, prove that he or she will suffer irreparable harm[25] if the interdict is not granted, but that the respondent will not suffer irremediable harm if the interdict is granted.

The position in regard to interim interdicts may be summarised as follows: an applicant need not establish the existence of the right that he or she seeks to protect on a balance of probabilities, but may submit *prima facie* evidence of the existence of the right provided that in such case he or she must also prove that he or she will suffer irreparable harm if the interdict is not granted, while the respondent will not suffer such harm if the interdict is granted. This last requirement is often called 'the balance of convenience'.[26]

4.2.2 *An injury*

This requirement is also sometimes referred to as a wrongful infringement of the applicant's rights.

The applicant seeking an interim order as well as a final interdict must prove that the respondent is conducting himself or herself in a manner which interferes

---

[21] For a full treatment, see C B Prest *Interlocutory Interdicts* (Juta, 1993) chapter 5 at 53.

[22] 1948 (1) SA 1186 (W) at 1189.

[23] In *Gool v Minister of Justice & another* 1955 (2) SA 682 (C) at 688E–F Ogilvie Thompson J (as he then was) held that this proposition was unduly favourable to the applicant. He decided, consequently, that the sentence ought to read 'should (not could) the applicant on those facts obtain final relief at the trial'. Cf also *Ndauti v Kgami & others* 1948 (3) SA 27 (W); *South African Bus & Taxi Association v Cape of Good Hope Bank Ltd* 1987 (4) SA 315 (C) at 318C. See also *Marais v Marais* 2012 JOL 28338 (GSJ) at 3–4; *Cipla Medpro (Pty) Ltd v Aventis Pharma SA and Related Appeal* 2013 (4) SA 579 (SCA) para 40.

[24] See *Erasmus & others v Senwes Ltd & others* 2006 (3) SA 529 (T).

[25] See *Molteno Bros v SAR* 1936 AD 408; *Setlogelo v Setlogelo* (supra) at 227. 'Irreparable harm' may be defined as the loss of property (including incorporeal property) and money in circumstances in which their recovery is impossible or unlikely. See also *Edrei Investments 9 Ltd (In Liquidation) v Dis-Chem Pharmacies (Pty) Ltd* 2012 (2) SA 553 (ECP) at 555F.

[26] *LF Boshoff Investments (Pty) Ltd v Cape Town Municipality, Cape Town Municipality v LF Boshoff Investments (Pty) Ltd* 1969 (2) SA 256 (C) at 267.

with the exercise of the applicant's rights or that the applicant, from an objective point of view, has a well-grounded apprehension that the respondent will conduct himself or herself in such a manner. The applicant must set out in his or her application the grounds for this apprehension.

The injury must give rise to prejudice or possible prejudice to the applicant, otherwise an interdict will not be granted.[27]

The injury must be ongoing. The court will not grant an interdict in relation to conduct already completed.[28] In such a case, the appropriate remedy will be an action for damages in delict.

The prejudice which results from the conduct of the respondent must be capable of being quantified in pecuniary terms and value must fall within the jurisdictional limits of the lower court before a magistrate may grant an interdict.

4.2.3 *No other legal remedy is available*

In applications for both final and interim interdicts the applicant must also prove that no other adequate relief is available to him or her.[29] This requirement is closely connected with the concept of 'irreparable harm'. If the prejudice will be irreparable unless the conduct complained of is terminated, an interdict will be the only legal remedy available.

An interdict will also not in general be granted where damages will adequately compensate the applicant or where other relief is available to him or her.[30] To this rule there are, however, exceptions. The court will grant an interdict even though the prejudice or harm is capable of being compensated by means of an award of damages if:

(1)   the respondent has no or very few assets;

(2)   the amount of the damages is extremely difficult to ascertain; or

(3)   the interference with the rights of the applicant is of an ongoing nature.

The applicant who seeks a prohibitory or a mandatory interdict must persuade the court that he or she has a clear right, that there is an injury to the applicant and that no other adequate legal remedy is available to him or her.[31]

To the rule that an applicant must prove that all three of the above requirements are satisfied before an interdict will be granted there exist, however, two exceptions, viz in regard to applications for interdicts relating to a pending vindicatory action (*actio rei vindicatio*) or a pending possessory action (also known as a quasi-vindicatory action).

A *vindicatory action* is an action in which a plaintiff claims delivery of property of which he or she is the owner or lawful possessor. An action is *quasi-vindicatory*

---

[27] *PGB Boerdery Beleggings (Edms) Bpk & another v Somerville 62 (Edms) Bpk & another* 2008 (2) SA 428 (SCA) para 8; *Mettenheimer & another v Zonquasdrif Vineyards CC & others* 2014 (2) SA 204 (SCA); *Motswagae & others v Rustenburg Local Municipality & another* 2013 (2) SA 613 (CC).

[28] *Philip Morris Inc v Marlboro Shirt Co SA Ltd* 1991 (2) SA 720 (A) at 735B.

[29] *Motswagae v Rustenburg Local Municipality* (supra); *Hotz & others v University of Cape Town* 2017 (2) SA 485 (SCA).

[30] *Celliers v Lehfeldt* 1921 AD 509.

[31] *Gugu & another v Zongwana & others* [2014] 1 All SA 203 (ECM) para 35.

if delivery of the property is claimed in terms of a right to be put in possession.[32] The best-known example of the latter action is an action for delivery or transfer of property in terms of a contract of sale: an interdict may prohibit the seller from selling the property pending the action.

5 *MANDAMENTEN VAN SPOLIE*

5.1 General[33]

The *mandament van spolie* is a restitutory interdict that accrues to a possessor[34] where another has deprived him or her of possession on the pretext that the latter was entitled to do so, or where the possessor has otherwise been deprived of possession unlawfully.

Public policy requires that no one may take the law into his or her own hands. All possessors, whether in lawful possession of an item or not, who are deprived of their possession must first have their possession restored to them before the lawfulness or unlawfulness of their possession is investigated.

This principle is reflected in the Latin maxim *spoliatus ante omnia restituendus est*: the possessor whose right of possession has been disturbed must first have possession restored to him or her (before the court will consider the matter at all).

The object of the *mandament* is to prevent people from taking the law into their own hands, and for this reason it is not permissible to go into the merits of the case before the person whose possession has been disturbed is again placed in possession of the item.

5.2 Procedure for obtaining the *mandament*

The *mandament van spolie* is a form of interdict.

The *mandament* may be brought by way of *ex parte* application.[35] The *ex parte* application is brought on affidavit, in which the applicant sets out briefly the facts upon which the application is made and the nature of the order applied for.[36]

Before the court will grant a spoliation order, the applicant must prove on a balance of probabilities that:
(1) he or she was in peaceful and undisturbed possession of the item in question; and
(2) the respondent deprived him or her of possession in a violent or unlawful manner and against his or her will.[37]

---

[32] *Stern & Rusk in NO v Appleson* 1951 (3) SA 800 (W) at 810–11; *Berman v Winrow* 1943 TPD 213.

[33] In general, see *Erasmus Superior Court Practice* D7–1 *et seq*; Jones & Buckle Act 102 *et seq*.

[34] For example, a lessee (*Nino Bonino v De Lange* 1906 TS 120) or a depositary (*Meyer v Glendinning* 1939 CPD 84). Where a person is deprived partially of use of a thing, this is likewise a case of spoliation (*Zinman v Miller* 1956 (3) SA 8 (T)); *Buffelsfontein Gold Mining Co Ltd en 'n ander v Bekker en andere* 1961 (3) SA 381 (T)).

[35] Rule 56(1).

[36] Rule 56(2).

[37] *City of Tshwane Metropolitan Municipality v Mamelodi Hostel Residents Association & others* 2012 JOL 28434 (SCA) para 6; *Gowrie Mews Investments CC v Calicom Trading 54 (Pty) Ltd & others* 2013 (1) SA 239 (KZD).

It is not necessary for the applicant to make out a *prima facie* case that he or she was lawfully in possession. Indeed, it is not even necessary for the applicant to prove that he or she had a right to be in possession.[38] The respondent cannot assume that the applicant was in unlawful possession or that he or she (the respondent) had a superior right to the item than the applicant.[39]

The onus of proving that deprivation of possession was lawful rests upon the respondent. The fact that the respondent is the owner of the item or that he or she sold the item on credit and that the applicant has not paid him is no defence to an application for a spoliation order. The rule still applies that no one may take the law into his or her own hands and disturb the possessor in his or her right of possession. If the owner of property is unlawfully deprived of possession, he or she must approach the court for relief. The dispossessed may not himself or herself go in search of his or her property and take it back from the possessor.

Only in the most exceptional circumstances is counter-spoliation permissible. Counter-spoliation occurs where a possessor who is deprived of possession of his or her property takes the item back again.[40]

One cannot bring a counter-application to a *mandament van spolie*.[41]

The following is an example of an application for a *mandament van spolie*:

---

* For use in the District Court

In the Magistrate's Court for the District of ....

held at ....

                                        Case No .... of 20 ....

In the matter between

               .... Applicant

                      and

               .... Respondent.

APPLICATION FOR *MANDAMENT VAN SPOLIE*

TAKE NOTICE that application is hereby made to the above Honourable Court for an order directing the Respondent to restore possession of Volkswagen .... (registration number) to the Applicant.

TAKE NOTICE FURTHER that the affidavit of .... attached hereto will be used in support of the application.

DATED at .... on this .... day of .... 20 ....

                            ....

                                   ATTORNEY

                    Address:

                            ....

                            ....

---

[38] *Ngqukumba v Minister of Safety and Security & others* 2014 (5) SA 112 (CC) para 21.

[39] In *Jigger Properties CC v Maynard NO & others* 2017 (4) SA 569 (KZP) paras 18–25, the court held that a mere threat of termination of the right to possession is insufficient to justify the granting of a *mandament van spolie*.

[40] *Mans v Loxton Municipality & another* 1948 (1) SA 966 (C).

[41] *Willowvale Estates CC & another v Bryanmore Estates Ltd* 1990 (3) SA 954 (W) at 961G.

To the Clerk of the Court

....

To the Respondent

....

The applicant's founding affidavit reads as follows:

In the Magistrate's Court for the District of ....

held at ....

Case No .... of 20 ....

In the matter between

.... Applicant

and

.... Respondent

APPLICANT'S FOUNDING AFFIDAVIT

I, the undersigned

....

do hereby make oath and say that:

1. I am the Applicant in this matter. I reside at ....

2. The Respondent is .... and resides/is employed at ....

3. On .... and at .... I entered into an oral agreement of sale with the Respondent in terms of which I purchased a Volkswagen registration number .... from the Respondent. The purchase price was R .... and was payable as follows: a deposit of R .... followed by .... two monthly instalments of R .... each.

4. I paid the deposit of R .... to the Respondent on .... 20 .... and the Respondent thereupon placed me in possession of the vehicle.

5. On .... 20 ...., before the first instalment became payable, the Respondent arrived at my residence and without my consent and without having good reason to do so removed the said vehicle.

6. Through the aforesaid conduct the Respondent has deprived me of the lawful possession and use of the said vehicle.

WHEREFORE I pray that the above Honourable Court will grant an order in terms of the notice of application.

....

APPLICANT

Signed and sworn to before me at .... on this the .... day of .... 20 ....

....

COMMISSIONER OF OATHS

Capacity ....

Area ....

Should the magistrate decide to grant the *mandament van spolie*, he or she may make the following order:

---

* For use in the District Court

In the Magistrate's Court for the District of ....

held at ....

                                                               Case No .... of 20 ....

In the matter between

                     .... Applicant

                               and

                     .... Respondent

COURT ORDER

IT IS ORDERED

1. That a rule *nisi* be granted and that .... (Respondent) of ....
   (address) be called upon to show cause before this Court on the .... day of 20
   .... at 09h00 or so soon thereafter as the matter may be heard why he should not be
   ordered to restore possession of motor vehicle .... (description and registration
   number) to the Applicant and why the costs of the application should not be awarded against
   the Respondent.

2. That this rule *nisi* operate as an interim interdict in terms of which the Respondent is
   prohibited from alienating the aforesaid motor vehicle or from otherwise allowing it to leave
   his custody.

DATED at .... on this .... day of .... 20 ....

By order of the Court.

                                           ....

                                              CLERK OF THE COURT

It should be noted that, where the spoliation order is sought by means of an *ex parte* notice of motion, the court, in accordance with general principles, issues a rule *nisi*. Where, however, the spoliator has received notice of the application and has placed his or her case before the court, a rule *nisi* is unnecessary.

Chapter 8

THE SUMMONS

1 GENERAL

Reference has already been made to the two ways (trial action procedure and application procedure) in which a matter may be conducted in the courts. As already explained, procedure by way of action culminates in a trial at which oral evidence is led, and the object of the procedure followed before the hearing is to formulate in writing the respective cases of the plaintiff and the defendant.

The trial action procedure is commenced by the issue of a summons. The summons is the first of the various processes that are exchanged in the course of conduct of the case prior to the stage when pleadings are, as it is termed, 'closed'—ie prior to the stage at which no further exchange of pleadings formulating the dispute may take place.

The summons is therefore the first process in the case. It is the process by which the proceedings are commenced. The summons may be defined as a court process in which the defendant is called upon to enter appearance to defend the action within a stipulated time and to answer the claim of the plaintiff, and in which he or she is warned of the consequences of failure to do so.[1]

According to Annexure 1 Form 2, the simple summons, which is to be used for claims in respect of a debt or a liquidated demand, reads as follows:

No. 2
Simple Summons
(Claim in respect of debt or liquidated demand)

* For use in the District Court

In the Magistrates' Court for the District of ....

held at ....

                                                      Case No .... of 20 ......

In the matter between:

.... Plaintiff

and

.... Defendant

To the sheriff or his/her deputy:

INFORM A.B., of .... (state residence or place of business and if known, gender, occupation and place of employment) ....

(hereinafter called the defendant), that C.D., (state gender and occupation), of ....

(state residence or place of business) .... hereby institutes action against him or her in which action the plaintiff claims:

(Here set out in concise terms plaintiff's cause of action)

INFORM the defendant further that if defendant disputes the claim and wishes to defend the action he or she shall within .... days of the service upon him or her of this summons file with the clerk of this court at .... (here set out the physical address of the clerk of the court's office) notice of his or her intention to defend and serve a copy thereof on the plaintiff or plaintiff's attorney, which notice shall give an address referred to in rule 13(3) for the service upon the defendant of all notices and documents in the action.

INFORM the defendant further that if he or she fails to file and serve notice as aforesaid, judgment as claimed may be given against him or her without further notice to him or her.

And immediately thereafter serve on the defendant a copy of this summons and return the same to the clerk of the court with whatsoever you have done thereupon.

DATED at .... this .... day of .... 20......

....

Clerk of the Court

....

Plaintiff/Plaintiff's Attorney
(15km Physical Address)

---

[1] Rule 5.

....

Postal Address

....

Facsimile number

....

Electronic Mail Address

* The plaintiff is prepared to accept all subsequent documents and notices at the facsimile/ electronic mail address stated herein.

Defendant must take notice that—

(a) in default of defendant paying the amount of the claim and costs within the said period, or of defendant delivering a notice of intention to defend, he or she will be held to have admitted the said claim and the plaintiff may proceed therein and judgment may be given against defendant in his or her absence;

(b) if defendant pays the said claim and costs within the said period judgment will not be given against defendant herein and he or she will save judgment charges. Defendant will also save judgment charges if, within the said period, he or she lodges with the clerk of the aforesaid Court a consent to judgment;

(c) if defendant admits the claim and wishes to consent to judgment or wishes to undertake to pay the claim in instalments or otherwise, defendant may approach the plaintiff or plaintiff's attorney.

Notice:

(i) Any person against whom a court has, in a civil case, given judgment or made any order who has not, within 10 days, satisfied in full such judgment or order may be called upon by notice in terms of section 65A(1) of the Act to appear on a specified date before the court in chambers to enable the court to enquire into the financial position of the judgment debtor and to make such order as the court may deem just and equitable.

(ii) If the court is satisfied that–

(aa) the judgment debtor or, if the judgment debtor is a juristic person, a director or officer of the juristic person has knowledge of the abovementioned notice and that he or she has failed to appear before the court on the date and at the time specified in the notice; or

(bb) the judgment debtor, director or officer, where the proceedings were postponed in his or her presence to a date and time determined by the court, has failed to appear before the court on that date and at that time; or

(cc) the judgment debtor, director or officer has failed to remain in attendance at the proceedings or at the proceedings so postponed, the court may, at the request of the judgment creditor or his or her attorney, authorise the issue of a warrant directing a sheriff to arrest the said judgment debtor, director or officer and to bring him or her before a competent court to enable that court to conduct a financial inquiry. [Section 65A(6) of the Act]

(iii) Any person who–

(aa) is called upon to appear before a court under a notice in terms of section 65A(1) or 65A(8)(b) of the Act (where the sheriff, in lieu of arresting a person, hands to that person a notice to appear in court) and who wilfully fails to appear before the court on the date and at the time specified in the notice; or

(bb) where the proceedings were postponed in his or her presence to a date and time determined by the court, wilfully fails to appear before the court on that date and at that time; or

(cc) wilfully fails to remain in attendance at the relevant proceedings or at the proceedings so postponed,

shall be guilty of an offence and liable on conviction to a fine or to imprisonment for a period not exceeding three months. [Section 65A(9) of the Act]

(iv) On appearing before the court on the date determined in the notice in terms of section 65A(1) or (8)(b) of the Act in pursuance of the arrest of the judgment debtor, director or officer under a warrant referred to in section 65A(6) of the Act or on any date to which the proceedings have been postponed, such judgment debtor, director or officer shall be called upon to give evidence on his or her financial position or that of the juristic person and his or her or its ability to pay the judgment debt. [Section 65D of the Act]

(v) Any person against whom a court has, in a civil case, given any judgment or made any order who has not satisfied in full such judgment or order and paid all costs for which he or she is liable in connection therewith shall, if he or she has changed his or her place of residence, business or employment, within 14 days from the date of every such change notify the clerk of the court who gave such judgment or made such order and the judgment creditor or his or her attorney fully and correctly in writing of his or her new place of residence, business or employment, and by his or her failure to do so such judgment debtor shall be guilty of an offence and liable upon conviction to a fine or imprisonment for a period not exceeding three months. [Section 109 of the Act)]

(1) Consent to judgment.

I admit that I am liable to the plaintiff as claimed in this summons (or in the amount of R ....
and costs to date) and I consent to judgment accordingly.

Dated at .... this .... day of .... 20......
....

Defendant

WITNESSES:

1 (full names) .... (signature) ....
  (address) ....
2 (full names) .... (signature) ....
  (address) ....

OR

* (2) Notice of intention to defend.

To the Clerk of the Court

Kindly take notice that the defendant hereby notifies his or her intention to defend this action.

Dated at .... this .... day of .... 20......
....

Defendant/Defendant's attorney
Address
....
....
....

Postal address
....
....
....

Facsimile (fax) number (where available) ....
Electronic mail (e-mail) address (where available) ....

(Give full address for acceptance of service of process or documents within 15 kilometres from the issuing Court-house and also the postal address.)

* The original notice must be filed with the clerk of the court and a copy thereof served on the plaintiff or plaintiff's attorney.

Costs if the action is undefended will be as follows:

Summons .... R	
Judgment .... R	
Attorney's charges .... R	
Sheriff's fees .... R	
Sheriff's fees on re-issue .... R	
Total: .... R	

According to Annexure 1 Form 2B, the combined summons, which is to be used for claims that are not based on a debt or a liquidated demand, reads as follows:

No. 2B

Combined Summons

[Form 2B substituted by GN R545 of 30 June 2015 (wef 31 July 2015).]

*For use in the District Court

Case No .... of 20 ....

In the matter between:

.... Plaintiff

and

.... Defendant

To the sheriff or his/her deputy:

INFORM A.B., of .... (state residence or place of business and if known, gender, occupation and place of employment) .... (hereinafter called the defendant), that C.D., (state gender and occupation), of .... (state residence or place of business) .... (hereinafter called the plaintiff), hereby institutes action against him or her in which action the plaintiff claims the relief and on the grounds set out in the particulars annexed hereto.

INFORM the defendant further that if he or she disputes the claim and wishes to defend the action he or she shall—

(i) within .... days of the service upon him or her of this summons file with the clerk of this court at .... (set out the physical address of the clerk of the court) notice of his or her intention to defend and serve a copy thereof on the plaintiff or plaintiff's attorney, which notice shall give an address referred to in rule 13(3) for the service upon the defendant of all notices and documents in the action;

(ii) thereafter, and within 20 days after filing and serving notice of intention to defend as aforesaid, file with the clerk of the court and serve upon the plaintiff or plaintiff's attorney a plea, exception, notice to strike out, with or without a counter-claim.

INFORM the defendant further that if defendant fails to file and serve notice as aforesaid judgment as claimed may be given against him or her without further notice to him or her, or if, having filed and served such notice, defendant fails to plead, except, make application to strike out or counter-claim, judgment may be given against him or her. And immediately thereafter serve on the defendant a copy of this summons and return the same to the clerk of the court with whatsoever you have done thereupon.

DATED at .... this .... day of .... 20..........

....

Clerk of the Court

....

Plaintiff/Plaintiff's Attorney
(15 km Physical Address)

....

Postal Address

....

Facsimile Number

....

Electronic Mail Address

....

* The plaintiff is prepared to accept all subsequent documents and notices at the facsimile address/electronic mail address/other address stated herein.

(Delete whichever is not applicable)

If a claim is based on a liquidated sum of money, the defendant must take note that–

(a) in default of defendant paying the amount of the claim and costs within the said period, or of defendant delivering a notice of intention to defend, he or she will be held to have admitted the said claim and the plaintiff may proceed therein and judgment may be given against defendant in his or her absence;

(b) if defendant pays the said claim and costs within the said period judgment will not be given against defendant herein and he or she will save judgment charges. Defendant will also save judgment charges if, within the said period, he or she lodges with the clerk of the aforesaid Court a consent to judgment;

(c) if defendant admits the claim and wishes to consent to judgment or wishes to undertake to pay the claim in instalments or otherwise, defendant may approach the plaintiff or plaintiff's attorney.

Notice:

(i) Any person against whom a court has, in a civil case, given judgment or made any order who has not, within 10 days, satisfied in full such judgment or order may be called upon by notice in terms of section 65A(1) of the Act to appear on a specified date before the court in chambers to enable the court to enquire into the financial position of the judgment debtor and to make such order as the court may deem just and equitable.

(ii) If the court is satisfied that–

(aa) the judgment debtor or, if the judgment debtor is a juristic person, a director or officer of the juristic person has knowledge of the above-mentioned notice and that he or she has failed to appear before the court on the date and at the time specified in the notice; or

(bb) the judgment debtor, director or officer, where the proceedings were postponed in his or her presence to a date and time determined by the court, has failed to appear before the court on that date and at that time; or

(cc) the judgment debtor, director or officer has failed to remain in attendance at the proceedings or at the proceedings so postponed,

the court may, at the request of the judgment creditor or his or her attorney, authorise the issue of a warrant directing a sheriff to arrest the said judgment debtor, director or officer and to bring him or her before a competent court to enable that court to conduct a financial inquiry. [Section 65A(6) of the Act]

(iii) Any person who–

(aa) is called upon to appear before a court under a notice in terms of section 65A(1) or 65A(8)*(b)* of the Act (where the sheriff, *in lieu* of arresting a person, hands to that person a notice to appear in court) and who wilfully fails to appear before the court on the date and at the time specified in the notice; or

(bb) where the proceedings were postponed in his or her presence to a date and time determined by the court, wilfully fails to appear before the court on that date and at that time; or

(cc) wilfully fails to remain in attendance at the relevant proceedings or at the proceedings so postponed,

shall be guilty of an offence and liable on conviction to a fine or to imprisonment for a period not exceeding three months. [Section 65A(9) of the Act]

(iv) On appearing before the court on the date determined in the notice in terms of section 65A(1) or (8)*(b)* of the Act in pursuance of the arrest of the judgment debtor, director or officer under a warrant referred to in section 65A(6) of the Act or on any date to which the proceedings have been postponed, such judgment debtor, director or officer shall be called upon to give evidence on his or her financial position or that of the juristic person and his or her or its ability to pay the judgment debt. [Section 65D of the Act]

(v) Any person against whom a court has, in a civil case, given any judgment or made any order who has not satisfied in full such judgment or order and paid all costs for which he or she is liable in connection therewith shall, if he or she has changed his or her place of residence, business or employment, within 14 days from the date of every such change notify the clerk of the court who gave such judgment or made such order and the judgment creditor or his or her attorney fully and correctly in writing of his or her new place of residence, business or employment, and by his or her failure to do so such judgment debtor shall be guilty of an offence and liable upon conviction to a fine or imprisonment for a period not exceeding three months. [Section 109 of the Act)]

*Consent to judgment.

I admit that I am liable to the plaintiff as claimed in this summons (or in the amount of R...............
and costs to date) and I consent to judgment accordingly.

DATED at .... this .... day of .... 20..........

....

Defendant

WITNESSES:

1. (full names).., (signature) ....
   (address) ....

2. (full names).., (signature) ....
   (address) ....

OR

* Notice of intention to defend.

To the Clerk of the Court.

Kindly take notice that the defendant hereby notifies his or her intention to defend this action.

DATED at .... this .... day of .... 20..........

....

Defendant/Defendant's attorney

15 km physical address from the courthouse for acceptance of service of process or documents

....

Postal address

....

Facsimile (fax) number (where available) ....

Electronic mail (e-mail) address (where available) ....

* The defendant is prepared to accept all subsequent documents and notices at the facsimile address/electronic mail address/other address stated herein.

(Delete whichever is not applicable)

*The original notice must be filed with the clerk of the court and a copy thereof served on the plaintiff or plaintiff's attorney.

Costs if the action is undefended will be as follows:

Summons	R
Judgment	R
Attorney's charges	R
Sheriff's fees	R
Sheriff's fees on re-issue	R
Total:	R

ANNEXURE
Particulars of Plaintiff's Claim

....

....

....

Dated at .... this .... day of .... 20.......

....
Plaintiff/Plaintiff's Attorney
Address of Plaintiff/Plaintiff's Attorney

....

The summons is issued by the clerk or registrar of the court and served by the sheriff upon the defendant. All other pleadings exchanged between plaintiff and defendant in the course of the proceedings are usually delivered directly, without the intercession of the sheriff.[2]

2 THE FORM OF THE SUMMONS

In terms of rule 1(4)*(b)* a summons should substantially comply to either Form 2 (simple summons), Form 2A (provisional sentence summons), Form 2B (combined summons) or Form 3 (summons in which is included an automatic rent interdict) contained in Annexure 1 to the magistrate's court rules. (Examples of the simple and combined summonses appear above. An example of the summons in which is included an automatic rent interdict appears at para 4 below.)

Rule 5(2)*(a)* provides that where a claim is not for a debt or liquidated demand, a combined summons (Form 2B) *must* be used. Attached to the summons must be a statement of material facts relied upon by the plaintiff in support of his or her claim. Said statement must comply with rule 6, ie the rule relating to pleadings generally.

Rule 5(2)*(b)* states that in those cases where the claim is for a debt or liquidated demand, a simple summons *may* be used (Form 2). Form 2 requires that the plaintiff's cause of action must be set out in 'concise terms'.[3] It must be described

---

[2] Rule 2(1) defines 'deliver' as follows: '(except when a summons is served on the opposite party only, and in rule 9) means to file with the registrar or clerk of the court and serve a copy on the opposite party either by hand-delivery, registered post, or, where agreed between the parties or so ordered by court, by facsimile or electronic mail (in which instance Chapter III, Part 2 of the Electronic Communications and Transactions Act, 2002 will apply), and "delivery", "delivered" and "delivering" have corresponding meanings.'

[3] *All Purpose Space Heating Co of SA (Pty) Ltd v Schweltzer* 1970 (3) SA 560 (D) at 466–467. See also *Volkskas Bank Ltd v Wilkinson and Three Similar Cases* 1992 (2) SA 388 (C) at 397I–398C.

with sufficient clarity 'for a court to decide whether judgment should be granted, and for the defendant to be made aware of what is being claimed from him'.[4]

If it is not possible to set out the cause of action in concise terms, a combined summons should be used regardless of whether the claim is for a debt or liquidated demand. The term 'debt or liquidated demand' is a claim for a fixed, certain or ascertained amount or thing.[5]

A simple summons is not a pleading. An exception raised against it will therefore not succeed.[6]

The summons, including the notices that must be embodied in it, must be in printed form. The summons must be on A4-size paper.[7]

3 THE CONTENTS OF THE SUMMONS

The most important provisions concerning the contents of the summons are contained in rules 5 and 6. According to these rules, certain particulars must appear in both simple and combined summonses. Every summons must:

(1) be addressed to the sheriff;[8]
(2) direct the sheriff to inform the defendant that if the defendant disputes the claim and intends to defend the action, the defendant must within the time stated in the summons give notice of his or her intention to defend the action;[9]
(3) be signed by the plaintiff's attorney or, if no attorney is acting for the plaintiff, by the plaintiff;[10]
(4) indicate the physical address of the plaintiff's attorneys at which the plaintiff will accept service of all subsequent documents and notices in the action; the address must be within 15 kilometres of the court;[11] if no attorney is acting for the plaintiff, the address must be that of the plaintiff;[12]
(5) indicate the attorney's postal address and, where available, the attorney's facsimile and electronic mail address;[13] if no attorney is acting for the plaintiff, the aforementioned addresses must be those of the plaintiff;[14]
(6) contain the first names and surname or initials of the defendant, the defendant's residential address or place of business and, where known, the defendant's occupation and employment address; if the defendant is sued in a representative capacity, it must indicate such capacity;[15]

---

[4] *ABSA Bank Ltd v Studdard & another* [2012] ZAGPJHC 26 (13 March 2012) para 10.
[5] See Jones and Buckle Rule 5-4 and the cases cited therein.
[6] *Icebreakers No 83 (Pty) Ltd v Medicross Health Care Group (Pty) Ltd* 2011 (5) SA 130 (KZD) at 131F–H and 134E–G.
[7] Rule 1(4)*(c)*.
[8] Rule 5(1).
[9] Rule 5(1)*(a)* and (3)*(a)*(ii).
[10] Rule 5(3)*(a)*(i).
[11] Ibid.
[12] Rule 5(3)*(a)*(ii).
[13] Rule 5(3)*(a)*(i).
[14] Rule 5(3)*(a)*(ii).
[15] Rule 5(4)*(a)*.

(7) contain the full names, gender and occupation and the residence and place of business of the plaintiff; if the plaintiff sues in a representative capacity, it must indicate such capacity;[16]

(8) include a form of notice of intention to defend;[17]

(9) include a form of consent to judgment;[18]

(10) include a notice drawing the defendant's attention to the provisions of s 109 of the Act;[19]

(11) include a notice drawing the defendant's attention to the provisions of ss 57, 58, 65A and 65D of the Act (where the action is based on a debt referred to in s 55 of the Act);[20]

(12) where the plaintiff relies on s 28(1)(*d*) of the Act, contain an averment that the whole cause of action arose within the district or region and set out the particulars in support of such averment;[21]

(13) where the plaintiff relies on s 28(1)(*g*) of the Act, contain an averment that the property is situated within the district or region;[22] and

(14) indicate any abandonment in terms of s 38 of the Act or deduction of an admitted debt under s 39 of the Act.[23]

Some of the topics listed above and related issues are briefly discussed below.

3.1 The *dies inducia* (intervals between pleadings or notices)

The defendant is called upon in the summons to enter an appearance to defend the action within a stipulated period after service of the summons (the *dies inducia*).

The period within which the defendant may enter appearance through delivery of a notice of intention to defend must, in terms of rule 13, be at least 10 days after service of the summons. The days between 16 December and 15 January shall not be counted in the time allowed within which to deliver the notice.[24]

In terms of rule 13(2), the State may enter appearance to defend at any time within 20 days after service of the summons.

The provisions of s 4 of the Interpretation Act 33 of 1957 must be borne in mind in calculating the number of days within which notice of intention to defend must be given.

Section 4 of the Interpretation Act provides that, when any particular number of days is prescribed for the doing of any act, the same shall be reckoned exclusively of the first and inclusively of the last day, unless the last day happens to fall on a Sunday or on any public holiday, in which case the time shall be reckoned exclusively of the first day and exclusively also of every such Sunday or public holiday.

---

[16] Rule 5(4)(*b*).
[17] Rule 5(5)(*a*).
[18] Rule 5(5)(*b*)(i). This does not apply to a divorce summons.
[19] Rule 5(5)(*b*)(ii). This does not apply to a divorce summons.
[20] Rule 5(5)(*b*)(iii). This does not apply to a divorce summons.
[21] Rule 5(6)(*a*).
[22] Rule 5(6)(*b*).
[23] Rule 5(6)(*c*).
[24] Referred to as *dies non*.

A distinction must therefore be drawn between 'calendar days' (to which the provisions of the Interpretation Act relate) and 'court days' (to which the rules of court apply). The most important distinction between the two is that in the calculation of 'calendar days' Saturdays, Sundays and public holidays falling within the period calculated must be taken into account, while in the computation of 'court days' Saturdays, Sundays and public holidays are *not* taken into consideration. It is important, however, to note that 'calendar days' are counted when time periods are calculated in accordance with the sections of the Act. Only where time periods are calculated according to the rules of court are only 'court days' counted.[25]

In terms of rule 2(2) a Saturday, Sunday or public holiday must not be reckoned as part of any period calculated in terms of the rules. Suppose, for example, that the *dies induciae* in a summons are five days, that the summons is served on a Friday and that the Monday immediately following is a public holiday. The *dies induciae* are then calculated as follows: the Friday on which the summons was served is not regarded as the first day, because, according to s 4 of the Interpretation Act, the first day is excluded. The Saturday, Sunday and the public holiday on the Monday may also not be counted, in terms of rule 2(2). The Tuesday immediately thereafter thus counts as the first of the five days. Since s 4 of the Interpretation Act stipulates that the last day, Thursday in this example, must be included in the calculation, the defendant must give notice of his or her intention to defend by the following Monday at the latest.

3.2 A form of consent to judgment

In terms of rule 5(5)(*b*)(i) this form must appear in the summons in order that the defendant may notify the plaintiff of his consent to judgment in the plaintiff's favour.

3.3 A form of appearance to defend

The inclusion of this form in the summons is required by rule 5(5)(*a*). The defendant may use it to notify the plaintiff of his or her intention to defend the action.

3.4 A notice drawing the defendant's attention to the provisions of s 109 of the Act

This notice is required by rule 5(5)(*b*)(ii). Section 109 of the Act provides that any person against whom the court has, in a civil case, given any judgment or made any order, who has not satisfied such judgment or order in full and paid all costs for which he or she is liable in connection therewith, shall be guilty of an offence if he or she has changed his or her place of residence, business or employment and failed within 14 days from the date of such change to notify the clerk of the court which gave the judgment or made the order fully and correctly in writing of such change. He or she is also obliged to give notice of his or her change of address to

---

[25] *Geregsbode, Oberholzer v Engelbrecht, Dupper en Vennote* 1984 (2) SA 638 (T).

the judgment creditor or the latter's attorney (or, if his or her estate is under administration, to the administrator).

3.5 The requisite notice in the case in which the action is based on a debt

In terms of rule 5(5)(*b*)(iii), in cases where the action is based on a debt[26] a notice directing the attention of the defendant to the provisions of ss 57, 58, 65A, and 65D of the Act must appear in the summons.

Section 57 provides that a defendant, after service of a letter of demand or summons upon him or her, may in writing admit liability to the plaintiff for the amount of the debt and costs claimed in the letter of demand or summons or for any other amount, and that he or she may offer to pay such amount in instalments or otherwise. The section further provides that the defendant may agree that, in the event of his or her failure to carry out the terms of his or her offer, the plaintiff shall, without notice to the defendant, be entitled to apply for judgment for the amount of the outstanding balance of the debt for which he or she admits liability and for an order of court for payment of the judgment debt in instalments or otherwise in accordance with his or her offer.

Section 58 provides that after receipt of a letter of demand or service of the summons upon him or her, the defendant may consent in writing to judgment in favour of the plaintiff for the amount of the debt and costs claimed or for any other amount and that he may likewise consent to an order of court for the payment of such amounts in instalments or otherwise.

Section 65A provides, in essence, that if the court has given judgment for the payment of a sum of money or has ordered the payment in specified instalments of such an amount, and the judgment or order has remained unsatisfied for a period of 10 days from the date on which the amount became payable, the judgment creditor may issue a notice calling upon the judgment debtor to appear before the court in chambers on a date specified in the notice to show cause why he or she should not be ordered to pay the judgment debt in instalments or otherwise.

Section 65D provides in essence that the judgment debtor must appear in court on the return day of the notice referred to in s 65A(1) to give evidence and be examined in regard to his or her financial position.

3.6 The address at which the plaintiff will accept service of process

The full physical address at which the plaintiff will accept service of process, notices or documents and also the postal address of the person signing the endorsement must be given in the summons.[27] The former address may not be more than 15 kilometres from the court out of which the summons has been issued unless there are fewer than three attorneys or firms of attorneys practising independently of each other within the court's area of jurisdiction.[28] Where available, a facsimile and electronic mail address should also be provided.

---

[26] In terms of s 55, 'debt' means any liquidated sum of money due—in other words, an amount due that is certain and definite.

[27] Rule 5(3)(*a*)(i) and (ii).

[28] Rule 5(3)(*a*)(i) and (ii).

3.7 The descriptions of the parties

The summons must also contain descriptions of the parties.

The first name(s), surname or initials, by which the defendant is known to the plaintiff must be set out in the summons. The summons must also contain the defendant's residence or place of business. Where known, the defendant's occupation and employment address must be indicated and, if the defendant is sued in a representative capacity, such capacity must be indicated.[29]

The full names and gender of the plaintiff (if the plaintiff is a natural person) as well as the occupation and residence or place of business must be indicated in the summons. If the plaintiff sues in a representative capacity, this must also be indicated in the summons.[30]

If the first name or the initial of the defendant is not known to the plaintiff, or is incorrectly set out in the summons or is not reflected in it, the plaintiff may request the insertion of such name or initial in the summons if the first name or initial or the correct or correctly spelt first name is, or all of the first names of the defendant are, furnished to the sheriff by the person on whom service of the summons is effected and the information is noted by the sheriff on his or her return. The correct information is inserted on the summons by the registrar or clerk of the court at the request of the plaintiff. It is not necessary for the plaintiff to give notice to the defendant of the amendment or correction to the summons. The amendment to the summons is for all purposes deemed to have been made before service of the summons.[31]

3.8 Averments of jurisdiction

It must be clear from the summons that the court in which the plaintiff has instituted action has jurisdiction.

By issuing summons out of a particular court, the plaintiff implies that that court has jurisdiction. The jurisdictional facts may appear from the description of the defendant's address and the size and nature of the claim.

It is therefore not normally necessary for the plaintiff to aver specifically in the summons that the court in fact has jurisdiction. It would appear, though, that there are two exceptions to this rule:

(1) Where the plaintiff relies upon the court having jurisdiction in respect of the person of the defendant by virtue of the fact that the cause of action arose wholly within the district, he or she must make an express averment to that effect.[32]

(2) Where the plaintiff relies, in terms of s 28(1)(*g*), upon the court having jurisdiction in respect of the defendant on the basis that the latter is the owner of immovable property within the district or region and the action is in respect of such property or in respect of a mortgage bond thereon, the

---

[29] Rule 5(4)(*a*).

[30] Rule 5(4)(*b*).

[31] Rule 7(3)(*a*). The incorrect citation of corporate entities raises the vexed question as to whether an amendment is merely correcting an error, which is allowed, or introducing a new party, which is not. See *Four Tower Investments (Pty) Ltd v Andre's Motors* 2005 (3) SA 39 (N).

[32] Rule 5(6)(*a*).

plaintiff must expressly aver that the property concerned is situated within the district or region of the court out of which summons has been issued.[33]

3.9 Particulars of claim

In the particulars of claim the basis of the action and the relief sought by the plaintiff are set out. The plaintiff, in other words, gives a description of the facts that give rise to the claim.

According to rule 5(2)(a), where the claim is not for a debt or liquidated demand, a combined summons must be used. Annexed to the summons must be a particulars of claim, ie a statement that contains the material facts upon which the plaintiff relies in support of his or her claim.

Where the plaintiff issues a simple summons, however, the summons itself should contain abbreviated particulars of the claim ie there is no annexed statement containing the material facts. The simple summons must briefly indicate the cause of action, refer to the court's jurisdiction and the parties' *locus standi*, draw a legal conclusion from the material facts and contain a request for legal relief. If the defendant then delivers a notice of intention to defend, the plaintiff must, within 15 days after receipt of the notice, deliver a declaration.[34] The declaration must set out the nature of the claim, the conclusions of law which the plaintiff is entitled to deduce from the facts stated therein and a prayer for the relief claimed.[35] This is essentially the equivalent of a particulars of claim used with a combined summons. Rule 15(3) further states that where the plaintiff seeks relief in respect of several distinct claims founded upon separate and distinct facts, such claims and facts shall be stated separately and distinctly.

The particulars of claim attached to the combined summons constitutes a pleading and must comply with rule 6, ie the rule relating to pleadings generally.[36] This is not the case with a simple summons. The subsequent declaration does, however, constitute a pleading. This explains why rule 5(1)(b) provides that if the summons is a combined summons, within 20 days after the defendant gives notice of his or her intention to defend the action, he or she may deliver a plea, an exception or an application to strike out. This would not be possible in relation to the simple summons as the summons does not constitute a pleading and is therefore not excipiable, and because the next step in the process is for the plaintiff to file his or her declaration (which would be excipiable).[37]

The prayer forms part of the particulars of claim. It is the request made by the plaintiff to the court on the basis of the facts set out by him or her in the particulars. The plaintiff says in effect in his particulars of claim: 'Such-and-such happened; the defendant is consequently legally liable to me for damages (or for the

---

[33] Rule 5(6)(b).
[34] Rule 15(1). See also rule 5(7).
[35] Rule 15(2).
[36] Rule 5(2)(a).
[37] See *Icebreakers No 83 (Pty) Ltd v Medicross Health Care Group (Pty) Ltd* 2011 (5) SA 130 (KZD) para 12 where it is stated that 'a simple summons is not a pleading and therefore not susceptible of being attacked by way of exception'.

performance of whatever obligation may be due) and so I am going to ask the court to grant me the relief stated in my prayer.'

The simple summons may be used when the plaintiff's claim is for a debt or liquidated demand. It often happens that the plaintiff summonses the defendant for 'services rendered by the plaintiff and materials supplied by him or her at the defendant's special instance and request'[38] or that the plaintiff summonses the defendant for 'goods sold and delivered to the defendant at the latter's special instance and request'. The latter type of claim is mostly found where the defendant has purchased goods from the plaintiff on credit and has subsequently failed to pay his or her account. This type of cause of action is so frequently found in lower court practice that the wording of the simple summons has become standardised. It is not necessary for the plaintiff to indicate the date and amount of each purchase or the total balance due thereafter.

The plaintiff advises the defendant in the summons that the claim against him or her is based on the purchase of goods by him or her from the plaintiff. In most cases the defendant will be well aware of the fact that he or she has purchased goods from the plaintiff and has yet to pay his or her account. The defendant will in all probability have received the plaintiff's account (and a demand for payment). The defendant knows, therefore, what the plaintiff's claim is all about. It is thus not necessary in such a case for the plaintiff to give a full account of every purchase.

Where the cause of action is based on a document, the simple summons should make reference to the document and the document should be attached to the summons. If this is not done, the summons will be regarded as failing to disclose a cause of action.[39]

It should be noted that where the plaintiff issues a simple summons in respect of a claim regulated by legislation, the summons may contain a bare averment of compliance with the legislation. However, when the defendant enters appearance to defend, the plaintiff's declaration must allege full particulars of compliance with the requirements of the regulating legislation.[40]

It is no longer possible to claim further particulars for the purpose of pleadings in the magistrates' courts.[41] Rather, the scope of rule 6 has been extended. Rule 6(4) provides that all pleadings must contain 'a clear and concise statement of the material facts upon which the pleader relies for his or her claim, defence or answer to any pleading, as the case may be, with sufficient particularity to enable the

---

[38] *San Sen Woodworks v Govender* 1984 (1) SA 486 (N). At 487H the court stated: 'The claim for "work done and material supplied by the plaintiff to the defendant at the latter's special instance and request" is a time-honoured one in the magistrate's court.' Cf also *Beaufort Furniture & Joinery Manufacturing Co (Pty) Ltd v De Vos* 1950 (1) SA 112 (C) and *Indecor v Hanekom* 1977 (3) SA 375 (NC).

[39] Jones & Buckle Rule 5-6A.

[40] Rule 5(7). The rule provides further that if the cause of action falls under the National Credit Act 34 of 2005, the summons must deal with ss 129 and 130 and allege compliance.

[41] GN 888 in *GG* 33620 of 8 October 2010.

opposing party to reply thereto'. Further particulars may, however, still be sought after the close of pleadings and for the purposes of trial.[42]

Section 43 of the Act provides that if two or more claims based upon a different cause of action are combined in one summons, the court will have the same jurisdiction to decide each claim as it would have had if each claim had formed the sole subject of a separate action. The summons may thus contain more than one claim, but the particulars of each claim and the relief sought in respect of each must be stated separately.[43] Failure to comply with this provision will render the particulars of claim or declaration excipiable.[44]

Where the defendant has, for example, defamed the plaintiff on two separate occasions in the presence of two different groups of people, it will not be possible for the plaintiff to claim a single sum by way of damages from the defendant. He or she will have to bring a separate claim in the summons in respect of each incident and set out in respect of each such claim a separate prayer in which he or she claims a specified amount in damages for the use of the particular defamatory words on each occasion.[45]

Where, however, the plaintiff claims the price of manufacturing a number of cabinets in terms of a single agreement, he or she may bring a single claim for the agreed contract price for his or her labour and materials in producing all of the cabinets.[46] The plaintiff may, however, claim payment of a single amount of money for professional services rendered on a number of occasions. While each service gives rise to a distinct claim, he or she may for the sake of convenience combine these claims in his or her particulars.[47]

The crux of the matter is always whether there was a single cause of action or whether there were several. Where the claim is based upon 'services rendered . . . and goods supplied', it is necessary to ascertain whether there was a contract in terms of which a single amount was payable for both the rendering of the services and the supply of the goods[48] or whether there was a contract in terms of which a stipulated amount would become payable for the supply of the goods alone. In the latter event, one is dealing with two causes of action, namely, the rendering of services for a fee and a contract of sale in regard to the provision of the goods in question.[49] Where two causes of action appear in the particulars of claim, they must be separately averred.

3.10 The prayer

In the prayer the plaintiff sets out his or her request for relief. This request is based upon the averments made by him or her in the particulars of claim.

---

[42] Rule 16.

[43] Section 43 of the Act read with rule 6. Cf *Grant v Vereeniging Motors (Pty) Ltd* 1954 (2) SA 627 (T); *Bothma v Laubscher* 1973 (3) SA 590 (O) and *Indecor v Hanekom* (supra).

[44] Rule 19.

[45] *Argus Printing & Publishing Co Ltd v Weichardt* 1940 CPD 453 at 461; *Kock v Zeeman* 1943 OPD 135 at 138.

[46] *Beaufort Furniture & Joinery Manufacturing Co v De Vos* (supra) at 114 and *San Sen Woodworks v Govender* (supra).

[47] *Fouche v Brandt* 1936 OPD 26.

[48] *Grant v Vereeniging Motors (Pty) Ltd* (supra) at 631D–G.

[49] *Fouche v Brandt* (supra) at 30.

The particulars of claim should show:
(1) the nature and amount of the claim;
(2) if the claim bears interest, the rate at which the interest is calculated; and
(3) the amount claimed for attorney's costs and court fees if the action is not defended.

The relief usually claimed in the prayer is:
(1) judgment against the defendant in favour of the plaintiff for the amount claimed;
(2) interest;
(3) costs; and
(4) alternative relief.

The following is an example of a prayer:

Wherefore[50] the Plaintiff claims:
(1) judgment against the Defendant in the amount of R ....;
(2) interest at the rate of .... % per annum *a tempore morae* to date of payment;
(3) costs of suit; and
(4) further and/or alternative relief.

Attention is given briefly below to the various aspects of the prayer.

3.10.1 *A request for the relief sought*
In the magistrates' courts the request usually made is for judgment against the defendant for the payment of a sum of money.

3.10.2 *A request for interest, should such a request be applicable*
Interest may be claimed only if the parties have agreed that interest shall be payable or if the defendant is *in mora*.[51]

If the parties have agreed on a specific rate of interest, interest at that rate is claimed in the summons. If no agreement has been reached as to the applicable rate of interest or if no rate of interest has been stipulated in the summons, the interest is calculated at the rate prescribed in terms of s 1(2) of the Prescribed Rate of Interest Act 55 of 1975.[52]

Where a party is *in mora*, interest is calculated from the date on which performance ought to have been made.[53] If no date for performance has been set, then interest is computed from the date on which the defendant fell *in mora* following *interpellatio*. The defendant will be *in mora* if performance has been demanded of him, he has been given a reasonable time in which to perform and he remains in default after the expiry of that time.[54]

---

[50] The Afrikaans equivalent is 'derhalwe' or the archaic 'weshalwe'.
[51] Voet 22.1.10; *Turner & Wright v Versatile Pump & Foundry Works (Pty) Ltd* 1951 (3) SA 556 (T) at 561.
[52] *UAL Leasing Corporation Ltd v Frew* 1977 (4) SA 249 (W) at 254A–D.
[53] *Becker v Stusser* 1910 CPD 289.
[54] *Nel v Cloete* 1972 (2) SA 150 (A) at 159H–160A.

In respect of unliquidated debts, which includes damages, a 1997 amendment of the Prescribed Rates of Interest Act provides that interest at the legal rate 'shall run from the date on which payment of the debt is claimed by the service on the debtor of a demand or summons, whichever date is earlier'.[55] However, interest on the present value of a future loan only runs from the date upon which the quantum is determined by a judgment.[56]

3.10.3 *A request for costs of suit*
The prayer for costs is governed by the general rule that the successful litigant is entitled to recover his or her legal costs from the loser.[57]

3.10.4 *A request for further or alternative relief*
The final request made at the end of the prayer asks the court to award the plaintiff any relief not specifically requested in the summons, but to which the latter is entitled on the basis of the averments made in the particulars of claim. In this way the plaintiff may prevent himself or herself from being penalised by a pure oversight in his or her formulation of the claim where it is clear that he or she is entitled to relief on the basis of the facts averred by him or her in the particulars of claim.[58]

4 THE SUMMONS CONTAINING AN AUTOMATIC RENT INTERDICT
When the lessor of premises summonses the lessee for the payment of arrear rent, he or she may, as plaintiff, include in the summons a notice prohibiting any person from removing any of the furniture or other effects on the premises which are subject to the plaintiff's hypothec for rent until an order relative thereto has been made by the court.[59]

This is a distinctive species of summons, since not only does the plaintiff claim the rent due to him or her, but at the same time he or she obtains an interdict to protect his or her tacit hypothec. The notice included in the summons operates to interdict any person who knows of it from removing any furniture or effects from the premises.[60]

The form of the summons containing the automatic rent interdict is set out in Form 3 of Annexure 1 to the rules.[61] This summons reads as follows:

---

[55] Section 2A(2)(*a*) of Act 55 of 1975.
[56] Section 2A(3).
[57] See chapter 16 below.
[58] A description of the origin and ambit of this prayer may be found in *Queensland Insurance Co Ltd v Banque Commerciale Africaine* 1946 AD 272 at 286.
[59] Section 31(1).
[60] Section 31(3).
[61] Rule 5(8).

No. 3

Summons

(in which is included an automatic rent interdict)

* For use in the District Court

In the Magistrate's Court for the District of ....

held at ....

Case No ....

between

.... Plaintiff

and

.... Defendant

To: .... of .... (state residence or place of business and if known, gender, occupation and place of employment) .... (hereinafter called the defendant).

You are hereby summoned that you do within .... days of the service of this summons deliver or cause to be delivered to the clerk of the aforesaid court and also the plaintiff or plaintiff's attorney, at the address specified herein, a notice in writing of your intention to defend this action and answer the claim of .... (state gender and occupation), of .... (residence or place of business) .... (hereinafter called the plaintiff), particulars whereof are endorsed hereunder.

And take notice that—

(a) in default of your paying the amount of the claim and costs within the said period or of your delivering a notice of intention to defend you will be held to have admitted the said claim and the plaintiff may proceed therein and judgment may be given against you in your absence;

(b) if you pay the said claim and costs within the said period judgment will not be given against you herein and you will save judgment charges. You will also save judgment charges if, within the said period, you lodge with the clerk of the aforesaid court a consent to judgment;

(c) if you admit the claim and wish to consent to judgment or wish to undertake to pay the claim in instalments or otherwise, you may approach the plaintiff or plaintiff's attorney.

And further take notice that you, the defendant, and all other persons are hereby interdicted from removing or causing or suffering to be removed any of the furniture or effects in or on the premises described in the particulars of claim endorsed hereon which are subject to the plaintiff's hypothec for rent until an order relative thereto shall have been made by the court.

Costs, if the action is undefended, will be as follows:

Summons .... R

Judgment .... R

Attorney's charges .... R

Sheriff's fees .... R

Sheriff's fees on re-issue .... R

Totals R .... R ....

Total R ....

Notice:

    (i) Any person against whom a court has, in a civil case, given judgment or made any order who has not, within 10 days, satisfied in full such judgment or order may be called upon by notice in terms of section 65A(1) of the Act to appear on a specified date before the court in chambers to enable the court to enquire into the financial position of the judgment debtor and to make such order as the court may deem just and equitable.

    (ii) If the court is satisfied that—

        (aa) the judgment debtor or, if the judgment debtor is a juristic person, a director or officer of the juristic person has knowledge of the abovementioned notice and that he or she has failed to appear before the court on the date and at the time specified in the notice; or

        (bb) the judgment debtor, director or officer, where the proceedings were postponed in his or her presence to a date and time determined by the court, has failed to appear before the court on that date and at that time; or

        (cc) the judgment debtor, director or officer has failed to remain in attendance at the proceedings or at the proceedings so postponed,

      the court may, at the request of the judgment creditor or his or her attorney, authorise the issue of a warrant directing a sheriff to arrest the said judgment debtor, director or officer and to bring him or her before a competent court to enable that court to conduct a financial inquiry. [Section 65A(6) of the Act]

  (iii) Any person who–

        (aa) is called upon to appear before a court under a notice in terms of section 65A(1) or 65A(8)*(b)* of the Act (where the sheriff, in lieu of arresting a person, hands to that person a notice to appear in court) and who wilfully fails to appear before the court on the date and at the time specified in the notice; or

        (bb) where the proceedings were postponed in his or her presence to a date and time determined by the court, wilfully fails to appear before the court on that date and at that time; or

        (cc) wilfully fails to remain in attendance at the relevant proceedings or at the proceedings so postponed,

      shall be guilty of an offence and liable on conviction to a fine or to imprisonment for a period not exceeding three months. [Section 65A(9) of the Act]

  (iv) On appearing before the court on the date determined in the notice in terms of section 65A(1) or (8)*(b)* of the Act in pursuance of the arrest of the judgment debtor, director or officer under a warrant referred to in section 65A(6) of the Act or on any date to which the proceedings have been postponed, such judgment debtor, director or officer shall be called upon to give evidence on his or her financial position or that of the juristic person and his or her or its ability to pay the judgment debt.

  (v) Any person against whom a court has, in a civil case, given any judgment or made any order who has not satisfied in full such judgment or order and paid all costs for which he or she is liable in connection therewith shall, if he or she has changed his or her place of residence, business or employment, within 14 days from the date of every such change notify the clerk of the court who gave such judgment or made such order and the judgment creditor or his or her attorney fully and correctly in writing of his or her new place of residence, business or employment, and by his or her failure to do so such judgment debtor shall be guilty of an offence and liable upon conviction to a fine or imprisonment for a period not exceeding three months. [Section 109 of the Act]

(1) Particulars of claim.

Plaintiff's claim is—

  (i) for arrears of rent due in respect of the defendant's tenancy of .... and for confirmation of the interdict appearing in this summons.

Particulars:

....

Date

Period

Amount

R

....

....

....
and
    (ii) for ejectment.
Particulars: ....
....
(2) Consent to judgment.
I admit that I am liable to the plaintiff as claimed in this summons (or in the amount of R ....
and costs to date) and I consent to judgment accordingly.
Dated at .... this .... day of ...., 20.......
....
Defendant
WITNESSES:

1   (full names) ...., (signature) ....
      (address) ....
2   (full names) ...., (signature) ....
(address) ....

ALTERNATIVE TO (2)

*(3) Notice of intention to defend.
To the Clerk of the Court
Kindly take notice that the defendant hereby gives notice of defendant's intention to defend this
action.
Dated at .... this .... day of ...., 20.......
....
Defendant/Defendant's Attorney
Physical address where service of process or documents will be accepted (within 15 kilometres
from the Court-house)
....
Postal address
....
....

* The original notice must be filed with the clerk of the court and a copy thereof served on the
plaintiff or plaintiff's attorney.

The sheriff shall, if required by the plaintiff and at the plaintiff's expense, make an inventory of the furniture or other effects on the premises.[62]

Any person affected by the interdict may apply to court to have it set aside.[63]

Where a landlord would prefer to secure the property to obtain payment of arrear rental, as opposed to imprisoning the lessee, the procedure in s 32 can be used. It essentially entails that the landlord may apply to court for an order permitting the attachment of movable property on the rented premises. In order to succeed with such an application, the landlord must show that:

---

[62] Section 31(2).
[63] Section 31(4). The granting of the order is interlocutory of the main action, and accordingly it is not appealable. See *Halstead v Durant NO* 2002 (1) SA 277 (W).

- an amount which does not exceed the court's monetary jurisdiction is due and in arrear;[64] and
- the rent has been demanded in writing and more than seven days have passed without payment; or
- the landlord believes that the tenant is about to remove the movable property to avoid paying rent.[65]

Section 32(2) states that the landlord must provide security to the satisfaction of the clerk or registrar of the court that he or she will pay all damages, costs and charges which the tenant or any other person may incur as a result of the attachment.

5 AMENDMENTS TO THE SUMMONS PRIOR TO SERVICE

A summons may be amended before service by the plaintiff as he or she may think fit.[66]

Any alteration or amendment made to a summons before service (whether before or after issue) must be initialled by the registrar or clerk of the court in the original before the summons is served; and until the summons is so initialled, the alterations and amendments are of no effect.[67]

6 AMENDMENTS TO THE SUMMONS AFTER SERVICE

The summons may be amended after service by way of application upon proper notice or, with leave of the court, at the trial itself.[68]

Rule 55A, which was added to the rules in 1977, has greatly simplified the procedure for amending pleadings. A party who now desires to amend a pleading is required to give notice to all other parties of his or her intention to amend and the particulars of the amendment.

The notice must state that, unless objection in writing to the proposed amendment is made within 10 days of delivery of the notice, the pleading will be deemed to be so amended. If objection is made, the party wishing to pursue the amendment must apply to court for leave to amend.

When a pleading is deemed to have been amended, the other party may plead to the amendment or amend consequentially any pleading already filed by him or her within 15 days after receipt of the notice of amendment.

Unless the court otherwise orders, the party giving notice of amendment is liable to any other party for the costs occasioned by the amendment.

---

[64] Currently the monetary limits are R200 000 in the District Court and R400 000 in the Regional Court.
[65] Section 32(1).
[66] Rule 7(1).
[67] Rule 7(2).
[68] Rule 7(3)(*b*) provides that rule 55A shall apply to the amendment of summonses after service.

7 ISSUE OF THE SUMMONS

The summons is issued by the clerk or registrar of the court. The issue takes place when the registrar or clerk of the court allocates to the summons a consecutive number[69] and signs the summons.[70]

In the larger centres, the summons is issued mechanically. A member of the staff of the office of the registrar or clerk of the court prints the number of the process, the signature and date on the summons by machine. Rule 3(1) makes provision for the registrar or clerk of the court to machine a facsimile of his or her signature onto the summons.

The registrar or clerk need therefore not sign every summons personally when it is issued.

The issue of the summons entails certain consequences. First, the action is instituted at the time the summons is issued.[71]

There exists uncertainty in our law on the question whether the action is instituted by issue of the summons or by service of the summons on the defendant. In a number of decided cases the view has been adopted that it is the issue of the summons that is decisive.[72] There are, however, other cases in which the view was adopted that the action is instituted only by the service of summons.[73]

The view that the action is instituted by the issue of summons is preferable. It is adopted on the basis of the greater certainty that it affords the plaintiff. The plaintiff must determine, prior to the issue of summons, which court will have jurisdiction to decide the action.

Secondly, the issue of summons establishes jurisdiction. The issue of summons out of a particular court implies that the court has jurisdiction to try the case and, unless the court itself decides that it does not have jurisdiction, all further steps in the proceeding, including the trial itself, will take place in that court.

The date on which action is instituted, and not the date on which the matter is heard, is decisive of the question whether the court has jurisdiction in respect of the value of the claim.[74]

It must be noted, however, that prescription is interrupted only by the *service* of the summons. The mere issue of the summons does not interrupt the running of prescription.[75]

8 DELAY IN THE PROSECUTION OF AN ACTION

Previously, a summons in an action lapsed if it was not served within 12 months of the date of its issue or, where it has been served, if the plaintiff did not within a period of 12 months after service take further steps in the prosecution of the

---

[69] Rule 3(2).
[70] Rule 3(1).
[71] Rule 5(1).
[72] *During v Kerr* 1946 TPD 412 at 421; *Marine & Trade Insurance Co Ltd v Reddinger* 1966 (2) SA 407 (A) at 413D; *Labuschagne v Labuschagne; Labuschagne v Minister van Justisie* 1967 (2) SA 575 (A) at 584B–D and the authorities there cited; *Glen v Glen* 1971 (3) SA 238 (R) at 240–1.
[73] *Buck v Parker* 1908 TS 1100 at 1104; *Ex parte Minister of Native Affairs* 1941 AD 53 at 58–9.
[74] *Grand Wholesalers v Ladysmith Metal Industry* 1985 (4) SA 100 (N).
[75] Section 15(1) of the Prescription Act 68 of 1969.

action.[76] Rule 10 has been entirely amended and the rules no longer contain such a provision.

9 CESSIONARY

According to rule 5(9), where the plaintiff sues as cessionary, he or she must indicate the name, address and description of the cedent at the date of cession, as well as the date of the cession.

10 DECLARING IMMOVABLE PROPERTY EXECUTABLE

A summons in which an order is sought to declare executable immovable property which is the home of the defendant shall contain a notice in the following form:

> 'The defendant's attention is drawn to section 26(1) of the Constitution of the Republic of South Africa which accords to everyone the right to have access to adequate housing. Should the defendant claim that the order for eviction will infringe that right it is incumbent on the defendant to place information supporting that claim before the Court.'[77]

11 FAILURE TO COMPLY

A failure to comply with rule 5 will result in the summons being deemed to constitute an irregular step.[78]

---

[76] *Manyasha v Minister of Law and Order* 1999 (2) SA 179 (SCA).
[77] Rule 5(10).
[78] The opposite party shall be entitled to act in accordance with rule 60A. Rule 5(11).

Chapter 9

SERVICE OF THE SUMMONS

Once the summons has been issued, the plaintiff takes the original and as many copies of it as there are defendants to the sheriff of the court for service.[1] The plaintiff should, as a salutary administrative practice, retain a copy signed by the registrar or clerk of the court in his or her file as proof of the fact that the summons has been issued in case the original is later misplaced.

The sheriff and his or her duties have already been dealt with above; he or she is required to serve the summons, being the document instituting action, upon the defendant. In this chapter the general rules relating to service of process are described, after which the manner of service of the summons is dealt with specifically.

1 GENERAL RULES RELATING TO SERVICE

As a general rule, process of the court may be served or executed only by the sheriff,[2] and so it must be to him or her that the plaintiff must hand the original summons together with as many copies as he or she requires the sheriff to serve.

---

[1] Rule 8(1).
[2] Rule 8(2).

A sheriff may serve documents only within the jurisdictional area of the court to which he or she is appointed.[3]

When the sheriff serves the summons upon someone, he or she hands that person the copy, explains the nature of the claim to the person and warns him or her of the consequences of failing to defend the action.

On demand by the person upon whom the summons is served, the sheriff must exhibit to him or her the original of the summons.[4]

Judicial process must be served or executed without any unreasonable delay by the sheriff. The sheriff cannot be regarded as the agent of the party who instructs him or her to serve the summons (or other process); rather, he or she is an officer of the court.[5] Should the sheriff thus fail to act in accordance with the rules of court, he or she will not be liable in terms of any contract of agency. He or she may, however, be held liable for intentional or negligent failure to discharge his or her duty to carry out his or her instructions properly. In *Weeks & another v Amalgamated Agencies Ltd*[6] the court investigated the basis of the sheriff's liability. While this case dealt with an instance in which a sheriff attached certain property in a negligent manner, the court discussed the basis of the sheriff's liability in general. The basis of liability is to be found in the law of delict. As an official of the court, the sheriff is under a duty to execute his or her instructions scrupulously within the limits of the law. Should the sheriff not carry out his or her instructions in such manner, he or she will be liable for damage that may be sustained by any party as a result of his or her conduct.[7]

The sheriff may not serve any process, notices or other documents on a Sunday or a public holiday.[8] The prohibition upon service on a Sunday or public holiday does not affect the service of an interdict, a warrant of arrest or a warrant of attachment of property under s 30*bis*. The service of the interdict (or any of these warrants) may be executed on any day at any hour and at any place.[9]

In any case where resistance to the due service or execution of the process of the court has been met with or is reasonably anticipated, the sheriff has the power to call upon any member of the Force as defined in the Police Act 7 of 1958 to render him or her aid.[10]

Any person who obstructs the sheriff or deputy sheriff in the execution of his or her duties is guilty of an offence and liable upon conviction to a fine not exceeding R500 or, in default of payment, to imprisonment for a period not exceeding six months, or to such imprisonment without the option of a fine.[11]

---

[3] Section 3(1) of the Sheriffs Act 90 of 1986.

[4] Rule 9(4).

[5] Rule 8(2). See also *Cyster v Du Toit* 1932 CPD 345 at 348.

[6] 1920 AD 218.

[7] At 225 and 234–5. See too *Smit v Van Wyk* 1966 (3) SA 210 (T) at 217G; *Trust Bank van Afrika Bpk v Geregsbode, Middelburg* 1966 (3) SA 391 (T) at 393F–G; *Meevis v Sheriff, Pretoria East* 1999 (2) SA 389 (T).

[8] Rule 9(2)*(a)*.

[9] Rule 9(2)*(c)*.

[10] Rule 8(2).

[11] Section 107(1).

The sheriff reports on the service or attempted service of process in a document known as a *return*.

Where the process served by the sheriff is a summons, the return of service and the original summons are returned by the sheriff to the party who sued out the summons.[12] Where the process is not a summons, the sheriff is required to notify both the court and the party who sued out the process that service has been duly effected, stating the date and the manner of service or the result of the execution, and to return the original process to the registrar or clerk of the court.[13]

If the sheriff has been unable to effect service of process or execution, he or she is required to notify the party who sued out the process of that fact, setting out the reason for such inability, and to return the process in question to such party.[14] The sheriff is required also to keep a record of any process so returned.

If the sheriff has succeeded in serving summons, his or her return is known as a *return of service*. If he or she has not been able to serve the summons, the return is known as a *return of non-service*.

Normally the sheriff sends the original summons together with the original return back to the registrar or clerk of the civil court, where they become the first documents to be filed in the court file. A copy of the summons is, of course, handed to the defendant and the copy of the return is sent to the plaintiff so that he or she is informed of the service of the summons.

In any court for which an officer of the Public Service has been appointed sheriff, the return of any process is deemed to have been properly effected if it is placed in a receptacle specially set apart for the attorney of that party in the office of the sheriff.[15]

After service or attempted service, the sheriff, other than a sheriff who is an officer of the Public Service, specifies the amount of each of his charges on the original and all copies of the return.[16] The tariff of charges claimable by the sheriff is set out in Part I and Part II of Table C of Annexure 2.

In terms of s 17 the return of a sheriff (or of any person authorised to perform any of the functions of a sheriff) constitutes *prima facie* proof of the matters stated in it.

Since the return constitutes only *prima facie* proof of such matters, a party may place it in dispute. The court will, however, have to be persuaded that the return does not set out the true facts and the party seeking to challenge the averments made in the return will have to prove that those averments do not accurately reflect the true state of affairs.[17]

---

[12] Rule 8(4).
[13] Rule 8(3)*(a)*.
[14] Rule 8(3)*(b)*.
[15] Rule 8(5).
[16] Rule 8(6).
[17] *Deputy-Sheriff for Witwatersrand District v Harry Goldberg & the Assignees of Goldberg Bros & Gerson* 1905 TS 680 at 684.

A sheriff may supplement an incomplete return[18] or give evidence to rectify an ambiguous statement contained in a return.[19]

If the return is erroneous but evidence is given to the court proving that service was effected in terms of the rules, the service will be valid.[20]

The service of a subpoena may be effected at a reasonable time before attendance at court is required, using any of the methods discussed below, but the service need not be effected through the sheriff.[21]

The service of any notice, request, statement or other document which is not process of the court likewise need not be effected through the sheriff, but may be effected by delivery by hand at the address for service given in the summons (or appearance to defend) or may be effected by sending the document in question by registered post to the postal address given in the summons (or appearance to defend).[22]

The address given for service or the postal address may be changed by the delivery of notice of a new address, and thereafter service may be effected at the new address by delivery by hand or by registered post.[23] The service by registered post is deemed, unless the contrary appears, to have been effected at 10h00 on the fourth day after the postmarked date upon the receipt for registration.[24]

2 PARTICULAR METHODS OF SERVICE

Service of process takes place when the process is formally delivered to an opposing litigant in accordance with the rules of court. Through service of the summons the sheriff certifies that the claim has been formally brought to the attention of the defendant.

Rule 9 makes provision for the following methods of service:
(1) personal service;
(2) service upon an agent;
(3) service at the residence or place of business of the defendant;
(4) service at the defendant's place of employment;
(5) service at the defendant's *domicilium citandi*;
(6) service upon a body corporate;
(7) service by registered post;
(8) service upon State organs and State officials;
(9) service by affixing a copy of the summons to a door;
(10) service upon a partnership;
(11) service upon curators, executors, guardians, etc;
(12) service upon clubs, societies, etc; and
(13) service in terms of an order of court.

---

[18] *Vermeulen v Vermeulen* 1940 OPD 25.
[19] *Botha v Measroch* 1916 TPD 142.
[20] *Botha v Measroch* (supra) at 146.
[21] Rule 9(8).
[22] Rule 9(9)(*a*).
[23] Rule 9(9)(*c*).
[24] Rule 9(9)(*c*)(i).

2.1 Personal service

The summons may be served by the delivery of a copy of the summons by the sheriff to the defendant personally.[25] On demand by the defendant, the sheriff is required to exhibit to him or her the original of the process as proof that the copy handed to him or her is a true copy of the original.[26]

Personal service is required in all matters involving the status of the defendant, such as divorce and insolvency.

2.2 Service upon an agent

The summons may also be served upon the duly authorised agent of the defendant.[27]

2.3 Service at the residence or place of business of the defendant

The sheriff may serve the summons at the residence or place of business of the defendant to some person apparently not less than 16 years of age and apparently residing or employed there.[28]

In this event the sheriff is required to indicate in his return of service the name of the person to whom it has been delivered and the capacity in which such person stands in relation to the person affected by the process. The court may, if there is reason to doubt whether the process served has come to the actual knowledge of the person to be served, and in the absence of satisfactory evidence, treat such service as invalid.[29]

2.4 Service at the defendant's place of employment

The summons may be served at the place of employment of the defendant to some person apparently not less than 16 years of age and apparently in authority over the defendant or, in the absence of such person in authority, to a person apparently not less than 16 years of age and apparently in charge at his or her place of employment.[30]

The same duty rests upon the sheriff as set out in the previous section.

2.5 Service at the defendant's *domicilium citandi*

The *domicilium citandi* is the address stipulated by a party in an agreement as being the place at which any process, notices or documents relating to the agreement may be delivered to him or her.

The sheriff may serve the summons at the *domicilium citandi* of the defendant.[31] The manner of service will be as set out above.

---

[25] Rule 9(3)*(a)*.
[26] Rule 9(4).
[27] Rule 9(3)*(a)*.
[28] Rule 9(3)*(b)*. This rule provides also that 'residence', when a building is occupied by more than one person or family, means that portion of the building occupied by the defendant.
[29] Proviso to rule 9(3).
[30] Rule 9(3)*(c)*.
[31] Rule 9(3)*(d)*.

2.6　Service upon a body corporate

If the defendant is a body corporate (a juristic person), the summons may be served at its registered office or principal place of business within the area of jurisdiction of the court to a responsible employee or by affixing a copy to the main door of such office of place of business, or it may be served in any other manner specially provided by law.[32]

In this event the sheriff is required to indicate the name of the person to whom it is has been delivered and the capacity in which such person stands in relation to the body corporate affected by the process.[33]

2.7　Service by registered post

The plaintiff or his or her authorised agent may give the sheriff written instructions to serve the summons by registered post, in which event it will not be necessary for the sheriff to serve the summons personally. This method of service would, for example, be appropriate where the defendant is a farmer who lives a considerable distance out of town. To expect the sheriff to drive out to the defendant's farm to serve the summons there will often merely result in unnecessary costs being incurred, especially where the farm is situated very far from the seat of the sheriff. In *Geregsbode, Meyerton v KGK (Edms) Bpk*[34] the question arose whether the sheriff may serve a summons by registered post where the address of the defendant is situated outside the area of jurisdiction of the court for which the sheriff has been appointed. At 778F–G Boshoff AJP (as he then was) essentially stated that the sheriff's powers and duties occur within the legal area from which the letter is sent. Delivery of the letter outside this area makes no difference. The place of such service is thus deemed to be the place of posting and not the place of residence of the addressee.

Rule 9(13)*(a)* provides that where service of process takes place by registered post, it is effected by the sheriff placing a copy thereof in an envelope, addressing it and posting it by prepaid registered letter to the address of the party to be served. At the time of registration the sheriff makes application for an acknowledgment by the addressee of the receipt of the registered letter as provided in reg 44(5) of the regulations published under GN R550 of 14 April 1960.

A receipt form completed as provided for in reg 44(8) of the above regulations constitutes a sufficient acknowledgment of receipt for this purpose.[35]

If no such acknowledgment is received, the sheriff mentions this fact in his return of service of the process.[36]

Every such letter is required to have on the envelope a printed or typewritten notice in the following terms:

---

[32] Rule 9(3)*(e)*.
[33] Proviso to rule 9(3).
[34] 1978 (1) SA 774 (T).
[35] Rule 9(13)*(b)*.
[36] Rule 9(13)*(c)*.

'This letter must not be readdressed. If delivery is not effected before.....................
.... 20........., this letter must be delivered to the Sheriff of the
Magistrate's Court at ....'[37]

Where the summons has been served by registered post in terms of rule 9(3)(*f*) and there is reason to doubt whether the process served has come to the actual knowledge of the person to be served, the court or the registrar or clerk of the court, as the case may be, may, in the absence of satisfactory evidence, treat such service as invalid.[38]

2.8 Service upon State organs and State officials

In cases where a minister, deputy minister or administrator is sued in his or her official capacity or where the State, or a province, is sued, the summons is served at the office of the state attorney in Tshwane or at a branch of that office which serves the area of jurisdiction of the court out of which the process was issued.[39]

The sheriff is required to indicate in the return of service the name of the person to whom the summons has been delivered and the capacity in which such person stands in relation to the institution affected by the process.[40]

2.9 Service by affixing a copy of the summons to a door

Where the person upon whom a summons is to be served keeps his or her residence or place of business closed and thus prevents the sheriff from serving the process upon him or her, the sheriff may affix a copy of the summons to the outer or principal door or security gate of the premises or place such copy in the post box at such residence or place of business.[41]

2.10 Service upon a partnership

The summons may be served upon a partnership at the office or place of business of the partnership or, if there is no such office or place of business, it may be served on any member of the partnership in any manner described above.[42]

2.11 Service upon curators, executors, guardians, etc

In the event of two or more persons being summonsed in their capacity as curators of an insolvent estate, liquidators of a company, executors, curators or guardians, the summons may be served upon any one of them in any manner described above.[43]

2.12 Service upon clubs, societies, etc

In the case of a syndicate, unincorporated company, club, society, church, public institution or public body, the summons may be served at the local office or place

---

[37] Rule 9(13)(*d*).
[38] Proviso to rule 9(3).
[39] Rule 9(3)(*g*).
[40] Proviso to rule 9(3).
[41] Rule 9(5).
[42] Rule 9(7)(*a*).
[43] Rule 9(7)(*b*).

of business of that body or, if there is no such office or place of business, it may be served on the chairperson or secretary or similar officer in any manner described above.[44]

2.13 Service in terms of an order of court

Where service cannot be effected in any manner described above, the court may, if the action is within its jurisdiction, make an order allowing service to be effected in the manner specified in the order.[45]

Normally the court in these cases orders substituted service. Substituted service takes place where the defendant is within the Republic but service cannot be effected upon him or her in terms of the rules of court. This will occur where, for example, the defendant is a debtor who constantly moves around from one place to another so that his or her place of residence or employment can never be ascertained with certainty. The plaintiff may then, by making application to court, ask the court to order that the summons be served in a different manner to the methods of service provided for in the rules of court which have been discussed above. The court may in such a case order that substituted service be effected by requiring, for example, that the summons be sent by registered post to the last-known address of the defendant and advertised in a local newspaper.[46] The court may likewise direct other forms of substituted service, for example, that the summons be served upon a friend or a relative of the defendant. The factor which will determine the method of service is whether the court believes that the summons will come to the attention of the defendant if it is served in the substituted manner authorised by the court.[47]

Rule 10 regulates substituted service and provides for edictal citation. Where service cannot be effected in terms of rule 9 (ie substituted service is necessary) or if service must occur outside the country (ie edictal citation is necessary), an application must be made to court.[48] The application must set out the nature and extent of the claim, the grounds upon which the claim is based and upon which the court has jurisdiction to entertain the claim, and the manner of service that the court is asked to authorise. Where the manner of service proposed is not personal service, the application must also address the last-known whereabouts of the person to be served and the inquiries made to ascertain his or her present whereabouts.[49]

---

[44] Rule 9(7)(*c*).
[45] Rule 9(10).
[46] *Estate Mahomed v Mahomed* 1925 WLD 107 at 108.
[47] In *CMC Woodworking Machinery (Pty) Ltd v Pieter Odendaal Kitchens* 2012 (5) SA 604 (KZD), service of a notice of set-down and pre-trial directions via substituted service was permitted. What makes this case significant is that the substituted service entailed service through social media, specifically transmission of a Facebook message.
[48] Rule 10(1).
[49] Rule 10(2)(*a*).

The court may make any order regarding the manner of service that it deems fit, and the court will order the amount of time within which a notice of intention to defend must be given or any other step that the person to be served must take.[50]

It is important to note that where a person wants to serve a document, not commencing court proceedings, inside or outside the country, it is not required that an application be brought. The party may rather request such leave at any hearing at which the court is dealing with the matter. This would not require that papers be filed in support of the request.[51]

According to Annexure 1 Form 4, the notice for substituted service reads as follows:

No. 4

Edictal Citation/Substituted Service: Short Form of Process

(Notice under Rule 9(12) for Substituted Service)

* For use in the District Court

In the Magistrate's Court for the District of ....

held at ....

Case No ....of 20...................

In the matter between:

....Plaintiff

and

.... Defendant

To:

A... B .... formerly residing at ...., but whose present whereabouts are unknown (defendant herein):

TAKE NOTICE that by summons sued out of this court, you have been called upon to give notice, within .... days after publication hereof, to the clerk of this court and to the plaintiff/plaintiff's attorney of your intention to defend (if any) in an action wherein

C .... D .... (plaintiff herein) claims:

  (a) ....

  (b) ....

  (c) ....

TAKE NOTICE FURTHER that if you fail to give such notice, judgment may be granted against you without further reference to you.

DATED at .... this .... day of ...., 20.......

Plaintiff/Plaintiff's Attorney

Address for service:

Physical address 15 km from court house

....

....

Clerk of the Court

---

[50] Rule 10(2)(*b*).
[51] Rule 10(3).

2.14 Objections to service

Where a summons has not been properly served, the defendant may apply to have it set aside as an irregular step in terms of rule 60A.[52] The application must be on notice and must set out particulars of the irregularity.[53] The applicant may not have taken a further step in the proceedings with knowledge of the irregularity, ie knowledge that service of the summons was defective. The applicant must, within 10 days of becoming aware of the irregular step, give written notice to the opposing party and afford him or her 10 days within which to remove the cause of complaint. An application may be brought within 15 days after the expiry of the 10-day period.[54]

At the hearing of the above application, the court may set the irregular step aside in whole or in part and grant leave to amend or make any such order as the court deems fit.[55] The party who has performed the irregular step may not perform any further steps until he or she has complied with the court order.[56]

---

[52] Rule 5(11). See also *SA Instrumentation (Pty) Ltd v Smithchem (Pty) Ltd* 1977 (3) SA 703 (D). However, in *Prism Payment Technologies (Pty) Ltd v Altech Information Technologies (t/a Altech Card Solutions) & others* 2012 (5) SA 267 (GSJ) para 24, Lamont J expressed doubt as to whether High Court Uniform Rule 30, the High Court equivalent to rule 60A, is appropriate for setting aside of an irregularity regarding service.

[53] Rule 60A(2).

[54] Rule 60A(2).

[55] Rule 60A(3).

[56] Rule 60A(4).

Chapter 10

SATISFACTION OF CLAIMS, JUDGMENT BY CONSENT AND DEFAULT JUDGMENT

1 INTRODUCTION

After the combined summons, or the simple summons followed by a declaration, has been served upon the defendant, he or she has various options open to him or her:

(1) The defendant may decide to oppose the action on the basis of some or other defect in the formulation of the claim. In this event he or she may make use of the exception procedure, the application to strike out or the special plea.[1]

(2) The defendant may decide to oppose the claim on its merits. In that event, he

---

[1] Chapter 12 below.

or she will deliver a notice of his or her intention to defend and thereafter deliver a plea.[2]

(3) The defendant may decide to give notice of intention to defend purely for the purpose of delaying the proceedings.[3]

(4) The defendant may decide to try to settle the matter by means of a tender or a payment into court.[4]

(5) Finally, the defendant may decide that he or she does not wish to defend the matter. He or she decides, in other words, not to oppose the plaintiff's claim. This decision may be manifested in three ways by the defendant:

- First, he or she may satisfy the plaintiff's claim by, for example, paying to the plaintiff the amount claimed or by offering to pay the amount claimed in instalments.

- Secondly, he or she may consent to the plaintiff's taking judgment against him or her.

- Thirdly, the defendant may simply do nothing. His or her failure to take any steps at all will usually result in the plaintiff obtaining default judgment.

In this chapter each of these three procedures, namely, satisfaction of the plaintiff's claim, judgment by consent and default judgment, is dealt with in greater detail.

2 SATISFACTION OF THE PLAINTIFF'S CLAIM

In its wide meaning, this entails meeting the plaintiff's claim as set out in the summons.

In its simplest form, satisfaction of the claim takes place if the defendant, after receipt of a letter of demand or summons, immediately meets the claim. In this event the plaintiff will not be entitled to proceed with the claim, since it will have been satisfied.

In cases in which the defendant is summonsed or receives a letter of demand for a debt and he or she is not in a financial position to satisfy the claim *immediately*, there exists a procedure by which the claim may be satisfied.

When the defendant admits liability to the plaintiff in the amount claimed plus the costs claimed in the summons or letter of demand or for some other amount, the defendant may tender to pay the amount of the claim and the costs in respect of which he or she admits liability in instalments or otherwise;[5] and he or she may likewise undertake, on payment of any instalment in terms of his or her offer, to

---

[2] Chapters 11 and 14 below respectively. Where a simple summons is issued, delivery by the defendant of a notice of intention to defend is followed by the plaintiff's declaration. Only thereafter does the defendant file a plea.

[3] Chapters 11 and 12 below.

[4] Chapter 13 below.

[5] Section 57(1)(*b*). Section 57(1A) provides that the offer must set out full particulars of the monthly or weekly income and expenditure, supported where reasonably possible by the most recent proof in the possession of the defendant and other court orders or agreements, if any, with other creditors for payment of a debt and costs in instalments. It must also indicate the amount of the offered instalment.

pay the collection fees for which the plaintiff is liable in respect of the recovery of that instalment.[6]

The defendant may also agree that in the event of his or her failure to carry out the terms of his or her offer, the plaintiff shall, without further notice to him or her, be entitled to apply for judgment for the amount, or the amount of the outstanding balance, of the debt for which he or she admits liability, with costs, and for an order of court for payment of the judgment debt and costs in instalments or otherwise in accordance with his or her offer.[7]

If the plaintiff or his attorney accepts this offer of the defendant, he or she is required to advise the defendant by registered letter of the acceptance of the offer.[8]

In this event the admission of liability is coupled with an offer to pay the debt in instalments and the acceptance of the offer therefore means that the claim is satisfied—provided, of course, that the defendant pays in regular instalments.

If, after having been advised by the plaintiff or his or her attorney in writing that his or her offer has been accepted, the defendant fails to carry out the terms of his or her offer, the court may upon the written request of the plaintiff or his or her attorney enter judgment in favour of the plaintiff for the amount, or the outstanding balance of the amount, of the debt for which the defendant has admitted liability, with costs. The court may order the defendant to pay the judgment debt and costs in specified instalments or otherwise in accordance with his or her offer.[9]

If the defendant was not present or represented when the judgment was entered by the court, the judgment creditor or his or her attorney must, within 10 days after it has received knowledge that judgment has been entered and an order made, advise the judgment debtor by registered letter of the terms of the judgment and order.[10]

A judgment entered in favour of the plaintiff in terms of s 57(2) has the effect of a judgment by default.[11]

Section 57 is subject to the relevant provisions of the National Credit Act 34 of 2005 (NCA) where the request for judgment is based on a credit agreement under said Act.[12]

The request for judgment is made using the wording given in the example set out in Annexure 1 Form 5A.

A 'defendant' may also admit liability after receiving a letter of demand as contemplated in s 56 in which payment of a debt is demanded.[13] In that event satisfaction of a claim takes place without the defendant having been summonsed.

This demand is made by registered post and the 'plaintiff' is entitled to recover

---

[6] Section 57(1)*(c)*.
[7] Section 57(1)*(d)*.
[8] Section 57(1).
[9] Section 57(2). Section 57(2A) contains information that must accompany the written request whereas s 57(2B) sets out the powers of the court in this regard.
[10] Section 57(3).
[11] Section 57(4).
[12] Section 57(5).
[13] Section 57(1)*(a)*. For further details, see chapter 19 below.

the costs of the letter of demand.[14] The letter of demand will constitute the first document to be filed in the action and must contain the particulars prescribed in the rules.[15]

The same procedure as set out above applies by which the 'defendant' may make an offer to pay in instalments and by which the 'plaintiff' may accept such an offer.

If the plaintiff or his attorney accepts such an offer made by the defendant, he or she is required to advise the defendant by registered letter of the acceptance of the offer.[16]

If, after having been advised by the plaintiff or his or her attorney in writing that his or her offer has been accepted, the defendant fails to carry out the terms of the offer, the court may in terms of s 57(2) upon the written request of the plaintiff or his or her attorney enter judgment in favour of the plaintiff.

According to Annexure 1 Form 5A, this request for judgment reads as follows:

No. 5A

Request for Judgment where the Defendant Has Admitted Liability and Undertaken to Pay the Debt in Instalments or Otherwise—Section 57 of the Magistrates' Courts Act, 1944 (Act 32 of 1944)

[Form 5A substituted by GN R632 of 22 June 2018 (wef 1 August 2018).]

* For use in the District Court

In the Magistrate's Court for the District of ....

held at .... Case No .... of 20 ....

In the matter between

.... Plaintiff

and

.... Defendant

Plaintiff requests that judgment in the above-mentioned matter in terms of section 57 of the Magistrates' Courts Act, 1944, be entered in his/her favour against the defendant as follows:

Judgment debt: R   c

Costs: R   c

Outstanding balance of the debt   ....

Interest at .... per cent per annum accounted from ....

Collection fees ....

Summons, if any (attorney's charges, sheriff's fees and sheriff's fees on re-issue)..........................

....

Cost of affidavit or affirmation by plaintiff/certificate by plaintiff's attorney..............

Cost of registered letter ....

Cost of notice in terms of rule 54(1) ....

Letter of demand (section 56) ....

Request for judgment (section 57) ....

Admission of liability and undertaking to pay (section 57)

Totals R   R

Total   R

---

[14] Section 56.

[15] Section 59.

[16] Section 57(1).

plus further interest at .... per cent per annum as from the date of judgment to the date of payment, and that payment thereof take place in accordance with defendant's offer. The following documents are attached:

(a)   the summons, or if no summons has been issued, a copy of the letter of demand;

(b)   the defendant's written acknowledgment of liability and offer indicating the amount of the instalment offered by the defendant;

(c)   full particulars and documentary evidence of the defendant's–

    (i) monthly or weekly income and expenditure, supported where reasonably possible by the most recent proof thereof in the possession of the defendant;

    (ii) other court orders or agreements, if any, with other creditors for payment of a debt and costs in instalments in order for the court to be apprised of the defendant's financial position at the time the offer was made and accepted; and

    (iii) if the written consent contains a consent to an emoluments attachment order, the notice to the employer and the judgment debtor of the intention to request the court to authorise an emoluments attachment order;

(d)   a copy of the plaintiff's or his or her attorney's written acceptance of the offer and proof of postage thereof to the defendant; and

(e)   an affidavit by the plaintiff or a certificate by his or her attorney stating in which respects the defendant has failed to carry out the terms of his or her offer and, if the defendant has made any payments since the date of the letter of demand or summons, showing how the balance claimed is arrived at.

Dated at .... this ...... day of .... 20......

Plaintiff/Plaintiff's attorney

....

(Address)

....

Judgment granted on the .... day of .... 20.............. in favour of the plaintiff for the amount of R .... and the amount of R .... costs.

The defendant is further ordered to pay the said judgment and costs in monthly/weekly instalments of R .... / The defendant is further ordered to pay the said judgment and costs in accordance with the offer.* **

The first instalment must be paid on or before .... and thereafter on or before the .... day of every succeeding month/week* until the outstanding balance of the judgment debt and costs has been paid in full.

....

Court

*   Delete whatever is not applicable

** Emoluments Attachment Order may only be issued if the court is satisfied that there is compliance with section 65J(2A)

Satisfaction may, however, also take place simply by a consent to judgment on the part of the defendant, and it is necessary to discuss this possibility in greater detail.

3 JUDGMENT BY CONSENT

3.1 How consent to judgment is given

After the summons claiming payment of a debt[17] has been served upon him or her,[18] or upon receipt of a letter of demand, the defendant may consent in writing to judgment in favour of the plaintiff for the amount of the debt and the costs claimed in the summons or demand, or he or she may consent to judgment in some other amount.[19]

The court may, on the written request of the plaintiff or his or her attorney, enter judgment in favour of the plaintiff for the amount of the debt and the costs for which the defendant has consented to judgment.[20] The request must be accompanied by the information listed in s 57(1B) and the court will be entitled to act in accordance with s 57(1C).

If it appears from the defendant's written consent to judgment that he or she has also consented to an order of court for payment in specified instalments or otherwise of the amount of the debt and costs in respect of which he or she has consented to judgment, the court may also order the defendant to pay the judgment debt and costs in specified instalments or otherwise in accordance with this consent, and such order shall be deemed to be an order of the court mentioned in terms of s 65A(1).[21]

Where the defendant consents to an order of court for payment in specified instalments, the consent must set out full particulars of his or her monthly or weekly income and expenditure, supported where reasonably possible by the most recent proof in the possession of the defendant and other court orders or agreements, if any, with other creditors for payment of a debt and costs in instalments. It must also indicate the amount of the offered instalment.[22]

Section 58 applies, subject to the relevant provisions of the NCA, where the application for judgment is based on a credit agreement under said Act.[23]

If the consent is given before entry of appearance to defend, the registrar or clerk of the court is required to notify the plaintiff of the consent.[24] The defendant need not notify the plaintiff of his or her consent to judgment.

The defendant may consent to judgment by signing the form of consent endorsed on the original summons[25] or by lodging with the registrar or clerk of the court the copy of the summons served upon him or her with the form of consent endorsed on it duly signed by him or her.[26]

---

[17] In terms of s 55, 'debt' means 'any liquidated sum of money due'.

[18] It should be noted that the defendant may likewise react to a letter of demand sent to him by the plaintiff by registered post in terms of s 56, in which payment of a debt is claimed. This eventuality is discussed in chapter 19 below.

[19] Section 58(1).

[20] Section 58(1)*(a)*.

[21] Section 58(1)*(b)*.

[22] Section 58(1A).

[23] Section 58(3).

[24] Rule 3(6)*(a)*.

[25] Rule 11(1)*(a)*.

[26] Rule 11(1)*(b)*.

There is no real difference between these two instances except that, in the first, consent is given on the original summons filed at the office of the registrar or clerk of the court, while in the second instance the consent is signed on the copy of the summons served by the messenger of the court upon the defendant.

The defendant may, in addition, consent to judgment by signing a similar form of consent to that endorsed on the summons. The defendant may therefore make a copy of the summons and sign it or copy out the wording of the form of consent embodied in the summons and then sign it.

In the latter event, the consent must be signed in front of two witnesses, whose addresses must be given.[27] The defendant then returns this form to the registrar or clerk of the court. The registrar or clerk has a discretion to determine whether the consent corresponds with the form of consent endorsed on the summons and to decide whether the defendant has validly consented to judgment in favour of the plaintiff.[28]

In no case where consent is given to judgment is it necessary for summons to have been served upon the defendant. The defendant will then not be liable for costs of service, provided that he or she consented to judgment before the sheriff was given instructions to serve the summons.[29]

If the defendant consents to judgment before the expiry of the period in which he or she is required to give notice of his intention to defend, he or she is not liable for judgment charges, except in those cases in which he or she has consented in terms of s 58 to judgment for the debt and costs.[30]

The defendant may also consent to judgment after he or she has already entered appearance to defend. In this event the consent is given on a form similar to that endorsed on the summons. Such consent may be signed by the defendant himself or herself or by his or her attorney on his or her behalf.[31]

It would appear from the provisions of rule 11(4) that an attorney may consent to judgment on behalf of a defendant only after the attorney has entered appearance to defend on the defendant's behalf. In all cases in which the defendant wishes to consent to judgment before entry of appearance to defend, therefore, the defendant must sign the consent to judgment personally.

The final manner in which the defendant may consent to judgment is by admitting in his or her plea that he or she indeed owes a certain portion of the sum claimed from him or her by the plaintiff, and then simply giving his or her consent to the plaintiff to take judgment against him or her in that amount. The plaintiff may take judgment in the amount for which consent has been given, but the claim for the balance of the amount for which summons was issued remains and the plaintiff will have to prove that portion of his or her claim as he or she would in a normal trial.[32] The plaintiff is entitled, before the trial in respect of the balance of the claim takes place, immediately after obtaining judgment for portion of the

---

[27] Rule 11(1)(*c*).
[28] *Pio v Button* 1946 TPD 733 at 734; *Jaffer v De Wet* 1972 (3) SA 38 (C) at 40H–41E.
[29] Rule 11(2).
[30] Rule 11(3).
[31] Rule 11(4).
[32] Rule 11(5) and (6).

claim on the basis of the consent, to have a warrant of execution issued for the amount in respect of which the defendant consented.[33]

3.2 How judgment is obtained on the basis of consent

The defendant's consent to judgment places the plaintiff in a position to make application to court in terms of the consent for judgment in his or her favour against the defendant. When a plaintiff makes application for judgment on the basis of the defendant's consent, he or she does so by means of a request similar to the example set out below. This request, the copy of the letter of demand referred to in s 56 (if there was one) and the defendant's written consent to judgment and costs are handed in to the registrar or clerk of the court.

The request for judgment reads as follows:

No. 5B

Request for Judgment where the Defendant Has Consented to Judgment—Section 58 of the Magistrates' Courts Act, 1944 (Act 32 of 1944)

[Form 5B substituted by GN R632 of 22 June 2018 (wef 1 August 2018).]

*For use in the District Court

In the Magistrate's Court for the District of ....

held at ....

                                          Case No .... of 20...............

In the matter between

.... Plaintiff

and

.... Defendant

Plaintiff requests that judgment in the above-mentioned matter in terms of section 58 of the Magistrates' Courts Act, 1944, be entered in plaintiff's favour against the defendant as follows:

Judgment debt: R   c

Costs: R   c

Amount of debt ....

Interest at .... per cent per annum accounted from ....

Letter of demand (section 56) ....

Summons, if any (attorney's charges, sheriff's fees and sheriff's fees on re-issue) ....

Cost of notice in terms of rule 54(1) ....

Request for judgment (section 58) ....

Consent to judgment (section 58) ....

Totals ....   R   R

Total ....   R

and that payment thereof takes place in accordance with defendant's consent.

The following documents are attached:

(a) the summons or, if no summons has been issued, a copy of the letter of demand;

(b) the defendant's written consent to judgment; and

(c) if the defendant consents to an order of court for payment in specified instalments–

     (i) the written consent indicating the amount of the specified instalments; and

    (ii) full particulars and documentary evidence of the defendant's–

        (aa) monthly or weekly income and expenditure supported where reasonably possible by the most recent proof in the possession of the defendant;

---

[33] *Packaree v Ash* 1949 (2) SA 822 (N) at 823.

> *(bb)* other court orders or agreements, if any, with other creditors for payment of a debt and costs in instalments in order for the court to be apprised of the defendant's financial position at the time the defendant consented to judgment; and
>
> *(cc)* if the written consent contains a consent to an emoluments attachment order, the notice to the employer and the judgment debtor of the intention to request the court to authorise an emoluments attachment order.
>
> Dated at .... this..... day of .... 20.......
>
> Plaintiff/Plaintiff's attorney:
>
> ....
>
> (Address)
>
> ....
>
> Judgment granted on the .... day of .... 20 ....
> in favour of the plaintiff for the amount of R............ and the amount of R .... costs for which the defendant has consented to judgment.
>
> The defendant is further ordered to pay the said judgment and costs in monthly/weekly instalments of R............. / The defendant is further ordered to pay the said judgment and costs in accordance with the offer.
>
> * **The first instalment must be paid on or before .... and thereafter on or before the .... day of every succeeding month/week* until the outstanding balance of the judgment debt and costs has been paid in full.
>
> ....
>
> Court
> *   Delete what is not applicable
> ** Emoluments Attachment Order may only be issued if the court is satisfied that there is compliance with section 65J(2A)

The rules distinguish between the situation when the registrar or clerk of the court shall enter judgment and when the registrar or clerk *may* refer the matter to the court. In general, the registrar or clerk should not decide any issue of law and should refer the matter to the court if there is any doubt. In this regard the registrar or clerk is in the same position as the registrar in the High Court.[34]

Rule 11(6) provides that the clerk of the court *shall*, subject to the provisions of s 58 and rule 12(5), (6) and (7), enter judgment in terms of the defendant's consent.

Where the claim is based on a liquid document, the plaintiff is required to file the original document duly stamped with the registrar or clerk of the court or to hand in an affidavit setting out reasons to the satisfaction of the court why the original liquid document cannot or should not be filed.[35]

In two cases the registrar or clerk of the court may not himself or herself grant judgment on the basis of the consent to judgment but must first refer the request for judgment to the court. These cases are:

(1)   where the request for judgment is based on a cause of action arising out of or

---

[34] Cf *Erf 1382 Sunnyside (Edms) Bpk v Die Chipi BK* 1995 (3) SA 659 (T); *Standard Bank of SA Ltd v Ngobeni* 1995 (3) SA 234 (V).
[35] Rule 11(6) read with rule 12(6).

based on an agreement governed by the NCA, the Credit Agreements Act 75 of 1980, or the Consumer Protection Act 68 of 2008 (CPA);[36] and

(2)   where the consent to judgment is contained in the defendant's plea.[37]

The reference to the 'court' in these instances does not mean that a trial in open court must take place. Section 5(1) provides that the proceedings in all criminal cases and all defended civil actions must be carried on in open court. The hearing on the request for judgment by consent does not fall within the category of proceedings referred to in this section and need not, therefore, take place in open court. The court may thus sit in an office or other place to which members of the public do not have access.

The magistrate may require the plaintiff to produce evidence to satisfy the court that the consent has been signed by the defendant and is a consent to the judgment sought.[38] The court may give judgment only for so much of the plaintiff's claim as has been established to its satisfaction.[39] In the case of a judgment by consent it is not necessary to prove the quantum of the claim—that is admitted and the defendant consents to judgment in a specified amount that appears from the consent itself. The court may give judgment[40] or refuse it,[41] or the court may make such other order as may be fit.[42]

4   DEFAULT JUDGMENT

4.1   When will default judgment be granted?

A default judgment is 'a judgment entered or given in the absence of the party against whom it is made'.[43]

It is important to bear in mind throughout that while default judgment is granted for the most part in cases in which the defendant has failed timeously to give notice of his intention to defend, it may likewise be granted in other instances in which the defendant is in some respect in default. Sometimes it may also happen that default judgment is granted against a plaintiff.

Default judgment may be granted in the following circumstances:

(1)   if the defendant fails to enter appearance to defend within the time limited by the summons;[44]

(2)   where the defendant enters appearance to defend, but thereafter fails to deliver a plea within the time limited by notice of bar;[45]

(3)   if the plaintiff or applicant does not appear at the time set down for the hearing in the trial of the action or in the application; since 'plaintiff' or 'applicant' includes also the legal representative of the party in question,

---

[36] Rule 12(5).
[37] Rule 11(6) read with rule 12(7).
[38] Rule 12(7)*(b)*.
[39] Rule 12(7)*(c)*.
[40] Rule 12(7)*(d)*.
[41] Rule 12(7)*(e)*.
[42] Rule 12(7)*(f)*.
[43] Rule 2(1).
[44] Rule 12(1)*(a)*.
[45] Rule 12(1)*(b)*.

judgment will be granted only if there is no appearance by or on behalf of the plaintiff;[46]

(4) if a party fails to comply with an order of court obliging him or her to comply with the provisions of the rules of court;[47] judgment may not be taken against a party merely on the basis of his or her failure to comply with the terms of the court order without further notice to him or her.

The first two instances of default judgment mentioned above are the ones most commonly encountered in practice. When one talks of default judgment, one is usually referring to these two cases. Rule 12, which is headed 'Judgment by default', in fact deals only with these two instances.

These two forms of default are referred to in what follows respectively as non-appearance and failure to deliver a plea, and they are discussed separately below.

4.1.1 *Non-appearance*
Three instances of what can be called non-appearance may be distinguished:
(1) the defendant fails to deliver notice of intention to defend;
(2) the defendant delivers a defective notice of intention to defend; or
(3) the defendant delivers the notice of intention to defend after the expiry of the time prescribed for its delivery.

The effect of each of these will differ in practice.

4.1.1.1 *The defendant fails to deliver notice of intention to defend*
In this case the plaintiff may proceed to apply for default judgment subject to the requirements mentioned below.

A situation that warrants special consideration is that in which the plaintiff seeks judgment on the basis of non-entry of appearance to defend but the summons is not in order. Can the plaintiff in that instance proceed to obtain judgment against the defendant even though the summons is void or invalid?

A defendant is entitled to raise an exception upon the basis that the summons is invalid and the clerk of the court likewise ought not to grant default judgment if it is clear that the plaintiff's summons is defective in some or other respect.

As a simple summons does not constitute a pleading, no exception may be taken against a simple summons which does not disclose a cause of action. As a result, if no cause of action is set out in the simple summons, no default judgment can be obtained. Where a simple summons is defective, rule 60A provides that a party may apply to set the summons aside in so far as it constitutes an irregular step.

When one or more of several defendants in an action consent to judgment or fail to enter appearance or to deliver a plea, judgment may be entered against the defendant or defendants in default, and the plaintiff may proceed on such

---

[46] Rule 32(1). Where a party's legal representative is present in court, the court cannot grant *default* judgment against that party: *Du Plessis v Goldblatt's Wholesale (Pty) Ltd* 1953 (4) SA 112 (O) at 114D–E; *De Allende v Baraldi t/a Embassy Drive Medical Centre* 2000 (1) SA 390 (T).
[47] Rule 60(2) and (3).

judgment without prejudice to his or her right to continue the action against another defendant or other defendants.[48]

Another question that arises is whether the plaintiff is entitled to take judgment against a defendant after the latter's death. Rule 52(3) provides that if a party dies or becomes incompetent to continue an action, the action shall thereby be stayed until such time as an executor, trustee, guardian or other competent person has been appointed in his or her place or until such incompetence shall cease to exist. The courts have also ruled that a default judgment obtained against a person after his or her death is not binding on his or her estate and that the executor thus has the authority to launch an application to have the default judgment obtained against the deceased set aside.[49]

4.1.1.2 *The defendant delivers a defective notice of intention to defend*

The defendant is required to enter proper appearance to defend. Rule 12(2)(a) sets out four respects in which the notice of intention to defend may be defective. These are where the notice:

(1) has not been properly delivered;
(2) has not been properly signed;
(3) does not set out the postal address of the person signing it or an address for service of further pleadings; or
(4) exhibits some or other defect of form.

In these cases, the plaintiff is obliged to notify the defendant in writing that he or she is required to deliver a notice of intention to defend in due form within five days after having been called upon to do so. In his or her notification, the plaintiff must set out clearly in what respect the defendant's entry of appearance to defend is defective. On failure of the defendant to deliver a memorandum of entry of appearance in due form, the failure to file such memorandum will constitute a ground for the granting of default judgment.[50]

The defendant is required to give proper notice of his or her intention to defend in accordance with the provisions contained in rule 13.[51] If, therefore, the defendant gives notice of his or her intention to defend the matter and such notice consists merely of a letter, it cannot be said that the defendant has given proper notice of his or her intention to defend.[52]

---

[48] Rule 12(8).

[49] In *Ohlsson's Cape Breweries Ltd v R W & A L Hamburg* 1908 TS 134 at 140, Solomon J (as he then was) said: 'But it must now be taken to be well established under our law and practice that the executor alone is the legal representative of the deceased, and that no action can be brought . . . claiming damages out of the assets of an estate without making the executor of the estate a party to the action.' This decision was followed in *Dykstra v Emmenis* 1952 (1) SA 661 (T). With regard to costs, it is submitted that the plaintiff should not be penalised if he or she was unaware of the death of the defendant. The executor ought in such a case to be in the same position as a defendant who in the normal course of an action makes an application for the rescission of a judgment (at 663E–F).

[50] Rule 12(2)(a), (b) and (c).

[51] See chapter 11 below.

[52] Cf *Anastassiades v Central Mining & Investment Corporation Ltd* 1955 (3) SA 53 (W) at 54E–G.

4.1.1.3 *The defendant delivers the notice out of time*

The third instance that requires attention occurs where the defendant's notice of intention to defend is not defective but is delivered late, ie not within the time allowed in the summons for delivery of notice of intention to defend.[53]

Rule 13(5) provides that a notice of intention to defend may be delivered after the above period has expired but before default judgment is granted. Where the plaintiff has lodged a request for default judgment, and the notice is only filed thereafter, the plaintiff will be entitled to costs.

The position in the rules accords with the position in the common law, which regards a late appearance as valid,[54] and it is in accordance with this rule that in the High Court a late notice of intention to defend will also be valid, but such a late defendant will have to pay the costs of an application for default judgment.[55]

4.1.2 *Failure to deliver a declaration*

Rule 15 provides that where the defendant has delivered a notice of intention to defend, the plaintiff must within 15 days after receipt of the notice deliver a declaration. Failure to deliver the declaration enables the defendant to serve a notice of bar on the plaintiff in terms of which the plaintiff is required to file the declaration within five days of receipt of the notice of bar, failing which he or she will be *ipso facto* barred from delivering further pleadings. The defendant may then apply for absolution from the instance or judgment and the court may make such order as it deems fit.[56]

A notice of bar usually reads as follows:

NOTICE OF BAR

KINDLY TAKE NOTICE that the Defendant hereby requests the Plaintiff to deliver her Declaration within 5 (five) days after receipt hereof. Should she fail to do so she will *ipso facto* be barred from delivering her Declaration in which event the Defendant will request that default judgment be given against her.

4.1.3 *Failure to deliver a plea*

It may happen that the defendant delivers a notice of his or her intention to defend the action and that he or she thereafter fails to take any further steps to defend the action.

In the normal course of the action, the defendant must answer the averments made in the summons by delivering his or her plea. The defendant must deliver his or her plea within 20 days after having given notice of his or her intention to defend the action or after receipt of the declaration. If the defendant fails to deliver the plea within 20 days, he or she is in default of a plea.[57]

In the absence of a plea from the defendant, the plaintiff may not simply

---

[53] Rule 13(1) and chapter 11 below.
[54] *Pugin v Pugin* 1963 (1) SA 791 (W) at 794F–795C and the authorities cited there.
[55] D E Van Loggerenberg *Erasmus Superior Court Practice* 2 ed (Service 6, 2018) D1-248.
[56] Rule 15(5).
[57] Rule 17(1).

proceed and request that judgment be granted against the defendant. The plaintiff must first deliver a notice of bar.[58]

Only if the defendant ignores the notice of bar will the plaintiff be able to obtain default judgment against him or her.

4.2 The contents of the request for default judgment

Rule 12(1)(*a*) prescribes that the request for default judgment must be in writing and that the request must be lodged in duplicate with the registrar or clerk of the court. The written request for judgment must be accompanied by the original summons and the return of service. If the original summons cannot be filed together with the request for default judgment, a copy or duplicate original and a copy of the return of service received from the sheriff may be filed. Also, the plaintiff may file an affidavit stating the reasons why the original summons and return of service cannot be filed.[59]

Rule 12(1)(*a*) provides that judgment may be sought for any sum not exceeding the sum claimed in the summons as well as for other relief sought in the summons, together with the costs of the action and interest at the rate specified in the summons to date of payment or, if no rate is specified, at the rate prescribed under s 1(2) of the Prescribed Rate of Interest Act 55 of 1975.[60]

The request for judgment where the defendant is in default of appearance to defend is made using the wording of the following example:[61]

No. 5
Request for Default Judgment
* For use in the District Court
In the Magistrate's Court for the District of ....
held at ....
Case No .... of 20............
In the matter between
.... Plaintiff
and
.... Defendant
The plaintiff hereby applies that—
   (*a*) the defendant having been duly served on ....;
   (*b*) the time for entering appearance to defend having expired; and
   (*c*) the defendant not having entered an appearance to defend,
judgment be given against the defendant, as claimed in the summons for R .... (state particulars if judgment is applied for something less than that claimed in the summons), together with interest at .... per cent.
Dated at .... this .... day of ...., 20.......
....
Plaintiff/Plaintiff's Attorney

---

[58] Rule 12(1)(*b*).
[59] Rule 12(1)(*e*).
[60] The current interest rate is 10 per cent as published under GN 435 in *GG* 41581 of 20 April 2018 (with effect from 1 May 2018).
[61] Annexure 1 Form 5.

The forms provide no example of a request for judgment where the defendant is in default of delivering a plea. The same example may be used with the necessary modifications to request default judgment in such a case. The relevant portion may, for example, read:

The plaintiff hereby requests that whereas—

(a) the defendant has been duly served on ....;

(b) the defendant has entered appearance to defend; and

(c) the defendant has failed to plead or otherwise to answer the claim of the plaintiff notwithstanding the fact that the plaintiff has requested her by means of written notice in terms of rule 12(1)*(b)* to deliver her plea within five days,

judgment be given . . . etc.

Although a prescribed form exists for the request for default judgment, and the procedure for obtaining judgment is at first blush very simple, a number of aspects warrant special mention.

It is especially important to bear in mind throughout that all of the relevant facts must be placed before the court. The complete version of all of the facts leading to the application for default judgment must be set out.

In the case where a defective notice of intention to defend has been delivered, express mention must be made of the fact that the defendant has been given an opportunity to rectify the defective notice.[62]

The legal relief sought in the request for judgment must correspond with that in the summons.

In particular, it must be borne in mind that the plaintiff may in terms of rule 12(1)*(a)*(i) request judgment for any amount not exceeding the sum claimed in the summons.

In the nature of things, the summons forming the basis of the claim must be correct.

The summons must not have lapsed.[63]

When the plaintiff asks for judgment in a lesser amount than that claimed in the summons, it is desirable that full particulars be supplied in the request for default judgment in order to present a complete picture to the registrar or clerk of the court (or to the court itself).

It is not necessary for the plaintiff to confirm the cause of action in the request for default judgment by means of a complete statement repeating the particulars contained in the summons.[64]

The registrar or clerk of the court must refer to the court every request for default judgment where the cause of action arises out of or is based on an agreement governed by the NCA, the Credit Agreements Act 75 of 1980 or the CPA.[65]

---

[62] Rule 12(2).

[63] Rule 10, which previously provided that, subject to certain exceptions, a summons lapses if it is not served within 12 months of the date of its issue, has been amended and the rules no longer contain a provision regarding the lapsing of summonses.

[64] *Durban City Council v Petersen* 1970 (1) SA 720 (N) at 724H.

[65] Rule 12(5).

The only case in which it is necessary for the plaintiff to supplement the request for default judgment by affidavit is where the plaintiff seeks default judgment in respect of an unliquidated claim.[66] Rule 12(4) provides that the registrar or clerk of the court shall refer to the court any request for default judgment for an unliquidated amount and that the plaintiff shall furnish to the court evidence, either oral or by affidavit, of the nature and extent of the claim.

It often occurs in practice that the registrar or clerk of the civil court takes the request for default judgment together with any affidavit(s) pertaining to it to a magistrate in chambers, who then decides whether or not judgment may be granted.[67] If the magistrate refuses to grant judgment, he or she should afford the applicant or the latter's attorney the opportunity to address him or her, to supplement the affidavits or to present oral evidence.

This provision, viz that the registrar or clerk of the court is required to refer to the court a request for default judgment in an unliquidated amount, is most commonly applicable in practice in cases in which the plaintiff claims compensation for damage caused in a motor collision. The quantum (amount) of the damage must be proved by giving evidence. The easiest way of placing evidence before the court in such a case is by attaching to the request for default judgment an affidavit deposed to by an expert.

The following must be borne in mind in drafting the affidavit:

- The expert must lay a basis for the averment that he or she is an expert. It would, for example, not be adequate to attach an affidavit deposed to by the *owner* of a garage in which he or she states that the vehicle in question has been repaired.
- It is necessary that evidence be placed before the court of an expert as to the actual nature and extent of the damage. The differences frequently encountered between quotations for the same panelbeating work are a matter of general knowledge.

According to the general wording of rule 12(4), the plaintiff must, whenever he or she requests default judgment for an unliquidated amount, place evidence before the court of the nature and extent of the amount. It is submitted that he or she is required to give evidence not only in cases in which the claim is based on damage sustained in a motor collision but also in cases in which his or her claim is for reasonable remuneration for services rendered by him or her. According to this argument, the plaintiff who sues on the basis of professional services rendered by him or her must likewise give evidence that the amount claimed represents reasonable remuneration for his or her services, unless, of course, he or she accepts that it was agreed that the defendant would remunerate him or her in accordance with a set tariff of charges for his or her professional services.

In cases where the plaintiff has had the summons served by registered post, he or she must remember before making application for default judgment that the court will not grant judgment unless the acknowledgement of receipt of the

---

[66] For the definition of this term, see below.
[67] *Briel v Van Zyl; Rolenyathe v Lupton-Smith* 1985 (4) SA 163 (T).

registered article has been filed by the sheriff with his or her return of service.[68] If the plaintiff is unable to persuade the court that the summons came to the notice of the defendant, the court may treat such service as invalid.

If the action is based on a liquid document, the plaintiff is required to file together with the request for default judgment the original of the liquid document duly stamped or an affidavit setting out reasons why the original liquid document cannot be attached to the request.[69]

4.3 Liquid and illiquid amounts

As already mentioned, the registrar or clerk of the court refers to the court any request for default judgment for an unliquidated amount, ie the matter is referred to a magistrate in chambers.[70] The plaintiff is required to place evidence before the court either orally or on affidavit of the nature and extent of his or her claim. The magistrate then assesses the amount recoverable by the plaintiff and determines in what amount judgment will be granted.

Where the claim is for a debt or liquidated amount of money and the defendant has failed to enter appearance or has failed to timeously deliver a plea, the registrar or clerk may grant judgment or refer the matter to court.[71]

It is necessary, therefore, to decide what an 'unliquidated amount' is. The simplest way of answering that question is to determine what is a 'liquid' (or a 'liquidated') amount and then to classify all other amounts as unliquidated.[72]

A liquid amount is an amount that is fixed and certain.[73] In *Fatti's Engineering Co (Pty) Ltd v Vendick Spares (Pty) Ltd*[74] the court held that a liquidated demand is a claim for a 'monetary amount capable of prompt and speedy ascertainment'. This does not mean that the amount must be determined to the last cent: a liquid amount is fixed and certain in the sense that the amount may be calculated readily and quickly.[75]

In *SA Fire & Accident Insurance Co Ltd v Hickman*[76] Ogilvie Thompson J (later CJ) accepted the definition given by the *Encyclopaedia of the Laws of England* of

---

[68] Rule 12(3). For details, see above.

[69] Rule 12(6). Cf, for example, *Barclays Western Bank Ltd v Creser* 1982 (2) SA 104 (T), where the court held that a microfilm reproduction of a credit agreement is admissible in evidence to prove the plaintiff's claim. The bank followed the practice of destroying the original contractual documents as soon as they had been copied onto microfilm.

[70] Rule 12(4).

[71] Rule 12(3A). Rule 5(2)*(b)* states that a simple summons may be used when the plaintiff's claim is founded on a 'debt or liquidated demand'.

[72] See also rule 14(1)*(b)* in connection with summary judgment. The High Court cases on liquidity can also be consulted: see *Erasmus Superior Court Practice* D1-386 *et seq.*

[73] Cf the definition given by Pothier in his *Traité des Obligations* para 592, cited in *Du Toit v Grobler* 1947 (3) SA 213 (SWA) at 216: '[A] debt is liquidated when it is evident that it is due, and to what amount, *cum certum est an et quantum debeatur.*'

[74] 1962 (1) SA 736 (T) at 739A–G.

[75] *Maritime & General Insurance Co Ltd v Colenbrander* 1978 (2) SA 262 (D) at 264F–G; *Lester Investments (Pty) Ltd v Narshi* 1951 (2) SA 464 (C) at 469F–G.

[76] 1955 (2) SA 131 (C) at 132H.

a liquidated claim, namely that the claim must be such that 'the ascertainment of the amount is a mere matter of calculation'.[77]

It has been said that a liquidated claim is one in which the amount of the claim has already been fixed by agreement or by an order of court, or in which the assessment of the amount of the claim is a question of pure arithmetical calculation. In contrast, a claim for damages is not usually a liquidated claim.[78]

According to this definition, the following may be regarded as liquid amounts and a plaintiff whose claim arises from one of these causes of action need not give evidence on affidavit of the nature and extent of his or her claim in default judgment proceedings. These amounts are:

- the amount set out in an account rendered by a shop for goods sold by it provided that there was express or implied agreement as to the price;[79]
- rental agreed upon between the parties;[80]
- the purchase price of goods sold that the plaintiff is prepared to deliver;[81]
- an amount shown in a balance sheet that has been accepted as correct by a defendant;[82]
- insurance premiums.[83]

In the case of an assault, however, it will be necessary for the plaintiff to place evidence before the court as to the amount claimed by him or her.[84]

Where a plaintiff requests default judgment in respect of a claim based upon enrichment, he or she will also have to prove the amount of the claim by way of affidavit.

Where the plaintiff's claim was for fair and reasonable remuneration for services rendered and material supplied, it is generally accepted that the claim is liquid unless it is put in dispute by the defendant.[85] The reason for this is that a reasonable price for the goods delivered and for services rendered can easily be ascertained. However, the same does not apply to professional services. These are not regarded as liquid unless a fee has been agreed between the parties.[86]

---

[77] In *Kleynhans v Van der Westhuizen NO* (1970) 3 All SA 105 (A) at 108–109 the Appellate Division stated authoritatively that a liquidated claim is one whose amount is fixed and certain.

[78] *Pick 'n Pay Retailers (Pty) Ltd h/a Hypermarkets v Dednam* 1984 (4) SA 673 (O).

[79] *Paver Bros v De Beer* 1916 OPD 236.

[80] *Oblewitz v Cortis* (1902) 19 SC 162.

[81] *Highman & Marks v Graham & Smith* (1903) 13 CTR 219.

[82] *Rooknodien v Kahn* 1915 CPD 394.

[83] *London & Lancashire Insurance Co Ltd v De Wet* 1938 CPD 577.

[84] *Marais v Mdowen* 1919 OPD 34 at 37.

[85] The decision of *Fatti's Engineering Co v Vendick Spares* (supra), which rejected the decision of *Kark v Proctor* 1961 (1) SA 752 (W), is now followed. Cf *Neves Builders & Decorators v De La Cour* 1985 (1) SA 540 (C); *Commercial Bank of Namibia Ltd v Trans Continental Trading (Namibia) & others* 1992 (2) SA 66 (Nm); *S Dreyer & Sons Transport v General Services* 1976 (4) SA 922 (C).

[86] *Consolidated Fish Distributors (Pty) Ltd v Sargeant, Jones, Valentine & Co* 1966 (4) SA 427 (C); *Pick 'n Pay Retailers v Dednam* (supra).

4.4 The decision to grant or refuse default judgment

The registrar or clerk of the court has the general power in every case to refer any request for judgment (whether for judgment by consent or for default judgment) to the court.[87]

The magistrate has the power in terms of rule 12(7) to make any of the following six orders should a request for judgment be referred to him or her:

(1) The magistrate may call upon the plaintiff to adduce such evidence, either written or oral, in support of the claim as the court deems necessary.[88]

(2) Where the plaintiff seeks judgment by consent, he or she may ask the plaintiff to adduce evidence to satisfy the court that the consent has been signed by the defendant and is a consent to the judgment sought. The magistrate may give judgment in terms of the plaintiff's request.

(3) The magistrate may give judgment for so much of the claim as has been established to his or her satisfaction.

(4) He or she may give judgment in terms of the defendant's consent.

(5) The magistrate may refuse judgment.

(6) The magistrate has the power make such other order as he or she deems fit.

The judgment is entered either by the registrar or clerk of the court or by the magistrate who grants the judgment. In practice the judgment is entered by stamping the request for default judgment with a rubber stamp and signing the request. Rule 12(9) provides that a judgment will be recorded once a minute thereof has been made on the cover of the court file and it is dated and signed.

If the request for default judgment is refused, the registrar or clerk of the court is required to notify the plaintiff forthwith in writing of the fact.[89]

The registrar or clerk of the court is also required to note the following on a certified copy of the judgment at the request of the party entitled to it:

(1) particulars of any other judgment by the court in that case; and

(2) any costs incurred after judgment and payable by the judgment debtor.[90]

In practice it is usual for the plaintiff or his or her legal representative to file a warrant of execution with the registrar or clerk of the court together with the request for default judgment. The intention is then that the warrant of execution should be issued when the judgment is granted.[91]

In terms of the provisions of rule 36(7) the warrant may not be issued before the day following that on which the judgment is given, except with the leave of the court. This rule, however, expressly does not apply where judgment has been entered by consent or default. The registrar or clerk of the court may therefore at the same time as he or she grants default judgment also issue the warrant of execution.

---

[87] Rule 12(7).

[88] *Credex Finance (Pty) Ltd v De Villiers NO & others* 1978 (2) SA 25 (N) at 31G–H and 32B.

[89] Rule 3(6)*(b)* and *(c)*.

[90] Rule 3(7)*(a)*.

[91] Section 62(1) provides that any court which has jurisdiction to try an action shall have jurisdiction to issue against any party to it any form of process in execution of its judgment in such action. For the warrant, see chapter 17 below.

4.5 Appeal against an order of court

When one of the orders mentioned above is made in terms of rule 12(7), the question arises whether an aggrieved party may appeal against such an order.

The general rule is that a party against whom judgment is given in his or her absence may apply for the rescission of that judgment. It is not necessary to appeal against it.[92] In practice this usually results in the defendant bringing an application for the rescission of a judgment entered against him or her, while the plaintiff in turn will take the matter on appeal if judgment is not granted against the defendant.

An aggrieved party may appeal against a decision of a magistrate only if that decision has the effect of a final order.[93] It is clear that a refusal to grant default judgment has the effect of a final order. There is nothing more that a plaintiff can do where he or she has requested default judgment and the court refuses to grant this request.[94]

Likewise, where a plaintiff is aggrieved as to the amount in which judgment has been granted by the court or as to any other judgment given by the court in terms of rule 12(7), he or she may appeal. The question is always simply whether that judgment has the effect of a final order or not: as long as it has the effect of a final order, he or she is entitled to appeal.

5 RESCISSION OR SETTING ASIDE OF A DEFAULT JUDGMENT

Section 36 of the Act refers to the 'rescission' of a judgment. For the sake of uniformity, this expression is also used in the discussion which follows. The expression 'setting aside' of a judgment is, however, often encountered as a synonym and is well established in practice.

5.1 Which judgments may be rescinded

Rescission (or setting aside) of a judgment is in issue not only in cases in which default judgment has been granted but also in cases in which application is made for the rescission of a summary judgment,[95] as well as in cases in which judgment has been granted in the absence of a defendant in terms of rule 60(3).[96]

Section 36 provides:[97]

'(1) The court may, upon application by any person affected thereby, or, in cases falling under paragraph *(c)*, *suo motu*–

---

[92] See the discussion immediately below.

[93] See chapter 18 below.

[94] *Durban City Council v Petersen* 1970 (1) SA 720 (N).

[95] For an instance in which application was made (without success) to set aside a summary judgment, see *Duncan t/a San Sales v Herbor Investments (Pty) Ltd* 1974 (2) SA 214 (T). In *Tlholoe v Maury (Earns) Bpk h/a Franelle Gordyn Boutique* 1988 (3) SA 922 (O) the court decided that a summary judgment granted in the absence of the defendant and his legal representative constituted a default judgment which could be rescinded in terms of s 36(*a*). See also *Sundra Hardeware v Mactro Plumbing* 1989 (1) SA 474 (T).

[96] *Cabral v Bank van die Oranje-Vrystaat Bpk* 1986 (4) SA 768 (T).

[97] The section was recently amended by the Courts of Law Amendment Act 7 of 2017.

(a)   rescind or vary any judgment granted by it in the absence of the person against whom that judgment was granted;

(b)   rescind or vary any judgment granted by it which was void *ab origine* or was obtained by fraud or by mistake common to the parties;

(c)   correct patent errors in any judgment in respect of which no appeal is pending;

(d)   rescind or vary any judgment in respect of which no appeal lies.

(2) If a plaintiff in whose favour a default judgment has been granted has consented in writing that the judgment be rescinded or varied, a court may rescind or vary such judgment on application by any person affected by it.

[Sub-s. (2) substituted by s. 2 *(a)* of Act 7 of 2017 (wef 1 August 2018).]

(3) *(a)* Where a judgment debt, the interest thereon at the rate granted in the judgment and the costs have been paid in full, whether the consent of the judgment creditor for the rescission of the judgment has been obtained or not, a court may, on application by the judgment debtor or any other person affected by the judgment rescind that judgment.

(b) The application contemplated in paragraph *(a)*–

(i)   must be made on a form which corresponds substantially with the form prescribed in the rules;

(ii)   must be accompanied by reasonable proof that the judgment debt, the interest and the costs have been paid;

(iii) must be accompanied by proof that the application has been served on the judgment creditor, at least 10 court days prior to the hearing of the intended application;

(iv)   may be set down for hearing on any day, not less than 10 court days, after service thereof; and

(v)   may be heard by a magistrate in chambers.

[Sub-s. (3) added by s 2 *(b)* of Act 7 of 2017 (wef 1 August 2018).]

(4) A court may make any cost order it deems fit with regard to an application contemplated in paragraph *(a)*.

[Sub-s. (4) added by s 2 *(b)* of Act 7 of 2017 (wef 1 August 2018).]

[S 36 substituted by s 1 of Act 55 of 2002 (wef 17 January 2003).]'

It does not matter, therefore, whether a default judgment has been obtained as a result of the failure of the defendant to enter appearance to defend or as a result of the failure of the defendant to plead.[98]

5.2   The procedure in the application for rescission of a judgment

Rule 49 was the subject of extensive amendment in 1997, and earlier cases must be used with caution in the interpretation of the rule.[99] In certain important respects the amended rule appears to revise the position as set out in the old cases.

Rule 49(1) provides that:

'A party to proceedings in which a default judgment has been given, or any person affected by such judgment, may within 20 days after obtaining knowledge of the judgment serve and file an application to court, on notice to all parties to the proceedings, for a rescission or variation of the judgment and the court may, upon good cause shown, or if it is satisfied that there is good reason to do so, rescind or

---

[98] *Meyer v Beyleveld NO & another* 1958 (4) SA 539 (T) at 542D.

[99] *Grant v Plumbers (Pty) Ltd* 1949 (2) SA 470 (O); *Silber v Ozen Wholesalers (Pty) Ltd* 1954 (2) SA 345 (A); *De Witts Auto Body Repairs (Pty) Ltd v Fedgen Insurance Co Ltd* 1994 (4) SA 705 (E).

vary the default judgment on such terms as it may deem fit: Provided that the 20 days' period shall not be applicable to a request for rescission or variation of judgment brought in terms of sub-rule (5) or (5A).'

Thus, the application may be made by any party, or any person affected thereby. The applicant is not necessarily the defendant in default. It may be, for instance, that there has been non-joinder and a person may seek to set aside the judgment because he or she is materially affected by it.[100]

The application must be served and filed within 20 days after obtaining knowledge of the judgment. Rule 49(2) provides that an applicant is presumed to have had knowledge of the default judgment 10 days after the date on which it was granted, unless the applicant proves otherwise. This subrule places an onus on the applicant to rebut the presumption and to prove that he or she has brought the application within the 20-day period.

The rule appears to lay down two different but related grounds upon which a court may grant rescission. The first is 'upon good cause shown'; the second is 'if it is satisfied that there is good reason to do so'.[101]

In the cases on the previous rule 'good cause' was held to include a reasonable explanation for the default, that a *bona fide* defence exists, and that the application is made *bona fide*. The first two of these requirements are set out in the rule 49(3), which requires that the application must be supported by an affidavit setting out the reasons for the defendant's absence or default and on the grounds of the defendant's defence to the claim. It is submitted that the previous case law still applies in regard to this subrule, since 'good cause' would only be shown if the explanation was reasonable, and the application and the defence *bona fide*.[102]

In the case of *Wright v Westelike Provinsie Kelders BPK*,[103] Binns–Ward AJ, as he then was, held as follows regarding the meaning of 'good cause shown or good reason to do so' in rule 49(1): 'In other words, the court is empowered by the introduction of the phrase to grant a rescission application if the exigencies of justice require it in an exceptional case, notwithstanding the existence of what would previously have been fatal deficiencies in the applicant's founding papers. It allows the court to have regard *mero motu* to the justice of the case untramelled by the incidence of onus.'

Rule 49(4) deals with the situation in which a defendant wishes to rescind the judgment when he or she does not wish to proceed with the proceedings, that is, he or she is prepared to make arrangements to satisfy the judgment. It is in these circumstances that the subrule requires an applicant to show that he or she was not in wilful default and that the judgment was satisfied, or arrangements were made

---

[100] *Standard Bank of South Africa Ltd v Swartland Municipality & others* 2011 (5) SA 257 (SCA) paras 13–14.

[101] *Philips t/a Southern Cross Optical v SA Vision Care (Pty) Ltd* 2000 (2) SA 1007 (C) at 1013.

[102] *Vhembe District Municipality v Stewarts & Lloyds Trading (Booysens) (Pty) Ltd & another* [2014] 3 All SA 675 (SCA) para 4. See also *Madinda v Minister of Safety and Security* 2008 (4) SA 312 (SCA); *Naidoo & another v Matlala NO & others* 2012 (1) SA 143 (GNP); *Subramanian v Standard Bank Ltd* 2013 JOL 30321 (KZP); *EH Hassim Hardware (Pty) Ltd v Fab Tanks CC* [2017] ZASCA 145 (13 October 2017).

[103] 2001 (4) SA 1165 (C) at 1181H–1182A.

to satisfy the judgment, within a reasonable time after it came to his or her knowledge. It does not mean that it is only in these circumstances that the absence of wilful default is a requirement. The absence of wilful default applies to all applications and it still remains part of demonstrating 'good cause'.[104]

It is submitted that in the circumstances of rule 49(4) the onus of demonstrating the absence of wilful default rests on the applicant. With regard to the previous rule, it was held that the onus of demonstrating that the applicant was in wilful default rested on the respondent.

The second possibility is that the applicant may show that there is 'good reason to do so'. While this requirement overlaps with 'good cause', it should be given an independent meaning. It is submitted that the 'good reason' relates to a wider discretion than that contained in good cause relating to the general equities of the situation. The prejudice to both parties will be considered together with all the other factors set out above.[105]

Rule 49(5) provides for rescission or variation of a judgment where the plaintiff consents to the rescission or variation. In *Venter v Standard Bank of South Africa* Joffe J held that this provision was *ultra vires* the Act.[106] This decision was not approved and not followed by Josman J and Van Reenen J in *RFS Catering Supplies v Barnard Bigara Enterprises CC*.[107] There are, thus, competing decisions in different divisions. With respect, the Cape decision is to be preferred.[108]

Subrule (5A) was recently introduced into rule 49.[109] It provides that where a judgment debt, the interest thereon at the rate granted in the judgment and the costs have been paid in full, a court may, on application by the judgment debtor or any other person affected by the judgment, rescind that judgment. The application must be made on a form corresponding substantially with Form 5C of Annexure 1 and must be accompanied by an affidavit with annexures providing reasonable proof that the judgment debt, the interest and the costs have been paid. It must further be served on the judgment creditor not less than 10 days prior to the hearing of the application.

---

[104] *Mountain View Investments (Pty) Ltd v Janse Van Rensburg t/a Alfa Loodgieters in re: Sarel Jacob Janse van Rensburg t/a Alfa Loodgieters (P); Mountain View Investments (Pty) Ltd* 2018 JOL 39464 (GP) paras 26–32; *Harris v Absa Bank Ltd t/a Volkskas* 2006 (4) SA 527 (T) at 529E–R; *Vhembe District Municipality v Stewarts & Lloyds Trading (Booysens)* (supra) para 4.

[105] *Mnandi Property Development CC v Beimore Development CC* 1999 (4) SA 462 (W) at 466A.

[106] 1999 3 All SA 278 (W) at 283e.

[107] 2002 (1) SA 896 (C).

[108] The decision in the *RFS Catering Supplies* case was followed in *TP and CY Damon v Nedcor Bank Ltd* 2006 JOL 18550 (C) and in *DS Cassisa and R Radomsky v Standard Bank of SA Ltd* (unreported, WCC case no 4057/2003, 26 March 2008). However, see *Vilvanathan & another v Louw NO* 2010 (5) SA 17 (WCC) where the court held that '[f]or a number of reasons I am firmly of the view that the *RFS Catering Supplies* case, was wrongly decided, and that it ought not to be followed'. See also the discussion in *Haffejee v Bytes Technology Group South Africa (Pty) Limited t/a Bytes Document Solutions & others* 2016 JOL 36006 (WCC).

[109] GN R632 in *GG* 41723 of 22 June 2018.

No. 5C

Application for Rescission of Judgment in terms of Section 36(3) of the Magistrates' Courts Act, 1944 (Act 32 of 1944)

[Form 5C inserted by GN R632 of 22 June 2018 (wef 1 August 2018).]

* For use in the District Court

In the Magistrate's Court for the District of ....

held at ....

Case No .... of 20..........................

In the matter between

.... Applicant

and

.... Respondent

KINDLY TAKE NOTICE that application will be made, to the above honourable court, on .... at 9:00, or so soon thereafter as the matter may be heard for an order in the following terms:

1   Rescinding the judgment that was granted in this matter against the applicant on .... (specify date of judgment).
2   No costs order/Costs to be paid by respondent if opposed.*

TAKE NOTICE FURTHER that the attached affidavit of the applicant containing reasonable proof that the judgment debt, the interest and the costs have been paid and that the application has been served on the judgment creditor, at least 10 court days prior to the hearing, will be used in support of this application.

Signed at... on this day of... 20......

....
Signature of Applicant/Applicant's Attorney

Address of Applicant/Applicant's Attorney

....

....

....

To: The Clerk of the Court

....

....

To: Respondent/Respondent's Attorney

....

Address of Respondent/Respondent's Attorney

....

....

....

* Delete whichever is not applicable.

If the rescission or variation is sought on the ground that the judgment is void from the beginning or was obtained by fraud or mistake, rule 49(8) provides that the application must be served and filed within one year after the applicant first had knowledge of such voidness, fraud or mistake.

Chapter 11

NOTICE OF INTENTION TO DEFEND, SUMMARY JUDGMENT, AND PROVISIONAL SENTENCE

The first two topics are dealt with together in this chapter for the sake of convenience. The application for summary judgment follows chronologically after the delivery of notice of intention to defend.

This is not to imply, however, that an application for summary judgment is always made after notice is given of intention to defend. The application is brought only if the defendant lacks a *bona fide* defence and gives notice of his or her intention to defend the action solely for the purpose of delaying the finalisation of the matter.

Provisional sentence is dealt with here because, as with summary judgment, it provides a speedy remedy; but it must be noted from the outset that the procedures are quite distinct.

1 NOTICE OF INTENTION TO DEFEND

1.1 The form of the notice

If the defendant decides to oppose the claim instituted against him or her by the plaintiff, he or she is obliged to give notice of his or her intention to defend. The rule provides that a defendant intending to defend the action shall within 10 days after service of the summons enter an appearance to defend by delivery of a notice that he or she intends to defend the action.[1] Where the action is instituted against any minister, deputy minister, provincial premier, officer or servant of the State in such official capacity, the State or the administration of a province, the applicable time period is 20 days after service of summons.[2] The defendant is obliged to give notice of intention to defend not only in cases in which he or she decides to resist the plaintiff's claim on the merits but also when his or her defence rests upon some or other special ground unconnected with the merits of the claim.[3]

It is possible to deliver the notice of intention to defend after the period to enter appearance has lapsed, but before default judgment is granted. However, the plaintiff will generally be entitled to costs if the notice of intention to defend is delivered after the plaintiff lodged the request for default judgment.[4]

The notice states that the defendant intends to defend the action.[5]

The notice must contain the defendant's full physical, residential or business address, postal address and, where available, facsimile and e-mail address.[6]

The notice must further contain a preferred address at which the defendant will accept service of any further process, notices or documents relating to the action.[7] This address is usually the address of the defendant's attorney and it should be noted that this address may not, in places where there are three or more attorneys or firms of attorneys practising independently of one another, be more than 15 kilometres distant from the courthouse.[8]

The notice of intention to defend must indicate whether the defendant is prepared to accept service of all subsequent documents and notices in the suit through any manner other than the physical address or postal address and, if so, shall state such preferred manner of service.[9] The defendant may request the

---

[1] Rule 13(1). In Afrikaans, 'die verweerder teken verskyning aan'. In this chapter preference is given to the expression 'to give notice of intention to defend'.

[2] Rule 13(2).

[3] Rule 13(4) provides expressly that the entry of an appearance to defend shall be without prejudice to the defendant's right to object to the court's jurisdiction or to any irregularity or impropriety in the proceedings.

[4] Rule 13(5).

[5] Rule 13(1).

[6] Rule 13(3)*(a)*(i). In terms of the Civil Practice Directives for the Regional Courts in South Africa, adopted by resolution of the Regional Court Presidents' Forum on 28 May 2013 (with effect from 1 August 2013), before any documents or pleadings are delivered by fax or email, a written agreement must be lodged with the registrar in which the parties agree to deliver in that manner. The 'Civil Practice Directives for the Regional Courts in South Africa' 4 ed (2017) do not make mention of such a requirement.

[7] Rule 13(3)*(a)*(ii).

[8] Rule 13(3)*(a)*(iii).

[9] Rule 13(3)*(b)*.

plaintiff to deliver a consent in writing to the exchange or service by both parties of subsequent documents and notices in the suit by way of facsimile or electronic mail.[10] If the plaintiff refuses or fails to deliver the consent, the court may, on application by the defendant, grant such consent, on such terms as to costs and otherwise as may be just and appropriate in the circumstances.[11]

The notice of intention to defend is signed by the defendant or his or her attorney. Where a legal representative signs the notice of intention to defend on behalf of the defendant, he or she need not file in court any written authority to do so. A person's authority to act on behalf of the defendant may, however, be challenged by the plaintiff within 10 days after it has come to his or her attention that the defendant is represented. The person whose authority to act is thus challenged may not thereafter act further without the leave of the court until he or she has satisfied the court that he or she has the necessary authority to represent the defendant.[12]

In the normal course of events, the plaintiff will bring an application to have the notice of intention to defend set aside by the court on the ground that the legal representative lacked the authority to execute the matter on the defendant's behalf. This application may effectively be resisted by, for example, filing in court a written power of attorney signed by the defendant.

The following persons need not file a written power of attorney: the state attorney, any deputy state attorney or any professional assistant to the state attorney or to a deputy state attorney, or any attorney instructed in writing by or on behalf of the state attorney or a deputy state attorney in matters in which the state attorney or a deputy state attorney is acting in his or her official capacity.

A local authority, company or other incorporated body may nominate one of its officers to defend a lawsuit on its behalf[13] and that officer will then sign all process, notices or documents. A partnership or group of persons associated for a common purpose may likewise nominate one of its members to act on its behalf in this way.[14]

Where the notice of intention to defend does not comply with the above requirements or has not been delivered, the notice is defective. Nevertheless, the plaintiff will not be permitted to obtain default judgment against the defendant on that ground alone. The rules provide[15] that if the defendant has given notice of intention to defend and this notice is defective in that it:

(1) has not been properly delivered;

(2) has not been properly signed;

(3) does not set out the postal address of the person signing it or an address for service; or

(4) exhibits any two or more of such defects or defect of form,

the registrar or clerk of the court may not enter default judgment against the defendant at the plaintiff's request unless the plaintiff has delivered written notice to the defendant stating in what respect the notice of intention to defend is

---

[10] Rule 13(3)(*c*).
[11] Rule 13(3)(*d*).
[12] Rule 52(2).
[13] Rule 52(1)(*b*).
[14] Rule 52(1)(*c*).
[15] Rule 12(2)(*a*) and (*b*).

defective and calling upon the defendant to deliver a notice of intention to defend in due form within five days of the receipt of such notice. Only upon the failure of the defendant thereafter to deliver a fresh notice of intention to defend in proper form may the plaintiff make application for default judgment.[16]

The defendant is free, after he or she has been summonsed, to enter appearance to defend in person by completing the printed form appearing on the summons and handing it to the clerk or registrar of the court.[17]

The registrar or clerk of the court may then notify the plaintiff or his or her attorney by letter or by telephone that the defendant has entered appearance.[18]

While it sometimes happens that a defendant gives notice of his intention to defend by completing the printed form on the summons, this form of notice does not comply strictly with the provisions of the rules of court. Rule 13(1) therefore provides that a defendant intending to defend the action is obliged to deliver a notice of intention to defend. According to the meaning given by rule 2(1) to the expression 'deliver', a copy of the notice of intention to defend must be served on the opposing litigant and the original must be handed in at court. This rule is thus not complied with in the case where only the notice of intention to defend appearing on the summons form served upon the defendant is signed. This is anomalous and requires rectification.

Nevertheless, the defendant who acts in this way will succeed in preventing the plaintiff from taking default judgment against him. At the time the plaintiff brings an application for default judgment he or she will be advised by the registrar or clerk of the court that default judgment may not be entered against the defendant because the latter has already given notice of his or her intention to defend.

1.2 Delivery of the notice

The defendant is obliged to deliver the notice of intention to defend.[19]

As mentioned, the expression 'deliver' means that the original document must be filed with the registrar or clerk of the court and a copy of the pleading or document served upon the opposite party.[20] In practice, every pleading or document that has to be delivered to the opposite party is prepared in an original with two copies. Usually only the original process, notices or documents are signed by the party himself or herself or by his or her legal representative. The name of the signatory is typed on the copies. A candidate attorney or a messenger then takes the three documents to the address supplied by the opposite party for the delivery of process, notices or documents. This address is usually that of the opposite party's attorney. At the foot of the process provision is made for the

---

[16] Rule 12(2).

[17] The summonses forms (Annexure 1 Forms 2 and 2A) make provision for a notice of intention to defend. Rule 5(5)(a) expressly provides that the summons shall include a form of appearance to defend.

[18] There is, however, no *obligation* on the registrar or clerk of the court to notify the plaintiff or his or her attorney that the defendant has entered appearance. Rule 3, which sets out the duties of the registrar and clerk of the court, does not list that as being one of their duties.

[19] Rule 13(1).

[20] Rule 2(1).

opposite party or his or her attorney to append his or her signature and the date on which he or she received a copy of the documents. The original and the second copy are handed back to the candidate attorney or messenger and the first copy is filed by the opposite party in his or her office file. The candidate attorney or messenger takes the original process to the court, where it is filed in the court file. The second copy is taken back to his or her office and serves as proof of the fact that the process has been delivered as well as proof of the date on which it was received by the opposite party.

The following may be given as an example of a notice of intention to defend. The addresses of the parties' representatives and the place at which the plaintiff's legal representative signs for receipt of the notice appear in the example.

---

* For use in the District Court

In the Magistrate's Court for the District of ....

held at ....

Case No .... of 20.........

In the matter between

.... Plaintiff

and

.... Defendant

NOTICE OF INTENTION TO DEFEND

TAKE NOTICE that the Defendant herewith gives notice of his/her intention to defend the action and gives the following addresses as required by rule 13(3)*(a)*:

1. Business and postal address: ....
2. Facsimile address: ....
3. Electronic mail address: ....

TAKE FURTHER NOTICE that the Defendant hereby appoints the below-mentioned attorneys as his/her attorneys of record and elects the below-mentioned address as that at which he/she will accept service of all processes, notices and documents in the action:

1.   ....
2.   ....

TAKE FURTHER NOTICE that the Defendant is not prepared to accept service of subsequent documents and notices in the suit through any manner other than by hand at the physical address of his/her attorneys of record as set out herein.

SIGNED at .... on this .... day of .... 20.........

....
DEFENDANT'S ATTORNEY
Address: ....
....

To the Clerk of the Court

....

And to: ....

....
(Plaintiff's Attorney)

Received copy hereof on this .... day of .... 20........
.... For: PLAINTIFF'S ATTORNEY

1.2.1 *Delivery to the 'wrong' defendant*

In those instances in which the person upon whom the summons was served wishes to allege that he or she is not in fact the defendant named in the summons, it is suggested that he or she first enters appearance to defend and then objects to the fact that the summons was served upon him or her. Failure to do so may result in default judgment being granted against the person incorrectly served and execution against his or her property. It is not possible for the court to order that costs be paid by or to the person incorrectly served who enters appearance to defend. He or she would need to issue summons against the plaintiff.[21]

1.3 The period within which notice of intention to defend must be given

The defendant is obliged to give notice of his or her intention to defend the action within the period set out in the summons, which will ordinarily be 10 days,[22] but when the defendant is the State the period shall be 20 days.[23]

The various problems associated with failure to give notice of intention to defend have been dealt with in the section on default judgment.

1.4 The duty of the plaintiff on receipt of the notice of intention to defend

Upon receipt of the notice of intention to defend, the plaintiff must forthwith lodge with the registrar or clerk of the court the original summons and the return of service.[24]

When rules 8(4) and 12(1)(*a*) are read together, it becomes clear that the sheriff returns the original summons together with the return of service to the plaintiff after service has been effected. The sheriff no longer remits the original summons and the return of service to the registrar or clerk of the court, as was done in the past.

The duty now rests upon the plaintiff to keep the original summons and the return of service safely in his or her possession, and these documents are delivered to the registrar or clerk of the court only when the plaintiff applies for default judgment in terms of rule 12(1)(*a*) or when the plaintiff receives the defendant's notice of intention to defend. If the returned summons has been endorsed by the defendant by completion of the printed notice of intention to defend, the notice is no longer required and the summons is delivered to the registrar or clerk.

2 SUMMARY JUDGMENT

2.1 General

The application for summary judgment is a procedure that protects the plaintiff in certain types of cases against an ill-disposed defendant who defends the matter purely in order to delay its finalisation.

---

[21] Jones & Buckle Rule 13-2.
[22] Rule 13(1).
[23] Rule 13(2).
[24] Rule 13(6).

A civil case, even without undue delay, lasts a long time from the time of issue of summons to the time when judgment is given. It would be a sad state of affairs if a plaintiff with a meritorious claim had to wait patiently until the court was able, only months later, to award him or her the legal relief he or she sought—and that simply because the defendant, whose case was devoid of merit, had the temerity to defend the matter.

The possibility is thus created by the application for summary judgment that the plaintiff may truncate the suit and obtain the legal relief that he or she seeks shortly after the defendant has given notice of his or her intention to defend.

Viewed against this background, the application for summary judgment is a remedy that may be used to prevent an abuse of the court procedure by a recalcitrant defendant.[25]

The remedy has repeatedly been called 'extraordinary and drastic' and this approach influences the interpretation of the rules.[26]

2.2 Claims in respect of which summary judgment may be granted

Rule 14(1) provides that a plaintiff in convention may apply to court for summary judgment on one or more of the following claims set out in the summons:
(1) based on a liquid document;
(2) for a liquidated sum of money;
(3) for the delivery of specified movable property; or
(4) for ejectment,
together with any claim for interests and costs.

It is clear that the application for summary judgment may be used only where the merits of the claim are easily ascertainable without the necessity of holding a trial with evidence and cross-examination. The claim must appear from the documents placed before the court and the legal relief sought must be fixed and certain.

Against this background it is clear why applications for summary judgment may be brought only where the claim is based on a liquid document or for a liquidated amount in money, delivery of specified movable property or ejectment.

A liquid document is a document which on the face of it, and without the need for the leading of further evidence, indicates that its signatory is indebted to the creditor in a stipulated amount in money and that such amount has become payable.[27]

---

[25] See *Meek v Kruger* 1958 (3) SA 154 (T) at 158C: 'The adoption of summary judgment procedure in our judicial practice was evidently also to prevent cunning and unwilling debtors from exploiting our system of legal procedure in order to withhold from creditors that to which they are justly entitled.'

[26] See *Maharaj v Barclays National Bank Ltd* 1976 (1) SA 418 (A) at 423F. The cases on the procedure in the High Court are good authority in the lower courts; see D E Van Loggerenberg *Erasmus Superior Court Practice* 2 ed (Service 6, 2018) D1-379 *et seq.* However, see also *Joob Joob Investments (Pty) Ltd v Stocks Mavundla Zek Joint Venture* 2009 (5) SA 1 (SCA) at 11G–D where the court stated that, inter alia, '[a]fter almost a century of successful application in our courts, summary judgment proceedings can hardly continue to be described as extraordinary'. The court suggested doing away with labels such as 'extraordinary' and 'drastic'.

[27] *Harrowsmith v Ceres Flats (Pty) Ltd* 1979 (2) SA 722 (T); *Rich & others v Lagerwey* 1974 (4) SA 748 (A) at 754; *Western Bank Ltd v Pretorius* 1976 (2) SA 481 (T) at 483. Examples of liquid documents are cheques and promissory notes.

The concept of a 'liquidated amount in money' is used to indicate an amount that is fixed and certain. In other words, it is an agreed amount in money or an amount that has been precisely quantified or that is readily capable of accurate determination and that is not in dispute.[28] An amount claimed by way of damages, for example, is not 'liquidated' until the court has determined the precise amount.

The question arises as to what is meant by an amount in money that is 'readily capable of accurate determination'. It means simply that the presiding officer should be able to ascertain *ex facie* the document precisely what amount is due and payable, for example by making a simple arithmetical calculation.[29]

The following may serve as examples of liquidated amounts in money:
- an amount outstanding in terms of a balance sheet that is admitted by the defendant;[30]
- an account rendered by a shopkeeper;[31]
- arrear maintenance payments;[32]
- insurance premiums;[33]
- rental payable on a weekly basis;[34]
- a taxed bill of costs.[35]

The claim must be for the delivery of movable property and may not be for transfer of immovable property.[36]

2.3 The period within which the application for summary judgment must be made

The plaintiff is required to bring the application for summary judgment within 15 days after the date of service of the defendant's notice of intention to defend. The notice of application for summary judgment must be accompanied by an affidavit made by the plaintiff or by any other person who can swear positively to the facts verifying the cause of action and the amount (if any) claimed, and stating that in his or her opinion there is no *bona fide* defence to the action and that notice of intention to defend has been served solely for the purposes of delay.[37]

If the plaintiff does not bring an application for summary judgment but instead takes some further step in the proceedings, he or she will be deemed to have waived his or her right to apply for summary judgment. Where, however, the

---

[28] *Lester Investments (Pty) Ltd v Narshi* 1951 (2) SA 464 (C); *Fatti's Engineering Co (Pty) Ltd v Vendick Spares (Pty) Ltd* 1962 (1) SA 736 (T).

[29] *Consolidated Fish Distributors (Pty) Ltd v Sargeant, Jones, Valentine & Co* 1966 (4) SA 427 (C); *Leymac Distributors Ltd v Hoosen & another* 1974 (4) SA 524 (D); *S Dreyer & Sons Transport v General Services* 1976 (4) SA 922 (C).

[30] *Rooknodien v Kahn* 1915 CPD 394.

[31] *Mahomed Essop (Pty) Ltd v Sekhukhulu & Son* 1967 (3) SA 728 (D); *Jacobsen van den Berg SA (Pty) Ltd v Triton Yachting Supplies* 1974 (2) SA 584 (O).

[32] *Martin v Le Vatte* 1914 CPD 212.

[33] *London & Lancashire Insurance Co Ltd v De Wet* 1938 CPD 577.

[34] *Oblewitz v Cortis* (1902) 19 SC 162.

[35] *Wolhuterskop Beleggings (Edms) Bpk v Bloemfontein Engineering Works (Pty) Ltd* 1965 (2) SA 122 (O).

[36] *Van Wyngaardt NO v Knox* 1977 (2) SA 636 (T).

[37] Rule 14(2).

plaintiff does not *mero motu* take any further procedural step but is compelled to take such a step, the plaintiff may nevertheless proceed with the application for summary judgment.[38]

Rule 14 provides that a 'plaintiff' in convention may make application for summary judgment. According to Jones & Buckle, should the defendant in convention be allowed to claim summary judgment, it would frustrate the principle that claims should be set off against one another.[39] For this reason the court may likewise not grant summary judgment against a defendant who has no defence but only a counterclaim.[40]

2.4 The procedure in applying for summary judgment

The plaintiff proceeds by way of application. The application is drafted in accordance with the example given in Annexure 1 Form 7, which reads as follows:

No. 7
Notice of Application for Summary Judgment
* For use in the District Court

In the Magistrate's Court for the District of ....
held at ....

Case No .... of 20.........

In the matter between

.... Applicant

and

.... Respondent

Take notice that application will be made to the above-mentioned court on the .... day of ...., 20...., at .... (time), for summary judgment against the respondent in this action for R .... and costs;

And further take notice that the document on which the claim is based or the affidavit of .... (copy served herewith) will be used in support of such application and that respondent may reply thereto by affidavit.

Dated at .... this .... day of ...., 20.........

....
Applicant/Applicant's Attorney

To: ....

....

and: Clerk of the Court,

....

---

[38] *Paul v Peter* 1985 (4) SA 227 (N), where the court refused to follow *Jacobs v FPJ Finans (Edms) Bpk* 1975 (3) SA 345 (O) but followed *Hire-Purchase Discount Co (Pty) Ltd v Ryan Scholz & Co (Pty) Ltd & another* 1979 (2) SA 305 (SE) instead. Cf also *Northern Cape Scrap & Metals (Edms) Bpk v Upington Radiators & Motor Graveyard (Edms) Bpk* 1974 (3) SA 788 (NC) and *Parma Bouers v Môrelig Engineering (Edms) Bpk* 1990 (4) SA 188 (O).

[39] Rule 14-6A.

[40] *Weinkove v Botha* 1952 (3) SA 178 (C).

If the claim is based on a liquid document, the plaintiff is required to attach a copy of the liquid document to the application.[41] It is not necessary to attach the original document: a copy will be sufficient. The original liquid document must, however, be handed in to court at the hearing of the application.[42]

If the claim is for a liquidated amount in money or for the delivery of specified movable property or for ejectment, the plaintiff must attach a copy of an affidavit deposed to by him or her or by someone else who is able to confirm the facts under oath. In this affidavit the cause of action and the amount (if any) claimed must be confirmed and the plaintiff must aver that in his or her belief there is no *bona fide* defence to the claim and that notice of intention to defend has been given solely for the purpose of delaying the action.

Annexure 1 Form 8 may be used as an example of the affidavit. It reads as follows:

No. 8

Affidavit in Support of Application for Summary Judgment

[Form 8 substituted by GN R318 of 17 April 2015 (wef 22 May 2015).]

* For use in the District Court

In the Magistrate's Court for the District of ....

held at ....

Case No .... of 20........

In the matter between

.... Applicant

and

.... Respondent

I, ..., of ....

.... (address), declare under oath/affirm as follows:

(a) I am the plaintiff (or state the relationship on which the authority to represent the plaintiff is based) in this action and am duly authorised to make this affidavit, the contents of which are within my personal knowledge.

(b) I verify that the defendant is indebted to me/to the plaintiff in the amount of R............. and on the grounds stated in the summons.

(c) I believe that the defendant does not have a *bona fide* defence to the claim and that the notice of intention to defend has been served solely for purposes of delay.

(d) A copy of the notice of intention to defend served on .... (date) is annexed hereto.

(e) *(If the claim is founded on a liquid document)* A copy of the .... (describe the relevant liquid document) is annexed hereto.

....

Signature

The deponent has acknowledged that he/she knows and understands the contents of this affidavit.

Signed and sworn to/affirmed before me at .... on this .... day of ...., 20........

---

[41] Rule 14(2)(c); *Credcor Bank Ltd v Thomson* 1975 (3) SA 916 (D) and *Bank van die Oranje Vrystaat Bpk v OVS Kleiwerke (Earns) Bpk en andere* 1976 (3) SA 804 (O).
[42] *Lishman v Scaife* 1927 EDL 137.

....
Commissioner of Oaths
....
Area
....
Office held if appointment is held *ex officio.*

Provided that the rules of court are complied with, it is not necessary that the affidavit should be drafted precisely in accordance with the above example.[43]

Three things must, however, be clearly apparent from the affidavit (or affidavits):[44]

(1)   the facts of the case must be confirmed;
(2)   the existence of the cause of action must be confirmed;
(3)   it must be averred that the plaintiff believes that the defendant
    (a)   has no *bona fide* defence; and
    (b)   has given notice of his intention to defend for the sole purpose of delaying the finalisation of the matter.

These three requirements are dealt with briefly below.

(1)   First, it is important that the facts set out in the particulars of claim be confirmed under oath or affirmed by the plaintiff or a person acting on his or her behalf who has first-hand knowledge of the facts. Where the plaintiff is a company, for example, the affidavit will have to be signed by someone within the company who has personal knowledge of the facts set out in the summons. The mere fact that a managing director of a company is deemed to have knowledge of all of the company's affairs does not necessarily imply that he or she is always able to confirm the facts stated in the summons on the company's behalf.[45] The test ought to be whether the person deposing to the affidavit could be called as a witness to give evidence of those facts in court and to be cross-examined as to them.[46]

(2)   Secondly, there must be, in addition to the confirmation of the facts mentioned in the particulars of claim, confirmation of the cause of action. The plaintiff or someone acting on his or her behalf is thus required to confirm that the plaintiff is entitled to the legal relief sought.[47]

(3)   Thirdly, the affidavit must state expressly that the plaintiff believes that the defendant has no *bona fide* defence to the claim and that he or she has given

---

[43] *Pillay v Andermain (Pty) Ltd; Runganarden v Andermain (Pty) Ltd* 1970 (1) SA 531 (T) at 536.

[44] It is quite in order for one person to depose to an affidavit in respect of some of the three matters mentioned hereafter while another person deposes in regard to the remainder of those matters (*International Shipping Co (Pty) Ltd v F C Bonnet (Pty) Ltd* 1975 (1) SA 853 (D)).

[45] *Conradie v Landro en Van der Hoff (Edms) Bpk* 1965 (2) SA 304 (GW) at 309. An official may, however, be able to gain the information from records or subordinates. *B Kaplan Estates (Pty) Ltd v Eastern Metropolitan Substructure* 1999 (2) SA 1017 (W); *Cape Town Transitional Metropolitan Substructure v Ilco Homes Ltd* 1996 (3) SA 492 (C).

[46] *Pinepipe (Pty) Ltd v Nolec (Pty) Ltd* 1975 (4) SA 932 (W); *Jeffrey v Andries Zietsman (Edms) Bpk* 1976 (2) SA 870 (T); *B Kaplan Estates v Eastern Metropolitan Substructure* (supra).

[47] *Pillay v Andermain (Pty) Ltd; Runganarden v Andermain (Pty) Ltd* 1970 (1) SA 531 (T).

notice of his or her intention to defend solely for the purpose of delaying the finalisation of the action.[48]

The plaintiff must make this affidavit in good faith. He or she need not give any explanation as to why he or she believes that the defendant lacks a *bona fide* defence and has entered appearance only in order to delay the action.[49] The plaintiff must, however, personally believe that that is indeed the case.[50]

The plaintiff may not attach any annexure to this affidavit if such annexure would constitute an attempt to place evidence before the court.[51] The cause of action must merely be verified. No evidence in support of the cause of action may be presented in the application.

2.5 Steps that may be taken by the defendant

Rule 14(3) creates two possible courses of action for the defendant if he or she wishes to resist summary judgment. The defendant may:
(1)   give security to the plaintiff to the satisfaction of the registrar or clerk for any judgment including costs which may be given;[52] or
(2)   satisfy the court by affidavit delivered not later than noon of the day preceding the hearing of the application or, with the court's leave, through oral evidence, that he or she has a *bona fide* defence to the claim on which summary judgment is being sought.[53]

Such affidavit and evidence must disclose the nature and bases of the defence and the relevant material facts relied upon.

These possibilities are discussed briefly below.

2.5.1 *Give security to the satisfaction of the registrar or clerk for any judgment including costs which may be given*

In this event the defendant shows by his or her conduct that he or she has not given notice of intention to defend solely for the purpose of delay. The defendant shows that he or she is serious in the desire to defend the action—that it is not so much a question of the money involved as a matter of principle.

The money paid into court is quite safe and the plaintiff may claim payment of it if at the conclusion of the trial the court acknowledges the merit of his or her claim by granting judgment in his or her favour.[54]

---

[48] Jones & Buckle 14–20G.

[49] *Wright v McGuinness* 1956 (3) SA 184 (C); *Sand & Co Ltd v Kollias* 1962 (2) SA 162 (W).

[50] *Group Areas Development Board v Hassim & others* 1964 (2) SA 327 (T); *H K Gokal (Pty) Ltd v Muthambi* 1967 (3) SA 89 (T). For cases as to whether an opinion is the same as a belief for these purposes, see the cases cited by Jones & Buckle Rule 14–20F.

[51] *Kosak & Co (Pty) Ltd v Keller & another* 1962 (1) SA 441 (W); *Venter v Kruger* 1971 (3) SA 848 (N); *Trust Bank of Africa Ltd v Hansa & another* 1988 (4) SA 102 (W).

[52] Rule 14(3)(*a*).

[53] Rule 14(3)(*b*).

[54] It is submitted that, in the current constitutional dispensation, it is arguably discriminatory to enable a person who is able to give security to escape summary judgment whereas an individual who is financially unable to do so is expected to satisfy the court that he or she has a *bona fide* defence and possibly incur costs in this regard as well.

The defendant may escape the grant of summary judgment by way of a payment into court only in those cases in which the plaintiff claims payment of a sum of money, and not in cases in which the delivery of specified movable property or ejectment is sought.[55]

The amount paid by the defendant into court is affected by the magistrate's assessment of the costs that will be incurred in the action if it is allowed to proceed. These future legal costs will be determined by the magistrate at the hearing of the application for summary judgment.

If the defendant pays into court the amount of the claim together with costs, the court is obliged to give him or her leave to defend the matter and the action then proceeds as though no application for summary judgment was made.[56]

2.5.2 *The defendant gives evidence that he or she has a* **bona fide** *defence or counterclaim against the plaintiff*

This is the method most commonly employed in order to resist an application for summary judgment.

The defendant seeks to persuade the court by affidavit, possibly supplemented (with the leave of the court) by oral evidence, that he or she has a *bona fide* defence or counterclaim.[57]

In the affidavit the defendant is required to disclose the nature and grounds of his or her counterclaim or defence.

The defendant may depose to this affidavit in person, unless he or she lacks personal knowledge either of the nature or the grounds of the defence. In that event the defendant may rely upon an affidavit of someone who has personal knowledge of the relevant facts.[58]

The 'nature and grounds' of the defence or counterclaim must be set out. By this is meant that the defendant must categorise his or her defence or put a name to it[59] and must then set out the facts on which the defence is based. Merely to state that he or she has no knowledge of the claim, as might be done in a plea, will not be sufficient.[60]

---

[55] *Doyle v Nash* 1953 (1) SA 77 (T).

[56] Rule 14(5) and (7).

[57] Rule 14(3)*(b)*. From these provisions it is clear that the court ought to afford the defendant every reasonable opportunity to place his or her defence before the court (*Hugh Holdings (Pvt) Ltd v Gamberini* 1968 (3) SA 157 (R) at 158). Cf in general in regard to the contents of the affidavit: *Benati v Morelli* 1968 (4) SA 111 (N); *Van Eeden v Sasol Pensioenfonds* 1975 (2) SA 167 (O); *Golding v Abrahams* 1911 (1) SA 350 (C); *Forhat Stud Farm (Edms) Bpk v Barclays Nasionale Bank Bpk* 1978 (3) SA 118 (O); *Verrijdt v Honeydew Tractors & Implements (Pty) Ltd* 1981 (1) SA 787 (T); *Slabbert v Volkskas Bpk* 1985 (1) SA 141 (T).

[58] *Estate Potgieter v Elliott* 1948 (1) SA 1084 (C) at 1086; cf the discussion above in relation to the position where affidavits are made by the plaintiff. (In this connection see *International Shipping Co (Pty) Ltd v F C Bonnet (Pty) Ltd* 1975 (1) SA 853 (D) at 854.) Cf also the cases mentioned in the previous footnote. The affidavit may not contain inadmissible hearsay evidence; *Chairperson, Independent Electoral Commission v Die Krans Ontspanningsoord (Edms) Bpk* 1997 (1) SA 244 (T).

[59] For example, 'waiver', 'novation' or 'payment'.

[60] *Herbst en 'n ander v Solo Boumateriaal* 1993 (1) SA 397 (T).

No obligation rests on the defendant to satisfy the court that the facts set out by him or her are true or that the balance of probabilities in the case lies in his or her favour.[61] The only question on which the court is called upon to decide is whether the defendant has disclosed a *bona fide* defence which, if proved at the trial, would constitute a complete defence to the plaintiff's claim.[62]

The defendant need not set out his or her defence in the affidavit with the precision that will subsequently be necessary in his or her plea if the application for summary judgment fails and he or she is given leave to defend the action.[63] The defendant must nevertheless formulate the defence sufficiently clearly to place the magistrate in a position to determine whether the defence, if true, will constitute a real defence to the action.

The defendant is required to disclose a *defence* to the plaintiff's claim or a *counterclaim* against the plaintiff. If the defendant attacks the form of the summons or alleges that it fails to disclose a cause of action, the defendant must set the summons aside as an irregular step[64] or raise an exception.[65]

If the defendant discloses a *bona fide* counterclaim against the summary judgment application, it will be sufficient to resist the application for summary judgment. If the counterclaim is lower than the claim in convention and the defendant cannot show that he or she has a defence in respect of the balance, the court may grant summary judgment for such balance.[66]

2.6 Orders that may be made by the court

At the hearing of the summary judgment application the presiding officer must decide on the two sets of affidavits whether to grant the application or not.

The magistrate may, however, permit the defendant to give oral evidence at the hearing of the application in order to supplement his or her affidavit.[67]

The defendant is, however, not permitted simply to give oral evidence as to the nature and grounds of his or her defence or counterclaim on the day of the hearing of the application. If the defendant has neglected to deliver an answering affidavit, the court will grant summary judgment against him or her unless he or she can furnish good reasons as to why the case should be postponed to allow him or her to file an affidavit. On an application for postponement, the defendant will be required to explain what the nature and grounds of the defence that he or she intends to set out in his or her affidavit will be.[68]

---

[61] *Arend & another v Astra Furnishers (Pty) Ltd* 1974 (1) SA 298 (C); *Maharaj v Barclays National Bank Ltd* 1976 (1) SA 418 (A) at 426; *Venter v Kruger* 1971 (3) SA 848 (N) at 852; *Davis v Terry* 1957 (4) SA 98 (SR).

[62] *Breitenbach v Fiat SA (Edms) Bpk* 1976 (2) SA 226 (T).

[63] *Wright v Van Zyl* 1951 (3) SA 488 (C) at 492; *Herb Dyers (Pty) Ltd v Mahomed & another* 1965 (1) SA 31 (T) at 32; *Maharaj v Barclays National Bank* (supra) at 426.

[64] Rule 5(11) read with rule 60A.

[65] Cf chapter 12 below.

[66] Rule 14(6)(*b*).

[67] Rule 14(3)(*b*).

[68] *Stofberg & others v Lochner* 1946 OPD 333; *Loots v Van Staden* 1962 (1) SA 152 (O).

The magistrate has a discretion whether to grant a postponement in such an event, and each case will be decided on its own merits.[69]

The plaintiff is not permitted to give oral evidence at the hearing of the application. The plaintiff must stand or fall on the original supporting affidavits attached to his or her application for summary judgment. The plaintiff, therefore, may likewise not hand in at the hearing of the application further documents or letters in further support of the application.[70] A contract or liquid document from which a cause of action arises may, however, be attached to the particulars of claim contained in the summons.[71] The terms of the contract from which the cause of action arises must, however, be set out in full in the particulars of claim. If the plaintiff, instead of repeating all of the terms of the contract in the particulars of claim, simply annexes the contract, then the contract will form part of the pleadings prior to the application for summary judgment.

If the defendant, or someone acting on the defendant's behalf, is permitted by the court to give oral evidence at the hearing of the application, the person who gives evidence in this manner may not be cross-examined by the plaintiff, but the witness may, after examination by the defendant, be examined by the court.[72]

When deciding the application for summary judgment, the presiding officer must always bear in mind that summary judgment is a drastic remedy. It is drastic because the granting of summary judgment amounts in essence to a disregard of the *audi alteram partem* principle. If the court grants summary judgment, it issues a final order against the defendant without a trial involving a thorough investigation of the merits of the case having taken place.

If at the hearing of an application for summary judgment it appears that one defendant is entitled to leave to defend and another not, or that a defendant is entitled to leave to defend as to part only of the plaintiff's claim, the court may:
(1) give leave to defend to a defendant so entitled and give judgment against a defendant not so entitled;
(2) give leave to defend to the defendant as to such part of the claim and give judgment against the defendant as to the balance of the claim, unless the defendant has paid such balance to the plaintiff; or
(3) make both such orders.[73]

Rule 14 provides that a court may, at the hearing of an application for summary judgment, make such order as to costs as it deems fit. Where the plaintiff applies for summary judgment, where the case is not within the terms of rule 14(1) or

---

[69] *Benati v Morelli* (supra).

[70] *Kosak & Co (Pty) Ltd v Keller & another* 1962 (1) SA 441 (W); *South African Trade Union Assurance Society Ltd v Dermot Properties (Pty) Ltd & others* 1962 (3) SA 601 (W); *Venter v Kruger* (supra); *Trust Bank of Africa Ltd v Hansa & another* 1988 (4) SA 102 (W) at 105A–F.

[71] *Kosak & Co v Keller* (supra); *South African Trade Union Assurance Society v Dermot Properties* (supra); *Venter v Kruger* (supra). These decisions were, however, criticised in *Beresford Land Plan (Pvt) Ltd v Urquhart* 1975 (3) SA 619 (RA). See, however, the detailed discussion by Flemming J in *Trust Bank of Africa v Hansa* (supra) at 107–9, where it was stated clearly that the *Beresford* case is not followed in South Africa. See also *Rossouw & another v FirstRand Bank Ltd* 2010 (6) SA 439 (SCA).

[72] Rule 14(4).

[73] Rule 14(6)*(b)*.

where the plaintiff, in the opinion of the court, knew that the defendant relied on a contention which would entitle him or her to leave to defend, the court may order that the action be stayed until the plaintiff has paid the defendant's costs and that such costs be taxed as between attorney and client. Furthermore, in any case in which summary judgment was refused and in which the court after trial gives judgment for the plaintiff substantially as prayed, and the court finds that summary judgment should have been granted had the defendant not raised a defence which in its opinion was unreasonable, the court may order the plaintiff's costs to be taxed as between attorney and client.[74]

Usually the court, if it grants leave to defend, orders that the costs of the summary judgment application will be costs in the cause.[75]

The court will then make an order of costs at the time final judgment is given at the trial, and this will take into account the costs of the summary judgment application.

If the court grants summary judgment, costs are usually ordered in favour of the plaintiff.

Where summary judgment is granted in the absence of a defendant, we are dealing with a judgment falling within the ambit of s 36(a). Consequently, application may be brought in the magistrate's court for the rescission of such a judgment.[76]

3 PROVISIONAL SENTENCE

Prior to GN R498 of 1994, provisional sentence proceedings could be brought only in the High Court. A party wishing to sue on a liquid document was obliged to serve a normal summons and then possibly to make application for summary judgment. By the 1994 amendment the High Court Uniform Rule 8 has been introduced to the lower courts as rule 14A. All authority on the High Court practice should be followed in the lower courts.[77]

Provisional sentence proceedings provide a speedy remedy for a creditor in possession of a liquid document. Should the debtor not be able to dispute the validity of the document, a provisional judgment will be entered against him or her, and the debtor will be able to enter into the merits of the matter only after giving satisfactory security or paying the judgment debt and costs.

The Constitutional Court, in *Twee Jonge Gezellen (Pty) Ltd & another v Land and Agricultural Development Bank of South Africa t/a The Land Bank & another*,[78] held that the provisional sentence procedure was inconsistent with the Constitution and invalid to the extent that it does not give the court a discretion to

---

[74] Rule 14(10).

[75] *Venter v Kruger* (supra) at 852; *H H Robertson (Africa) (Pty) Ltd v N L Builders & Construction Co (Pty) Ltd* 1974 (3) SA 776 (N) at 777.

[76] *Tlholoe v Maury (Edms) Bpk h/a Franelle Gordyn Boutique* 1988 (3) SA 922 (O). Cf in general in regard to the procedure that must be followed, at chapter 10 para 4.5 above.

[77] See *Erasmus Superior Court Practice* D1-98 *et seq*; F R Malan et al *Provisional Sentence on Bills of Exchange, Cheques and Promissory Notes* 2 ed (Butterworths, 1995). In *Ndamase v Functions 4 All* 2004 (5) SA 602 (SCA) it was held that rule 14A was not *ultra vires* the Act.

[78] 2011 (3) SA 1 (CC) at 22H–J.

refuse provisional sentence in certain circumstances. These circumstances include where the nature of the defence raised did not allow the defendant to show a balance of success in his or her favour without the benefit of oral evidence and where the defendant was unable to satisfy the judgment debt. The court had no discretion, outside 'special circumstances', to refuse provisional sentence. The Constitutional Court held that the common law had to be developed so that courts would in future have a discretion to refuse provisional sentence in the above circumstances, ie where there is an inability to satisfy the judgment debt, where there is an even balance of success in the main case on the papers, and where there is a reasonable prospect that oral evidence might tip the balance of success in the defendant's favour.[79]

The document upon which provisional sentence is brought has to fulfil rigid requirements. These are not set out in the rule and one has to look to the common law. The document must in itself, and without resort to extrinsic evidence, reveal 'an unconditional acknowledgement of indebtedness in an ascertained amount of money, the payment of which is due to the creditor'.[80]

The question whether a particular document fulfils this requirement has been the subject of a great deal of case law. Difficulties arise over the following issues:

(1)   There must be an acknowledgment of debt

Despite much misgiving, an acknowledgment of debt given in consideration of an undertaking by the creditor to advance monies in the future is liquid provided an unconditional obligation to pay is undertaken.[81]

The acknowledgment must be unconditional. However, where the payment of the indebtedness is conditional on a simple event or condition, evidence of fulfilment is permitted.[82]

(2)   The debt must be in an ascertained amount of money

Some documents provide for a debt in an unspecified amount. Such a document cannot be made liquid for the purpose of provisional sentence by the production of a certificate of the actual amount owing.[83]

In addition to bills of exchange, promissory notes and cheques, provisional sentence may also be obtained on certificates of architects and engineers which are issued in terms of the contract,[84] taxed bills of costs in conjunction with a power of attorney,[85] foreign judgments, a lease, and mortgage bonds.

---

[79] At 23A–B.
[80] *Rich & others v Lagerwey* 1974 (4) SA 748 (A) at 754H. See also, for example, *Joob Joob Investments (Pty) Ltd v Stocks Mavundla Zek Joint Venture* 2009 (5) SA 1 (SCA) at 10C–D and *Twee Jonge Gezellen v Land and Agricultural Development Bank* (supra) at 8C–D.
[81] *Inglestone v Pereira* 1939 TPD 357.
[82] *Pepler v Hirschberg* 1920 CPD 438 at 443; *Western Bank Ltd v Pretorius* 1976 (2) SA 481 (T) at 487F–H; *Joosub v Edelson* 1998 (3) SA 534 (W); *First National Bank Ltd v Avtjoglou* 2000 (1) SA 989 (C).
[83] *Harrowsmith v Ceres Flats (Pty) Ltd* 1979 (2) SA 722 (T); *Wollach v Barclays National Bank Ltd* 1983 (2) SA 543 (A).
[84] *Longtill Construction Ltd v Lirhobern (Pty) Ltd* 1978 (2) SA 240 (W).
[85] *Gelb, Benjamin & Kaplan v Melzer* 1987 (1) SA 917 (T).

3.1 The procedure for applying for provisional sentence

A special summons is used which must follow Form 2A of Annexure 1. This summons is served in the usual way. The *dies induciae* in the summons are 10 days.[86]

No. 2A

Summons: Provisional Sentence

[Form 2A substituted by GN R545 of 30 June 2015 (wef 31 July 2015).]

* For use in the District Court

In the Magistrate's Court for the District of ....

held at ....

Case No .... of 20 ....

In the matter between

.... Plaintiff

and

.... Defendant

To the sheriff or his/her deputy:

INFORM A.B., of .... (state residence or place of business and if known, gender, occupation and place of employment) .... (hereinafter called the defendant), that C.D. (state gender and occupation), of .... (residence or place of business) .... (hereinafter called the plaintiff), hereby institutes action against him or her in which action:

(1) Defendant is hereby summoned to pay to the plaintiff herein immediately after service of this summons an amount of .... together with interest thereon at the rate of ....% per annum as from ....

Plaintiff's claim against defendant for payment of the above-mentioned amount is for: (set out the cause of action)

....

....

and a copy of which document is annexed hereto.

(2) By failing such payment, defendant is hereby called upon to appear before this court personally or by a practitioner at .... (place and court if necessary) on the .... day of .... 20 .... at .... (time) in the forenoon (or as soon thereafter as the matter can be heard) to admit or deny defendant's liability for the said claim.

(3) If defendant denies liability for the claim, defendant shall not later than the .... day of .... 20 ...., file an affidavit with the clerk of this court, and serve a copy thereof on the plaintiff or plaintiff's attorney at the address indicated for service on the summons, which affidavit shall set forth the grounds of defendant's defence to the said claim, and in particular state whether defendant admits or denies defendant's or defendant's agent's signature which appears on the said .... and if it is defendant's agent's signature whether defendant admits or denies the signature or authority of defendant's agent.

---

[86] Rule 14A(1).

Defendant is further informed that in the event of defendant not paying the amount and interest above-mentioned to the plaintiff immediately and if defendant further fails to file an affidavit as aforesaid, and to appear before this court at the time above stated, provisional sentence may be granted against defendant with costs, but that against payment of the said amount, interest and costs, defendant will be entitled to demand security for the restitution thereof if the said sentence should thereafter be reversed.

Dated at .... this .... day of .... 20..........

....
Clerk of the Court

....
Plaintiff/Plaintiff's Attorney
(15 km Physical Address)

....
Postal Address

....
Facsimile Number

....
Electronic Mail Address

....

* The plaintiff is prepared to accept all subsequent documents and notices at the facsimile address/electronic mail address/other address stated herein.

(Delete whichever is not applicable)

Costs, if the action is undefended, will be as follows:

Attorney's charges
   (i) Issue of summons
     (Item 2 of Part II of Table A) R............
   (ii) Attending court
     (Item 7 of Part II of Table A) R............
   (iii) Judgment fees
     (Item 3 of Part II of Table A) R............
     Court fees R............
     Sheriff's fees R............
     Sheriff's fees on re-issue of summons R............
     Total R............

And take notice that–

(a) if defendant pays the said claim and costs immediately judgment will not be given against defendant herein and defendant will save judgment charges;

(b) if defendant admits the claim and wishes to consent to judgment, defendant may file with the clerk of the court an admission of liability signed by defendant and witnessed by defendant's attorney, or otherwise verified by affidavit, and if defendant wishes to undertake to pay the claim in instalments or otherwise, defendant may approach the plaintiff or plaintiff's attorney.

  Notice:

   (i) Any person against whom a court has, in a civil case, given judgment or made any order who has not, within 10 days, satisfied in full such judgment or order may be called upon by notice in terms of section 65A(1) of the Act to appear on a specified date before the court in chambers to enable the court to enquire into the financial position of the judgment debtor and to make such order as the court may deem just and equitable.

   (ii) If the court is satisfied that—

(aa) the judgment debtor or, if the judgment debtor is a juristic person, a director or officer of the juristic person has knowledge of the above-mentioned notice and that he or she has failed to appear before the court on the date and at the time specified in the notice; or

(bb) the judgment debtor, director or officer, where the proceedings were postponed in his or her presence to a date and time determined by the court, has failed to appear before the court on that date and at that time; or

(cc) the judgment debtor, director or officer has failed to remain in attendance at the proceedings or at the proceedings so postponed,

the court may, at the request of the judgment creditor or his or her attorney, authorise the issue of a warrant directing a sheriff to arrest the said judgment debtor, director or officer and to bring him or her before a competent court to enable that court to conduct a financial inquiry. [Section 65A(6) of the Act]

(iii) Any person who–

(aa) is called upon to appear before a court under a notice in terms of section 65A(1) or (8)(b) of the Act (where the sheriff, *in lieu* of arresting a person, hands to that person a notice to appear in court) and who wilfully fails to appear before the court on the date and at the time specified in the notice; or

(bb) where the proceedings were postponed in his or her presence to a date and time determined by the court, wilfully fails to appear before the court on that date and at that time; or

(cc) wilfully fails to remain in attendance at the proceedings or at the proceedings so postponed,

shall be guilty of an offence and liable on conviction to a fine or to imprisonment for a period not exceeding three months. [Section 65A(9) of the Act]

(iv) On appearing before the court on the date determined in the notice in terms of section 65A(1) or (8)(b) of the Act in pursuance of the arrest of the judgment debtor, director or officer under a warrant referred to in section 65A(6) of the Act or on any date to which the proceedings have been postponed, such judgment debtor, director or officer shall be called upon to give evidence on his or her financial position or that of the juristic person and his or her or its ability to pay the judgment debt. [Section 65D of the Act]

(v) Any person against whom a court has, in a civil case, given any judgment or made any order who has not satisfied in full such judgment or order and paid all costs for which he or she is liable in connection therewith shall, if he or she has changed his or her place of residence, business or employment, within 14 days from the date of every such change notify the clerk of the court who gave such judgment or made such order and the judgment creditor or his or her attorney fully and correctly in writing of his or her new place of residence, business or employment, and by his or her failure to do so such judgment debtor shall be guilty of an offence and liable upon conviction to a fine or to imprisonment for a period not exceeding three months. [Section 109 of the Act.]

1: Admission of liability
Kindly take notice that the defendant admits liability to the plaintiff as claimed in this summons.

DATED at .... this .... day of .... 20.........
....
Defendant
(Must be witnessed by defendant's attorney or otherwise verified by affidavit)
OR
2: Notice of intention to defend*
To: THE CLERK OF THE COURT

Kindly take notice that the defendant denies liability and that defendant's affidavit setting forth the grounds upon which defendant disputes liability is attached hereto.

Dated at .... this .... day of .... 20..........

....

Defendant/Defendant's attorney

....

....

(15 km physical address where service of process and documents shall be accepted)

....

....

....

(Postal address)

* The original notice and affidavit must be filed with the clerk of the court and a copy thereof served on the plaintiff or plaintiff's attorney.

A copy of the document upon which the claim is founded must be attached to the summons.[87]

Once the summons is served, the plaintiff may set the matter down not later than three days before the day upon which it is to be heard.[88] The matter may not simply be postponed since the summons stipulates a particular day, but on that day the matter may be held over for another day in order, for instance, for the defendant to file an affidavit.

The defendant may oppose the provisional sentence summons by appearing personally, or by a practitioner on the day named in the summons, or he or she may not later than three days prior to that date deliver an affidavit setting forth the grounds upon which he or she disputes liability.[89] If the opposing affidavit is delivered, the plaintiff will be given a reasonable opportunity to reply.[90] This may lead to a postponement of the action on the day set out in the summons. When the matter is heard, there are thus two affidavits before the court: the opposing affidavit and a reply from the plaintiff.

The defendant may admit liability either prior to or at the hearing. A written admission of liability must be signed by the defendant personally and must be witnessed by an attorney not acting for the defendant—in which case, the court will award a final judgment to the plaintiff.[91]

The summons should set forth the grounds of the defendant's defence to the said claim, and in particular state whether the defendant admits or denies the defendant's or defendant's agent's signature which appears on the said (document) and if it is the defendant's agent's signature, whether the defendant admits or denies the signature or authority of the defendant's agent.

A defence against a provisional sentence summons is therefore directed in two directions, namely, (1) at the authenticity of the signature on the document or the authority of the person signing, and (2) at the merits of the claim itself. If the

---

[87] Rule 14A(3).
[88] Rule 14A(4).
[89] Rule 14A(5)*(a)*.
[90] Rule 14A(5)*(b)*.
[91] Rule 14A(6).

defence is based upon a lack of authenticity of the signature or a lack of authority in the person signing, then oral evidence on these points is permissible at the hearing.[92]

In the adjudication of the action, the parties bear the onus of proof in respect of different issues. The plaintiff bears the onus to prove the authenticity of the signature, the authority of any agent and the fulfilment of any condition.

If the defence is aimed at the merits of the transaction lying behind the document, for example, a defence based on duress, then the defendant bears the onus of proving that the probabilities are against the plaintiff in the principal case. This onus is discharged on the normal civil onus of a preponderance of probability. The defendant must place facts before the court and cannot argue from inferences.[93] The defendant may raise a counterclaim, which may be illiquid, as a defence.

If provisional sentence is refused, the defendant may be ordered to file a plea within a stated time, and the court may award any fitting order of costs.[94] This is a discretionary step which the court will take only if it is satisfied that there is a case for the defendant to answer. If the court does not order the defendant to file a plea, the matter is at an end.[95]

Should a defendant not succeed in warding off provisional sentence, this is not the end of the matter for him or her. The court will grant the plaintiff provisional sentence. The sentence is provisional in the sense that the defendant may defend the matter by referring the matter to a full trial, but only on certain conditions. The defendant may demand from the plaintiff security *de restituendo* to the satisfaction of the clerk of the court.[96] Such security is designed to cover the defendant should he or she succeed in the principal action. Should the plaintiff not provide such security, the defendant may file a plea and enter into the principal case. But should the plaintiff provide the security, the defendant must pay the amount of the judgment together with costs.[97] The defendant initiates this process within two months of the granting of provisional sentence by delivering a notice of intention to enter the principal case and by delivery of a plea 10 days after the notice. Should the defendant not take these steps timeously, the provisional sentence becomes a final judgment.[98]

Once the plea has been filed, the matter is conducted as a normal trial action.

---

[92] Rule 14A(7). In *Twee Jonge Gezellen (Pty) Ltd & another v Land and Agricultural Development Bank of South Africa t/a The Land Bank & another* 2011 (3) SA 1 (CC) it was held, inter alia, that a court should retain a discretion to allow oral evidence where there is a reasonable prospect that it may tip the balance of success in the defendant's favour.

[93] *Syfrets Mortgage Nominees Ltd v Cape St Francis Hotels* 1991 (3) SA 276 (SEC) at 286C–F and *Twee Jonge Gezellen v Land and Agricultural Development Bank* (supra) at 11C.

[94] Rule 14A(8)*(a)*.

[95] The better position is that the refusal of provisional sentence does not make the matter *res judicata* between the parties. The plaintiff would therefore be at liberty to prosecute his action by means of an ordinary summons. See *Erasmus Superior Court Practice* D1-98 *et seq.*

[96] Rule 14A(9).

[97] Rule 14A(10).

[98] Rule 14A(11).

Chapter 12

THE EXCEPTION AND THE APPLICATION TO STRIKE OUT

1 GENERAL

There are various ways in which a defendant may defend himself or herself against an action instituted against him or her. These methods of response are generally also available to the plaintiff in relation to pleadings filed by the defendant.[1]

One such way is to apply to have an irregular step set aside in accordance with rule 60A.[2] Alternatively, an exception may be raised on the basis that the pleading is vague and embarrassing or lacks averments necessary to sustain a cause of

---

[1] Not all of the options mentioned below are limited to the defendant. Indeed, the plaintiff may also apply to set aside an irregular step, raise an exception or bring an application to strike out. A special plea, however, is only available to a defendant.

[2] Rules 5(11), 6(13) and 17(6). Rule 60A's equivalent in the High Court Rules is rule 30. The subrule is identical to High Court rule 30.

action or a defence. Alternatively, the plaintiff or defendant can apply to strike out content from a pleading that is scandalous, vexatious or irrelevant.[3]

The defendant can also substantively aver that the plaintiff ought not to succeed on the merits of his or her case. Here, the defendant joins issue with the plaintiff on the merits and defends himself or herself against the averments made by the plaintiff. The procedure employed by the defendant if he or she wishes to defend the matter on the merits is to file a plea.

This chapter will consider the various responses referred to above other than a plea on the merits.[4]

2 SETTING ASIDE AN IRREGULAR STEP

An irregular step is a step which advances the proceedings one stage nearer to completion.[5] The defendant may apply to court to have the irregular step set aside as envisaged by rule 60A. Of particular importance in this regard are the rules regulating summonses[6] and pleadings.[7] Non-compliance with these rules may give rise to such an application.[8] Rule 60A mostly applies to irregularities of form, not substance.[9] Examples of irregular steps include improper service of a summons,[10] where the address for service was not set out in the summons,[11] and where pleadings were not properly signed or are otherwise non-compliant with the rules as to form.[12]

The application to have the summons set aside as an irregular step must be on notice, specifying the particulars of the irregularity.[13] However, an affidavit is not required. All that is required is that the defendant or applicant may not have taken a further step with knowledge of the irregularity.[14] The defendant must, within 10 days of becoming aware of the irregularity, afford the plaintiff written opportunity to remove the cause of complaint within 10 days.[15] Furthermore, the application

---

[3] Exceptions and applications to strike out are regulated by rule 19.

[4] The defence on the merits of the claim is dealt with in chapter 14.

[5] *Cyril Smiedt (Pty) Ltd v Lourens* 1966 (1) SA 150 (O) at 152E; *Market Dynamics (Pty) Ltd t/a Brian Ferris v Grögor* 1984 (1) SA 152 (W) at 153C; *Henred Fruehauf (Pty) Limited t/a Henred Fruehauf Trailers & another v Els: In re: Els v Henred Fruehauf (Pty) Limited t/a Henred Fruehauf Trailers & another* 2015 JOL 33567 (GP) at 4.

[6] Rule 5.

[7] Rule 6 regulates pleadings generally and rule 17 relates to the defendant's plea.

[8] Rules 5(11), 6(13) and 17(6).

[9] *Singh v Vorkel* 1947 (3) SA 400 (C) at 406; *Odendaal v De Jager* 1961 (4) SA 307 (O) at 310F–G; *Nyaniso v Head of the Department of Sports, Recreation, Arts and Culture, Eastern Cape Province & another* [2016] ZAECBHC 8 (27 September 2016) para 11.

[10] *SA Instrumentation (Pty) Ltd v Smithchem (Pty) Ltd* 1977 (3) SA 703 (D).

[11] *Minister of Prisons & another v Jongilanga* 1983 (3) SA 47 (E); 1985 (3) SA 117 (A).

[12] See *Suliman v Karodia* 1926 WLD 102; *Union & SWA Salt Snoek Corporation (Pty) Ltd v Lancashire Agencies* 1959 (2) SA 52 (N); *Bredenkamp v Dart* 1960 (3) SA 106 (O). See also rules 5(11), 6(13) and 17(6).

[13] Rule 60A(2).

[14] Rule 60A(2)(*a*).

[15] Rule 60A(2)(*b*).

must be delivered within 15 days of expiry of the 10-day period mentioned above.[16]

A further step is one that advances the proceedings one stage nearer to completion[17] which, objectively viewed, evidences an intention to pursue the claim or defence despite the irregularity.[18] It does not include the delivery of the defendant's notice of intention to defend.

At the hearing of the application the court can set aside the irregular step in whole or in part[19] and grant leave to amend or make any such order as the court deems fit.[20] No further step may be taken until the party has complied with the court order, except to apply for an extension of time within which to comply with such order.[21]

In order to succeed with an application to set aside an irregular step, the party who applies to have it set aside must show that he or she will be substantially prejudiced should the litigation continue without the step being set aside.[22] A court has a discretion whether or not to grant the application even if the irregularity is established.[23]

3 THE EXCEPTION

3.1 The purpose of the exception

The exception is used in order to object to any pleading.[24] An exception cannot therefore be taken against a simple summons as it is not a pleading, as opposed to a combined summons. The objection relates to an inherent defect in the pleading. The key consideration is, assuming that all the allegations in the particulars of claim, declaration or plea are true, whether the pleading nevertheless fails to disclose a cause of action or defence or is vague and embarrassing.[25] If so, then an exception can be raised by the excipient and the pleading is regarded as being excipiable.

The exception procedure is used because it is unfair to the plaintiff or defendant to allow the entire trial procedure to run its course up to and including the trial

---

[16] Rule 60A(2)*(c)*.

[17] *Market Dynamics (Pty) Ltd t/a Brian Ferris v Grögor* 1984 (1) SA 152 (W) at 153C.

[18] *Jowell v Bramwell-Jones & others* 1998 (1) SA 836 (W) at 904.

[19] *Sasol Industries (Pty) Ltd t/a Sasol 1 v Electrical Repair Engineering (Pty) Ltd t/a L H Marthinusen* 1992 (4) SA 466 (W).

[20] Rule 60A(3).

[21] Rule 60A(4).

[22] *Uitenhage Municipality v Uys* 1974 (3) SA 800 (E) at 805D–E; *Pinro Building & Steel Merchants (Edms) Bpk v Yawa* [2003] 1 All SA 318 (C); *Concrete 2000 (Pty) Ltd v Lorenzo Builders CC t/a Creative Designs & others* [2014] 2 All SA 81 (KZD) at 36–37.

[23] *Northern Assurance Co Ltd v Somdaka* 1960 (1) SA 588 (A) at 595B.

[24] Rule 19(1).

[25] *Champion v J D Celliers & Co Ltd* 1904 TS 788 at 790–1; *Wellington Court Shareblock v Johannesburg City Council; Agar Properties (Pty) Ltd v Johannesburg City Council* 1995 (3) SA 827 (A) at 833F and 834D; *TWK Agriculture Ltd v NCT Forestry Co-operative Ltd & others* 2006 (6) SA 20 (N) at 23B–C.

stage if the plaintiff or defendant is prejudiced in his or her claim or defence by a defective pleading.[26]

For example, where the particulars of claim disclose no cause of action or the plea discloses no defence or answer to the plaintiff's claim, the exception procedure provides a cheap and quick way of settling a dispute, thus obviating the need for the lengthy, protracted and expensive procedure of a full trial.[27]

3.2 The bases upon which exception may be taken

According to the rules of court, the only exceptions that may be taken by a defendant against any pleading are the following:[28]

(1) where the pleading lacks averments which are necessary to sustain an action or defence; or

(2) where the pleading is vague and embarrassing.

The bases of exception set out above are the only grounds upon which an exception may be taken. The excipient is restricted to the exception taken by him or her. He or she may not raise any exception other than the one set out in the notice of exception.[29] Where, for example, exception is taken on the basis that the pleading does not disclose a cause of action, the court will not uphold the exception on the basis that the pleading is also vague and embarrassing. Likewise, in the case where exception is taken on the basis that the pleading is vague and embarrassing, the defendant may not at the hearing of this exception aver that the pleading does not comply with the formal rules governing pleadings.[30]

The abovementioned bases of exception are discussed in greater detail below.

3.2.1 *The pleading does not disclose a cause of action*

The expression 'cause of action' means 'every fact which is material to be proved in order to entitle a plaintiff to succeed'.[31] While reference is made in this quotation to 'every fact which is material to be proved', it is clear that the summons will disclose a cause of action as long as the *facta probanda* (the facts in dispute or the facts that have to be proved) are set out in the summons. It is not necessary to set out the *facta probantia* (the facts that relate to the facts in dispute and that are used to prove the facts in dispute) as well.

To give an example: where a plaintiff summonses the defendant on the basis of damage sustained by him or her in a motor collision caused by the alleged negligence of the defendant, the facts that the plaintiff must allege in order to disclose a cause of action are:

---

[26] See, for example, *Alphina Investments Ltd & another v Blacher* 2008 (5) SA 479 (C) at 483B; *Inzalo Communications & Event Management (Pty) Ltd v Economic Value Accelerators (Pty) Ltd* 2008 (6) SA 87 (W) at 101C–D.

[27] *Kahn v Stuart & others* 1942 CPD 386.

[28] Rule 19(1) and (2).

[29] *Feldman NO v EMI Music SA (Pty) Ltd; Feldman NO v EMI Music Publishing SA (Pty) Ltd* 2010 (1) SA 1 (SCA) at 5A; *Cotas v Williams & another* 1947 (2) SA 1154 (T); *Wicksteed & others v George* 1961 (1) SA 651 (FC).

[30] *Scheepers v Krog* 1925 CPD 9; *Jack Smith v Joe's (Pty) Ltd* 1929 TPD 323; *Kock v Zeeman* 1943 OPD 135 at 139; *Ritchie Motors v Moolman* 1956 (4) SA 337 (T).

[31] *McKenzie v Farmers' Co-operative Meat Industries Ltd* 1922 AD 16.

(1)   that he or she has suffered harm;
(2)   as a result of a collision with a vehicle driven by the defendant; and
(3)   that this collision was caused by the negligence of the defendant.

If the plaintiff does not state in the particulars of claim where or on what date the collision occurred, the omission of this information will not mean that a cause of action is lacking.

It is thus important in every case in which the defendant contemplates taking exception to analyse the elements of the cause of action in order to determine whether a basis has been established for the claim:[32]

'It does not seem to me that the Rules of the Magistrates' Courts . . . have gone so far as to relieve him [sc the plaintiff] from setting . . . out [the particulars of claim] in such a way that, when read by itself, it leads to the necessary conclusion that, if the allegations in it are established, the defendant is liable to the plaintiff, at least in principle.'[33]

This exception may also be taken where the pleadings contain more than one claim. In such a case exception may be taken to any of the claims.[34]

It may happen that the pleading has been drafted in such a way that it is susceptible of two or more differing interpretations. If any of these interpretations discloses a cause of action or defence, however, exception may not be taken on the basis that it fails to disclose a cause of action or defence. It may nevertheless be possible in such a case to take exception on the basis that the pleading is vague and embarrassing.

Where the pleadings filed up to the date of the exception contain sufficient allegations to persuade a court to dismiss the plaintiff's claim or to uphold the defendant's defence should all of the allegations made by the plaintiff be deemed correct,[35] exception *must* be taken. Should a party in such a case fail to do so, this results in the matter being unnecessarily delayed. In that event, the failure to take exception may be penalised by an adverse order of costs.[36] On the other hand, one must guard against undue haste in taking exception if it is doubtful that the exception will be upheld.[37]

Where a plaintiff relies on a contract that is partly oral and partly written and he or she refers in the particulars of claim only to the written portion of the contract (in other words, the necessary averments relating to the oral portion of the

---

[32] See in general in regard to *facta probanda* and *facta probantia*, *Dusheiko v Milburn* 1964 (4) SA 648 (A); *Herholdt v Rand Debt Collecting Co* 1965 (3) SA 752 (T). See also *Alphedie Investments (Pty) Ltd v Greentops (Pty) Ltd* 1975 (1) SA 161 (T). See above at pp 26–27.

[33] *Nees & Korving v Louters* 1950 (4) SA 300 (N) at 302G–H.

[34] *Kennedy v Steenkamp* 1936 CPD 113 at 115; *Amalgamated Footwear & Leather Industries v Jordan & Co Ltd* 1948 (2) SA 891 (C).

[35] *Fineberg v Horwitz* 1950 (3) SA 371 (T) at 372B–C: '[O]n the facts you allege, you have no case.'

[36] *Myers v Shraga* 1947 (2) SA 258 (T); *Scheepers v Vermeulen* 1948 (4) SA 884 (O); *Laingsburg Afdelingsraad v Luyt* 1959 (3) SA 679 (C).

[37] *Colonial Industries Ltd v Provincial Insurance Co Ltd* 1920 CPD 627 at 630; *City of Cape Town v National Meat Suppliers Ltd* 1938 CPD 59 at 63 and 64; *International Tobacco Co of SA Ltd v Wollheim & others* 1953 (2) SA 603 (A).

agreement have not been made), the particulars of claim will be excipiable if the written part of the agreement does not by itself disclose a cause of action.[38]

3.2.2 *The pleading is vague and embarrassing*

A pleading is vague and embarrassing if it is set out in such a way that the opposing party is prejudiced because he or she does not know precisely what case he or she is required to meet.[39] It does not speak to a single sentence or paragraph—the entire cause of action must be shown to be vague and embarrassing.[40] To determine whether the pleading is excipiable, the following test is applied: one must enquire whether it contains sufficient particularity to enable the opposing party to identify the case against him or her and to respond thereto.[41]

In this case, too, the rule applies that exception ought to be taken only where the pleading is substantially vague and embarrassing—and not in cases in which the pleading has merely been badly formulated. Where a particulars of claim therefore contains merely the averment that the plaintiff claims on the basis of work done and materials supplied, it is not necessarily vague and embarrassing on account of the fact that not all of the terms of the contract between the parties are set out. The mere fact that a particular defendant is summonsed for work done and materials supplied indicates that the plaintiff holds him or her (and no one else) liable for the cost of the materials and the work.[42]

Where exception is taken on the basis that a pleading is vague and embarrassing, it is furthermore important to bear in mind that the court will not uphold this exception unless the excipient has first given the opposing party the opportunity to remove the cause of complaint.[43] Rule 19(1) provides that the opposing party be provided 15 days' opportunity to remove the cause of complaint. The excipient may within 10 days from the date on which a reply to the aforementioned notice is received or from the date on which it is due, deliver the actual exception. In the case of an exception on the basis that a pleading fails to disclose a cause of action or defence, no such initial opportunity to remove the cause of complaint should be given—an exception may immediately be taken. Where an exception is taken, it is not necessary to file a plea, replication or any other pleading as the case may be.[44]

---

[38] *Du Pisanie v Van Rensburg* 1950 (2) SA 124 (E).

[39] *Scheepers v Krog* 1925 CPD 9; *Visser v Van der Merwe* 1925 CPD 373.

[40] *Venter & others NNO v Barritt Venter & others NNO v Wolfsberg Arch Investments 2 (Pty) Ltd* 2008 (4) SA 639 (C) at 644G–645B.

[41] *Cilliers v Van Biljon* 1925 OPD 4; *Quin v Oelofse & another* 1926 TPD 336; *Van Bassen v Retief* 1928 TPD 758 at 760.

[42] *Beaufort Furniture & Joinery Manufacturing Co (Pty) Ltd v De Vos* 1950 (1) SA 112 (C).

[43] Rule 19(1); *Viljoen v Federated Trust Ltd* 1971 (1) SA 750 (O); *Operative Furnishing Co (Pty) Ltd v Dragon Gas Services (Pty) Ltd* 1965 (4) SA 5 (E); *Chapman v Proclad (Pty) Ltd* 1978 (2) SA 336 (NC); *NKP Kunsmisverspreiders (Edms) Bpk v Sentrale Kunsmis Korporasie (Edms) Bpk en 'n ander* 1973 (2) SA 680 (T); *Crawford-Brunt v Kavnat & another* 1967 (4) SA 308 (C); *MN v AJ* 2013 (3) SA 26 (WCC).

[44] Rule 19(4).

3.3 How exception is taken

As mentioned, before an exception may be filed on the basis that a pleading is vague and embarrassing, a notice must first be delivered in terms of which the opposing party is afforded an opportunity to remove the cause(s) of complaint.[45] An example of such a notice follows:

---

* For use in the District Court

In the Magistrate's Court for the District of ....

held at ....

Case No .... of 20 ....

In the matter between

.... Plaintiff

and

.... Defendant

NOTICE IN TERMS OF RULE 19(1)

TAKE NOTICE THAT the Defendant excepts against the Plaintiff's Particulars of Claim because they are vague and embarrassing for the following reasons:

(a)   ...

(b)   ...

(c)   ...

TAKE FURTHER NOTICE that, unless the cause of complaint is removed within 15 days from receipt of this notice, the Defendant will approach the abovementioned Honourable Court and raise an exception against the Plaintiff's Particulars of Claim.

Dated on this .... day of .... 20.........

....

Defendant's Attorney

Address: ....

To: The Clerk of the Court

....

And to: Plaintiff's Attorney

Address ....

The excipient may take exception against the pleading within 10 days from the date on which a reply to such notice was received or from the date upon which such reply was due but has not yet been received.[46] In other words, exception may only be taken on the grounds of vagueness and embarrassment where there was a reply but the cause of complaint has not been removed or where no reply to the rule 19(1) notice has been received. The example below illustrates what the exception following on the rule 19(1) notice would look like:

---

[45] Rule 19(1). This notice is commonly referred to as a rule 19(1) notice.
[46] Rule 19(1).

---

* For use in the District Court

In the Magistrate's Court for the District of ....

held at ....

                                  Case No .... of 20 ....

In the matter between

               .... Plaintiff

                             and

               .... Defendant

NOTICE OF EXCEPTION

TAKE NOTICE THAT the Defendant having given the Plaintiff the opportunity to remove the cause of complaint rendering his/her Particulars of Claim vague and embarrassing by a notice in terms of rule 19(1) served on the Plaintiff on (insert date), hereby excepts to the Plaintiff's Particulars of Claim on the grounds set out in the aforementioned notice.

WHEREFORE the Defendant prays that the Plaintiff's claim be dismissed with costs.

Dated on this .... day of .... 20.........

                                 ....

                                 Defendant's Attorney

                                 Address: ....

To: The Clerk of the Court

....

And to: Plaintiff's Attorney

                                 Address ....

An exception clearly and concisely states the grounds upon which the exception is based.[47] A reference in the exception filed on the basis of a pleading being vague and embarrassing to the notice in terms of rule 19(1) and the grounds set out in such notice is generally sufficient.

An example of an exception filed on the basis that a pleading fails to disclose a cause of action is as follows:

---

* For use in the District Court

In the Magistrate's Court for the District of ....

held at ....

                                    Case No .... of 20 ....

In the matter between

               .... Plaintiff

                             and

               .... Defendant

NOTICE OF EXCEPTION

TAKE NOTICE THAT the Defendant hereby notes exception to the Plaintiff's particulars of claim on the basis that it fails to disclose a cause of action.

    The grounds upon which the Defendant excepts are:

(a)   no averment has been made that ....;

---

[47] Rule 19(3). *Alphina Investments Ltd & another v Blacher* 2008 (5) SA 479 (C) at 483D and 488G–I.

(b) *ex facie* the Plaintiff's averments it does not appear that the Defendant is liable to him/her.

WHEREFORE the Defendant prays that the Plaintiff's claim be dismissed with costs.

Dated on this .... day of .... 20.........

....
DEFENDANT'S ATTORNEY
Address: ....

To: The Clerk of the Court

....

And to: Plaintiff's Attorney
Address ....

At the end of the notice of exception appears a prayer asking that the exception be upheld with costs, or, as is more common, that the plaintiff's claim, for example, be dismissed with costs. The rule that a prayer should appear is a logical consequence of the nature of the exception as a request to the court to put a speedy end to the matter. Without this prayer at the end of the notice of exception, the exception is nothing more than a notice advising that the party objects to the pleading, and it is not a request to the court to uphold this objection and to dismiss the plaintiff's claim or defendant's defence with costs.[48]

An exception may not normally be raised orally during the trial, for it would be out of time. If a defect in the pleading is noticed only at the trial, the proper procedure is for the defendant to apply for absolution from the instance.[49] The court has, however, in the past allowed an exception to be taken informally by a party during the trial provided that his or her opponent agrees to the adoption of this unusual procedure.

3.4 The hearing of the exception

The exception must be enrolled for hearing as an application on the opposed roll. The excipient should apply to the registrar or clerk of the court for a hearing date within five days of delivery of the notice of exception.[50]

No evidence may be given at the hearing of the exception in so far as the fault that gives rise to the exception must be apparent *ex facie* the pleading.[51]

In cases in which the defendant has failed to take exception and the plaintiff applies for summary judgment on the basis of the (excipiable) particulars of claim, the court has a discretion to grant summary judgment in spite of the fact that the particulars of claim is defective.[52]

---

[48] *Bothma v Laubscher* 1973 (3) SA 590 (O).

[49] *Moodley v Bondcrete (Pty) Ltd & others* 1969 (2) SA 370 (N) at 374C–H.

[50] Rule 19(1) read with rule 55(1)(*j*).

[51] *Muller v Cook & others* 1973 (2) SA 247 (N). Regarding the court's ability to defer consideration of the exception to trial, see *Minerals & Quarries (Pty) Ltd v Henckert en 'n ander* 1967 (4) SA 77 (SWA) at 84A and *Versluis v Greenblatt* 1973 (2) SA 271 (NC) at 278A–C.

[52] *Car Bargains v Nhlanhla* 1971 (1) SA 214 (T), especially at 217C–D. The court will not grant judgment if no cause of action is disclosed but may grant judgment if the pleading is merely inelegantly set out and a cause of action may be gleaned from it.

The onus rests on the excipient to show that the pleading discloses no cause of action or defence on any construction that may be given to the averments contained in it.[53] The excipient must prove not only the grounds of exception but must also show that he or she will be prejudiced if the court does not uphold the exception.[54]

In *Ash v Venketsamy*[55] De Wet J said:

'I do not in any way wish to encourage practitioners to fall into the habit of being careless in drafting pleadings in the magistrate's court. At the same time practitioners should not resort to exceptions when there is no real prejudice. A careless pleading could always be penalised by an appropriate order as to costs.'

The High Court will not lightly interfere with the finding of a magistrate that an excipient is potentially prejudiced.[56]

Where the pleading discloses no cause of action or defence, it will readily be accepted that prejudice exists. If the plaintiff omits a salient averment from his or her particulars of claim, it may be argued that he or she thereby places the burden on the defendant of making that averment in his or her defence and proving it. If the plaintiff had made the necessary averment in his or her particulars, then he or she would have borne the onus of proving it. In this sense the defendant is thus prejudiced if the plaintiff fails to make an essential averment in his or her particulars in order to disclose a cause of action.[57]

The exception indicates that the pleadings are not in order. When the hearing of the exception takes place, therefore, argument is heard on the excipiable pleadings themselves and no evidence is led.[58]

3.5 The effect of the upholding of an exception

If an exception is dismissed, the excipient will have to file a pleading within the normal period allowed.

The usual prayer at the end of the notice of exception is usually as follows: 'Wherefore it is prayed that the exception be upheld with costs and that the [state

---

[53] *Amalgamated Footwear & Leather Industries v Jordan & Co Ltd* 1948 (2) SA 891 (C); *Kennedy v Steenkamp* 1936 CPD 113 at 115.

[54] See in general the well-known statement of Davis J in *Van Eck Bros v Van der Merwe* 1940 CPD 357 at 360: 'The cases show this, I think, clearly, that the use of the weapon of an exception in the magistrate's court is not one which the Court will encourage, and a defendant should not except to a summons unless it is really necessary for him to do so, because a defect in the summons so affects the root of the action that he cannot see from the summons what case he has to meet. In other words, he can use an exception when it really is a genuine defence on his part against vital embarrassment, but he cannot use it as in any way a means of embarrassing a plaintiff, or, shall we say, as a counter-vexation because he feels that the plaintiff has vexed him.' See also *Levitan v Newhaven Holiday Enterprises CC* 1991 (2) SA 297 (C) at 298A; *Living Hands (Pty) Ltd & another v Ditz & others* 2013 (2) SA 368 (GSJ) at 394D–E; *Gallagher Group Ltd & another v IO Tech Manufacturing (Pty) Ltd & others* 2014 (2) SA 157 (GNP) at 166G–H.

[55] 1949 (2) SA 617 (N) at 620.

[56] *Britz v Weideman* 1946 OPD 144 at 153; *Gordon v Pokroy* 1964 (2) SA 338 (T) at 340G.

[57] *Andrews v Pillay* 1954 (2) SA 136 (N) at 137G–H; *Gordon v Pokroy* (supra) at 340.

[58] If, for example, there is a dispute between the parties as to whether a certain condition within a contract is resolutive or suspensive and it is possible that oral evidence will have to be led, it is wrong to use the exception procedure: *Naidu v Naidoo* 1967 (2) SA 223 (N) at 227.

party and pleading] be set aside.' In reality, the proper order that the court should make is that the relevant pleading is set aside and that the party whose pleading is set aside may have leave to amend it.[59] Accordingly, the effect of the upholding of an exception does not mean that the claim or defence is dismissed in its entirety. Often a party will not be able to so amend the pleading because the supporting facts required simply do not exist. But it may happen that the party can amend the pleading so as to remove the cause of complaint. Only if the party against whom the exception was taken cannot amend, or fails to amend, does the granting of an exception amount to a final judgment in the defendant's favour.

Should the court uphold the exception and the party does want to amend the pleading, the latter party should apply immediately for leave to amend. Failure to do so will lead to a final judgment.

3.6　The difference between the exception and the special plea

It is necessary to take note of the difference between the exception and the special plea. These two legal procedures are sometimes confused.

The exception differs from the special plea in the following three respects:

(1)　The basis of the exception must appear *ex facie* the pleading to which exception is taken. The exception rests upon a legal argument and no new facts apart from those mentioned in the pleadings may be placed before the court on exception. For purposes of the decision on the exception it is assumed that the facts mentioned in the pleading are true. It must then be decided only whether those facts disclose a cause of action (or a defence).[60] Alternatively, a decision must be made whether the averments are excipiable on the basis that they are vague and embarrassing. In the case of a special plea, it does not appear (without further explanatory averments) from the particulars of claim that a special plea may be raised to the particulars of claim. The basis of the special defence does not appear from the pleading against which the defence is raised.

　　The defence of *res judicata*, for example, may not be raised by way of exception but should be raised by way of a special plea, since evidence will have to be led regarding the previous action. The defence that a matter is *res judicata* does not entail a legal argument; it is a factual matter, viz whether or not the claim has been adjudicated upon by a competent court at an earlier stage.[61] Likewise, the defence of *lis alibi pendens* must be raised by way of special plea and not by way of exception. It has been said that the principal difference between the exception and the special plea is the fact that evidence may not be led in the case of the former, while it may be led in the case of the latter.[62]

---

[59] *Group Five Building Ltd v Government of the RSA* 1993 (2) SA 593 (A).

[60] *Fineberg v Horwitz* 1950 (3) SA 371 (T) at 372B–C: '[O]n the facts you allege, you have no case.'

[61] *Hatfield Town Management Board v Mynfred Poultry Farm (Pvt) Ltd* 1963 (1) SA 737 (SR).

[62] *Muller v Cook & others* 1973 (2) SA 247 (N).

(2) The exception is taken to a pleading as a whole and not to a portion of the pleading unless such portion makes out a separate cause of action or defence.[63] The special plea is a defence to the *averments* made in a pleading.

(3) The exception may be raised by the plaintiff as well as by the defendant, while a special defence may be raised only by a defendant.

(4) A notice of exception is a pleading,[64] whereas a special plea is not in itself a pleading but merely a special defence adduced in the plea. No provision is made in the magistrates' courts' rules for a pleading known as a special plea.

The special plea is pleaded as a preliminary point in the defendant's plea, and the defendant thereafter usually 'pleads over' by answering each of the averments made in the particulars of claim.[65]

A special plea would read as follows:

---

* For use in the District Court

In the Magistrate's Court for the District of ....

held at ....

Case No .... of 20.........

In the matter between

.... Plaintiff

and

.... Defendant

PLEA

Special Plea

The Defendant pleads that

(1) the Plaintiff's claim arose on ....

(2) the summons was served on the Defendant in ....

(3) in the premises, ... in terms of section .... of the Prescription Act 68 of 1969 the claim has prescribed.

WHEREFORE the Defendant prays that the Plaintiff's claim be dismissed with costs.

ALTERNATIVELY the Defendant pleads as follows to the Plaintiff's particulars of claim:

(1) *Ad par* 1 ....

etc

Dated on this .... day of .... 20............

....

DEFENDANT'S ATTORNEY

Address: ....

To: The Clerk of the Court

....

And to: Plaintiff's Attorney

Address ....

---

[63] *Commissioner of Customs v Airton Timber Co Ltd* 1926 AD 1 at 4; *Millward v Glaser* 1949 (4) SA 931 (A) at 937.

[64] *Minerals & Quarries (Pty) Ltd v Henckert en 'n ander* 1967 (4) SA 77 (SWA).

[65] Rule 19(4) provides that it is not necessary to plead over.

4 THE APPLICATION TO STRIKE OUT

4.1 The difference between the application to strike out and the exception

The purpose of the application to strike out differs from the purpose of the exception. The exception is used in order to note an objection to the pleading as a whole, while the application to strike out is used in order to raise an objection to certain portions of a pleading.[66]

4.2 The bases of the application to strike out

The bases for the application to strike out are set out in rule 19(2). The rule reads as follows:

> 'Where any pleading contains averments which are scandalous, vexatious, or irrelevant, the opposite party may, within the period allowed for filing any subsequent pleading, apply for the striking out of the matter aforesaid, and may set such application down for hearing in terms of rule 55(1)(*j*), but the court shall not grant the same unless it is satisfied that the applicant will be prejudiced in the conduct of his or her claim or defence if it be not granted.'

These grounds are examined in greater detail below.

4.2.1 *The claims are mutually inconsistent and have not been made in the alternative*

The following may be given as an example of mutually inconsistent claims: the plaintiff claims, first, the balance of the purchase price due in terms of a contract of sale and, secondly, return of the item sold on the basis that the contract is void. These claims must be made in the alternative. If they are not, then they are mutually inconsistent in view of the fact that a plaintiff may not claim the outstanding balance of the purchase price together with the return of the thing sold on the basis that the contract is void.

A further example is that of a plaintiff who claims, first, rental in respect of property let and, secondly, the eviction of the lessee on the basis of unlawful occupation. These claims are likewise mutually inconsistent if they are not made in the alternative. In both of these cases application may be made to strike out one of the claims.

---

[66] '[B]ut there is a clear distinction between the two proceedings [the exception and the application to strike out]. An exception goes to the root of a particular claim or defence contained in a pleading whereas an application to strike out attacks individual paragraphs in a pleading which do not comprise an entire claim or defence' (*Suid-Afrikaanse Sentrale Ko-operatiewe Graanmaatskappy Bpk v Shifren & others & the Taxing Master* 1964 (1) SA 162 (O) at 167C–D). Cf also *Salzmann v Holmes* 1914 AD 152, especially at 156, where Innes JA (as he then was) said the following: 'The distinction between an exception and an application to strike out is clear. An exception goes to the root of the entire claim or defence, as the case may be. The excipient alleges that the pleading objected to, taken as it stands, is legally invalid for its purpose. Whereas individual sections, which do not comprise an entire claim or defence, but are only portion of one, must, if objected to, be attacked by a motion to expunge.'

4.2.2 *The pleading contains scandalous, vexatious or irrelevant averments*

The terms 'scandalous', 'vexatious' and 'irrelevant' are grouped together.[67] Although they are specified separately in rule 19(2), they would appear to be tautologous. In any event, it is not clear what the practical value of distinguishing between them would be. The idea behind them is that the pleading should set out only the facts which form the basis of the claim or the defence. The pleading may not contain arguments and reasoning: only the salient averments may appear in it.

Irrelevant averments in the pleading ought to be struck out. In order to determine whether an averment is relevant, one must ask whether the averment is necessary in order to raise a disputed issue. It is the task of the court to adjudicate upon issues in dispute between the parties and when an averment does not contribute to the raising of an issue in dispute or assist in circumscribing the area of dispute, that averment is irrelevant.

In *Bosman v Van Vuuren & another*[68] Bristowe J was called upon to decide upon the meaning of rule 35 of the High Court Rules of that time, which provided that an 'argumentative or irrelevant or superfluous matter' could be struck out. At 832 he said:

> 'The rule [rule 35] is merely a rule of pleading, and I think it was only intended to apply to matter which is argumentative, irrelevant or superfluous from the point of pleading, that is having regard to the issues intended to be raised. If the matter complained of is relevant to an issue in the action, I cannot see how it can be said to be either irrelevant or superfluous. To say that it is irrelevant or superfluous because it raises a question which will have to be decided adversely at the trial would be to elevate [r]ule 35 from a mere rule of pleading to a rule providing for the determination of preliminary points of law.'

On the same page the judge refers to the earlier decision in *Champion v J D Celliers & Co Ltd*[69] and says: 'The learned Judge therefore applied the test which appears to me to be the correct one, namely, whether the matter objected to is or is not relevant to an issue in the action.'[70]

It has been said that the rule that no averments may be made which do not contribute to the delineation of the area of dispute is the same as the rule that evidence may not be pleaded.[71] Although any averments which form part of the evidence and set out the background to the case that has been made out on the pleadings may be led at the trial, it does not follow that they constitute a necessary

---

[67] Regarding the meaning of these terms, see *Vaatz v Law Society of Namibia* 1991 (3) SA 563 (NM) at 566C–E; *Tshabalala-Msimang & another v Makhanya & others* [2008] 1 All SA 509 (W) at 516e–f; *Breedenkamp & others v Standard Bank of South Africa Ltd & another* 2009 (5) SA 304 (GSJ) at 321C–E.

[68] 1911 TPD 825.

[69] 1904 TS 788.

[70] The statement made in *Botha v Botha* 1921 TPD 387 at 390 that 'relevant' is defined as any fact which may be led in evidence at the trial is clearly too wide. In *Stephens v De Wet* 1920 AD 279 at 282 the exposition of Bristowe J was accepted as authoritative. See also *Geyser & another v Geyser* 1926 TPD 590; *Edwards v African Guarantee & Indemnity Co Ltd* 1952 (4) SA 335 (O); *Katz v Saffer & Saffer* 1944 WLD 124.

[71] *Wells v Wells* 1952 (4) SA 586 (W).

part of the pleadings. The purpose of pleadings is only to outline clearly the issues in dispute.

In order to determine whether certain averments are relevant to the issues in dispute, the pleadings must be viewed as a whole.[72]

4.2.3 *The pleading contains contradictory matter*

An application may be brought to strike out averments which contain contradictory matter. In this case, the application to strike out is brought not in relation to inconsistent claims but against averments contained in the pleading itself that are mutually contradictory.

There can be no objection to a party's making two sets of contradictory factual averments in a pleading, provided that they are clearly made in the alternative. It would, however, expose a pleading to an application to strike out should a particular fact be denied and the same fact thereafter be admitted without the admission being made in the alternative.

4.3 How application is made to strike out

An example of an application to strike out reads as follows:

---

* For use in the District Court

In the Magistrate's Court for the District of ....

held at ....

Case No .... of 20.......

In the matter between

.... Plaintiff

and

.... Defendant

NOTICE OF APPLICATION TO STRIKE OUT

TAKE NOTICE that the Defendant hereby makes application to the above Honourable Court for the striking out with costs from the Plaintiff's particulars of claim of the matter set out below, on the basis that the aforesaid matter is scandalous, vexatious or irrelevant:

1. Paragraph 4 from the words 'and the Plaintiff ....' up to and including the words 'duty to act'.

etc

Dated on this .... day of .... 20....

....
DEFENDANT'S ATTORNEY
Address: ....

To: The Clerk of the Court

....

And to: Plaintiff's Attorney

Address ....

---

[72] *Union Government v Imperial Cold Storage & Supply Co Ltd* 1934 AD 193.

OFFER OR TENDER TO SETTLE

1 GENERAL

When a defendant is summonsed, he or she may decide to try to settle the case before it comes to trial. There are various ways in which he or she may try to do this.

It is possible to settle a dispute prior to or after the institution of litigation, but before judgment is given, at common law.[1] This means that the defendant enters into negotiations with the plaintiff and they come to a compromise by way of agreement. The matter is then settled. Settlement at common law entails the application of the usual contractual principles of offer and acceptance. The settlement agreement creates a new legal relationship between the parties which replaces the previous legal relationship that could have led or did lead to the institution of the action. If, after a settlement is reached, the plaintiff proceeds with the original action, the defendant will be able to plead successfully that the case has been settled.

In case the plaintiff is not prepared to negotiate a settlement with the defendant, however, the rules of court make provision for procedures in accordance with which the defendant may nevertheless attempt to reach a settlement. This procedure essentially entails:
(1) an unconditional offer or tender; and
(2) an offer or tender without prejudice to the rights of the party making the offer or tender.[2]

The unconditional offer or tender is a relatively simple procedure in which the defendant unconditionally offers to pay the amount or unconditionally tenders the performance of an act in an attempt to dispose of the matter and thereby save additional legal costs.[3]

---

[1] It is also possible to do so after litigation has been initiated, but it is usually made before litigation commences as the rules of court, specifically rule 18, is not applicable at that stage.

[2] Rule 18 regulates offers to settle in the magistrates' courts. It basically replicates rule 34 of the High Court Rules. These rules do not preclude common-law tender. The practice of actual payment into court in terms of the former rule 18 was abolished in 2010.

[3] *Van Rensburg v AA Mutual Insurance Co Ltd* 1969 (4) SA 360 (E); *South African Eagle Insurance Co Ltd v Serebro* 1985 (4) SA 50 (W).

The without-prejudice offer or tender is a procedure which obliges the plaintiff to reassess whether he or she wishes to persist in the original claim or whether he or she intends to accept the offer of payment or the performance of the act so tendered. The consequence of an offer or tender made without prejudice is to place the plaintiff in a position where he or she, upon rejecting it, will run the risk of liability for costs subsequently incurred, unless the plaintiff can prove liability in excess of the sum tendered.[4]

2 UNCONDITIONAL OFFER OR TENDER

This procedure is used when the defendant decides to throw in the towel and to satisfy the claim made by the plaintiff. It differs from a consent to judgment in that the claim is settled prior to judgment and the defendant will therefore avoid judgment being taken against him or her. The defendant's name will therefore not appear on lists of judgment debtors circulated amongst the business community. The defendant will also save the costs of judgment.

The unconditional offer or tender takes place in terms of rule 18(1) and (2). At any time after the issue of summons, in a claim sounding in money, the defendant may decide to unconditionally offer to settle the full amount claimed by the plaintiff.[5] This procedure cannot be applied in cases in which the plaintiff claims the delivery of property or an order of ejectment. In these instances, the defendant, where the plaintiff claims the performance of some act by the defendant, may unconditionally tender the performance of such act.[6]

An unconditional offer or tender may not take place after consent to judgment. If a defendant should so pay or perform, all he or she would be doing would be satisfying the judgment and there would be no settlement.

A defendant who makes an unconditional offer or tender also generally makes himself or herself liable for the legal costs incurred by the plaintiff prior to the payment or performance. These include the costs of summons, court fees and sheriff's charges. Rule 18(5) states that notice of any offer or tender in terms of the rule must be given to all the parties in the action and must state, inter alia, whether the defendant disclaims liability for the payment of costs or for part thereof. If the defendant does disclaim liability for costs, he or she must provide reasons. The action may then be set down on the question of costs alone.[7] If an offer or tender has been made in terms of the rule, it may be brought to the court after judgment has been given as being relevant to the question of costs.[8]

---

[4] *Visser v Visser* 2012 (4) SA 74 (KZD) at 89B–90F.
[5] Rule 18(1).
[6] Rule 18(2).
[7] See also rule 18(5) which provides that '[i]f an offer or tender accepted in terms of this rule is not stated to be in satisfaction of a plaintiff's claim and costs, the party to whom the offer or tender is made may apply to the court, after notice of not less than 5 days, for an order for costs.'
[8] Rule 18(11).

3 PAYMENT OR PERFORMANCE WITHOUT PREJUDICE BY WAY OF AN OFFER OR TENDER OF SETTLEMENT

To take a step 'without prejudice' means to do something without admitting liability.[9] The advantage of doing this lies mainly in the final adjudication of costs. If the defendant offers payment or tenders performance without prejudice for a part of the claim, and the matter goes to trial and the defendant is found to be liable only in that or a lesser part, then the plaintiff will not be able to recover his or her costs of the trial. That there has been a without-prejudice payment is not disclosed to the court hearing the matter until after the court decides liability.[10] The parties should ensure that prior to the trial all record of the without-prejudice offer or tender is removed from the court file. Any party who discloses an offer or tender in terms of rule 18 to the magistrate or court will be liable for costs even if he or she is successful.[11] After the court has made a decision, it is then informed of the without-prejudice offer or tender in so far as it is relevant to the question of costs.[12]

A defendant therefore has a valuable weapon in a without-prejudice offer or tender by which he or she can force a plaintiff to consider whether to proceed further or to accept the without-prejudice payment and so to settle the dispute.

As with the unconditional offer of payment, this procedure is appropriate in cases in which the claim sounds in money, and it is especially appropriate in claims for damages where the quantification of the amount to be awarded is difficult and where plaintiffs regularly inflate their claims and expect the claim to be cut down by the court. The offer must be in writing and signed by the defendant or his or her attorney.[13] Notice of the offer must state that it is a without-prejudice offer, whether it is accompanied by an offer to pay some or all of the costs of the party to whom the offer is made and the conditions that it is subject to. It must also indicate whether the offer is made by way of settlement of both claim and costs and whether the defendant disclaims liability for costs, in which case reasons must be given.[14]

Where a without-prejudice tender is made, the defendant may tender to perform the act personally or through another person on his or her behalf, in which case the tender must be accompanied by the delivery to the registrar or clerk of an irrevocable power of attorney authorising the performance of the act.[15] It is submitted that a tender to perform an act would also need to be in writing.[16]

The without-prejudice offer or tender is made by the defendant in an attempt to settle the case. The plaintiff is entitled to refuse the offer or tender, and he or she does so by ignoring it. However, should the plaintiff decide to accept the offer or tender, he or she must do so within 15 days of receipt of the above written notice,

---

[9] *KLD Residential CC v Empire Earth Investments 17 (Pty) Ltd* 2017 (6) SA 55 (SCA).
[10] Rule 18(10).
[11] Rule 18(13).
[12] Rule 18(11).
[13] Rule 18(1). See also *Van der Merwe v FirstRand Bank Ltd t/a Wesbank and Barloworld Equipment Finance* 2012 (1) SA 480 (ECG) at 483D–E.
[14] Rule 18(5). This rule also applies to performance tenders as provided for in rule 18(2).
[15] Rule 18(2).
[16] Rule 18(2) read with rule 18(5).

or at a later stage if the defendant consents. The registrar or clerk must then satisfy himself or herself that the requirements of rule 18 have been complied with and, if it is a tender to perform an act, he or she must hand the power of attorney to the plaintiff or his or her attorney.[17]

If the unconditional or without-prejudice offer or tender is accepted but the defendant fails to perform within 10 days after delivery by the plaintiff of a notice of acceptance of the offer or tender, the plaintiff may, on five days' notice in writing to the defendant, apply to the registrar or clerk for judgment in accordance with the offer or tender and costs.[18]

4 PLEADING A TENDER

Rule 17(5) provides that where a tender is pleaded as to part of an amount claimed, the defendant's plea must specify the items of the plaintiff's claim to which the tender relates. Such a plea of tender is not admissible unless the amount tendered is secured to the plaintiff's satisfaction on the delivery of the plea. Such amount may only be paid to the plaintiff upon the order of the court or upon agreement in writing between the parties. The rule further states that a tender under the rule implies an undertaking to pay the plaintiff's costs up to the date of tender, unless such an undertaking is expressly 'disavowed' at the time of making the tender.

The tender in terms of rule 17(5) is different from an offer or tender to settle in terms of rule 18. Rule 17(5) relates to an admission of liability regarding a claim sounding in money. Rule 18, as mentioned, also precludes disclosure of the offer or tender before judgment is given. Rule 17(5) also does not preclude settlement at common law.

---

[17] Rule 18(6).
[18] Rule 18(7).

CHAPTER 14

THE PLEA, CLAIMS IN RECONVENTION, THE REPLY AND CLOSE OF PLEADINGS

Although each of the topics mentioned in the heading to this chapter refers to a separate step in the course of the proceedings, they are grouped together here. The reason for this is that claims in reconvention (counterclaims), the reply (answer) and the close of pleadings are usually closely connected with the plea in magistrate's court practice. According to rule 20(1)(*b*), the claim in reconvention must be delivered at the same time as the plea. The reply, if one is necessary, follows after the plea. And the close of pleadings usually takes place within a stipulated period of time after the plea or reply has been delivered.

1 THE PLEA

1.1 General

There are various ways in which a defendant may defend himself or herself against a claim. The defendant may, for example, raise an exception, file a special plea or make a settlement offer or tender. The most common way of defending a matter, however, is to raise a defence on the merits. This defence is set out in the plea. The plea contains the defendant's answer to the averments made by the plaintiff in the particulars of claim attached to the summons or in the declaration.

1.2 The time for delivery of the plea

Rule 17(1) provides that the plea must be delivered by the defendant within 20 days:
(1) after the service upon him or her of a declaration;[1] or
(2) within 20 days after delivery of such notice in respect of a combined summons.

If the plaintiff's particulars of claim or declaration is excipiable and/or susceptible to an application to strike out, the exception and/or application to strike out can be delivered within the 20-day period without the need to deliver a plea.[2]

If the defendant fails to deliver a plea, the plaintiff may serve a notice of bar upon the defendant in which the defendant is called upon to deliver his or her plea within five days.[3]

1.3 The form of the plea

The plea sets out the defence and the factual basis of that defence and must answer every material allegation made by the plaintiff.[4] The plea must be a single document.[5] It must be dated and signed by the defendant or his or her attorney.[6] The plea must be filed with the registrar or clerk of the court and a copy served upon the plaintiff.[7]

---

[1] Where a simple summons was used.
[2] Rule 19, especially rule 19(4).
[3] Rule 21B. For a discussion of the notice of bar, see above at chapter 10, para 4.1.2.
[4] Rule 17(2). See below.
[5] *Du Plessis v Doubells Transport (Edms) Bpk* 1979 (1) SA 1046 (O).
[6] Rule 6(1).
[7] See rules 3 and 9(3).

1.4 The special plea

1.4.1 *General*

The defendant may, after entry of appearance to defend, decide to attack the summons by averring some or other basis, not apparent from the plaintiff's particulars of claim or declaration, for the dismissal or temporary postponement of the plaintiff's claim.

In the rules of the magistrates' courts no provision is made for the special plea as such. Likewise, in the High Court rules no express provision is made for the special plea.[8] In practice, the defendant raises the issue pertinent to the special plea in a section of the plea entitled 'Special Plea', and the defendant then goes on to plead over by pleading to the particulars of claim or declaration averment by averment. This is made necessary by rule 17(2), which requires the defendant either 'to admit or deny or confess and avoid all the material facts alleged in the particulars to the combined summons or declaration'. Should a defendant file a special plea only and not plead to the merits, the defendant will be taken to have admitted the averments contained in the particulars or declaration and to stake his or her whole defence upon the issue raised in the special plea.[9]

1.4.2 *The nature of the special plea*

The special plea in English law is called a plea in bar or a plea *in limine*. Using this nomenclature, the special plea has been defined as follows:

> 'Now a plea in bar is one which, part from the merits, raises some special defence, not apparent *ex facie* the declaration—for in that case it would be taken by way of exception—which either destroys or postpones the operation of the cause of action.'[10]

The special plea differs from the exception in three respects. First, it sets out, as its name indicates, special facts unconnected with the merits of the action in consequence of which the action is either finally determined or delayed.[11] Secondly, a special defence may be pleaded only in response to the plaintiff's particulars of claim or declaration, while an exception may be raised to any pleading. Thirdly, the correctness of the averments of the pleading to which exception is taken is assumed. No evidence is therefore led in exception proceedings, whereas the averments set out in the special plea will have to be proved if they are not admitted by the plaintiff.

1.4.3 *Grounds upon which a special plea may be raised*

The defendant must raise all special defences in the plea. If this is not done, it may be assumed that the defendant has condoned the errors or irregularities that gave rise to the special defence. However, in those cases in which the court objectively speaking would not have jurisdiction, the court will not acquire jurisdiction purely

---

[8] Rule 22, Uniform Rules of Court.

[9] Rule 17(3).

[10] *Per* Innes CJ in *Brown v Vlok* 1925 AD 56 at 58.

[11] If a defence deals with the merits of the claim, it cannot be labelled a special plea: *Glennie, Egan & Sikkel v Du Toit's Kloof Development Co (Pty) Ltd* 1953 (2) SA 85 (C).

because the defendant has failed to deliver a special plea of lack of jurisdiction. Similarly, the plea of prescription may be raised at any point in the proceedings, but such defences would have to be placed before the court through an application to amend the plea, which application could be refused if the previous neglect amounted to a tacit admission.[12]

A number of bases upon which a special plea may be raised are dealt with alphabetically below. This is not to say, however, that these are the only possible bases upon which a special plea may be raised.

1.4.3.1 *Arbitration*

Contracting parties often stipulate that future disputes about the contract or its performance should be referred to arbitration rather than to the courts. Such clauses do not automatically exclude the jurisdiction of the court. A defendant may raise the arbitration agreement in a special plea and the court will give effect to the arbitration clause unless there is a strong case made out by the plaintiff why the matter should not be referred to arbitration.[13] The matter is regulated by s 6 of the Arbitration Act 42 of 1965, sub-s (2) of which reads:

> 'If on any such application the court is satisfied that there is no sufficient reason why the dispute should not be referred to arbitration in accordance with the agreement, the court may make an order staying such proceedings subject to such terms and conditions as it may consider just.'

Although the Act refers to an application, the matter may be raised in a special plea.[14]

The defendant will bear the onus of proving that the dispute falls within the terms of the arbitration clause.[15]

The proper relief to seek, and the proper order to be made, is that the matter be stayed pending the arbitration, and not that the claim be dismissed.[16]

1.4.3.2 *Jurisdiction*

There are three possibilities. The first is that the court lacks jurisdiction because the cause of action in respect of which the plaintiff has issued summons is specifically excluded by s 46 from the jurisdiction of the court. Secondly, the defendant may raise a special defence of lack of jurisdiction because the amount claimed by the plaintiff is in excess of the maximum in respect of which the court has jurisdiction in terms of s 29.[17] Thirdly, the defendant may object that the court

---

[12] *Stolz v Pretoria North Town Council* 1953 (3) SA 884 (T); *Reuben v Meyers* 1957 (4) SA 57 (SR). See also *Glanfield v Asp Development Syndicate Ltd* 1911 AD 374; *Reitz Ko-operatieve Landbouw Vereeniging v Botha* 1923 OPD 49; *The Rhodesian Railways Ltd v Mackintosh* 1932 AD 359 at 368; *Stanhope v Combined Holdings & Industries Ltd* 1950 (3) SA 52 (E) at 57C.
[13] *The Rhodesian Railways Ltd v Mackintosh* (supra); *Universiteit van Stellenbosch v JA Louw* 1983 (4) SA 321 (A).
[14] *Delfante v Delta Electrical Industries Ltd* 1992 (2) SA 221 (C) at 226E–H.
[15] *Rogers v Mathews* 1926 TPD 21.
[16] See also *Foize Africa (Pty) Ltd v Foize Beheer BV & others* 2013 (3) SA 91 (SCA) at 99F–H.
[17] *Durban City Council v Kadir* 1971 (1) SA 364 (N).

lacks jurisdiction in respect of his or her person in terms of s 28. If a defendant pleads this point, he or she must provide a factual basis for the plea.[18]

1.4.3.3 *Costs in a previous suit between the same parties have not been paid*

The court does not permit a plaintiff who could not succeed in a previous action against the defendant to take further legal steps against the same defendant based upon the same cause of action before the plaintiff has paid the defendant the costs flowing from the prior unsuccessful claim.[19] The basis of the rule is that the previous decision is deemed to be correct and it is thus *prima facie* vexatious to reopen the case without paying the costs.[20]

Where, therefore, the court grants absolution from the instance, a plaintiff will not be permitted to issue summons against the defendant a second time on the basis of the same cause of action until he or she has paid the costs of the earlier action in which absolution was granted.

This rule has no application to interlocutory applications even if brought unsuccessfully by a plaintiff. The parties must wait until the case has been finalised to tax the bill of costs; claims on the costs have to wait until this is done.

In *Meyer v Meyer*[21] it was held that the court has a discretion to permit the raising of this special defence. The court will not order that the proceedings be suspended because the costs incurred in the previous action have not been paid where such suspension would lead to an unjust result.

This position under the common law is embodied in rule 32(3), which reads:

> 'The withdrawal or dismissal of an action or a decree of absolution from the instance shall not be a defence to any subsequent action, but if a subsequent action is brought for the same or substantially the same cause of action before payment of the costs awarded on such withdrawal, dismissal or decree of absolution, the court may on application, if it deems fit and if the said costs have been taxed and payment thereof has been demanded, order a stay of such subsequent action until such costs shall be paid and that the plaintiff shall pay the costs of such application.'

1.4.3.4 Lis pendens

The defendant may raise the special defence that an action is already pending between the same parties (or their successors in title) which arises from the same cause of action or in relation to the same subject-matter in dispute.[22]

It is not necessary that the two actions be precisely the same. If one of the cases necessarily requires that judgment be given on a point of law that may be *res judicata*, the same 'cause of action' requirement will be satisfied. In order to

---

[18] *Lubbe v Bosman* 1948 (3) SA 909 (O) at 915.

[19] *Town Council of Bloemfontein v Larsen* 1921 OPD 172; *Argus Printing & Publishing Co Ltd v Anastassiades* 1954 (1) SA 72 (W); *Du Plessis v Doubells Transport (Edms) Bpk* (supra).

[20] *Meyer v Meyer* 1945 TPD 118.

[21] Supra at 123.

[22] Voet 44.2.7; Van Leeuwen *Rooms-Hollands Regt* 5.17.16; Merula *Manier van Procederen* 4.40.1; *Wolff NO v Solomon* (1898) 15 SC 297 at 306; *Pretorius v Barkly East Divisional Council* 1914 AD 407; *Westphal v Schlemmer* 1925 SWA 127; *Richtersveld Community v Alexkor Ltd & another* 2000 (1) SA 377 (LCC).

determine upon precisely which points the court will have to give judgment, attention is directed to the pleadings and not to the evidence.[23]

The two actions need not be instituted in the same court; the plea of *lis pendens* may be raised also where the earlier action is pending in a different court in the same country.[24]

1.4.3.5   Locus standi

The defendant may at any time raise the special defence that the plaintiff lacks the necessary *locus standi* to institute action against him or her. If the lack of *locus standi* appears from the combined summons or declaration itself, it will be possible for the defendant to raise the issue by way of exception. If, however, it is not clear from the particulars or declaration that the plaintiff lacks *locus standi*, the defendant will raise the lack of *locus standi* by way of special defence.

1.4.3.6   Res judicata

The defendant may raise as a special defence the fact that the entire matter is *res judicata*. This defence amounts to a plea that a judgment has already been given by a competent court in a matter between the same parties in which the point in dispute was the same.[25]

The requirement that the court in the later case be requested to determine the same *lis* between the parties may also be interpreted as meaning that the same point must have been in dispute and that the same relief must have been sought or that the action must have been instituted on the same basis and must have been based on the same cause of action.

1.4.3.7   *Settlement*

The defendant may at any time raise by way of a special plea the defence that the matter has already been settled. Full particulars of the settlement must be given.

1.4.3.8   *Prescription*

Prescription is not a claim that deals with the merits. The date on which the plaintiff's claim arose has nothing to do with the nature of the claim but has a role to play in determining the enforceability of the action. When the special defence of prescription succeeds, this means simply that the claim has become unenforceable on account of prescription. It does not mean that the cause of action is unfounded, but merely that the claim may no longer be enforced.[26]

---

[23] *Shaw v Williams* (1883) 3 EDC 251; *Marks & Kantor v Van Diggelen* 1935 TPD 29.
[24] *Painter v Strauss* 1951 (3) SA 307 (O) at 312E–F.
[25] Voet 44.2.1–3; *R v Manasewitz* 1933 AD 165; *Boshoff v Union Government* 1932 TPD 345; *Sundays River Irrigation Board v Parkes Bros* 1938 AD 493; *Durban City Council v Standard-Vacuum Refining Co (Pty) Ltd* 1961 (2) SA 682 (N) at 685B; *Jacobson v Havinga t/a Havingas* 2001 (2) SA 177 (T); *National Sorghum Breweries Ltd (t/a Vivo African Breweries) v International Liquor Distributors (Pty) Ltd* 2001 (2) SA 232 (SCA); *Richtersveld Community v Alexkor* (supra).
[26] *Mostert v Mostert* 1913 TPD 255; *Conradie v Van Niekerk* 1970 (3) SA 164 (O) at 166C.

The periods for prescription are set out in numerous statutes, of which the Prescription Act 68 of 1969 is the most important.[27]

The defence of prescription must be averred in a special plea. If the defendant does not raise the defence of prescription, he or she is deemed to have waived his or her right to do so. The court may not *mero motu* raise the matter of prescription. The defendant may raise the defence at any time before the close of pleadings, and after that time he or she will have to make application to amend his or her plea, which application will be refused if the defendant cannot show that his or her neglect was inadvertent.[28]

(a)   Non-joinder and misjoinder

It is necessary that every party against whom relief is sought, or who has a direct substantial interest in the suit, should be joined as a party to it. If there has been non-joinder or a misjoinder, then the defendant must raise this point in a special plea.[29]

The most common instance where the plea of non-joinder will be successful is where only one owner of property owned by several co-owners is sued, or where there is joint financial or proprietary interest not based upon co-ownership.[30] Apart from these instances, the right of a defendant to raise non-joinder is limited.[31]

There will, of course, be much greater scope for the defendant to raise the plea of misjoinder.

In the event of these pleas being successful, the court will order a stay in the proceedings so that the pleading can be amended so as to bring the proper parties before the court.

1.5   The contents of the plea

1.5.1 *General*

The plea must be formulated sufficiently clearly to inform the plaintiff precisely of the basis of the defendant's defence. If the plaintiff is left at a loss as to what the defence is, he or she will be entitled to take exception to the plea on the ground

---

[27] See also *Moise v Transitional Local Council of Greater Germiston* 2001 (8) BCLR 765 (CC). The South African Law Reform Commission recently issued a revised discussion paper (147) titled 'Harmonisation of Existing Laws Providing for Different Prescription Periods', Project 125 (2 December 2017).

[28] *Stolz v Pretoria North Town Council* 1954 (1) SA 110 (T) at 113A; *Glaser v Millward* 1950 (4) SA 587 (W) at 590D; *Moult v Minister of Agriculture and Forestry, Transkei* 1992 (1) SA 688 (Tk).

[29] *Amos Legane & others v Webb* 1917 TPD 650; *Estate Vom Dorp v Scott* 1915 CPD 739; *Collin v Toffie* 1944 AD 456 at 467; *Skyline Hotel v Nickloes* 1973 (4) SA 170 (W).

[30] See *Morgan & another v Salisbury Municipality* 1935 AD 167 at 171.

[31] *Kock and Schmidt v Alma Modehuis (Edms) Bpk* 1959 (3) SA 308 (A) at 318; *Pillay v Harry & others* 1966 (1) SA 801 (D) at 804C–E; *Richards & another v Port Elizabeth Municipality* 1990 (4) SA 770 (SEC) 775E–776F; *New Garden Cities Incorporated Association Not for Gain v Adhikarie* 1998 (3) SA 626 (C). An admission in a pleading may be ignored by the court when it is contrary to all the evidence and it would lead to an injustice. *Fourie v Sentrasure Bpk* 1997 (4) SA 950 (NC).

that it fails to disclose a defence or that the defence that is disclosed is vague and embarrassing. Alternatively, it may be set aside as an irregular step in terms of rule 60A.[32]

Rule 17(2) deals with the contents of the plea and provides that:

'The defendant shall in defendant's plea either admit or deny or confess and avoid all the material facts alleged in the combined summons or declaration or state which of the said facts are not admitted and to what extent, and shall clearly and concisely state all material facts upon which defendant relies.'

The defendant responds to each averment contained in the plaintiff's particulars of claim by:
(1) admitting it;
(2) denying it; or
(3) confessing and avoiding it.

1.5.2 *Admission*

An admission on the part of the defendant means that he or she unconditionally accepts the averments of fact made by the plaintiff. The effect of an admission is that it becomes unnecessary for the party averring the admitted facts to prove these facts at the trial.[33] An admission must be made unambiguously. However, rule 17(3)*(a)* provides that '[e]very allegation of fact in the combined summons or declaration which is not stated in the plea to be denied or to be admitted, shall be deemed to be admitted'. The result of this is that any averment which the defendant does not contradict in the plea will be presumed to be admitted. It is submitted that, should the pleading be ambiguous, it will be presumed to be denied.

Great care should be taken to deal with each averment made. It is easy to overlook averments and to find that they have been admitted. Thus, where a defendant denies the existence of a contract but not the amount of the claim, he or she will be deemed to have admitted the amount. The plaintiff therefore has only to prove the existence of the contract to succeed in the claim.[34]

1.5.2.1 *The withdrawal of an admission*

An admission made in the pleadings may not be withdrawn except with leave of the court. The rules relating to the amendment pleadings apply. The court will authorise the withdrawal only if evidence is led regarding the circumstances under which the admission was made. A full explanation of how the admission came to be made will be required.[35] Such application can be made at any stage in the proceedings and can succeed only if there is no prejudice to the other party.[36]

---

[32] Rule 17(6).

[33] *Gordon v Tarnow* 1947 (3) SA 525 (A) at 531; *A A Mutual Insurance Association Ltd v Biddulph & another* 1976 (1) SA 725 (A) at 735A–H; see too s 15 of the Civil Proceedings Evidence Act 25 of 1965.

[34] *Hayes v Van Rensburg* 1964 (2) SA 641 (C); *Botha v Van Zyl* 1955 (3) SA 310 (SWA).

[35] *Van Deventer v De Villers* 1953 (4) SA 72 (C).

[36] *Gordon v Tarnow* (supra) at 531; *Bellairs v Hodnett & another* 1978 (1) SA 1109 (A) at 1150E–G.

1.5.3 *Denial*

1.5.3.1 *The general (or bare) denial*

The defendant must deal expressly with each individual averment made by the plaintiff in his or her particulars of claim. The defendant must guard against making a general or bare denial which has the effect of leaving the plaintiff in the dark as to which averments are denied.

Suppose that the plaintiff avers that his motor vehicle was damaged on 10 February in a collision with a vehicle driven by the defendant. To this averment the defendant answers simply: 'The contents of this paragraph are denied.' It is not then clear whether the defendant denies that:

(1)   it is the plaintiff's vehicle that has been damaged;
(2)   the collision occurred on 10 February;
(3)   a collision occurred at all; or
(4)   he (the defendant) was the driver of the other vehicle involved.

It is clear that a general denial of this nature is inadmissible.[37] According to rule 6(5), a bare denial of liability or a defence of general issue is not permitted but the defendant may, either as a sole defence or in combination with any other defence inconsistent therewith, deny specifically any of the allegations contained in the summons. Rule 17(2) further provides that the defendant must in the plea 'clearly and concisely state all material facts upon which defendant relies'.[38] In effect, the plea containing a general denial of this sort will be excipiable in so far as the plaintiff is not informed as to the basis of the defendant's defence. It will also constitute an irregular step, as provided for in rules 6(13) and 17(6).

In many courts the practice has developed in connection with the more formal elements of the pleadings for the defendant to plead that he or she denies each and every averment contained in a paragraph. This pleading has the effect of avoiding the ambiguity dealt with above, but this form of pleading should be used with caution.

Such general denials have the further difficulty that they do not place before the parties and the court the proper basis of the defendant's defence. In many instances the defendant may not rest content with even a specific denial, but the defendant is obliged to place the factual basis for his or her denial on record in the pleadings. Should the defendant fail to do so, he or she may be prevented at the trial from leading evidence to support his or her denial.

1.5.3.2 *The burden of proof*

The general rule that 'he who alleges must prove' applies in relation to the facts expressly denied by the defendant. The plaintiff must prove those facts by leading evidence at the trial.

---

[37] *Hillman Bros Ltd v Kelly & Hingle* 1926 WLD 153; *Hlongwane v Methodist Church of South Africa* 1933 WLD 165.

[38] A similar provision can be found in rule 6(4). Furthermore, rule 6(5) provides that '[w]hen in any pleading a party denies an allegation of fact in the previous pleading of the opposite party, he or she shall not do so evasively, but shall answer the point of substance'.

From this it is obvious that it is generally much safer for the defendant to deny averments made by the plaintiff than to admit them.

It sometimes happens that the defendant denies every averment made by the plaintiff purely in order to ensure that the burden of proof in relation to every fact rests upon the plaintiff. The denials are made, in other words, simply to make matters difficult for the plaintiff.

In order to avoid the impression that the defendant is denying certain facts for the sole purpose of placing an additional burden upon the plaintiff, it has become customary for the defendant to plead in relation to some averments that he or she has no knowledge of the facts set out by the plaintiff and that in consequence he or she refuses to admit them and puts the plaintiff to the proof thereof. The instances where this is done are especially common where the plaintiff avers that his or her motor vehicle has been damaged as a result of the defendant's negligence. The defendant will usually not be aware whether the plaintiff is the owner of the vehicle or whether he or she is merely a lessee of the vehicle or a purchaser in terms of an instalment sale transaction.

1.5.4 *Confession and avoidance*

The defendant may admit the facts pleaded by the plaintiff, but aver fresh facts which avoid the normal legal consequences of the facts upon which the plaintiff relies.[39]

Thus, the defendant may, for example, admit that he or she borrowed money from the plaintiff as alleged, but he or she may aver that the amount has been repaid in full to the plaintiff.

Confession and avoidance will be typical in the following instances: payment, discharge, necessity, novation, defences in defamation cases, tender and payment into court, and interruption of causality.

No absolute general rule can be set out with regard to the incidence of the onus in this and similar circumstances. Where the plea is a proper confession and avoidance, the defendant will usually assume the duty to place before the court evidence to substantiate his or her avoidance, but the plaintiff will still bear the overall onus.[40] A defendant who pleads that the contract in terms of which the plaintiff sues is subject to a condition precedent, will have to prove the condition.[41] These situations must not be confused with those in which a plaintiff retains the onus of proving a disputed term in a contract.[42]

---

[39] *Britz v Weideman* 1946 OPD 144 at 151.
[40] *Mabaso v Felix* 1981 (3) SA 865 (A).
[41] *Seedat v Tucker's Shoe Co* 1952 (3) SA 513 (T) at 515H–516A.
[42] *Stocks & Stocks (Pty) Ltd v TJ Daly & Sons (Pty) Ltd* 1979 (3) SA 754 (A).

1.6 The amendment of the plea

All defences must be pleaded.[43] If during the trial it becomes apparent that there is *prima facie* evidence of a defence on some other ground than that pleaded, the new defence should be placed on record and the plea would need to be amended.[44]

1.7 Separate hearing of a defence

Rule 17(7) provides that any defence which can be adjudicated upon without the necessity of going into the main case may be set down by either party for a separate hearing upon 10 days' notice at any time after the defence has been raised.

This provision creates the possibility of speedy adjudication without the need for a long, protracted trial. The procedure will be used in particular for the adjudication of defences raised by way of special plea.

No invariable rule can be laid down as to which defences may be the subject of a separate hearing. There may be defences pertaining to the facts of the case which are nevertheless distinguishable from the other defences raised and which, if upheld, may result in the disposal of the entire matter without any need for a finding on the remaining aspects of the claim.

The piecemeal disposal of the matter at the defendant's instance by having each defence adjudicated upon separately will constitute an abuse of procedure.

Should the matter be enrolled for separate hearing, the hearing amounts to a separate trial and the parties will be entitled to the costs of preparation for it.[45]

1.8 The exception to the plea

1.8.1 *The period within which exception must be noted*

If the plaintiff considers the plea to be vague and embarrassing, the plaintiff must by notice and within 15 days of the plea give the defendant an opportunity to remove the cause of complaint. The defendant then has 15 days to remove said cause of complaint. The excipient must deliver the exception within 10 days from the date on which a reply to such notice is received or from the date on which such reply is due. If an exception is brought on the ground that the plea fails to disclose a defence, the notice of exception must be delivered within 15 days of the plea.[46]

The exception may be set down for hearing by either party on 10 days' notice.[47]

1.8.2 *The grounds of exception to the plea*

Rule 19(1) stipulates two bases upon which exception may be taken to a plea. These are that the plea:

* discloses no defence to the plaintiff's claim;
* is vague and embarrassing.

---

[43] *Doyle v Botha* 1909 26 SC 245; *Naran v Rajoo* 1921 42 NLR 39; *Circle Construction (Pty) Ltd v Smithfield Construction* 1982 (4) SA 726 (N).

[44] *Cornelius & Sons v McClaren* 1961 (2) SA 604 (E).

[45] *Savopoulos v Nieman* 1973 (2) SA 767 (O) at 769B–C.

[46] Rule 19(1) read with rule 21(1).

[47] Rule 19(1) read with rule 55(1)(*j*).

These two grounds of exception are the most commonly encountered in practice.

In order to succeed in an exception that the plea discloses no defence, the plaintiff must show that the defence does not avail against the claim as a whole. If another defence is available against a portion of the claim, the exception must fail. The exception must be able to succeed against the entire defence.[48]

The plaintiff must distinguish clearly between cases in which the plea discloses no defence and cases in which the plea is vague and embarrassing. A distinction is drawn between a poorly formulated plea, which nevertheless discloses a defence, and a plea which discloses no defence at all.[49]

The plea is vague and embarrassing when it is not precisely clear to the plaintiff what the basis of the defence is. This type of exception may be brought in the event of a general denial, when the defendant fails specifically to admit, deny or confess and avoid each of the averments made by the plaintiff.

A plea will be vague and embarrassing, for example, when it is susceptible of different interpretations.[50] A plea is likewise vague and embarrassing if it contains an averment which is altogether inconsistent with a previous averment contained in the plea.[51]

1.9 The application to strike out matter from the plea

The plaintiff may apply to strike out from the plea any of two or more mutually contradictory defences not pleaded in the alternative, or any averments which are scandalous, vexatious or irrelevant.[52]

The same principles apply here as in the case of the application to strike out objectionable matter from the particulars of claim or declaration.

The application to strike out matter from the plea may be set down for hearing by either party on 10 days' notice.[53]

2 COUNTERCLAIMS

When delivering his or her plea, a defendant may, if he or she wishes, institute a counterclaim against the plaintiff.[54]

The counterclaim is also known as a 'claim in reconvention'.

---

[48] *Naylor v Central News Agency Ltd* 1910 WLD 90; *Salzmann v Holmes* 1914 AD 152; *Miller & others v Bellville Municipality* 1971 (4) SA 544 (C); *Rumanal (Pty) Ltd v Hubner* 1976 (1) SA 643 (E) at 646C; *Warren v Pirie (Pty) Ltd* 1959 (1) SA 419 (E) at 424F–G. Where several claims are brought, each independent of the others, an exception may be brought against one of the claims; *Barclays National Bank Ltd v Thompson* 1989 (1) SA 547 (A).
[49] *Gericke v Mangold Bros Ltd* 1961 (3) SA 901 (T) at 903A.
[50] *General Commercial & Industrial Finance Corp Ltd v Pretoria Portland Cement Co Ltd* 1944 AD 444 at 454; *Builders Ltd v Union Government (Minister of Finance)* 1918 AD 46 at 52; *Parow Lands (Pty) Ltd v Schneider* 1952 (1) SA 150 (SWA); *Trope v South African Reserve Bank & another and two other cases* 1992 (3) SA 208 (T).
[51] *Westphal v Schlemmer* 1925 SWA 127.
[52] Rule 19(2).
[53] Rule 19(2) read with rule 55(1)(*j*).
[54] Rule 20(1)(*b*). It is mandatory that the counterclaim be instituted within the time for delivery of the plea: *Leonard v Evbro (Edms) Bpk* 1976 (1) SA 227 (O); *Sekhoto v Qwa Qwa Auto Industries CC*

The defendant who institutes a counterclaim is known as the plaintiff in reconvention, while the plaintiff (in the main claim) is known as the defendant in reconvention.

The counterclaim may be based upon any right or claim of any amount, whether liquid or illiquid, liquidated or unliquidated. It may have arisen out of or be connected with the subject-matter of the plaintiff's claim or it may have nothing at all to do with the claim in convention.[55]

A defendant cannot obtain any order against the plaintiff without instituting a counterclaim.

The counterclaim may exceed the magistrates' court jurisdiction. When the counterclaim is in excess of the court's jurisdiction, the defendant (ie the plaintiff in reconvention) may apply to the magistrate's court on notice delivered together with his or her counterclaim, or within five days thereafter, for a pronouncement that the counterclaim exceeds the jurisdiction and for an order staying the action instituted by the plaintiff in order to afford the defendant the opportunity of instituting action in a competent court.[56]

Where the defendant does not request the court to pronounce that the counterclaim exceeds its jurisdiction, the court may itself pronounce that it lacks jurisdiction to entertain the counterclaim. In that event the defendant may apply to court on notice immediately or within five days after such finding for a stay of action.[57]

The magistrate will, however, stay the claim in convention (ie the main claim) only if it is clear that the defendant has *prima facie* a reasonable prospect of obtaining judgment in his or her favour on the counterclaim.[58] If the magistrate stays the action, he or she does so for a reasonable period in order to afford the defendant the opportunity of instituting his or her claim in a competent court.[59]

Should the defendant fail to institute the counterclaim in a competent court within the period for which the matter has been stayed, the magistrate may on application either stay the action for a further period or dismiss the counterclaim.[60] The magistrate may dismiss the counterclaim regardless of whether the defendant reduces it to an amount falling within the jurisdiction of the court.

If the claim in convention is stayed in the magistrate's court and the counterclaim is thereafter stayed, dismissed, withdrawn or abandoned, or if a competent court has granted absolution from the instance on the counterclaim, the magistrate's court is obliged, on application, to dismiss the counterclaim and to proceed to determine the main claim.[61]

Panel Beaters & Spray Painters 1998 (1) SA 164 (O). However, the plaintiff or the court may agree to it being delivered at a later stage.

[55] Jones & Buckle Rule 20-2.

[56] Rule 20(5) and s 47(1).

[57] Rule 20(6).

[58] Section 47(1).

[59] Ibid. Cf also *Esterhuizen v Holmes* 1947 (2) SA 789 (T); *Beznbo International Agencies (Pty) Ltd v Samuel A May (Pty) Ltd* 1971 (3) SA 349 (T).

[60] Section 47(2).

[61] Section 47(3).

If no application for a stay of action is made by the defendant in convention or if such an application is dismissed, the court must on application by the plaintiff or of its own motion dismiss a counterclaim pronounced to exceed its jurisdiction, unless the defendant, under s 38, at once abandons a sufficient amount of his counterclaim to bring it within the jurisdiction of the court.[62]

2.1 General rules pertaining to counterclaims

The same rules apply to the counterclaim as to the claim in convention.[63] In the nature of things, however, there are a number of rules peculiar to the counterclaim. For example, the counterclaim is not served upon the plaintiff in convention by the sheriff. Also, it is not necessary for the plaintiff to enter appearance to defend. All times which, in the case of a claim in convention, run from the date of entry of appearance to defend, in the case of a claim in reconvention run from the date on which the counterclaim is delivered.[64]

The rest of the procedure subsequent to the institution of a counterclaim is precisely the same as the procedure subsequent to the service of summons. The counterclaim is excipiable, an application to strike out may be brought or it may be set aside as an irregular step in terms of the rules. A plea is filed (by the plaintiff in convention) to the counterclaim. One therefore finds a repetition of the course of proceedings between the same two parties. The two actions are combined merely for practical purposes so that judgment on both may be delivered simultaneously.

It is not possible for a defendant in reconvention in turn to institute a claim in reconvention together with his or her plea to the counterclaim.[65]

If the claim in convention as well as the counterclaim are tried by the magistrate's court, the court has the power to try each action separately, but judgment must be given on both claim and counterclaim simultaneously.[66]

Since the actions may be heard separately, it is only logical that the counterclaim may be proceeded with even though the main action is withdrawn, stayed, discontinued or dismissed.[67]

3 THE REPLY

The final pleading that may be delivered by the parties during the exchange of pleadings in the course of a trial action in the magistrate's court is the reply. In Superior Court practice, this pleading is known as a replication.[68]

---

[62] Rule 20(7).

[63] Rule 20(1)(*a*).

[64] Rule 20(1)(*a*) provides that 'it shall not be necessary to deliver a notice of intention to defend and that all times which, in the case of a claim in convention, run from the date of delivery of a notice of intention to defend, shall, in the case of a claim in reconvention, run from the date of delivery of such claim in reconvention'.

[65] Rule 20(9).

[66] Rule 20(8). *Robot Paints, Hardware & Timber Co (Pty) Ltd v South African Industrial Equipment (Pty) Ltd* 1975 (4) SA 829 (T).

[67] Rule 20(10).

[68] Rule 21 now also refers to the word 'replication'.

The reply may be delivered by both the plaintiff in convention and the plaintiff in reconvention.

The purpose of the reply is to answer any *new* averments made by the defendant in his or her plea. The reply will therefore be necessary only if the defence consists of more than mere denials of the averments made in the particulars of claim or declaration.

The reply is commonly encountered where the defence consists of a confession and avoidance. But by virtue of the provisions of rule 21(3), it is not even necessary to deliver a reply in every such case. Rule 21(3) provides that, should the plaintiff fail to deliver a reply within the time period specified in the rules, he or she is taken to have denied all of the allegations of fact contained in the plea.

Only if the plaintiff wishes to qualify the averments made by the defendant in his or her plea will he or she deliver a reply. Suppose, for example, that the plaintiff claims payment of an amount of R3 000 for goods sold and delivered by him or her to the defendant. To this claim the defendant pleads that he or she purchased the goods but that he or she is entitled to refuse to pay for them on the ground that the plaintiff failed to deliver them on time. The plaintiff may reply to this by averring, for example, that the defendant condoned the late delivery by accepting the goods without demur.

The reply must be delivered within 15 days after the delivery of the plea.[69]

The rules applicable to the plea are *mutatis mutandis* applicable to the reply.[70]

4 CLOSE OF PLEADINGS

The close of pleadings is also known as *litis contestatio.*

Close of pleadings means that the exchange of all pleadings in which the plaintiff and defendant formulate their respective cases is complete. The litigants have thus reached finality in regard to all allegations of fact forming the basis of the claim and defence, and the parties may now begin to prepare for trial.

Rule 21A provides that the pleadings are deemed to be closed in the following circumstances:

> '(a) either party has joined issue without alleging any new matter, and without adding any further pleading;
>
> (b) the last day allowed for filing a replication or subsequent pleading has elapsed and it has not been filed;
>
> (c) the parties agree in writing that the pleadings are closed and such agreement is filed with the registrar or clerk of the court; or
>
> (d) the parties are unable to agree as to the close of pleadings, and the court upon the application of a party declares them closed.'

Certain procedural steps relating to preparation for trial may take place only after *litis contestatio.* But *litis contestatio* also has important substantive effects.

---

[69] Rule 21(1).

[70] Rule 21(1). It follows that the same exceptions may be raised to the reply as may be raised to the plea. The same procedure must be followed. An application to strike out may likewise be brought to strike out averments from the reply.

For instance, in an action for damages the claim was previously transmissible to the estate of the plaintiff only after *litis contestatio*.[71]

---

[71] *Executors of Meyer v Gericke* 1880 Foord 14, applied in *Jankowiak & another v Parity Insurance Co (Pty) Ltd* 1963 (2) SA 286 (W); *Potgieter v Sustein (Edms) Bpk* 1990 (2) SA 15 (T). See, however, *Nkala & others v Harmony Gold Mining Company Ltd & others* 2016 (5) SA 240 (GJ) where the court held that the common law should be developed to include transmissibility of claims for general damages where a plaintiff has died after the commencement of proceedings but before close of pleadings.

Chapter 15

THE TRIAL AND THE PREPARATION FOR IT

1 PREPARATION FOR TRIAL

Adjudication of the dispute between the parties takes place at the trial. The pleadings delimit the issues between the parties. But before the matter can go to trial the parties have to disclose to each other certain aspects of the evidence they wish to place before the court in the trial. The purpose of the pretrial procedures is to facilitate an orderly and speedy trial and to prevent the parties being taken by surprise at the trial by unexpected evidence. Such surprise would lead to an application for a postponement and in all probability to a further delay in the finalisation of the matter.

Between *litis contestatio* and the trial there is therefore a period in which various pretrial procedures take place. These procedures are all of great importance and a party who does not diligently prepare for trial can find himself or herself greatly prejudiced at the trial. It can also happen that the pretrial procedures further delimit the issues or bring evidence to light which leads to a settlement of the matter.

There are inevitably long delays in bringing matters to court. These delays are caused by long court rolls and the availability of magistrates. Practitioners should take care that their own neglect does not lead to yet further delay.

1.1 Set-down for trial

After the close of pleadings, the plaintiff ascertains from the registrar or clerk of the court on which date the matter may be heard. Once the date has been arranged with the registrar or clerk, the plaintiff delivers a notice of set-down.[1] The case is then enrolled for trial.

The notice of set-down reads as follows:

* For use in the District Court
In the Magistrate's Court for the District of ....
held at ....
Case No .... of 20......
In the matter between
.... Plaintiff
and
.... Defendant
<div align="center">NOTICE OF SET-DOWN</div>
TAKE NOTICE that the abovementioned case has been enrolled for hearing on .... 20...... at ....h........ or so soon thereafter as the parties may be heard.
DATED at .... on this .... day of .... 20......
.... <div align="center">PLAINTIFF'S ATTORNEY</div>

---

[1] Rule 22(1).

To: The Clerk of the Court

....

And to: ....

Address: ....

If the plaintiff does not deliver notice of set-down for trial within 15 days after the pleadings have closed, the defendant may make the arrangements and deliver the notice.[2] A defendant would set the matter down in this way only if he or she has instituted a counterclaim. The notice of the trial must be delivered at least 20 days before the trial date.[3] In practice it should preferably be delivered a few months prior to the allocated day. Furthermore, the delivery of the notice of the trial will automatically operate to set down for trial at the same time the defendant's claim in reconvention.[4]

1.2 Discovery

The process of discovery is the means by which each party can compel the other to reveal the documentary evidence[5] which he or she has in his or her possession or under his or her control, which relates to the action, irrespective of whether it arises between the party requiring discovery and the party required to make discovery.[6] The party called upon to discover does not need to disclose documents which tend to only advance his or her case, unless he or she intends to use it at the trial.[7] Documents that may directly or indirectly advance the case of the party requiring discovery, or which would enable him or her to damage the case of the party effecting discovery, would need to be disclosed. In this regard:

> 'It seems to me that every document relates to the matter in question in the action which, it is reasonable to suppose, contains information which may—not which must—either directly or indirectly enable the party requiring the affidavit either to advance his own case or to damage the case of his adversary. I have put in the words "either directly or indirectly" because, as it seems to me, a document can properly be said to contain information which may enable the party requiring the affidavit either to advance his own case or to damage the case of his adversary, if it is a document which may fairly lead him to a train of enquiry which may have either of these two consequences.'[8]

---

[2] Ibid.

[3] Rule 22(3).

[4] Rule 22(2).

[5] Rule 23(1) provides that 'all documents and tape, electronic, digital or other forms of recordings' are susceptible to discovery.

[6] Rule 23(1). Discovery in the magistrates' courts is now basically identical to discovery in the High Courts. The ambit of discovery and the category of documents to be discovered in the magistrates' courts are now wider than they were previously. For example, rule 23(10) now makes provision for a notice to admit. Importantly, documents and tape recordings previously in the possession or control of the party now also need to be discovered, where formerly only those that were currently in the party's possession or control had to be discovered.

[7] Jones & Buckle Rule 23-6 and the cases cited therein.

[8] *SA Neon Advertising (Pty) Ltd v Claude Neon Lights (SA) Ltd* 1968 (3) SA 381 (W).

The discovery procedure consists of a notice calling upon the other side to discover. Such discovery is effected by means of a discovery affidavit in which the litigant himself or herself states which documents are in his or her possession which will be used in the trial or which are relevant to the dispute.

Discovery is not an essential procedure and matters can go to trial without any discovery at all. However, if any party fails to discover, the party desiring discovery may apply to a court to order compliance with the rule and, failing such compliance, may dismiss the claim or strike out the defence.[9]

It is to the advantage of every party to call for discovery, because in this way one can prevent oneself being caught by surprise at the trial. A party who has made discovery will not be allowed to adduce documentary evidence which has not been discovered. At the trial the other party may call for these books or documents which were not discovered and may use such books or documents in his or her cross-examination.[10] A party forced into this predicament and prevented from leading evidence will have to apply to amend the discovery affidavit and may well be faced with an application for postponement and an adverse order of costs.

The notice to discover will call upon the other side to make discovery on oath within 20 days and such a notice may not, without the leave of the court, be given before the close of pleadings.[11]

Section 7 of the Promotion of Access to Information Act 2 of 2000 provides that this Act does not apply to a record of a public or private body if that record is requested for the purpose of civil proceedings or is requested after the institution of proceedings. Any record obtained contrary to the section is not admissible unless the exclusion would be detrimental to the interests of justice. The result is that this section cannot be used to circumvent the restrictions of the normal discovery process.[12]

The form calling for discovery reads as follows:

Notice to Deliver Schedule of Documents
* For use in the District Court
In the Magistrate's Court for the District of ....
held at ....
Case No .... of 20......
In the matter between
.... Plaintiff
and
.... Defendant

---

[9] Rule 23(8).

[10] Rule 23(4).

[11] Rule 23(1)*(a)* and *(b)*.

[12] In *Alliance Cash & Carry (Pty) Ltd v Commissioner, South African Revenue Service* 2002 (1) SA 789 (T) an unsuccessful attempt was made to invoke ss 32, 33 and 34 of the Constitution to compel the commissioner to disclose information outside of the normal discovery process.

Take notice that the .... requires you to, in accordance with rule 23, within 20 days after receiving this notice, make discovery on oath of all documents and tape, electronic, digital or other forms of recordings relating to any matter in question in such action which are or at any time have been in your possession or under your control.

Dated this .... day of.................20......

....

Attorney for ....
Address: ....

To: The Clerk of the Court,

....

and: ....

The party called upon to make discovery must verify on affidavit the following documents and recordings:

(1) documents and recordings that are currently in his or her possession or in the possession of his or her agent;

(2) documents and recordings to which he or she has a valid objection to produce;

(3) documents and recordings which were previously in his or her possession or that of his or her agent but are no longer in his or her possession or in the possession of his or her agent.[13]

If the party making discovery claims privilege for any of the books or documents scheduled, those books or documents must be separately listed and the grounds on which privilege is claimed for each book or document must be set out.[14]

The documents and books listed in the schedule must be described in such a way that they are readily identifiable and that it is clear at the trial that discovery of a relevant document has indeed been made. It is not sufficient merely to list correspondence in general: particular letters must be identified. All documents in the parties' possession or under the parties' control or previously in the parties' possession or under their control must be discovered. Therefore, even documents in the possession of another but which the party still controls must be listed.

The list of documents is verified on affidavit deposed to by the party himself or herself.[15] The reason for this is that no one besides the party knows the full extent of the documentation which might be relevant.

The discovery affidavit may be drafted in the following form:

---

[13] Rule 23(2)*(a)–(c)*.

[14] Rule 23(1).

[15] Only in highly exceptional circumstances will a legal representative be permitted to sign the affidavit on behalf of his or her client. In such a case, he or she will have to indicate clearly why he or she, and not the client, is signing the affidavit (cf *Gerry v Gerry* 1958 (1) SA 295 (W); *Ocean Accident & Guarantee Corp Ltd v Potgieter; Potgieter v Ocean Accident & Guarantee Corp Ltd* 1961 (2) SA 783 (O); *Rellams (Pty) Ltd v James Brown & Hamer Ltd* 1983 (1) SA 556 (N)).

No. 13
Discovery—Form of Affidavit

* For use in the District Court

In the Magistrate's Court for the District of ....

held at ....

Case No .... of 20......

In the matter between

.... Plaintiff

and

.... Defendant

DISCOVERY AFFIDAVIT

I, ..., the above-named defendant/plaintiff, make oath and say:

(1) I have in my possession or power the documents or recordings relating to the matters in question in this cause set forth in the first and second parts of the First Schedule hereto.

(2) I object to produce the said documents or recordings set forth in the second part of the said schedule hereto.

(3) I do so for the reason that .... (here state upon what grounds the objection is made, and verify the fact as far as may be).

(4) I have had, but no longer have in my possession or power, the documents or recordings relating to the matters in question in this action, set forth in the Second Schedule hereto.

(5) The last-mentioned documents or recordings were last in my possession or power .... (state when).

(6) The .... (here state what has become of the last-mentioned documents and recordings, and in whose possession they are now).

(7) According to the best of my knowledge and belief, I do not now have, and never have had in my possession, custody, or power, or in the possession, custody or power of my attorney, or agent, or any other person on my behalf, any document or recording, or copy of, or extract from any document or recording, relating to any matters in question in this cause, other than the documents or recordings set forth in the First and Second Schedules hereto.

DATED at .... this .... day of .... 20......

....

Defendant/Plaintiff

FIRST SCHEDULE
Part 1

(1) All pleadings and documents referred to therein.

(2) Original letter addressed by the Defendant's attorney to the Plaintiff's attorney dated ....

(3) Original letter addressed by the Plaintiff's attorney to Defendant's attorney dated ....

(4) Copies of invoices dated .... issued by...............................

FIRST SCHEDULE
Part 2

(1) Correspondence between attorney and client.

(2) Statements of witnesses.

Documents listed in the Schedule are not disclosed on the ground of privilege as between attorney and client.

After discovery has been made, the party discovering has to allow the other party the opportunity to peruse the documents and recordings and to make copies or transcriptions of them. A request to inspect has to be delivered.[16]

The notice to produce documents for inspection reads as follows:[17]

No. 15

Discovery—Notice to Produce—Rule 23(6)

* For use in the District Court

In the Magistrate's Court for the District of ....

held at ....

Case No .... of 20......

In the matter between

.... Plaintiff

and

.... Defendant

TAKE NOTICE that the .... (plaintiff or defendant) requires you to produce within five days for his or her inspection the following documents or recordings referred to in your affidavit, dated the .... day of .... 20 ....

(Describe documents or recordings required)

Dated at .... this .... day of .... 20......

....

Attorney for the ....

(Address)

To:

....

Attorney for ....

(Address)

The person who receives the above notice must deliver within five days a notice stating a time within five days from the delivery of such latter notice when the document or recording may be inspected at the office of his or her attorney or, if he or she is not represented by an attorney, at some convenient place mentioned in the notice.[18] A party who has received such a notice is entitled at the time therein stated, and for a period of five days thereafter during normal business hours and on any one or more of such days, to inspect such document or recording and to take copies or transcriptions thereof.

---

[16] Rule 23(6).
[17] Annexure 1 Form 15.
[18] Rule 23(6)*(b)*.

The abovementioned notice reads as follows:

No. 15A

Discovery—Notice to Inspect Documents

* For use in the District Court

In the Magistrate's Court for the District of ....

held at ....

Case No .... of 20......

In the matter between

.... Plaintiff

and

.... Defendant

TAKE NOTICE that you may inspect the documents or recordings mentioned in your notice of the .... day of .... 20 ......, at my office, or at .... and between the hours of .... and on the following days.

(or)

That the (plaintiff or defendant) objects to giving you inspection of the documents or recordings mentioned in your notice of the .... day of .... 20 ...., on the grounds that ....

(State the grounds)

DATED at .... this .... day of .... 20......

....

Attorney for the ....

(Address)

To:

....

Attorney for ....

(Address)

After *litis contestatio*, it is possible for a party to give notice to another party to specify in writing particulars of dates and parties of or to any document or recording intended to be used at the trial of the action on behalf of the party to whom notice is given. The party who receives such a notice must, not less than 15 days before the date of the trial, deliver a notice that specifies:

(1) the dates of and parties to and the general nature of any such document or recording which is in his or her possession; or

(2) such particulars as he or she may have to identify any such document or recording not in his or her possession, and at the same time furnishing the name and address of the person who is in possession such document or tape, electronic, digital or other form of recording.[19]

Any party proposing to prove any document or recording at a trial may give notice to any other party requiring him or her, within 10 days after the receipt of such notice, to admit that such document or recording was properly executed and is what it purports to be.[20] If no admission is forthcoming, the party who delivered the notice shall be entitled to produce the document or recording specified at the

---

[19] Rule 23(9).

[20] Rule 23(10)(*a*).

trial without proof other than proof, if it is disputed, that the document or recording is the document or recording referred to in the notice and that the notice was duly given.[21] Where the party who received the notice expressly states that the document or recording is not admitted, the other party would need to prove it before he or she is entitled to use it at the trial, but the party not admitting it may be ordered to pay the costs of its proof.[22]

Rule 23 provides that a party may at any time before the hearing deliver a notice to any other party in whose pleadings or affidavits reference is made to any document or recording to produce it for his or her inspection and to permit him or her to make a copy or transcription thereof.[23] The rule 23(13) notice reads as follows:

No. 15B
Discovery—Notice to Produce Documents in Pleadings, etc—Rule 23(13)(*a*)

* For use in the District Court

In the Magistrates' Court for the District of ....

held at ....

Case No .... of 20......

In the matter between

.... Plaintiff

and

.... Defendant

TAKE NOTICE that the plaintiff (or defendant) requires you to produce for his or her inspection the following documents or recordings referred to in your .... (declaration or plea, or affidavit).

(Describe documents or recordings required)

To:

....

Attorney for the ....
(Address)

....

Attorney for ....
(Address)

1.3 Medical examinations, inspection of things, expert testimony, plans, diagrams, models and photographs

Rule 24 contains detailed provisions regarding:
- medical examinations;
- inspection of things;
- expert testimony;
- the presentation in evidence of a plan, diagram, model or photograph.

This rule was incorporated into the magistrates' courts' rules in 1968. It is the equivalent of rule 36 in the High Court. The object of the High Court rule was

---

[21] Rule 23(10)(*b*).
[22] Rule 23(10)(*c*).
[23] In accordance with Annexure 1 Form 15B.

described in the following terms by Wessels JA in *Coopers (SA) (Pty) Ltd v Deutsche Gesellschaft fur Schadlingsbekämpfung mbH*:[24]

> 'In deciding whether there has been due compliance with . . . [the rule], it is, in my opinion, relevant to have regard to the main purpose thereof, which is to require the party intending to call a witness to give expert evidence to give the other party such information about his evidence as will remove the element of surprise, which in earlier times (regarded as an element affording a tactical advantage) frequently caused delays in the conduct of trials. Indeed, all the subrules of Rule 36 were formulated with that purpose in mind.'

1.3.1 *Medical examinations*

Any party to proceedings in which damages or compensation in respect of alleged bodily injury is claimed may require any party claiming such damages or compensation whose state of health is relevant to the determination of the damages or compensation claimed to submit to an examination by one or more duly registered medical practitioners.[25]

This procedure is followed in particular in third-party insurance claims. A notice is given to the plaintiff requiring him or her to report for a medical examination on a stipulated date at a stipulated place.

The notice must specify the nature of the examination required, the person or persons by whom it will be conducted, and the place where and the date (which must not be less than 15 days from the date of the notice) and time when the desired examination is to take place.[26]

The notice must in addition state that the party undergoing the medical examination shall be entitled to have his or her own medical adviser present.[27]

Accompanying the notice must be a remittance of an amount that the recipient may reasonably expect to incur by way of expense in attending the examination. The amount must be tendered on the scale applicable to a person attending court as a witness in a civil suit, with the proviso that:

(1) If the party in question is not physically capable of proceeding to the examination on his or her own, the amount to be paid to him or her must include the cost of his or her travelling by motor vehicle and, where required, the reasonable cost of a person attending upon him or her.

(2) Where the other party will actually forfeit any salary, wage or other remuneration during the period of his or her absence from work, he or she shall in addition to his or her expenses, on the basis of a witness in a civil case, be entitled to receive an amount not exceeding R75 per day in respect of the salary, wage or other remuneration which he or she will actually forfeit.

(3) Any amount paid by a party in terms of these provisions shall be costs in the cause, unless the court directs otherwise.[28]

Such a notice would read:

---

[24] 1976 (3) SA 352 (A) at 371D.
[25] Rule 24(1).
[26] Rule 24(2)(*a*).
[27] Rule 24(2)(*b*).
[28] Rule 24(2)(*c*).

---

*For use in the District Court

In the Magistrate's Court for the District of ....

held at ....

Case No .... of 20......

In the matter between

.... Plaintiff

and

.... Defendant

NOTICE IN TERMS OF RULE 24(1) AND (2)

TAKE NOTICE that the .... requires .... to undergo a medical examination in terms of the above rule by Dr .... on the .... day of .... 20...... at ....h...................

TAKE NOTICE FURTHER that the purpose of the medical examination is to ascertain the state of health of the ...., which is relevant to the determination of the claim for damages in the above matter.

TAKE NOTICE FURTHER that the ....'s own medical representative may be present at the above examination.

.... hereby tenders the amount of R...................., being the reasonable expense to be incurred in connection with the above examination and a cheque in the above amount is attached hereto.

SIGNED at .... on this .... day of .... 20......

....

Attorney for ....

Address: ....

To: The Clerk of the Court

....

And to: ....

....

It is a drastic step to compel a party to subject himself or herself to a medical examination; nevertheless, the rules permit a party so required to raise only a few specific objections. He or she may not refuse point blank to subject himself or herself to the medical examination. He or she must set his or her objections out in writing within 10 days of his or her receipt of the notice calling upon him or her to present himself or herself for medical examination. In the written objection he or she must state the nature and grounds of the objection to:

- the nature of the proposed examination;
- the person or persons by whom the examination is to be conducted;
- the place, date or time of the examination;
- the amount of the expenses tendered to him or her,

and the objector must in addition:

- if he or she objects to the place, date or time of the examination, suggest an alternative place, date or time for the examination;
- if he or she objects to the amount of the expenses tendered, furnish particulars of such increased amount as he or she may require.[29]

---

[29] Rule 24(3)(*a*).

If the party receiving the notice fails to object to it within a period of 10 days, he or she will be deemed to have agreed to the examination on the terms set forth by the party giving the notice.[30]

If the party to whom objection is made is of the opinion that the objection or any part of it is unfounded, he or she may apply to court to determine the conditions upon which the examination, if any, is to be conducted.[31]

The rule also provides for the inspection of X-rays and medical reports pertaining to the party claiming damages: the latter must, on notice by any other party, make available within 15 days any medical report, hospital record, X-ray photograph or other documentary information of a similar nature relevant to the assessment of the damages or compensation claimed.[32]

The notice requiring this inspection reads:

---

*For use in the District Court

In the Magistrate's Court for the district of ....

held at ....

Case No .... of 20......

In the matter between

.... Plaintiff

and

.... Defendant

NOTICE IN TERMS OF RULE 24(4)

TAKE NOTICE that the Defendant to this action requires the Plaintiff, in so far as he or she is able to do so, to furnish within 15 (fifteen) days of receipt hereof all medical reports, hospital records, X-ray photographs or other documentary information of a like nature which is/are relevant to the assessment of damages in the action.

SIGNED at .... on this .... day of .... 20......

....

ATTORNEY FOR DEFENDANT

Address: ....

To: The Clerk of the Court

....

And to: ....

....

If it appears from any medical examination that a further medical examination by any other medical practitioner is necessary or desirable in order to obtain full information on matters relevant to the assessment of damages or compensation, any party may require a second and final examination, and the provisions discussed above will likewise apply in respect of that examination.[33]

---

[30] Rule 24(3)*(b)*.
[31] Rule 24(3)*(c)*.
[32] Rule 24(4).
[33] Rule 24(5).

1.3.2 *Examinations of things in the possession of one's opponent*

The inspection before trial of a thing whose condition may be relevant may contribute considerably to the formulation of the issues in dispute, assist witnesses (especially expert witnesses) in the preparation of their evidence and facilitate the speedier and smoother resolution of the dispute. In this context, one thinks of an instance where the plaintiff avers that an incorrect part has been assembled into a machine, that goods delivered were of poor quality or that repair work has not been executed in a proper, workmanlike manner. In all of these instances, the court's task will be facilitated if the parties, together with all of the witnesses whom they wish to call to give evidence as to the condition of the thing in question, have taken the opportunity at the outset to inspect it.

If it appears that the condition of anything of any nature whatsoever, whether movable or immovable, may be relevant with regard to the decision of any matter at issue in any action, any party to the action may at any stage of proceedings—but not later than 15 days before the hearing—give notice to the party relying upon the existence of the state or condition of a thing in his or her possession or under his or her control to make it available for inspection or examination. He or she may stipulate in the notice that the recipient is required to have the thing in question or a fair sample of it available for inspection or examination for a period not exceeding 10 days from the date of receipt of the notice.[34]

The notice reads as follows:

---

* For use in the District Court

In the Magistrate's Court for the District of ....

held at ....

Case No.............. of 20......

In the matter between

.... Plaintiff

and

.... Defendant

NOTICE IN TERMS OF RULE 24(6)

TAKE NOTICE that the Defendant hereby requires the Plaintiff to make available to him or her for inspection and examination the .... in issue in the above action for a period not exceeding 10 (ten) days from the day of receipt of this notice, during normal office hours.

SIGNED at .... on this............... day of .... 20......

....

ATTORNEY FOR DEFENDANT

Address: ....

To: The Clerk of the Court

....

And to: ....

....

The party requested to submit the thing in question for inspection or examination may require the party making the request to specify the nature of the

---

[34] Rule 24(6).

inspection or examination to which the thing is to be subjected, and is not bound to submit it for inspection if he or she will be materially prejudiced by reason of the effect that the examination will have upon the thing to be examined.[35]

The wording of this notice may read simply:

TAKE NOTICE that the .... (party) requires the .... (party) to specify the nature of the inspection or examination to which the .... (thing) in issue in the above action will be subjected.

If the answer to this is 'The .... will be visually inspected', definitely no objection can be raised to the inspection. On the other hand, where the thing in question will be dismantled or subjected to chemical tests, objection may be raised on the basis that the proposed examination will have the effect of materially prejudicing the party who wishes to use the thing to establish his or her case.

If a dispute arises as to whether the thing should be submitted for inspection or examination, either party may on application to the court state that the inspection or examination has been required and objected to and the court may make such order as it may deem fit.[36]

1.3.3 *The report of the inspection or examination*
A party who requires his or her opponent to submit to a medical examination or to make a thing available for inspection must obtain from the person conducting the inspection or examination a full report in writing of the results of the examination or inspection and the opinions that he or she formed as a result.[37]

This report must then be furnished on request to the party who was medically examined or whose property was inspected.[38] This report does not form part of the pleadings. It is not necessary to supply the report to the party who was medically examined or whose property was inspected, in the absence of an express request for a copy of the report.

The party who requested the examination or inspection must bear the expense it entails, and such expense forms part of that party's costs in the action.[39]

When a party wishes, on the other hand, to call the person who conducted the examination or inspection to give evidence at the trial as an expert witness, that party is obliged to give notice at least 15 days before the hearing of his or her intention to do so, and at least 10 days before the hearing to deliver a summary of the expert's opinions and the reasons for them.[40]

If this notice is not delivered, the expert may be called to give evidence only with the leave of the court or the consent of all parties to the suit.[41]

---

[35] Rule 24(7)*(a)*.
[36] Rule 24(7)*(b)*.
[37] Rule 24(8)*(a)*.
[38] Rule 24(8)*(b)*.
[39] Rule 24(8)*(c)*.
[40] Rule 24(9)*(a)* and *(b)*.
[41] Rule 24(9).

The court has the power, if the prescribed time periods are not complied with, to postpone the trial.[42]

In *Coopers (SA) (Pty) Ltd v Deutsche Gesellschaft für Schädlingsbekädmpfung mbH*[43] the Appellate Division dealt with the content of this notice and went into the meaning of the expression 'a summary of such opinions of such expert and his reasons therefor' appearing in rule 24(9)*(b)*. The full report of the expert does not have to be set out in the summary required by rule 24(9)*(b)*, but the most important facts and data on which he or she bases his or her opinion must be furnished. Where the opinion is not based solely upon an inference from the facts set out in the notice, but a scientific formula or calculation is in issue, the formula or calculation in question must be set out briefly.

The following example illustrates the content of the notice required by rule 24(9):

---

* For use in the District Court

In the Magistrate's Court for the District of ....

held at ....

                                                    Case No .... of 20......

In the matter between

                             .... Plaintiff

                                  and

                             .... Defendant

NOTICE IN TERMS OF RULE 24(9)*(a)* AND *(b)*

(1)   TAKE NOTICE that the Plaintiff intends to call .... to give evidence as an expert witness at the trial of the above action.

(2)   TAKE NOTICE FURTHER that the following summary of the opinions of .... and the reasons therefor is furnished:

    (a)   .... is qualified as an expert to give the evidence summarised herein and his or her opinions are based on his or her knowledge and experience;

    (b)   he or she has examined .... and discovered the following:

        (i)   ....

        (ii)   .... (etc.);

    (c)   on the basis of the above examination and discovery he or she has arrived at the following conclusions:

        (i)   .... because ....

        (ii)   .... because ....

SIGNED on this .... day of .... 20......

                                    ....

                                    ATTORNEY FOR PLAINTIFF

To: The Clerk of the Court

....

And to: ....

....

---

[42] *Smit v Shongwe* 1982 (4) SA 699 (T).

[43] 1976 (3) SA 352 (A) at 370 *et seq*.

This notice may alternatively read as follows:

* For use in the District Court
In the Magistrate's Court for the District of ....
held at ....
Case No .... of 20......
In the matter between
.... Plaintiff
and
.... Defendant
NOTICE IN TERMS OF RULE 24(9)
TAKE NOTICE that .... intends to call .... as an expert witness in order to prove the quantum of damage sustained by ....
The abovementioned .... (expert witness) will give evidence to the effect that the cost of repair as set out in the Plaintiff's particulars of claim constitutes the fair and reasonable repair cost of the Plaintiff's vehicle damaged in the collision which occurred on ....
This opinion is based upon an investigation of the aforementioned vehicle conducted by him or her and on his or her training, knowledge and/or experience.
SIGNED on this .... day of .... 20......
....
ATTORNEY FOR PLAINTIFF
To: The Clerk of the Court
....
And to: ....
....

1.3.4 *Plans, diagrams, models or photographs*

No party may, except with the leave of the court or the consent of all the other parties, tender in evidence any plan, diagram, model or photograph unless he or she has given every other party notice of his or her intention to do so at least 10 days before the hearing of the action.[44]

The notice must state that every party receiving it shall be entitled to inspect such plan, diagram, model or photograph and must require such party, within five days of receipt of the notice, to state whether he or she has any objection to such plan, diagram, model or photograph being admitted in evidence without proof.[45]

If the party receiving the notice fails within the period specified in the notice to state whether he or she objects to the admission in evidence of the plan, diagram, model or photograph referred to in the notice, then such plan, diagram, model or photograph may be received in evidence upon its mere production and without further proof thereof.[46]

It is important to remember that a plan, diagram, model or photograph is admitted in evidence as such and not as proof of its content. Suppose that a plaintiff gives notice that in terms of the rule he or she intends to use a photograph of a damaged motor

---

[44] Rule 24(10)*(a)*.
[45] Rule 24(10)*(b)*.
[46] Rule 24(10)*(c)*.

vehicle at the trial. If the defendant does not object to the use of the photograph, it may be admitted in evidence at the trial. It is then unnecessary for the photographer to be called to give evidence concerning the taking of the photograph. The photograph will also be accepted as presenting a true image of what was photographed. But the photograph cannot be used in order to prove that the defendant negligently caused the damage to the vehicle or that the damage amounts to R*X*.

If a party objects to the admission in evidence of the plan, diagram, model or photograph, such plan, diagram, model or photograph, as the case may be, may be proved at the hearing of the action and the party receiving the notice may be ordered to pay the costs of such proof.[47] In this way, parties are discouraged from raising objections to the admission in evidence of plans, diagrams, models or photographs purely for the sake of the inconvenience that such objections may cause their opponents.

The tendering of such material in evidence is useful in order to assist the court at the trial to obtain a complete picture of the case, and it can also obviate the leading of unnecessary evidence.

1.4 Pretrial conferences

In order to curtail as far as possible the time taken up by the conduct of the trial itself, it is often desirable for the parties to attempt, before the trial, to restrict and delimit the points in dispute even further. The more the parties can reach agreement on matters that may be mutually admitted and the precise points in issue between them, the more the leading of unnecessary evidence can be curbed. In this way, the number of court days taken up by the trial may be considerably lessened, with a consequent saving of legal costs.

It is certainly true that the pleadings already go some way towards fulfilling the function of formulating the points in dispute. It is, however, also a fact that a litigant often denies his or her opponent's averments purely because he or she has no knowledge of whether the allegations are true or not.

However, after all of the pleadings have been delivered, possible reports of experts have been exchanged and inspections of things have been conducted, the parties are considerably better informed as to each other's cases than they were at the time of the delivery of pleadings.

For this reason, it is desirable for the parties to meet in order to examine the case as a whole and to determine which matters remaining in dispute at the time of close of pleadings they are prepared to admit and which matters they intend to canvass at the trial.

The High Court Rules now provide for a compulsory pretrial conference, which is usually conducted by the parties themselves.[48]

---

[47] Rule 24(10)(*d*).

[48] Rule 37, Uniform Rules of Court. The introduction of a new Uniform rule 37A, which deals with case flow management, was proposed early 2017, but has not yet been implemented. In this regard, see R Daya Deputy Chief State Law Adviser and Secretary to the Rules Board 'Proposed Amendments to Certain Uniform Rules and New Rules Submitted by the Judicial Case Flow Management Committee of the Office of the Chief Justice' 3 April 2017. See also para 2 of the 'Civil Practice Directives for the Regional Courts in South Africa' 4 ed (2017).

In the magistrates' courts the procedure laid down is not compulsory and takes place before a magistrate in chambers. The conference can be convened by the court or by one of the parties.[49] Often in practice it is convened by the court on the morning of the trial.

While the expression 'pretrial conference' is used here and the matter is dealt with as part of the pretrial procedure, it is important to remember that this procedure may be used at any stage of the proceedings.

The following matters may be discussed at the conference held in the presence of the magistrate:

(1) the simplification of the issues;
(2) the necessity or desirability of amendments to the pleadings;
(3) the possibility of obtaining admissions of fact and of documents with a view to avoiding unnecessary proof;
(4) the limitation of the number of expert witnesses; and
(5) such other matters as may aid in the disposal of the action in the most expeditious and least costly manner.

If a party wishes to request the parties to appear before the magistrate for a conference, he or she does so by directing a request in duplicate to the registrar or clerk of the court, indicating generally the matters which he or she desires should be considered at the conference.[50]

The request will read as follows:

---

* For use in the District Court

In the Magistrate's Court for the District of ....

held at ....

Case No .... of 20......

In the matter between

.... Plaintiff

and

.... Defendant

NOTICE IN TERMS OF SECTION 54(1)

TAKE NOTICE that the .... hereby requests you to issue an order in terms of s 54(1) of the Magistrates' Courts Act 32 of 1944 in terms of which the parties or their representatives are ordered to appear before the above Honourable Court in chambers for a conference to consider the following matters:

(1) ....

(2) ....

(Set out any of the matters referred to in s 54(1)*(a)–(e)*.)

SIGNED on this .... day of .... 20......

....

ATTORNEY FOR ....

---

[49] Section 54. See also para 2 of the 'Civil Practice Directives for the Regional Courts in South Africa' 4 ed (2017) which deal with judicial case management, specifically pre-trial conferences and trial-readiness certification.

[50] Rule 25(1).

> To: The Clerk of the Court
>
> ....
>
> And to: ....
>
> ....

The registrar or clerk of the court thereafter places the request before a judicial officer who, if he or she decides to call a conference, directs the registrar or clerk of the court to issue the necessary process.[51]

The procedure for requiring the attendance of parties or their legal representatives at a pretrial conference is by letter signed by the clerk of the court, together with a copy of the request set out above. The letter is delivered by hand or by registered post at least 10 days prior to the date fixed for the conference.[52]

The direction to attend the pretrial conference reads as follows:[53]

> **No. 19**
> **Direction to Attend Pretrial Conference**
>
> *** For use in the District Court**
>
> In the Magistrate's Court for the District of ....
>
> held at ....
>
> Case No .... of 20......
>
> In the matter between
>
> .... Plaintiff
>
> and
>
> .... Defendant
>
> [Direction in terms of section 54(1) of the Magistrates' Courts Act, 1944 (Act 32 of 1944.)]
>
> To the Plaintiff's Attorney/the Defendant's Attorney.
>
> You are hereby directed to attend a conference to be held before the magistrate in court .... on the .... day of .... 20 ...., at ....
> (time) to consider—
>
> (a) the simplification of the issues;
> (b) the necessity or desirability of amendments to the pleadings;
> (c) the possibility of obtaining admissions of fact and of documents with a view to avoiding unnecessary proof;
> (d) the limitation of the number of expert witnesses;
> (e) ....
>
> Dated at .... this .... day of .... 20......
>
> By Order of the Court,
>
> ....
>
> Clerk of the Court

If a party refuses or neglects to appear at the conference, the court may, without derogation from its power to punish for contempt of court, make such order as it considers equitable in the circumstances. Upon conclusion of the proceedings, the

---

[51] Rule 25(2).
[52] Rule 25(3) read with rule 9(9)(a).
[53] Annexure 1 Form 19.

court may order the party who has absented himself or herself from the pretrial conference to pay such costs as in the opinion of the court were incurred as a result of his or her absence.[54]

After the conference, the court issues an order reciting the action taken at the conference, the amendments allowed to the pleadings and the agreements made by the parties as to any of the matters considered, which limits the issues for trial to those not disposed of by admissions or agreements of the parties or their representatives.[55]

This order binds the parties, unless altered at the trial to prevent manifest injustice.[56]

The order reads as follows:[57]

No. 20
Order—Pretrial Conference

* For use in the District Court

In the Magistrate's Court for the District of ....

held at ....

Case No .... of 20......

In the matter between

.... Plaintiff

and

.... Defendant

Order in terms of section 54(2) of the Magistrates' Courts Act, 1944 (Act 32 of 1944).

To the Plaintiff's Attorney and the Defendant's Attorney.

At the pre-trial conference held in chambers/court .... at .... on the .... day of ...., 20...... between the parties and/or their representatives, the following was agreed upon:

(1) ....

(2) ....

(3) ....

(4) ....

(5) ....

As a result the court gave the following orders:

(1) ....

(2) ....

(3) ....

(4) ....

(5) ....

Dated at .... this .... day of ...., 20......

---

[54] Section 54(4).
[55] Section 54(2).
[56] Section 54(3).
[57] Annexure 1 Form 20.

By Order of the Court,
....
Clerk of the Court, To: Plaintiff's Attorney To: Defendant's Attorney

1.5 Subpoenas

A litigant may ask his witnesses to be present at court on the day of the trial to give evidence. Section 8 of the Civil Proceedings Evidence Act 25 of 1965 provides: 'Save in so far as this Act or any other law otherwise provides, every person shall be competent *and compellable*[58] to give evidence in any civil proceedings.'

The way in which a witness may be compelled to present himself or herself at a civil trial is by the service upon him or her of a subpoena.[59]

If no subpoena was served upon the witness, the absence of the witness may not be punished with the sanction provided for in the Act. (The word *subpoena* means, literally, 'subject to punishment'—should the witness not be present.)

A subpoena is issued by the registrar or clerk of the court and sued out by the party desiring the attendance of the witness.[60]

The subpoena is accompanied by the witness fees prescribed in terms of s 51*bis* by the Minister of Justice in consultation with the Minister of Finance by notice in the *Government Gazette*.[61] The witness fees are payable to a witness in civil proceedings or to any person necessarily required to accompany any such witness on account of his or her youth, old age or infirmity.[62]

The notice published in the *Government Gazette* may distinguish between persons according to the distances which they have to travel to attend the court to which they are summoned or subpoenaed, or according to their professions, callings or occupations, or between different classes of persons, and may empower certain officers in the service of the State, in cases where payment of witness fees in accordance with the prescribed tariff may cause undue hardship, to order payment of allowances in accordance with a higher tariff than the tariff so prescribed.[63]

The court may order that no allowances or only a portion of the allowances prescribed shall be paid to any witness.[64]

The subpoena may direct the witness to make books, papers or documents in his or her possession or under his or her control available at the trial and to produce them to the court. In this event, the subpoena is known as a subpoena *duces tecum* (meaning, literally, 'bring with you!').

The subpoena reads as follows:[65]

---

[58] My italics.
[59] Section 51(1) read with rule 26(1).
[60] Rule 26(1).
[61] The present tariff is contained in GN R2597 of 1 November 1991.
[62] Section 51*bis*(1).
[63] Section 51*bis*(2).
[64] Section 51*bis*(3).

No. 24
Subpoena

* For use in the District Court

In the Magistrate's Court for the District of ....

held at ....

Case No .... of 20......

In the matter between

.... Plaintiff

and

.... Defendant

To: the Sheriff/Deputy Sheriff:

INFORM:

(1) .... of ....

(2) .... of ....

(3) .... of ....

(4) .... of ....

that each of them is hereby required to appear in person before this court at court .... on the .... day of ...., 20......, at............................ (time) in the above-mentioned action to give evidence or to produce books, papers or documents on behalf of the .... (Where documents are required to be produced, add:) and to bring with each one of them and then produce to the court the several books, papers or documents specified in the list hereunder.

Payment of the witness fees for the witnesses as provided and allowed under section 51*bis* of the Magistrates' Courts Act, 1944 (Act 32 of 1944), as amended, is hereby tendered by the Plaintiff.

If any person, being duly subpoenaed to give evidence or to produce any books, papers or documents in his or her possession or under his or her control, which the party requiring the witness(es)' attendance desires to show in evidence, fails, without lawful excuse, to attend or to give evidence or to produce those books, papers or documents according to the subpoena or, unless duly excused, fails to remain in attendance throughout the trial, the court may, upon being satisfied on oath or by the return of the messenger that such person has been duly subpoenaed and that such person's reasonable expenses, calculated in accordance with the tariff prescribed under section 51*bis*, have been paid or offered to such person, impose upon the said person a fine not exceeding R300,00, and in default of payment, imprisonment for a period not exceeding three months, whether or not such person is otherwise subject to the jurisdiction of the court.

Dated at .... this .... day of ...., 20......

Clerk of the Court

LIST OF BOOKS, PAPERS OR DOCUMENTS TO BE PRODUCED

Date	Description	Original or Copy
....	....	....
....	....	....
....	....	....

(See back)

[Print on back, paragraphs *(a)* and *(b)* of section 51(2) of the Act.]

The subpoena must be served by the sheriff in the manner prescribed by rule 9, together with the amount offered by way of witness fees.[66]

---

[65] Annexure 1 Form 24.

[66] Rule 26(1) and (4).

The court may set aside the service of any subpoena if it appears that the witness upon whom it was served was not given reasonable time to enable him or her to appear pursuant to the subpoena.[67]

If any person, after being duly subpoenaed, fails, without lawful excuse, to attend or to give evidence or to produce those books, papers or documents stipulated in the subpoena or, unless duly excused, fails to remain in attendance throughout the trial, the court may, upon being duly satisfied upon oath or by the return of the sheriff that such person has been duly subpoenaed and that his or her reasonable expenses, calculated in accordance with the tariff prescribed under s 51*bis*, have been paid or offered to him or her, impose upon him or her a fine not exceeding R300 and, in default of payment, imprisonment for a period not exceeding three months, whether or not he or she is otherwise subject to the jurisdiction of the court.[68]

The relevant warrant issued by the court reads as follows:[69]

No. 25
Warrant for Payment of Fine or Arrest of Witness in Default
* For use in the District Court

In the Magistrate's Court for the District of ....

held at ....

Case No .... of 20......

In the matter between

.... Plaintiff

and

.... Defendant

Whereas .... of .... has been duly subpoenaed to give evidence (or to produce certain books, papers or documents, as the case may be) in the above matter before this court at .... (time) on the ....day of ...., 20 .... and has made default;

And whereas this court has imposed upon the said .... for his or her said default a fine of .... rand and for non-payment has committed him or her to the above-mentioned prison for a period of ....;

This is therefore to authorise and require you, the said sheriff of the court, to arrest the said .... and, unless he or she shall pay to you the said sum of .... rand, to deliver him or her to the officer in charge of the .... Prison together with this warrant to be safely kept there until he or she shall have paid the said sum of .... rand or until the expiration of the said period of .... from the day on which the said .... shall be received into or retained in the said prison by virtue of this warrant whichever of the two shall first happen or until the said .... shall be otherwise legally discharged;

And this is to command you, the said officer in charge of the .... Prison, to receive and safely keep the said .... as aforesaid.

Dated at .... this .... day of ...., 20......

....

Clerk of the Court

---

[67] Rule 26(5).
[68] Section 51(2)*(a)*.
[69] Annexure 1 Form 25.

The court also has the power to order the arrest of the witness who has failed to appear or who, without having been duly excused, has failed to remain in attendance throughout the trial, so that he or she can be brought before the court to give his or her evidence.[70]

In that instance, the court issues the following warrant:[71]

No. 26
Warrant for the Arrest of a Witness in Default

* For use in the District Court

In the Magistrate's Court for the District of ....

held at ....

Case No .... of 20......

In the matter between

.... Plaintiff

and

.... Defendant

(1) To the Sheriff:

Whereas .... of .... has been duly subpoenaed to give evidence (or to produce certain books, papers or documents, as the case may be) in the above matter before this court on the .... day of 20...... at (time), and has made default;

This is therefore to authorise and require you to arrest the said............................ and bring him or her before this court on the .... day of .... 20...... at .... (time), then and there to give evidence and to be otherwise dealt with according to law.

(2) To the Officer-in-Charge of the .... Prison:

You are hereby commanded to receive the said .... and to keep him or her safely until such time as he or she shall be removed to have him or her before the court in accordance with the first part of this warrant or until he or she shall be otherwise lawfully discharged.

Dated at .... this .... day of ...., 20......

....

Clerk of the Court

If good cause can be shown for doing so, the court may remit the whole or part of any fine or imprisonment which it has imposed under s 51(2).[72] The court may also order all or part of the costs of any postponement or adjournment occasioned by the default of a witness to be paid out of a fine imposed upon the witness in default.[73]

When a subpoena has been issued to procure the attendance of a judicial officer to give evidence or to produce any book, paper or document in a criminal case, civil action or other proceeding, if it appears that:

(1) he or she is unable to give any evidence or to produce any book, paper or document which would be relevant to any issue in the case, action or proceeding;

---

[70] Section 51(2)*(b)*.
[71] Annexure 1 Form 26.
[72] Section 51(2)*(c)*.
[73] Section 51*(2)(d)*.

(2) the book, paper or document could properly be produced by some other person; or

(3) to compel him or her to attend would be an abuse of the process of the court, the court may, after reasonable notice to the party suing out the subpoena, make an order cancelling the subpoena.[74]

1.6 The trial by interrogatory or by means of commission *de bene esse*

These two procedures may be used to obtain evidence where a witness lives or is outside of the district in which the trial is heard.

In trial by interrogatory, the court is approached for its approval of questions that the parties wish to have put to the witness. Those questions approved by the court are then transmitted, together with any further questions framed by the court itself, to the court of the district within which the witness resides or is.[75]

The latter court then subpoenas the witness to appear before it and, on his appearance, takes his or her evidence in the same manner and form as though he or she were a witness in a case pending before that court. The court puts to the witness the questions transmitted to it (which are termed the 'interrogatories'), together with such other questions as it thinks necessary in order to obtain full and true answers to the interrogatories. The court records the evidence of the witness and transmits the evidence to the court in which the case is pending. The record of the questions put to and the answers given by the witness are (subject to all lawful objections) then received as evidence in that case.[76]

Where the court has issued an order authorising the evidence of any witness to be taken on interrogatories, the interrogatories must be filed within four days of the court's order, and cross-interrogatories within five days thereafter.[77]

The witness who is subpoenaed to give evidence upon interrogatory before a court is liable to the same penalties in the case of non-attendance or failure to give evidence or to produce books, papers or documents as though he or she had been subpoenaed to give evidence in a trial action pending in the court of the district in which he or she resides or is.[78]

Should a party wish to have the evidence of a witness recorded, whether the witness is within the Republic or elsewhere, he or she may request the court to appoint a commissioner to take the evidence.[79] The evidence, in such a case, is therefore not recorded by a court but by a commission, known as a commission *de bene esse*.

The instruction issued to the commissioner reads as follows:[80]

---

[74] Section 51(3).
[75] Section 52(1).
[76] Section 52(2).
[77] Rule 29(15).
[78] Section 52(3).
[79] Section 53(1). It must be expedient and consistent with the ends of justice to do so.
[80] Annexure 1 Form 23.

No. 23
Commissions *de bene esse*

* For use in the District Court

In the Magistrate's Court for the District of ....

held at ....

Case No .... of 20......

In the matter between

.... Plaintiff

and

.... Defendant

To: ....

....

Greeting:

Under and by virtue of the authority vested in me by section 53 of the Magistrates' Courts Act, 1944 (Act 32 of 1944), I do hereby commit to you full power and authority as a Commissioner of this court to examine .... of .... (and such other witnesses as either of the parties to this suit may desire to call) and to take the evidence on oath of the said witness(es) in the above suit now pending in this court.

Given under my hand at .... this .... day of ...., 20 ......

....

Magistrate

In the case of evidence taken on commission, the subpoena summonsing the witness to appear is sued out by the party desiring the attendance of the witness and is issued by the commissioner.[81]

This procedure for the taking of evidence is used in cases in which it is in the interests of justice that the evidence be recorded and where there is some or other valid reason as to why the witness cannot give evidence at the trial, for example that the witness is resident outside South Africa,[82] or is sickly and bedridden or extremely old,[83] or intends to leave the Republic prior to the hearing.[84]

The commissioner puts to the witness such questions as have been mutually agreed upon by the parties and transmitted to him or her, or otherwise allows the parties to examine the witness, and may himself or herself question the witness as though the witness were being examined in court. He or she records the evidence or has it recorded, after which the record is read back to the witness and signed by him or her.[85] The record is then (subject to all lawful objections) received as evidence in the case.[86]

1.7 The final checking and preparation for trial

At this stage of proceedings (viz prior to the hearing of the action), the legal representative ought to have the following in his possession:

---

[81] Rule 26(2).
[82] *J Raw & Co v Hugh Parker & Co* (1890) 11 NLR 112.
[83] *Becker & others v Wolfaardt* (1906) 16 CTR 727.
[84] *Janisch v Herold* 1914 CPD 258.
[85] Section 53(2).
[86] Section 53(3).

(1) all pleadings;
(2) all discovered documents such as contracts, letters and other exhibits; and
(3) expert reports and documents obtained in terms of the provisions of rule 24.

In High Court practice it is customary for an advocate to be briefed to draft an Advice on Evidence. In such an Advice the following are discussed: the form of the pleadings, the nature of the claim and the onus of proof, and all the necessary and available evidence. Any further preparations for the trial are set out. From this document the attorney can thoroughly prepare for trial.

A similar practice is advisable in the magistrates' courts. A thorough review of the whole case should be undertaken with a view to leading evidence at the trial. All too often this is not done and some important aspect of the matter is overlooked. This step has great advantages for the trial itself because it makes the immediate preparation for trial so much easier.

The legal representative may use the following as a checklist to ascertain whether all of the necessary preparations for trial are complete:
(1) Have copies of all pertinent documents been obtained from his or her opponent?
(2) Have all notices served by his or her opponent been answered?
(3) Have all subpoenas been issued and served?
(4) Is an interpreter necessary? If so, have arrangements been made?
(5) Are there sufficient copies of the documents that may be used as possible exhibits?
(6) The documents must be arranged in a logical sequence.
(7) The documents, including those filed in court, must be paginated and an index must be drafted of all documents. The court file should then be prepared. This is the duty of the plaintiff, or of the defendant if the defendant has set the matter down.
(8) Consultations with witnesses should be arranged.

After final consultations have been held with all of the witnesses and statements have been taken from them, the legal representative goes over his case as a whole in order to prepare for trial. At this stage the actual presentation of evidence is organised. The legal representative should prepare notes as to the evidence to be led, and prepare, as far as is possible, for the cross-examination of the witnesses for the other side.

The legal representative ought to arrange his or her own file of relevant documents under the following headings:
(1) pleadings and notices;
(2) statements of witnesses;
(3) documentary exhibits;
(4) exhibits, such as X-rays; and
(5) reports of experts.

2 THE PROCEDURE AT TRIAL

Although the law of civil procedure is aimed to a large extent at enabling the dispute to be tried, there are relatively few provisions in the Act and rules pertaining directly to the trial.

The trial itself is governed principally by the rules of evidence. The law of evidence falls beyond the scope of this book, and only purely procedural aspects will therefore be considered here.

2.1 The place of the trial

The trial takes place in the building of the court out of which summons was issued, unless the court orders otherwise.[87] An action or proceeding may, however, be transferred by the court to any other court with the consent of all parties, or upon the application of any party and upon its being made to appear that the trial of the action or proceeding in the court out of which summons was issued may result in undue expense or inconvenience to that party.[88]

All cases must be heard in open court.[89]

The court may, in the interests of good order or public morals, direct that a civil trial shall be held behind closed doors or that (with such exceptions as the court may direct) minors or the public generally may not be present at the trial.[90]

If any person present at civil proceedings in any court disturbs the peace or order of the court, the court has the power to order that that person be removed and detained in custody until the rising of the court, and the presiding officer may, if he or she is of the opinion that order cannot otherwise be maintained, order the courtroom to be cleared and that the doors of the court be closed to the public.[91]

2.2 The opening address

Although it is not necessary for an opening address to be delivered by the plaintiff or the defendant at every trial, the parties may, if necessary, address the court before the first witness is called to explain some aspect of the case to the court. The court itself, prior to the taking of evidence, may require the parties to state briefly the issues of fact or questions of law in dispute and may record the issues so stated.[92]

2.3 The hearing of preliminary issues

If upon the pleadings it appears to the court that there is a question of law or fact which may conveniently be decided before any evidence is led or separately from any other question, the court may make an order directing the disposal of such question in such a manner as it may deem fit and may order that all further proceedings be stayed until such question has been disposed of. Such an order may also be sought by either party.[93] If the question in dispute is a question of law and the parties are agreed upon the facts, the facts may be admitted in court by the

---

[87] Rule 29(1).

[88] Section 35(1).

[89] Section 5(1).

[90] Section 5(2).

[91] Section 5(3).

[92] Rule 29(3).

[93] Rule 29(4). The court is obliged to order separation unless it appears that the issues cannot conveniently be decided separately. *Braaf v Fedgen Ltd* 1995 (3) SA 938 (C); *Edward L Bateman Ltd v CA Brand Projects (Pty) Ltd* 1995 (4) SA 128 (T).

parties, either orally or by written statement, and recorded by the court, and judgment may be given thereon without further evidence.[94]

If questions of law and issues of fact arise in the same case and the court is of the opinion that the case may be disposed of upon the questions of law only, the court may require the parties to argue upon only those questions. The court may give its decision on them before taking evidence as to the issues of fact and may then give final judgment without dealing with the issues of fact.[95]

2.4 The witnesses and the language medium used at the proceedings
A witness who is not a party to the action may be ordered by the court to:
(1)   leave the court until his or her evidence is required or after his or her evidence has been given; or
(2)   remain in court after his or her evidence has been given until the trial is terminated or adjourned.[96]

Every witness gives his or her evidence under oath or affirmation. The oath to be taken by any witness in any civil proceedings in any court must be administered by the presiding officer or by the clerk of the court (or any person acting in his or her stead) in the presence of the presiding officer, or if the witness is to give his or her evidence through an interpreter, by that officer through the interpreter or by the interpreter in the presiding officer's presence.[97]

The plaintiff and the defendant are entitled to be present in court throughout the trial and to listen to all of the evidence and arguments.

The Act still envisages only two official languages.[98] However, on 31 March 2017 the Heads of Courts Forum resolved that English must be the official language of record in all South African courts. No national directive has been issued by the Office of the Chief Justice as to the application of the resolution. The office of the Judge President of the Western Cape High Court has, however, issued a directive that '[a]ll court documents submitted to courts in both civil and criminal cases and which will form part of the eventual record shall be submitted in English'. It further states that '[t]he only limited exception permitted to the said directive will be the submission of witness statements in a language other than English and only if the witness is not sufficiently conversant in English'. Furthermore, '[c]ourt proceedings should as far as possible be conducted in English'. If a witness is not conversant in English, only the leading of evidence may be conducted in another language.

2.5 The course of the trial
The party on whom the onus of proof rests according to the pleadings has the duty to lead his or her evidence first.[99]

---

[94] Rule 29(5).
[95] Rule 29(6).
[96] Rule 29(2).
[97] Section 112.
[98] Section 6. The section must be interpreted in conformity with s 6(1) of the Constitution.
[99] Rules 29(7)(*a*) and 29(8).

Normally it is the plaintiff who is obliged to lead evidence first because the necessity for proof of a cause of action requires the plaintiff to establish the facts which give rise to his or her cause of action, while the defendant is required to prove a special defence raised by him or her.

Where the burden of proving one or more of the issues is on the plaintiff and that of proving others is on the defendant, the plaintiff is first required to lead evidence on any issues on which he or she bears the onus of proof, after which he or she may close his or her case and the defendant will then call his or her evidence on all of the issues in dispute.[100]

If the plaintiff has not called any evidence (other than that necessitated by evidence on issues in respect of which the onus rests upon him or her) on issues in relation to which the defendant bears the onus, then the plaintiff may call such evidence after the defendant has closed his or her case. If, however, the plaintiff has called any such evidence, he or she has no right to lead further evidence after the close of the defendant's case.[101]

Where a dispute arises as to which party bears the burden of proof, the court directs which party is to adduce evidence first.[102]

Suppose that the duty to adduce evidence first rests upon the plaintiff. In that event the plaintiff himself or herself will give evidence first. He or she is, of course, permitted to remain present in court throughout the duration of the trial. If he or she first has all of his or her witnesses give evidence and only thereafter gives his or her own evidence, the suspicion may arise that he or she has tailored his or her version of the facts to fit in with what his or her witnesses have already told the court. The other witnesses usually sit outside the court, and it is considerably better, from the point of view of the probative value of the evidence, to have the plaintiff give his or her evidence first and thereafter to call his or her witnesses who are waiting outside the court to give their evidence.

Each witness may be examined by the court and cross-examined by the opposite party to the one who called him or her.[103]

The plaintiff whose witness has been cross-examined on his or her evidence may also, in re-examination, question his or her witness on new matters arising out of the cross-examination.

In this way, the plaintiff calls his or her witnesses one after the other to give evidence.

After the plaintiff has called all of his or her witnesses and they have given their evidence and been cross-examined by the defendant, the plaintiff closes his or her case.

A party may, with the leave of the court, adduce further evidence at any time before judgment, but such leave may not be granted if it appears to the court that the evidence in question was intentionally withheld out of its proper order.[104] It is

---

[100] Rule 29(9)*(a)*. The rule refers to the 'calling' of evidence. This may be an inelegant translation of the Afrikaans 'aanvoer'. A better expression would be to 'lead' or 'adduce' evidence.

[101] Rule 29(9)*(b)*.

[102] Rule 29(10).

[103] Rule 29(13).

[104] Rule 29(11).

therefore only in exceptional cases that the court will permit a party who already closed his or her case to reopen it and lead further evidence. The court, however, has the power at any time before judgment to recall any witness for further examination on the application of any party or of its own motion.[105]

As soon as the plaintiff closes his or her case, the defendant may apply for absolution from the instance.

If the court refuses to grant the application for absolution, the defendant is given the opportunity to establish his or her case by calling witnesses to give evidence on his or her behalf.

Just as in the case of the plaintiff's witnesses, each witness called by the defendant may be subjected to examination-in-chief, cross-examination and re-examination. Once the evidence of all of his or her witnesses has been heard, the defendant closes his or her case.

After both parties have closed their cases, the legal representatives are given the opportunity to address the court. The party who first adduced evidence addresses the court first, and thereafter the other party; finally, the first party may reply to the address of his or her opponent.[106]

After the parties have been afforded the opportunity of addressing the court, the court may deliver judgment immediately, or may reserve judgment and adjourn.

The trial of an action or the hearing of an application may be adjourned or postponed by the court by consent of the parties or by the court, either on application or request or of the court's own motion.[107] The adjournment or postponement takes place on such terms as to costs as may be agreed upon by the parties or ordered by the court.[108]

2.6 Amendment of pleadings during the trial

In any civil proceeding, the court may, at any time before judgment, authorise the amendment of any summons or other document forming part of the record. No such amendment will be made, however, where the opposing party (notwithstanding adjournment) may be prejudiced in the conduct of his or her action or defence.[109]

The court may always order the amendment of the pleadings upon such terms as to costs and otherwise as the court may consider reasonable.[110]

A misnomer in regard to the name of any person or place does not vitiate the proceedings of the court if the person or place is described as he, she or it is commonly known, and the court may, on application, correct the misnomer at any time before or after judgment is given.[111]

---

[105] Rule 29(12). The court is not, however, competent *mero motu* to call a new witness in a civil case (*Rowe v Assistant Magistrate, Pretoria, & another* 1925 TPD 361).
[106] Rule 29(14).
[107] Rule 31(1).
[108] Rule 31(3).
[109] Section 111(1).
[110] Section 111(2).
[111] Section 111(3).

2.7 Inspections *in loco*

There is no specific statutory provision conferring upon the court the power to hold an inspection *in loco*. It has always been accepted, however, that our courts have an inherent power to hold such an inspection.[112]

Any party may therefore request that an inspection *in loco* be held. It is submitted that the court may likewise order an inspection acting on its own initiative.[113]

The court is obliged to keep minutes of the inspection *in loco* and such minutes form part of the record of proceedings. The parties should be given the opportunity of agreeing with it or challenging it.[114]

The inspection must be held in the presence of all interested parties.[115] It must take place before the parties have closed their cases, so that they will have the opportunity of putting forward explanations as to what has been observed at the inspection.[116]

2.8 The record of proceedings

The court is obliged to keep minutes of record of the following matters:

(1) any judgment given by the court;
(2) any oral evidence given in court;
(3) any objection made to any evidence received or tendered; and
(4) the proceedings of the court generally, including the record of any inspection *in loco*.[117]

To keep minutes of record of a case means to take the proceedings down in writing or in shorthand or to record the proceedings by mechanical means (viz by means of a tape recorder).[118]

In the larger centres, most civil courts are equipped with tape recorders, but in many smaller centres the minutes of the proceedings still have to be taken down by the presiding officer using those age-old tools, pen and paper.

Shorthand as a method of recording proceedings in court is even less common. The rules of court contain, however, a number of provisions pertaining to the keeping of shorthand records of proceedings. Rule 30(10) reflects, however, the burgeoning tendency to record court proceedings on tape.

Any reference in the rules to 'shorthand notes' or to a 'transcription' or 'transcript' of such notes, or to a copy of such a transcript, or to a person employed for the taking of shorthand notes or for the transcription of such notes, is to be construed as a reference to a record of proceedings made by mechanical means, to a transcription or transcript of such record, to a copy of such a transcript, or to a

---

[112] See *Kruger v Ludick* 1947 (3) SA 23 (A) at 31.
[113] *R v Sewpaul* 1949 (4) SA 978 (N); *East London Municipality v Van Zyl* 1959 (2) SA 514 (E).
[114] Rule 30(1)*(d)*; *Bayer South Africa (Pty) Ltd & another v Viljoen* 1990 (2) SA 647 (A).
[115] *Norwitz v The Magistrate of Fauresmith & Bane* 1928 OPD 109.
[116] *Goldstuck v Mappin & Webb Ltd* 1927 TPD 723.
[117] Rule 30(1).
[118] See definition in s 1.

person employed for the making of a mechanical record of proceedings or a person transcribing such mechanical record, as the case may be.[119]

The person who is employed for the taking of shorthand notes or for the transcription of shorthand notes taken by another person is deemed to be an officer of the court and is obliged, before entering on his or her duties, to take an oath or make an affirmation before the judicial officer.[120]

Shorthand notes are taken by the shorthand writer and must be certified by him or her as correct and thereafter filed with the record of the case by the registrar or clerk of the court.[121]

Shorthand notes are not transcribed unless a judicial officer so directs.[122]

The transcript must be certified as correct by the person making it and filed with the record of the case.[123]

Anyone may on notice to the clerk of the court request a transcription of any shorthand notes or of any recording on payment of the full cost thereof as predetermined by agreement between the contractor concerned and the State for such transcription.[124]

One copy of the transcript of the shorthand notes must then be supplied free of charge to the person at whose request the transcription was made.[125]

The original copy of the transcript of the shorthand notes must be certified as correct by the person making it and filed with the record of the case.[126]

Any shorthand notes and any transcript of them, certified as correct, are deemed to be correct and form part of the record of proceedings in question.[127]

A copy of any transcript made simultaneously with the transcription of any shorthand notes may, on application to the registrar or clerk of the court, be supplied to any person upon payment of the predetermined fee.

When it makes minutes of the proceedings, the court also marks each document put in evidence and notes these marks on the record.[128]

The arguments of the parties, the oral evidence given, any exception or objection taken in the course of the proceedings, the rulings and judgment of the court and any other portion of the proceedings may be recorded in any of the ways described above, viz in shorthand, verbatim or in narrative form, or mechanically.[129]

If it is alleged that the record of proceedings is in some respect erroneous, any party may, not later than 10 days after judgment, or, where proceedings have been noted in shorthand or by mechanical means, within 10 days after having been notified by the registrar or clerk of the court that the transcript of the shorthand

---

[119] Rule 30(10).
[120] Rule 30(5)*(a)*.
[121] Rule 30(6)*(a)*.
[122] Rule 30(6)*(b)*.
[123] Rule 30(6)*(c)*.
[124] Rule 30(7)*(a)*.
[125] Rule 30(7)*(b)*.
[126] Rule 30(7)*(c)*.
[127] Rule 30(8).
[128] Rule 30(2).
[129] Rule 30(4).

notes or mechanical record has been completed, apply to the court to correct any errors in the minutes of the proceedings or in the transcript of the shorthand notes or mechanical record, and the court may then correct any such errors.[130]

If, before the hearing of such an application, all of the parties affected file a consent to the corrections claimed, no costs of the application may be allowed; otherwise, the costs will be in the discretion of the court.[131]

The presiding officer is obliged to note on the record of proceedings which last for a quarter of an hour or longer the time of day at which the proceedings actually commenced and actually ended, as well as the time of commencement and conclusion of every adjournment.[132] The duration of the proceedings in court is recorded in this way so that, when the costs have to be determined, there is a note of how long the case lasted in court.

Members of the public are entitled to access to the records of civil cases heard in a magistrate's court. The records may be inspected under the supervision of the clerk of the court at convenient times and upon payment of the prescribed fees. A person who wishes for purposes of academic research to inspect the records of cases may, however, be exempted from the payment of the prescribed inspection fees.[133]

This request for inspection of the record of a case reads:[134]

No. 55
Request to Inspect Record

*For use in the District Court

In the Magistrate's Court for the District of ....

held at ....

I, ..., of ...., hereby apply to inspect the record of Case No .... of 20......

(If number of record is not known, then as follows:)

I, ..., of ...., hereby apply to inspect the record of the case between .... (plaintiff) and .... (defendant).

Search to begin with the month of .... 20......

....

Signature

(If the applicant is a party to the case or the attorney of such party, his or her capacity should be stated after his or her signature.)

2.9 Non-appearance of a party at the trial

It sometimes happens that one of the parties does not arrive at court on the day set down for the hearing of the trial or an application.

---

[130] Rule 30(11).
[131] Rule 30(12).
[132] Rule 33(7).
[133] Section 7(1).
[134] Annexure 1 Form 55.

If the plaintiff or applicant fails to appear at the appointed time, the action or application may be dismissed with costs.[135]

The action or application may not, however, be dismissed if the plaintiff or applicant is not present but his or her legal representative is. Since the expression 'plaintiff' or 'applicant' includes the attorney or advocate appearing on his or her behalf, that party is *de jure* present in court as long as his or her legal representative is present.[136]

Where the legal representative is present in court but the plaintiff or applicant, whose presence is necessary, is not, the court will usually postpone the case at the expense of the absent plaintiff or applicant. His or her legal representative may, however, ask the court for leave to be excused from further attendance at the proceedings. If such leave is granted, then the plaintiff or applicant is unrepresented and the court may dismiss the action or application.

The dismissal of the case for this reason has the same effect as the grant of an order of absolution from the instance.

The dismissal of the claim therefore does not mean that the matter is *res judicata*.[137]

If a defendant or respondent fails to appear on the day set aside for the hearing, a judgment (not exceeding the relief claimed) may be given against him or her with costs.[138]

2.10   The withdrawal of an action

It is possible for a plaintiff to withdraw an action instituted by himself or herself. He or she may withdraw the summons that has been issued if it has not yet been served or if the time allowed for entry by the defendant of appearance to defend has expired and appearance has not been entered.

Withdrawal of the summons takes place by way of notice to the registrar or clerk of the court.[139]

The notice of withdrawal reads as follows:[140]

No. 6
Notice of Withdrawal

* For use in the District Court

In the Magistrate's Court for the District of ....

held at ....

Case No .... of 20......

In the matter between

.... Plaintiff/Applicant

and

.... Defendant/Respondent

---

[135] Rule 32(1).
[136] Rule 2(1); *Serfontein v Bosch* 1930 OPD 75.
[137] Rule 32(3).
[138] Rule 32(2).
[139] Rule 27(1).
[140] Annexure 1 Form 6.

The plaintiff/applicant hereby withdraws the above-mentioned action/application and consents to pay the defendant's/respondent's taxed costs.

Dated at .... this .... day of ...., 20......

....

Plaintiff/Plaintiff's Attorney*

Applicant/Applicant's Attorney*

To: ....

....

and: The Clerk of the Court,

....

The withdrawal may not be raised by the defendant as a defence to a subsequent action, but should a subsequent claim be brought on the same cause of action before the plaintiff has paid the costs awarded upon the withdrawal of the initial claim, the court may, on application by the defendant, order a stay of the subsequent action until the costs occasioned by the withdrawal have been paid.[141]

Any party served with a notice of withdrawal may, within 20 days thereafter, apply to the court for an order that the party so withdrawing shall pay the applicant's costs of the action or application withdrawn, together with the costs incurred in so applying. In withdrawing, the plaintiff may consent to pay the costs, in which case the consent has the force of an order of court and the registrar or clerk of the court can be requested by the defendant to tax the costs.[142]

2.11 Settlement

The parties are free to settle the matter between them at any time before judgment is given. In practice, it very often happens that the case is settled even while the trial is in progress. Experience shows that the further a case progresses and the closer the date of trial, the more prepared the parties become to settle the case.

A party may, if he or she wishes, abandon a specific claim, exception or defence. In accordance with Annexure 1 Form 53, the notice of abandonment will take the following form:

No. 53

Notice of Abandonment of Specified Claim, Exception or Defence

* For use in the District Court

In the Magistrate's Court for the District of ....

held at ....

Case No .... of 20......

In the matter between

.... Plaintiff

and

.... Defendant

---

[141] Rule 32(3).

[142] Rule 27(3).

> Take notice that the plaintiff/defendant hereby abandons the under-mentioned claim/exception/
> defence (as the case may be) set up by him or her in his or her summons/plea/reply (as the case
> may be).
> Particulars: ....
> ....
> Dated at .... this .... day of ...., 20......
> ....
> Plaintiff/Plaintiff's Attorney or Defendant/Defendant's Attorney
> To: ....

If the parties settle the case, the cause of action giving rise to the claim is wiped out. The settlement constitutes an agreement between the parties which brings into existence a fresh legal relationship between them.[143]

When the matter is settled, the parties will agree upon settlement terms. They may agree, for example, that the defendant will pay an amount of RX to the plaintiff in full and final settlement, that the plaintiff will withdraw his or her claim against the defendant and that each party will bear his or her own costs. This agreement thus creates fresh rights and obligations to which the parties will be bound.

When the terms of settlement provide for the future fulfilment by any party of stated conditions and they have not been complied with by the party concerned, the other party may, at any time after the failure of the former to comply with the settlement terms, apply for the entry of judgment in terms of the settlement. This application must be brought on notice to the party alleged to be in default, setting forth particulars of the breach by the respondent of the terms of settlement.[144]

If the defendant in the above example does not pay the agreed amount of RX to the plaintiff, the latter will be able to apply to court for judgment in the amount of RX against the defendant. In this way it is possible to foil a person who wishes to settle a case simply in order to prevent it from coming to court, without carrying out his or her obligations in terms of the settlement agreement. In such a case, there would be no justification for expecting the plaintiff to begin entirely from scratch with a claim based upon the settlement agreement. This procedure therefore makes it possible for the plaintiff to apply to court for judgment in terms of the settlement agreement without other formalities having to be complied with.

After hearing the parties, the court may:
* dismiss the application;
* give judgment for the applicant in accordance with the terms of settlement;
* set aside the settlement and give such directions for the further prosecution of the action as it may deem fit;
* make such order as may be just as to the costs of the application.[145]

The parties may also have their agreement of settlement recorded by the court

---

[143] *Van Zyl v Niemann* 1964 (4) SA 661 (A) at 669–70; *Massey-Ferguson (SA) Ltd v Ermelo Motors (Pty) Ltd & others* 1973 (4) SA 206 (T); *Gollach & Gomperts (1967) (Pty) Ltd v Universal Mills & Produce Co (Pty) Ltd & others* 1978 (1) SA 914 (A) at 922.
[144] Rule 27(9).
[145] Rule 27(10).

and, in that way, make the settlement an order of court.[146] Such an order of court amounts to a judgment by consent and may support a defence of *res judicata*.[147]

The application to have the terms of the settlement agreement recorded by the court must be made on notice, except when the application is made in court during the hearing of any proceeding in the action at which the other party is represented, or when a written waiver (which may be included in the terms of settlement) by the other party is produced to the court.[148]

Should the parties thus settle the matter before trial, they may approach the court on application prior to the date of the hearing to have the terms of the agreement recorded. Alternatively, they may wait until the case is called on the day allocated for the hearing and then, during the hearing of the 'proceeding in the action', request the court to record the settlement and to make it an order of court.

In the latter case, it is desirable to inform the magistrate at the outset that the parties intend to announce a settlement of the matter on the day of the trial so that the necessary arrangements can be made to have another case heard on that day in order to prevent the day on which the former case was set down for trial from being lost.

At the hearing of the application, the applicant must lodge with the court a statement of the terms of settlement signed by all of the parties to the action and, if no objection is made by any other party, the court must note that the action has been settled on the terms set out in the statement. All further proceedings in the action are thereafter stayed.[149]

2.12 Absolution from the instance at the close of the plaintiff's case

As the discussion of the course of the trial has indicated, a defendant is entitled in cases in which the plaintiff bears the onus of proof to apply at the close of the plaintiff's case for an order of absolution from the instance.

When the defendant applies at this stage for absolution from the instance, he or she submits that the plaintiff has not made out a case for the relief he or she seeks and that in consequence there is no case for the defendant to answer. He or she avers, therefore, that no purpose would be served by proceeding with the trial.

The criterion that is applied in order to determine the outcome of the application for absolution from the instance is to enquire whether the evidence adduced by the plaintiff is such that a reasonable person might be able to reach a finding in the plaintiff's favour on the strength of that evidence.[150] It is sometimes said that the plaintiff must have made out a *prima facie* case.[151]

---

[146] Rule 27(6).
[147] *Baleta v Kandralides* 1948 (2) SA 1 (W) at 6.
[148] Rule 27(7).
[149] Rule 27(8). Subject to subrules (9) and (10).
[150] *Gascoyne v Paul & Hunter* 1917 TPD 170 at 173; *Robot Paints, Hardware & Timber Co (Pty) Ltd v South African Industrial Equipment (Pty) Ltd* 1975 (4) SA 829 (T) at 833D–F; *Claude Neon Lights (SA) Ltd v Daniel* 1976 (4) SA 403 (A) at 409G–H; *Rosherville Vehicle Services (Edms) Bpk v Bloemfontein Plaaslike Oorgangsraad* 1998 (2) SA 289 (O); *Paarlberg Motors (Pty) Ltd t/a Paarlberg EMW v Henning* 2000 (1) SA 981 (C).
[151] *Van Vuuren v Klopper Diskontohuis (Edms) Bpk* 1979 (1) SA 1053 (O) at 1057B–C.

If the application for absolution is granted, the plaintiff's claim fails, but the judgment does render the matter *res judicata* against him or her.

If the plaintiff presents his or her evidence first but the onus of proof rests in part upon him or her and in part upon the defendant, there is no room for an application for absolution, since it is not yet clear precisely which facts will ultimately be proved by the evidence still to be led. In such a case, one cannot say until all of the evidence in the case has been heard that the plaintiff's case had no prospect of succeeding.[152]

3 THE JUDGMENT AND THE CONCLUSION OF THE TRIAL

After the plaintiff and the defendant have closed their cases and presented argument, the court may grant:

- judgment for the plaintiff in respect of his claim in so far as he or she has proved it;
- judgment for the defendant in so far as he or she has proved his or her defence;
- absolution from the instance if it appears to the court that the evidence does not justify the court giving judgment for either party;
- such judgment as to costs (including costs as between attorney and client) as may be just;
- an order, subject to such conditions as the court thinks fit, against the party in whose favour judgment has been given suspending, wholly or in part, the taking of further proceedings upon the judgment for a specified period pending arrangements by the other party for the satisfaction of the judgment.[153]

These various possible orders are considered below.

3.1 Judgment in favour of the plaintiff

This order will be granted where the plaintiff has discharged the onus of proof resting upon him or her.

The court is bound by the amount set out by the plaintiff in his or her prayer for relief in the sense that the court may not award a higher amount than has been sought in the prayers, even though an entitlement to a higher amount has been established.[154]

3.2 Judgment in favour of the defendant

Where the onus of proof rests upon the defendant and he or she discharges it, thus establishing his or her defence as valid, the court grants judgment in his or her favour.

In the nature of things, judgment in the defendant's favour may be granted only where the defendant has presented his or her evidence and, in that way, proved the

---

[152] *Schoeman v Moller* 1949 (3) SA 949 (O).
[153] Section 48.
[154] *Charney v Paletz* 1924 SWA 5.

elements of his or her defence. Such an order cannot be issued if the plaintiff's case has collapsed but the defendant has not established his or her own case.

Where the onus of proof rests on the defendant and he or she fails to discharge it, the correct order is not absolution from the instance but judgment in favour of the plaintiff.

Where the defendant bears the onus of proof and he or she fails to discharge it—in other words, the evidence is evenly balanced—the plaintiff must succeed.[155] This can be illustrated by way of example: suppose that the plaintiff summonses the defendant for the repayment of money which the plaintiff has lent to the defendant. The defendant admits the loan, but avers that he or she has repaid it. In regard to this defence, a confession and avoidance, the defendant bears the onus of proof.[156]

If the defendant does not succeed in proving repayment, the court must grant judgment in favour of the plaintiff.

3.3 Absolution from the instance

An order of absolution granted at the close of the case must be distinguished from the order of absolution which may be granted at the close of the plaintiff's case.

Absolution is granted at the close of the case if it appears to the court that the evidence does not justify it granting judgment in favour of either the plaintiff or the defendant.

In cases in which the onus of proof rests upon the plaintiff and the court at the end of the case is unable to determine which side has spoken the truth, it must order absolution from the instance.

This occurs where the acceptance of one party's version necessitates the rejection of his or her opponent's version and there is no reason to reject the latter's version.[157]

Suppose that the plaintiff summonses the defendant for damage to the former's car, which was allegedly caused by the defendant in driving through an intersection in defiance of a red traffic light. The defendant's version of the facts is that it was not he or she but the plaintiff who drove through the intersection against the light. If at the conclusion of the case the magistrate is unable to reject either the plaintiff's or the defendant's version, in other words he or she cannot determine what happened, he or she will order absolution from the instance.

In cases in which the onus of proof rests upon the defendant and he or she fails to discharge it, the court cannot grant absolution from the instance but must grant judgment in favour of the plaintiff. The same reasoning is followed here as in the

---

[155] *Sebogo v Raath* 1947 (2) SA 624 (T); *Ramnath v Bunsee* 1961 (1) SA 394 (N); *Chetty v Naidoo* 1974 (3) SA 13 (A).
[156] *Pillay v Krishna & another* 1946 AD 946; *Asmal v Stanger Motor Centre (Pty) Ltd & others* 1973 (3) SA 642 (D).
[157] *Forbes v Golach & Cohen* 1917 AD 559; *National Employers Mutual General Insurance Association v Gany* 1931 AD 187 at 199; *Oliver's Transport v Divisional Council, Worcester* 1950 (4) SA 537 (C); *Koster Ko-operatiewe Landboumaatskappy Bpk v SA Spoorweën Hawens* 1974 (4) SA 420 (W).

case where the defendant bears the onus of proof and absolution is sought at the close of the plaintiff's case.[158]

3.4 Judgment as to costs
This topic is dealt with in chapter 16 below.

3.5 An order suspending further proceedings upon the judgment
In terms of s 48(e), the court may issue an order against the party in whose favour judgment has been given in terms of which all further proceedings in relation to that judgment are suspended, wholly or in part, for a specified period while the parties make arrangements for the satisfaction of the judgment.

---

[158] *Arter v Burt* 1922 AD 303 at 306; *Groenewald v Minister van Justisie* 1972 (3) SA 596 (O) at 600D–G; *Sentraalwes Personeel Ondernemings (Edms) Bpk v Nieuwoudt* 1979 (2) SA 537 (C) at 546A–B; *Build-a-Brick BK en 'n ander v Eskom* 1996 (1) SA 115 (O).

Chapter 16

COSTS

1 GENERAL

As part of the judgment, the magistrate is empowered by s 48*(d)* to 'grant such judgment as to costs (including costs as between attorney and client) as may be just'.

It is often difficult to lay down general guidelines governing the award of costs.[1] It has even been said: 'The existence of fixed rules governing awards of costs is doubted.'[2]

In spite of the problems that exist in relation to awards of costs, orders for the payment of costs are not something that the court may deal with lightly. The legal costs that have to be paid by a party may often in practice be the most important part of the order granted by the court.

The court exercises a discretion in making orders for the payment of costs. This discretion cannot, however, be exercised arbitrarily.[3] The order for the payment of costs must have a rational basis, in the same way as must any other order that the court grants. The discretion that the court possesses to grant an order of costs must be exercised judicially.[4]

In this chapter, attention is devoted to some of the most important aspects of legal costs and the guidelines for granting an order of costs.

In the first instance, it is necessary to obtain clarity regarding the scale on which costs of suit are awarded. Thereafter, attention must be given to the most important rules pertaining to the award of costs and, finally, one must deal with the manner in which costs are determined and recovered.

1.1 Party-and-party costs and attorney-and-client costs

In order to understand the workings of orders of costs in practice, it is essential to distinguish clearly between the concepts of *party-and-party costs* and *attorney-and-client costs*.[5]

The client is responsible to his or her attorney for the payment of the latter's fees. This liability flows from the contract that exists between the client and his or her legal representative. Regardless of the outcome of a case, the client is responsible to his or her attorney for payment for the attorney's services and expenses (which may include advocate's fees).

---

[1] *Nel v Nel* 1943 AD 280 at 287.

[2] A C Cilliers *Law of Costs* 2 ed (Butterworths, 1984) 1. The author of this book refers to more than 1 500 decisions in an attempt to lay down clear guidelines for the award of costs and concludes that it is often extremely difficult to determine fixed rules.

[3] 'Costs are usually regarded as a separate issue to be decided on their own peculiar principles': *per* Schreiner JA in *Pretoria Garrison Institutes v Danish Variety Products (Pty) Ltd* 1948 (1) SA 839 (A) at 872

[4] *Marks v Estate Gluckman* 1946 AD 289 at 314–15; *Merber v Merber* 1948 (1) SA 446 (A) at 453.

[5] There is a third scale of costs, namely, *attorney-and-own-client* costs. No provision for an award of such costs is made in the Act. It is submitted that such an award may, however, be made if provision is made for such an award in the contract between the parties. For a general discussion, see D E Van Loggerenberg *Erasmus Superior Court Practice* 2 ed (Service 6, 2018) D5-1 *et seq.* An award of costs making a special order relating to counsel's fees goes beyond the terms of s 80(1) and this is not competent. See *War Systems Technologies CC t/a Systems Technologies v United Computer Systems (JHB) CC* [2004] 1 All SA 457 (W).

This amount due for services rendered and expenses incurred for which the client is liable to his or her own attorney is known as *attorney-and-client costs*.

When the court, usually at the end of a case, makes an order of costs, it normally orders one of the parties to pay the legal costs incurred by the other. Suppose that the court orders the defendant to pay the costs incurred by the plaintiff. The defendant, in other words, is obliged to pay the plaintiff's costs. The costs must then be paid by the one party (the defendant) to the other (the plaintiff). Here we talk of *party-and-party costs*. It is important to note that these costs are payable to the plaintiff himself or herself, and *not* to the plaintiff's attorney. The defendant may be said to be liable to reimburse the plaintiff for the costs that the latter is obliged to pay to his or her own attorney. The matter may be represented diagrammatically as follows:

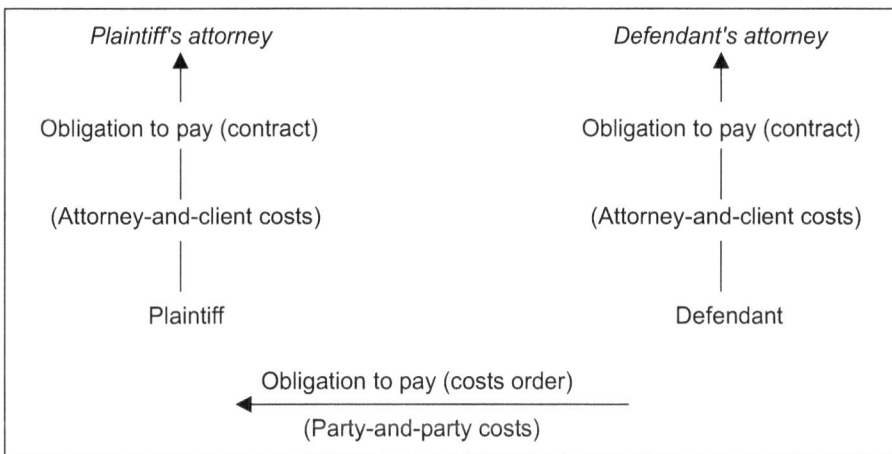

```
    Plaintiff's attorney                      Defendant's attorney
           ▲                                         ▲
           │                                         │
  Obligation to pay (contract)            Obligation to pay (contract)
           │                                         │
  (Attorney-and-client costs)             (Attorney-and-client costs)
           │                                         │
        Plaintiff                                 Defendant

              Obligation to pay (costs order)
        ◄─────────────────────────────────────
              (Party-and-party costs)
```

The reason for granting an order of costs is that the successful party (in this example, the plaintiff) must be compensated for the costs that he or she is obliged to pay to his or her attorney for conducting the case on his or her behalf.[6]

Annexure 2 of the Act sets out a tariff which lays down set fees for virtually every aspect of the preparation for and conduct of a matter. Nothing prevents an attorney charging more than the tariff. However, only the fee laid down in the tariff is recoverable from the other side if one obtains an order of costs in one's favour. Party-and-party costs are therefore determined by the tariff rather than the contract between attorney and client.

Any party, even if not ordered to pay costs, can require an attorney's bill to be taxed as between attorney and client.[7] In this instance there is no scale which is

---

[6] '[C]osts are awarded to a successful party in order to indemnify him for the expense to which he has been put through having been unjustly compelled either to initiate or defend litigation, as the case may be. Owing to the necessary operation of taxation, such an award is seldom a complete indemnity; but that does not affect the principle on which it is based': *per* Innes CJ in *Texas Co (SA) Ltd v Cape Town Municipality* 1926 AD 467 at 488. Cf in general also *Taylor v Mackay Bros & McMahon Ltd* 1947 (4) SA 423 (N); *Kerwin v Jones* 1958 (1) SA 400 (SR) at 401–2.

[7] Rule 33(18).

provided in the Act. The registrar or clerk has to determine what a reasonable fee for the services rendered is, bearing in mind the scales as between party and party. Such a bill can be taxed even though no action is pending and before judgment, provided the attorney's mandate has been terminated. Such taxation would be useful to a client only where there was no agreement between client and attorney as to fees to be charged, and where, as a result, the contract would contain an implied term that the amount allowed on taxation would be charged.

The costs recoverable after taxation from the other side are known as party-and-party costs. In practice, it happens almost without exception that the attorney collects these costs on behalf of his or her client. The plaintiff's attorney in our example will therefore recover the costs directly from the defendant. If it turns out that the defendant is unable to pay these costs, the plaintiff is, of course, not released from his or her obligation to pay his or her own attorney's account. Should the attorney (on behalf of his or her client) therefore not collect his or her costs from the party against whom the order of party-and-party costs has been made, he or she will recover the costs directly from his or her own client.

The rules relating to taxation lay down clearly what kinds of expenses can be included in the party-and-party costs and which are excluded. In general, all necessary and proper expenses are included. It used to happen that witness expenses were excluded unless the court specifically ordered. But since the deletion of rule 33(15) in 1977, this is no longer so. In general, witness expenses, including the qualifying expenses of expert witnesses, are included. On taxation, the registrar or clerk still has the discretion not to award witness expenses if these expenses were not necessary or proper in the context of the particular dispute.[8] It may happen that expenses incurred prior to the issue of summons will be properly included in these costs, but such expenses must be directly connected to the preparation and institution of the action.[9]

Although the award of costs is meant to indemnify the winning party for his or her costs, in practice the party-and-party costs that the attorney recovers on behalf of his or her client will rarely pay the attorney in full for the costs of suit.

Suppose, for example, that the attorney-and-client costs between attorney A and client X amount to R8 000. According to the order of costs, the party against whom the order has been granted, litigant Y, is obliged to reimburse X for his costs. Y is liable for costs on the party-and-party scale. These costs are calculated according to a fixed tariff. It very often happens that these party-and-party costs are less than the attorney-and-client costs because only certain items of cost may be recovered on the party-and-party scale, and even those which are recoverable can be recovered only at the tariff.[10] Y therefore pays only part of X's costs to attorney A—for instance, R7 200. X then remains liable for payment of the balance of the account, viz R800.

---

[8] Rule 33(16). See para 1.2.3.6 below.

[9] *Randall v Baisley* 1992 (3) SA 448 (E).

[10] Section 80(2) of the Act provides: 'As between attorney and client, the clerk of the court may in his discretion (subject to the review hereinafter mentioned) allow costs and charges for services reasonably performed by the attorney at the request of the client for which no remuneration is recoverable as between party and party and for which no provision is made in the rules.'

Only in those cases in which the court orders the unsuccessful party to pay costs on an attorney-and-client basis will Y in the above example be obliged to pay the full R800 to client X. In this case Y is therefore ordered by the court to reimburse X for the full amount of the costs that X has to pay to A.

1.1.1 *Interlocutory orders (also known as interim orders)*

An interlocutory application is an application ancillary to the main action, relating to some incidental issue which arises out of the main proceedings. At the conclusion of such an application, an interim order is granted.

Unless the court for good cause orders otherwise, costs of interim orders are not taxed until the conclusion of the action and a party may present only one bill for taxation up to and including the judgment or other conclusion of the action.[11]

It is difficult to lay down any fixed rule concerning costs in these matters because so much depends upon the circumstances of each particular case.

As a rule, it is usually ordered that the costs of interlocutory proceedings will be costs in the cause, but there is no rigid rule and in general the matter is in the hands of the presiding officer.[12]

Although normally only one bill may be presented for taxation, the court may for good cause direct that a separate bill be presented for taxation. It is submitted that a good reason for granting such an order would be, for example, that the matter is lengthy and complicated, so that it would be reasonable towards the attorney in question to allow his bill of costs to be taxed at some time during an interval in the proceedings.

Costs awarded in interlocutory proceedings may not be ceded without the consent of the court awarding such costs.[13]

The court may likewise order the costs of any interlocutory application to be costs in the cause. The result of such an order is that the order of costs made at the end of the main case will apply also in relation to the interlocutory application. The party to whom costs are awarded at the conclusion of the case will therefore be entitled also to the costs of the interlocutory application.

Sometimes an order that costs shall be costs in the cause may apparently operate unfairly. It may therefore be preferable that the court, when making the interim order, direct that the question of costs be reserved. It will then be left to the trial magistrate to make an appropriate order of costs on the basis of all the circumstances of the case.

The costs of any application or order or issue raised by the pleadings may:
(1) be awarded by the court irrespective of the judgment in the action;
(2) be made costs in the action (costs in the cause); or

---

[11] Rule 33(3).

[12] Although the court usually orders the costs of interlocutory proceedings to be costs in the cause, a court ought nevertheless to order, if it is clear that one of the parties is entitled to succeed at the interlocutory application stage, that that party is entitled to his costs in respect of the interlocutory application. The costs will then become payable, however, only after taxation, at the conclusion of the case: *Gering v Gering & another* 1974 (3) SA 358 (W) at 363H–364A; *Cape Underwear Manufacturers (Pty) Ltd v Consolidated Fashion Industries Ltd* 1948 (1) SA 175 (C).

[13] Section 49.

(3)   be reserved to be dealt with on the conclusion of the action.[14]

If the court makes no order of costs when it grants its interlocutory order, the costs will be costs in the cause.[15]

A magistrate must attempt, when making an order of costs at the conclusion of the case, to take into account the entire course of proceedings so that the order of costs granted by the court does justice between the parties.[16] The legal representatives ought to bring to the attention of the court any reason that may exist for declining to award all of the costs against one of the parties.[17] In that way, an order that costs shall be costs in the cause will not operate against one of the litigants with undue harshness.

1.2   General guidelines for the making of orders of costs

Although it is difficult to lay down a general rule for the award of costs, certain guidelines nevertheless exist. These guidelines are found, for the most part, in court decisions. There are, however, several rules of court which deal specifically with certain aspects of costs.

On closer scrutiny, there appear to be three general principles according to which orders of costs must be made. First, the principle applies that the courts always exercise a discretion in regard to the grant of an order of costs. Secondly, the order of costs usually follows the result of the case. Thirdly, certain rules of court expressly regulate the granting of orders of costs in particular cases.

1.2.1   *The court has a discretion as to the appropriate order of costs*

This general rule means that a judicial officer is free to decide on the costs in accordance with the merits of each case which comes before him or her.[18]

---

[14] Rule 33(2)*(a)*, *(b)* and *(c)*.

[15] Rule 33(2).

[16] 'A judicial officer has the jurisdiction and indeed should in suitable and proper cases in the exercise of his discretion order that the whole of the costs of an action (including the costs of any claim in reconvention) be paid by the parties in such proportions as he may direct. He is not obliged in every case to order that the costs follow the result of the claim and the counterclaim. He should only do so if he is satisfied that an order in that form when worked out will in substance effect the result he desires, and it may perhaps be desirable to impress upon judicial officers the necessity of adjusting critically their orders as to costs if these orders are not sometimes to produce results which are unintentional and unjust': *per* Boshoff J in *Botha v African Bitumen Emulsion (Pty) Ltd* 1960 (2) SA 6 (T) at 9H–10A.

[17] The Appellate Division in *Union Government v Gass* 1959 (4) SA 401 (A) at 412F held that, where a court awards costs against a party without giving him or her the opportunity to address the court on the question of costs, the award is always made on the understanding that he or she is free within a reasonable time to request the court to hear him or her on the matter. See also, in general, *Estate Garlick v Commissioner for Inland Revenue* 1934 AD 499 at 503–5. It is therefore always desirable for a magistrate to give the parties or their legal representatives the opportunity to address the court on the issue of costs.

[18] *Kruger Bros & Wasserman v Ruskin* 1918 AD 63 at 69. In *Cronje v Pelser* 1967 (2) SA 589 (A) at 593A–B Van Blerk JA stated: 'Gedurende die betoog is aandag gevestig op verskillende gewysdes wat moet dien as rigsnoere. Vorige vergelykbare gewysdes aangaande koste skep nie bindende beginsels nie. Dit kan hoogstens insiggewend wees. Dit kan nie sterk genoeg beklemtoon word nie dat die dogmatiese toepassing van ander gewysdes, as sou dit geykte beginsels vir kostebevele voorskryf, die ongewenste uitwerking het dat dié diskresie waarmee die Hof *a quo* beklee is aan

Section 48*(d)* expressly confers upon the court the power to make such order of costs as may be just. Rule 33(11) provides that the court may in its discretion order the costs of an action (including the costs of any claim in reconvention) to be paid by the parties in such proportions as it may direct.

The discretion must be exercised judicially.[19] 'Judicially' means that the presiding officer must not act arbitrarily but must consider all aspects of the case properly.[20] The wide discretion of the court enables a presiding officer to decide to penalise a party by means of an appropriate order of costs for the manner in which he or she has contested the case.[21]

If the magistrate has exercised his or her discretion judicially, it is highly unlikely that an appeal court will interfere with the order of costs.[22]

1.2.2 *The order of costs follows the outcome of the case*

It is a well-known general rule that the successful litigant is usually granted an order of costs in his or her favour.[23]

The question arises when, for purposes of an order of costs, a litigant can be said to have been successful in his or her claim or defence. To determine this, one must examine the essence of the judgment and not merely the formal order made at the end of the case. On the basis of this rule, a number of refinements to the general rule have crystallised. These subrules may be expounded as follows:

1.2.2.1 *A party may be substantially successful even though he or she recovers only a nominal amount*

If the plaintiff recovers only a nominal amount but has established a substantive right to relief, he or she is entitled to his or her costs.[24]

The fact that the plaintiff originally claimed a much larger amount than has been

---

bande gelê word.' See also *Gelb v Hawkins* 1960 (3) SA 687 (A) at 694A; *Graham v Odendaal* 1972 (2) SA 611 (A) at 616A; *Ward v Sulzer* 1973 (3) SA 701 (A) at 706G–707D, where the Appellate Division *per* Holmes JA summarised the most important principles relating to orders for the payment of costs.

[19] *Marks v Estate Gluckman* 1946 AD 289 at 314–15; *Van der Ploeg v Vivier & another* 1966 (3) SA 218 (SWA) at 222A; *Jordan v New Zealand Insurance Co Ltd* 1968 (2) SA 238 (E) at 245C–D; *Bruwer v Smit* 1971 (4) SA 164 (C).

[20] *Merber v Merber* 1948 (1) SA 446 (A) at 453; *Cronje v Pelser* (supra).

[21] For a more detailed discussion, see below at p 242. Cf also *Van der Merwe v Strydom* 1967 (3) SA 460 (A).

[22] *Fripp v Gibbon & Co* 1913 AD 354 at 363: 'Questions of costs are always important and sometimes complex and difficult to determine, and in leaving the magistrate a discretion the law contemplates that he should take into consideration the circumstances of each case, carefully weighing the various issues in the case, the conduct of the parties and any other circumstance which may have a bearing upon the question of costs, and then make such order as to costs as would be fair and just between the parties. And if he does this, and brings his unbiased judgment to bear upon the matter and does not act capriciously or upon any wrong principle, I know of no right on the part of a court of appeal to interfere with the honest exercise of his discretion.'

[23] *Fripp v Gibbon & Co* (supra); *Sackville West v Nourse & another* 1925 AD 516; *Pretoria Garrison Institutes v Danish Variety Products (Pty) Ltd* 1948 (1) SA 839 (A).

[24] *Brickman's Trustee v Transvaal Warehouse Co Ltd* 1904 TS 548; *Bhika v Minister of Justice & another* 1965 (4) SA 399 (W).

awarded to him or her at the conclusion of the case does not affect this principle.[25] The party who claimed the large amount, however, must not have had a blameworthy motive or have behaved irresponsibly.[26]

1.2.2.2 *In order to determine whether a party has been substantially successful, one must ascertain whether it is possible to distinguish between different issues in dispute*

Sometimes different issues are in dispute between the parties in one set of pleadings. At the time of the trial the court is then obliged to deliver judgment on various matters in issue, which are sometimes clearly distinguishable from one another. In general, the court may then make a separate order of costs in respect of each of these issues.[27]

It is often difficult, however, to determine whether the issues in dispute are distinguishable. Especially in cases in which the evidence led relates to a number of issues, it is hardly possible to determine what portion of the case (including the evidence) dealt with a particular aspect of the dispute.[28]

In attempting to obtain judgment against the defendant, the plaintiff may base his or her action on alternative grounds. On the other hand, a defendant may, of course, plead a number of defences in the alternative in an attempt to ward off liability.

These situations must be distinguished from those in which numerous different matters are in issue in a single case. Where alternative bases of claim and defences are placed before the court, the dispute relates to only a single matter, for example a motor collision or an alleged breach of contract or damage caused by an animal. There is one issue in dispute between the parties, but alternative bases of claim and alternative defences are possible.

Where claims are based on alternative grounds and the plaintiff succeeds in one of them, he or she 'wins the case'. If the defendant succeeds in one of his or her defences, he or she 'wins the case'. The general rule then applies that the successful plaintiff[29] or defendant[30] is entitled to his or her costs in these

---

[25] *Cohen v Engelbrecht* (1898) 15 SC 40; *Jonker v Schultz* 2002 (2) SA 360 (O). This rule applies especially where damages are claimed.

[26] *Gijzen v Verrinder* 1965 (1) SA 806 (D) at 815H–816C. In *Palmer v SA Mutual Life & General Insurance Co Ltd* 1964 (3) SA 434 (D) the court refused, however, to award the costs of the summons and particulars of claim to a plaintiff because the amount claimed by him was excessive and unreasonable. Cf also *Lutzkie v SAR & H & another* 1974 (4) SA 396 (W) at 398H ff.

[27] In *Estate Wege v Strauss* 1932 AD 76 at 86 the court stated: 'This Court has on several occasions laid down that if issues are distinct and severable the successful party on each issue is as a rule entitled to his costs on that issue. This is a general rule which all Courts should follow, but it is not a hard and fast rule and considerable discretion must be left to the trial Judge in regard to costs.' Cf also *Trollip v African Timbers* 1946 AD 1063 at 1076; *Nel v Nel* 1943 AD 280 at 288; *May v Union Government* 1954 (3) SA 120 (N) at 132F–G.

[28] In *Penny v Walker* 1936 AD 241 at 260 the court said: 'But if there are technically separate issues but all these issues had to be raised in order to lead evidence so as to enable the trial judge to give a correct judgment upon the issue on which the litigant succeeds, then there must be some exceptional reason for not adopting the general principle that the successful litigant is entitled to all his costs.'

[29] *Jenkins v SA Boiler Makers, Iron & Steel Workers & Ship Builders Society* 1946 WLD 15.

circumstances. The parties act within their rights if they plead alternative bases for the claim or alternative defences in an attempt to obtain a decision in their favour.

1.2.2.3 *Incidental costs might not be governed by the outcome of the case*

The question arises as to who is liable for those costs which are not directly and necessarily related to the conduct of the case from the time of issue of the summons until the handing down of judgment. In this regard, one thinks of costs occasioned by postponements or by interlocutory applications. Does the general rule apply that the party who at the conclusion of the case is substantially successful is entitled to these costs also? *Prima facie* it seems unfair to expect the unsuccessful party to be held liable for those costs which do not relate necessarily to the conduct of the case—especially if he or she was not the party who occasioned those incidental costs. Closely interwoven with this issue is the question whether a court, in giving judgment on a postponement or an interlocutory application, may make an order of costs before it has become clear—which it does only at a later stage, following a decision on the merits—who is the successful party to the case. Section 48 confers upon the magistrate's court the power to grant such judgment as to costs as may be just only *when it delivers judgment on the action.* By implication, the court lacks the capacity to make an order of costs at the time it grants an interlocutory order. On the other hand, s 49 makes express mention of costs awarded in interlocutory proceedings. These two provisions would therefore appear to be in conflict with each other.

In *Pretoria Garrison Institutes v Danish Variety Products (Pty) Ltd* the Appellate Division, however, accepted the general rule that success on the merits at the conclusion of the case entitles the successful party to all costs which have been incurred incidentally.[31]

The Appellate Division in the *Pretoria Garrison Institutes* case therefore expressly rejected the rule in *Erasmus v Daly & Co*[32] that in general a party who succeeds in obtaining an interlocutory order in his or her favour is entitled to the costs of those proceedings even though the case is ultimately decided against him or her.

For a discussion of the order of costs that a court ought to make in interlocutory proceedings, the reader may compare the section above at para 1.1.1.

1.2.2.4 *When an apportionment of damages is made, the costs likewise follow the outcome of the proceedings*

As already stated, costs are usually granted to the successful party even though the amount claimed by him or her was greater than the amount which was ultimately

---

[30] The defendant must not, however, have behaved unreasonably. See *Nel v Nel* (supra); *Scheepers & Nolte v Pate* 1909 TS 353 at 356 where Innes CJ stated: 'I think it is the duty of a litigant to avoid any course which unduly protracts a lawsuit, or unduly increases its expense. If there is a legal defence which can be effectively raised, by way of exception or otherwise, at an early stage, he ought at that stage to raise it. If he only takes it later on it may still be effective, but the fact that it came late, and that considerable expense was unnecessarily incurred in consequence, seems to me an element which may well affect the mind of the Court in apportioning the costs.'

[31] 1948 (1) SA 839 (A) at 863 and 864; cf also *Fortune v Versluis* 1962 (1) SA 343 (A) at 359H–360C.

[32] 1912 TPD 465.

awarded, and this is especially so where damages have been claimed—as long as the amount awarded is not out of all proportion to the size of the claim.[33]

A thorny problem arises as to the award of costs, however, in cases in which both a claim in convention and a counterclaim are instituted for damages arising from a motor collision, and in which each party points to the other as the party responsible for the damage. It often happens that the court in such cases decides that fault must be apportioned in the ratio of 60 per cent–40 per cent or 70 per cent–30 per cent and that the court then orders that the damages must be apportioned accordingly in terms of the Apportionment of Damages Act 34 of 1956.

The Appellate Division has decided that, where a court applies s 1(1)(*a*) of the Apportionment of Damages Act, it must assess the degree of the plaintiff's negligence and that of the defendant.[34] The assessment of the degree of negligence on the part of the plaintiff does not determine the degree of the defendant's negligence.[35]

Where both parties have behaved negligently, the court is obliged to assess the degrees of fault on the part of both the plaintiff and the defendant in order to determine for what percentage of the damage each party must be held liable.[36]

When making an order of costs, the court may in its discretion order that the whole of the costs of an action (including the costs of any claim in reconvention) be paid by the parties in such proportions as it may direct.[37]

According to what guidelines is the court obliged to make an order of costs when an apportionment of damages is made in consequence of the counterclaim launched by the defendant?

Cases in which a counterclaim is brought are discussed here separately from other claims. Where there is a claim in reconvention, the defendant (as plaintiff in reconvention) must also incur legal costs in order to recover his or her share of the harm suffered. The position in such cases therefore differs from that in cases in which only a claim in convention was instituted and the plaintiff merely recovered less compensation than he or she claimed. (In the latter instances, the plaintiff is entitled to recover the full amount of his or her legal costs.)

In cases of apportionment as a result of a counterclaim, the court may award costs in convention and costs in reconvention to different parties. The registrar or clerk of the court must on taxation allow each party to submit a bill of costs in respect of all costs and charges incurred in instituting and defending the claim in convention and reconvention, and defending the claim in convention and reconvention, respectively, and award the successful parties a proportionate amount of their costs in accordance with the award given by the court.[38]

---

[33] *Rabie v Stewart* 1927 OPD 74; *Janisch v Hall* 1946 CPD 553. Cf also in general *Norwich Union Fire Insurance Society Ltd v Tutt* 1960 (4) SA 851 (A) at 854D–F.

[34] *South British Insurance Co Ltd v Smit* 1962 (3) SA 826 (A) at 836B–D.

[35] *Jones NO v Santam Bpk* 1965 (2) SA 542 (A) at 555B–D, where the contrary proposition stated in *South British Insurance Co Ltd v Smit* (supra) at 835H was rejected.

[36] *Jones NO v Santam Bpk* (supra).

[37] Rule 33(11).

[38] Rule 33(13).

1.2.2.5 *The court has the discretion to penalise a party by means of an order of costs*

As already explained, the fundamental rule governing awards of costs is that the court exercises a discretion in making its award. It is therefore obvious that the court has the power to penalise a party by means of an adverse order of costs.

The court will do this in order to arrive at a just result.[39]

Without derogating from the general rule that the court has a discretion to make an appropriate order of costs, some instances of the court's power to penalise a party for certain types of conduct are mentioned below.

Subject to this general guideline, three aspects warrant particular mention, viz the refusal of costs to a successful party in whole or in part, attorney-and-client costs and costs *de bonis propriis.*

(a) The refusal of costs to a successful party in whole or in part

The court may deprive a successful plaintiff of his or her costs in whole or in part where he or she has deliberately claimed an amount considerably in excess of that in which he or she has obtained judgment.[40]

The court may also order a successful party to pay all the costs incurred by his or her opponent, or a portion of those costs. Such an order will be made in consequence of serious misconduct on the part of the successful party[41] or where he or she has followed the wrong procedure.[42]

In cases where the successful party has taken unnecessary steps, the court may likewise refuse him or her all or part of his or her costs.[43]

The court may also, where it is of the opinion that at the hearing the party to whom costs are awarded has occupied time unnecessarily or in relation to matters not relevant to the issue, disallow a proportionate part of the hearing fee payable to the attorney or counsel.[44]

---

[39] The Appellate Division has indicated that costs are a matter resting within the discretion of the court and that ethical considerations may well play a part in the exercise of that discretion (*Mahomed v Nagdee* 1952 (1) SA 410 (A) at 420H).

[40] *Rowles v Isipingo Beach Revision Court & another* 1966 (3) SA 751 (D) at 753C.

[41] Examples of serious misconduct are, for example, that the plaintiff claims the delivery of property in the knowledge that it belongs to someone else and that he or she is not entitled to it (*De Wet v Brink* 1910 TPD 336 at 341), that he or she pleads his case dishonestly (*SA Tungsten Mines Ltd (in liquidation) v Van Zyl* 1928 CPD 122 at 130) and that he or she attempts to mislead the court (*Van der Merwe v Strydom* 1967 (3) SA 460 (A)).

[42] Where, for example, a party uses the application procedure even though he or she foresees a material dispute of fact (cf chapter 5 above; *Less & another v Bomstein & another* 1948 (4) SA 333 (C) at 340–1).

[43] Where the court is of opinion that expense has been unnecessarily incurred because of the successful party's failure to take a course which would have shortened the proceedings and decreased the costs, it awards only such costs as would have been incurred if the successful party had taken the correct course (rule 33(12)).

[44] Rule 33(10). See also the remark of Innes CJ in *Scheepers & Nolte v Pate* 1909 TS 353 (cited in note 30). This *dictum* has been followed on many occasions: cf, for example, *Gerritsen v Dorpsbestuur, Aurora* 1969 (4) SA 556 (A); *Algoa Milling Co Ltd v Arkell & Douglas* 1918 AD 145 at 159–60; *Laingsburg Afdelingsraad v Luyt* 1959 (3) SA 679 (C); *Giuliani v Diesel Pump Injector Services (Pvt) Ltd* 1966 (3) SA 451 (R); *Feinstein & another v Taylor & others* 1962 (2) SA 54 (W); *Allen & others NNO v Gibbs & others* 1977 (3) SA 212 (SE).

(b) Attorney-and-client costs

The court may also express its displeasure at the conduct of a party by ordering him or her to pay the costs incurred by his or her opponent on an attorney-and-client scale.

Such an order is not lightly made.[45] The courts have, however, issued such orders in cases where a party has made himself or herself guilty of fraudulent conduct,[46] where he or she has behaved vexatiously or maliciously,[47] where he or she has litigated unnecessarily[48] and where he or she has been deliberately dishonest.[49]

Section 50(2) of the Act provides expressly for an award of costs on an attorney-and-client scale to a plaintiff who succeeds in an action which, upon the application of the defendant, was removed to the High Court.

(c) Costs *de bonis propriis*

Costs *de bonis propriis* are costs of suit which the court directs are to be paid by the unsuccessful party out of his or her own pocket where he or she instituted proceedings or defended the matter in a representative capacity.[50] Only in exceptional circumstances will the court make an order that costs be paid *de bonis propriis*.[51]

The particular circumstances in which a court will make such an order are set out by Innes CJ in the *locus classicus* in this regard[52] as follows:

'The whole question was very carefully considered by this Court in *Potgieter's* case [*Re Estate Potgieter* (1908 TS 982)], and a general rule was formulated to the effect that in order to justify a personal order for costs against a litigant occupying a fiduciary capacity his conduct in connection with the litigation in question must have been *mala fide*, negligent or unreasonable.'

It would serve no purpose to attempt to compile a comprehensive list of the particular circumstances in which the court will make an order of costs *de bonis propriis*. It is clear from the tenor of the decision of Innes CJ as well as from other cases[53] that the Chief Justice meant only to lay down a general guideline and not a closed list of circumstances in which the court will direct the payment of costs *de bonis propriis*.

---

[45] *De Villiers v Murraysburg School Board* 1910 CPD 535 at 538.

[46] *Nel v Waterberg Landbouwers Ko-operatieve Vereeniging* 1946 AD 597.

[47] *Real Estate & Trust Corporation v Central India Estates Ltd* 1923 WLD 121.

[48] *In re Alluvial Creek Ltd* 1929 CPD 532.

[49] *Herold v Sinclair & others* 1954 (2) SA 531 (A) at 537A.

[50] *Moller en andere v Erasmus en andere* 1959 (2) SA 465 (T) at 467B–D; *Zalk v Inglestone* 1961 (2) SA 788 (W) at 795A.

[51] *Grobbelaar v Grobbelaar* 1959 (4) SA 719 (A) at 725B.

[52] *Vermaak's Executors v Vermaak's Heirs* 1909 TS 679 at 691.

[53] *Moller en andere v Erasmus en andere* (supra) at 467; *Zalk v Inglestone* (supra) at 795; *Grobbelaar v Grobbelaar* (supra) at 725B–C; *Estate Orr v The Master* 1938 AD 336; *Gangat v Bejorseth NO* 1954 (4) SA 145 (D); *Re Estate Potgieter* 1908 TS 982; *Joubert v Ruddock & others* 1968 (1) SA 95 (E); *Stapelberg v Schlebusch NO en 'n ander* 1968 (3) SA 596 (O) at 605H; *Conradie en andere v Smit* 1966 (3) SA 368 (A) at 377H.

The court may make an order of costs *de bonis propriis* against an attorney, but it will do so only if the attorney has been guilty of unprofessional conduct and not merely because the attorney has conducted the case ineptly.[54]

1.2.3 *Miscellaneous provisions in the Act and rules pertaining to costs*

Additional guidelines relating to orders of costs in the magistrates' courts are found in a number of express rules appearing in the Act and the rules of court. Some of these provisions are briefly referred to below.

1.2.3.1 *Further particulars*

A party may, in accordance with rule 16, after the close of pleadings but before the trial, request further particulars that are strictly necessary to enable him or her to prepare for trial.[55] At the conclusion of the trial the court must *mero motu* consider whether the further particulars were strictly necessary 'and shall disallow all costs of and flowing from any unnecessary request or reply, or both, and may order either party to pay the costs thereby wasted, on an attorney and client basis or otherwise'.[56]

1.2.3.2 *Costs of adjournments and amendments of pleadings*

The court, in making any order, including an order pertaining to an adjournment or amendment, may award such costs as it deems fit.[57]

1.2.3.3 *Costs on a higher scale*

The tariff provides two scales. The first applies to matters which fall within the quantum of the small claims court and the second to other matters. However, the court may in certain circumstances direct that costs be taxed on a higher scale than that on which they are normally taxed.

The court may award costs on a higher scale at the request of a party made at or immediately after the giving of judgment. The order for the taxation of costs on a higher scale is made only in opposed actions or proceedings. Furthermore:
(1) the action must have involved a difficult question of law or of fact;
(2) the plaintiff must have made two or more claims other than in the alternative;
(3) the claim or defence must have been frivolous or vexatious; or
(4) costs were reasonably incurred, and in respect of which costs there is no specific provision in the rules.[58]

1.2.3.4 *Costs of applications, orders or issues raised by the pleadings*

Costs falling within this category may be:
(1) awarded by the court irrespective of the judgment in the action;
(2) made costs in the cause; or

---

[54] *Nkosi v Caledonian Insurance Co* 1961 (4) SA 649 (N); *David v Naggyah & another* 1961 (3) SA 4 (N) at 7D–F; *Washaya v Washaya* 1990 (4) SA 41 (ZHC) at 45G–46A.
[55] Rule 16.
[56] Rule 16(5).
[57] Rule 33(1).
[58] Rule 33(8).

(3)   reserved to be dealt with on the conclusion of the action.
    If no order is made, then these costs will be costs in the cause.[59]

1.2.3.5   *Costs necessarily incurred*

When it is reasonable in any proceedings for a party to employ the services of an attorney other than a local attorney, the court may on proof thereof, and if costs are awarded to him or her, order that such costs shall include the reasonable travelling time, travelling expenses and subsistence expenses of such attorney as determined by the court. The court may order that the determination of such costs be done on taxation by the registrar or clerk of the court.[60]

What other costs are necessary and proper will vary from case to case.[61] In *Randall v Baisley*[62] Erasmus J held that previous cases which would not allow the costs incurred prior to the issue of summons were incorrect. In that case the costs of an out-of-town private investigator were allowed. The investigation was necessary for the institution of the action.

1.2.3.6   *Witness fees*

Rule 33(16) provides that witness fees shall not be allowed in taxation unless properly vouched for. The tariff is contained in Appendix A to the Act. The court may order that no allowance or only a portion of an allowance should be paid to a witness.[63]

1.2.3.7   *Costs on the discharge of orders obtained* ex parte

The court has the power to make orders of costs on the discharge of orders granted *ex parte*. The rules provide:[64] 'Any order made *ex parte* may be confirmed, discharged or varied by the court on cause shown by any person affected thereby and on such terms as to costs as the court may deem fit.'

1.2.3.8   *Assessors' fees*

Fees and expenses of assessors, unless otherwise ordered by the court, are costs in the cause.[65]

1.2.3.9   *Security for costs*

Rule 62 provides that a defendant may protect himself or herself from the eventuality of gaining an empty award of costs against a plaintiff. As soon as practicable after the commencement of proceedings, a party may call upon another

---

[59] Rule 33(2).

[60] Rule 33(9). Under normal circumstances the attorney's travelling expenses do not form a portion of the party-and-party costs and a successful party will have to pay them as part of his or her liability to his or her own attorney for attorney-and-client costs without being able to recover the travelling expenses from his or her opponent. For a case involving two attorneys, see *Fedmech EFS (Edms) Bpk v Saaiman* 1990 (4) SA 637 (O).

[61] Rule 33(16). The phrase 'necessary expenses' in rule 33(5)*(a)* should be interpreted with regard to rule 33(16).

[62] 1992 (3) SA 448 (E).

[63] Section 51*bis*(3).

[64] Rule 55(3)*(g)*.

[65] Rule 59(6).

party to provide security.[66] Where the amount is contested, the registrar or clerk must determine the amount and his or her decision is final.[67] If liability is contested, or there is a failure to furnish security within 10 days of the demand or the registrar's or clerk's decision, the other party may apply to court for an order for security and those proceedings be stayed pending compliance with the order.[68] Failure to provide security within a reasonable time will enable the court to dismiss the proceedings or strike out pleadings by the party in default, or to make any other order as the court may deem fit.[69] Any security for costs must be given in the form, amount and manner directed by the registrar or clerk of the court, unless the court directs otherwise or the parties agree otherwise.[70]

2 DRAWING UP THE BILL OF COSTS

After the court has made an order of costs, the successful party's attorney must draw up a bill of costs.[71] The purpose of the bill of costs is to set out the costs and expenses that the loser is obliged to pay to the winning party. As we have already seen, these costs are usually recovered from the losing party by the attorney acting for the winning litigant.[72]

The successful party is entitled to recover from his or her opponent only those party-and-party costs for which the rules provide.[73] Only if costs are awarded to him or her on an attorney-and-client scale is a party entitled to recover more from his or her opponent than the costs provided for in the rules of court.

It must be remembered that the successful party is liable to his or her own attorney for the costs of bringing or defending the matter on his or her behalf. Quite possibly, the successful party will not recover from his or her opponent in terms of the party-and-party bill of costs all of the costs that he or she has incurred, and the successful party is then liable to his or her attorney for the difference between what he or she recovers from his or her opponent and his or her attorney's fees and expenses on an attorney-and-client scale.

The amounts allowed by way of party-and-party costs in district court civil matters are set out in Table A of Annexure 2 to the rules.[74] In regional court civil matters, the scale of fees are set out in scale D of Table A of Annexure 2.[75]

---

[66] Rule 62(1).

[67] Rule 62(2).

[68] Rule 62(3).

[69] Rule 62(4).

[70] Rule 62(5).

[71] Rule 33(15). See also rule 33(19), which provides that '[w]here liability for costs is determined without judgment of the court by virtue of the provisions of these rules or by a settlement recorded in terms of rule 27(8), such costs shall be taxable by the registrar or clerk of the court as if they had been awarded by the court'.

[72] 'Where a judgment or order for costs is made against two or more persons it shall, unless the contrary is stated, have effect against such persons severally as well as jointly' (rule 33(4)).

[73] Section 80(1) provides: 'The stamps, fees, costs and charges in connection with any civil proceedings in magistrates' courts shall, as between party and party, be payable in accordance with the scales prescribed by the rules.'

[74] Rule 33(5)*(a)* and *(b)*.

[75] Rule 33(5)*(c)*.

The fees prescribed in the rules are recoverable whether the work has been done by the attorney himself or herself or by his or her clerk.[76]

In view of the fact that certain items of cost are calculated on an hourly basis, the officer presiding in civil proceedings which last for a period of a quarter of an hour or longer is obliged to note on the record of proceedings the times of commencement and adjournment of the proceedings.[77]

The purpose of drawing up a bill of costs is to set out the costs that the one party is entitled to recover from the other. Because the costs are calculated in accordance with fixed tariffs, the party who is obliged to pay the costs is afforded a measure of protection: he or she is in the position of a client to whom an account in a stipulated amount must be rendered, containing particulars of the various items and the costs that he or she is required to pay.

The party who has to pay the bill of costs enjoys still further protection in that the bill must be placed before the taxing master of the court, who is then required to check that the bill has been drawn up in accordance with the provisions of the rules of court.

A client is likewise protected: the items for which he or she is liable to his or her own attorney on an attorney-and-client scale are also taxable.[78] A client is thus entitled to require the drawing up of a bill of costs as between attorney and client and its submission for taxation. Section 80(4) reads:

> 'Any person who is liable to pay or who is sued for costs of any civil proceedings in a court otherwise than under an award by the court or under a special agreement, may require that those costs shall be taxed by the clerk of the court as between attorney and client; and thereupon any action for the recovery of those costs shall be stayed pending the taxation. The costs of and incidental to such a taxation shall be borne, if not more than one-sixth of such costs is disallowed on taxation, by the person requiring the taxation, and, if more than one-sixth is so disallowed, by the person claiming the costs.'

This is of assistance to parties against whom an attorney-and-client order is made and to those clients of attorneys where there is no special agreement as to fees. In practice, virtually every attorney makes a special agreement as to the payment of fees, which agreement stipulates a scale higher than that of the tariff.

The clerk or registrar of the court may in his or her discretion as between attorney and client allow costs and charges for services reasonably performed by the attorney at the request of the client for which no remuneration is recoverable as between party and party and for which no provision is made in the rules.[79]

3 TAXATION

Once the bill of costs has been drawn up in accordance with the provisions of the rules of court, it must be delivered, meaning that the original of the bill must be

---

[76] Rule 33(6).
[77] Rule 33(7).
[78] Section 80(4).
[79] Section 80(2).

handed to the registrar or clerk of the court and a copy served upon the opposite party (or, more commonly, his or her legal representative).[80]

At the same time, the registrar or clerk of the court is requested to set a date and time on which the bill may be taxed. At least five days' notice of the date and time of taxation must be given to his or her opponent by the party having the bill taxed.

Where a bill of costs as between attorney and client is to be taxed, taxation may take place on at least five days' notice by the attorney to the client, whether or not an action for costs is pending. A bill of costs as between attorney and client may be taxed at any time after termination of the mandate.[81]

At the appointed time on the appointed day, the parties (or, more usually, their legal representatives) meet at the office of the registrar or clerk of the court. The bill is then taxed.[82]

At the taxation the registrar or clerk of the court checks the bill of costs item by item in the presence of the parties.

The parties are given the opportunity either to explain the various items and, if necessary, to justify them, or to object to certain items. The registrar or clerk of the court then decides whether or not to allow the item in question. The registrar or clerk may reduce the amount reflected in the bill in respect of any item, a process known as 'taxing off', or he or she may disallow a certain item (or certain items) altogether.

At the end of the bill the total amount allowed and the total taxed off are indicated. The costs of taxation are added to the amount allowed. The party at whose instance the bill is taxed is entitled to recover the costs of taxation for drawing up the bill.[83]

Where more than one-quarter of the costs claimed in the bill (excluding expenses) is taxed off by the taxing master, the party presenting the bill is not allowed any costs of taxation.[84]

If the party who gave notice of the taxation fails to appear at the appointed time for the taxation, the bill may be taxed in his or her absence, but he or she is not then allowed any costs of taxation.[85]

A taxed bill of costs, together with the relevant court order or power of attorney, is regarded as a liquid document for the purposes of summary judgment or provisional sentence proceedings.[86]

4 REVIEW OF TAXATION

A party who is dissatisfied with the taxation by the registrar or clerk of the court may place a taxed bill of costs and expenses before a judicial officer of the district

---

[80] Rule 33(15).
[81] Rule 33(18).
[82] Rule 33(20).
[83] Items 6, 7 and 8 of Part IV of Table A of Annexure 2 stipulate the amounts to which the party is entitled by way of costs of taxation.
[84] Rule 33(17)(*a*).
[85] Rule 33(20).
[86] See *Erasmus Superior Court Practice* D1-389.

or region for review, and this judicial officer (a magistrate) must review the taxed bill free of charge.[87]

In order to have a taxed bill reviewed, the dissatisfied party must place before the judicial officer for review, within 15 days after the taxation has come to his or her knowledge and on 10 days' notice to the party entitled to receive or liable to pay the costs, or to the sheriff, as the case may be:[88]

(1)   the costs and expenses claimed in any undefended action;
(2)   the assessment by the registrar or clerk of the court of any costs and expenses;
(3)   the taxation by the registrar or clerk of the court of any costs awarded in any action or matter;
(4)   the taxation by the registrar or clerk of the court of any fees or charges of the sheriff.[89]

It is important to note that the rule provides for review not only of the taxation and assessment by the registrar clerk of the court of the costs and expenses but also of any costs and expenses claimed in any undefended action. A party is therefore at liberty to take on review the costs and expenses claimed where default judgment has been granted.

Of further importance is that, in terms of rule 35(1)(d), any account rendered by a sheriff may likewise be taxed.[90] The fees and charges that may be levied by a sheriff who is an officer of the Public Service are prescribed in Part I of Table C of Annexure 2, while those that may be levied by a sheriff who is not an officer of the Public Service are set out in Part II of the Table.[91]

The taxation of an account rendered by a sheriff likewise takes place before the registrar or clerk of the court on notice, in the same way as the taxation of a bill of costs between parties, and a fee for attending the taxation is allowed.[92]

Rule 35(1) refers to an 'interested party'. When this provision is read with rule 35(2), it is apparent that both the plaintiff and the defendant are at liberty to place a taxed bill of costs before the magistrate for review.

The rules make no provision as to the manner in which the magistrate conducts the review. He or she may decide on the correctness of the costs and expenses purely on the basis of the written objection to the bill and possibly any answer that may have been delivered to it. There is no indication in the rules that the magistrate is obliged to follow the motion procedure, for example by hearing argument, or to conduct the review in open court. In addition, there is no obligation on him or her to give his or her decision within a stipulated time. One may infer only that the review must take place within a reasonable time.

It is possible to obtain a further review of the decision given by the magistrate.

Rule 35(3) appears to limit this right of further review to items to which objection was made at the taxation before the registrar or clerk of the court. This

---

[87] Section 81 read with rule 35.
[88] Rule 35(1) and 35(2).
[89] Rule 35(1).
[90] Indeed, in terms of rule 34(2) every account of fees or charges furnished by a sheriff must contain the statement: 'You may require this account to be taxed and vouched before payment.'
[91] Rule 34(1).
[92] Rule 34(3)(a), (b) and (c).

rule is in conflict with an unfettered right of review provided for in s 81 of the Act. In so far as the rule is in conflict with the section, it is *ultra vires*.[93]

The rule further provides that an applicant for a review must within 10 days of the decision of the judicial officer ask the judicial officer (that is, the magistrate) to state a case for the decision of a judge, and that he or she shall not do so if the disputed amount is less than R1 000.

Within 10 days after the magistrate has drawn up the stated case, the parties may submit contentions in writing to him or her.[94] The magistrate must then lay the case, together with the written contentions submitted to him or her and his or her own report, before a judge of the court of appeal not later than 15 days after receipt of the contentions.[95]

The judge may then decide the matter upon the case and contentions submitted to him or her, together with any further information which he or she may require from the magistrate. He or she may decide it after hearing the parties or their counsel or attorneys in chambers, or he or she may refer the case for decision to the court of appeal.[96]

The decision of the registrar or clerk of the court should be interfered with only by the judicial officer or the judge on review where such reviewing officers are satisfied that the registrar or clerk acted on a wrong principle or that he or she did not exercise his or her discretion at all.[97]

When the matter is decided, such order may be given as the judge or court deems fit, including an order that the unsuccessful party shall pay to the opposing party a sum fixed by the judge or the court as costs.[98]

Although no such procedure is provided in the rules, it is possible to take the decision of the reviewing judge on appeal in terms of the Superior Courts Act.[99]

---

[93] *Krull v Bursey* 1966 (4) SA 448 (E); *Paruk v Lallo* 1979 (3) SA 653 (D); *Louw v Gleeson* 1991 (3) SA 219 (O); contra *Sacca Bpk v Burger* 1974 (3) SA 732 (C).

[94] Rule 35(4).

[95] Rule 35(5).

[96] Rule 35(5).

[97] *De Villers v Estate Hunt* 1940 CPD 518.

[98] Rule 35(6).

[99] See *Vaaltyn v Goss & another* 1992 (3) SA 549 (E), decided under the Supreme Court Act 59 of 1959, the predecessor of the Superior Courts Act 10 of 2013. See also s 22 of the Superior Courts Act.

EXECUTION

1 INTRODUCTION

If a judgment or order of court could not be enforced by the party in whose favour it has been given, there would be no purpose in approaching a court for relief. The reason why people turn to the courts is precisely to obtain payment of money, or other relief, due to them.

It is therefore necessary for there to be rules enabling a judgment of the court to be enforced in a case in which the party against whom judgment has been given does not comply with the court's order voluntarily. The procedure in terms of which any judgment or order of the court is enforced is known as 'execution'.

The litigant who obtains a judgment in his or her favour is known as *the judgment creditor* and the party against whom the judgment has been awarded is known as the *judgment debtor*.

A *defendant* who has obtained judgment in his or her favour is therefore known as a *judgment creditor* even though he or she was the defendant in the suit.

After the court has granted judgment in his or her favour,[1] the judgment creditor is entitled to have a warrant of execution for the enforcement of the court's order issued by the registrar or clerk of the court and delivered to the sheriff for execution.

The execution procedure consists, first, of the attachment of the judgment creditor's assets and, secondly, of the sale in execution of those assets.

Civil imprisonment has been expressly abolished by the legislature.[2] Section 106 of the Act provides that any person wilfully disobeying, or refusing or failing to comply with any judgment or order of a court or with a notice lawfully endorsed on a summons for rent prohibiting the removal of any furniture in effect shall be guilty of contempt of court and shall, upon conviction, be liable to a fine, or to imprisonment for a period not exceeding six months or to such imprisonment, without the option of a fine. This provision creates an offence. It is not applicable to a judgment debtor who fails to satisfy a judgment. The section is therefore not part of the execution process.

The judgment must be executed within three years of the date on which it was granted.[3]

2 THE WARRANT OF EXECUTION

2.1 Types

Suppose that the court grants judgment in favour of the plaintiff in a case in which ejectment of the defendant was sought. After the plaintiff has obtained the order of ejectment, the court may issue a warrant of ejectment. According to Annexure 1 Form 30, this warrant reads as follows:

No. 30
Warrant of Ejectment
* For use in the District Court
In the Magistrate's Court for the District of ....
held at ....
Case No .... of 20......
In the matter between
.... Plaintiff
and
.... Defendant

---

[1] Section 64 provides for execution also in the case of a judgment debt which has been ceded. The section provides: 'Any person who has, either by cession or by operation of law, become entitled to the benefit of a judgment debt may, after notice to the judgment creditor, and the judgment debtor, be substituted on the record for the judgment creditor and may obtain execution in the manner provided for judgment creditors.'

[2] The Civil Imprisonment Restriction Act 21 of 1942, repealed by the Abolition of Civil Imprisonment Act 2 of 1977.

[3] Section 63.

To the Sheriff.

Whereas in this action the said plaintiff on the .... day of ...., 20......
obtained judgment for the ejectment of the said defendant from the premises or land known as
.....................................;

This is to authorise and require you to put the said plaintiff into possession of the said premises or
land by removing therefrom the said defendant for which this shall be your warrant;

And return to this court what you have done by virtue hereof.

Dated at .... this .... day of ...., 20......

By Order of the Court.

....

Clerk of the Court

....

Plaintiff/Plaintiff's Attorney

....

Address: ....

....

Suppose that the court grants judgment in favour of the plaintiff in a case in
which the delivery of property was claimed. After the plaintiff has obtained
judgment, the court may issue a warrant for the delivery of the property which,
according to Annexure 1 Form 31, will read as follows:

No. 31
Warrant for Delivery of Goods
* For use in the District Court

In the Magistrate's Court for the District of ....

held at ....

Case No .... of 20......

In the matter between

.... Plaintiff

and

.... Defendant

To the Sheriff.

Whereas in this action the court ordered that the defendant should deliver to the plaintiff a certain
.... (describe the thing to be delivered);

This is to authorise and require you to take the said .... (describe the thing)
from the defendant and place the plaintiff in possession thereof, for which this shall be your
warrant;

And return to this court what you have done by virtue hereof.

Dated at .... this .... day of ...., 20......

By Order of the Court

....

Clerk of the Court

....

Plaintiff/Plaintiff's Attorney

Address: ....

....

Suppose that the court grants judgment against a party for the payment of a sum of money but that he or she does not pay the amount due in terms of the judgment. In this instance a warrant of execution against property is issued. According to Annexure 1 Form 32, the warrant will read as follows:

No. 32
Warrant of Execution Against Property
* For use in the District Court

In the Magistrate's Court for the District of ....

held at ....

Case No .... of 20......

In the matter between

.... Execution creditor

and

.... Execution debtor

To the Sheriff.

Amounts to be levied (with costs execution)

Whereas in this action the said .... of .... on the .... day of ...., 20...... obtained judgment in the abovementioned court against the said .... of .... for the several sums set out in the margin hereof amounting in all to the sum of R............ of which R............ has since been paid;

This is therefore to authorise and require you to raise on the property of the said .... the sum of R .... together with your costs of this execution and pay to the said .... the aforesaid sum of R................ and return to this court what you have done by virtue hereof.

R   c

Judgment Debt ....

Judgment debt Costs ....

Cost of issuing warrant ....

Costs of appeal ....

SUBTOTAL

Less amount paid since judgment ....

TOTAL DUE ....

Dated at .... this .... day of ...., 20......

Clerk of the Court

....

Attorney for Execution Creditor

Address: ....

....

NOTE: (1) If the execution debtor pays the amounts specified in the margin hereof with Sheriff's charges of R...................... within half an hour of the entry of the sheriff he or she will not be required to pay any further costs of execution. The amount of any payment made by the execution debtor and the date thereof shall be endorsed on the original and copy hereof, which endorsement shall be signed by the sheriff and countersigned by the execution debtor or execution debtor's representative.

(2) This execution may be paid out before sale, subject to the payment of the Sheriff's fees and charges of execution, which may be required to be taxed.

> (3) The only immovable property upon which this warrant may be executed is .... (set out its situation and nature sufficiently to enable it to be identified).
>
> (4) In case of reissue the fact and date of reissue and any increase or reduction in the amounts to be levied shown on the face hereof shall be set out in a note endorsed hereon and signed by the execution creditor or execution creditor's attorney and by the clerk of the court.
>
> (5) Any alterations made herein shall be initialled by the clerk of the court before the warrant is issued or reissued by him or her.

The sheriff then attaches movable property belonging to the judgment debtor of sufficient value to pay the judgment debt. If the value of the movable property is insufficient or if the court authorises the sheriff to do so, then the sheriff may also attach immovable property belonging to the debtor. The goods attached are then sold in execution and the proceeds of the sale are applied to pay the claim of the judgment creditor.

2.2 The issue of a warrant of execution

After a party has obtained judgment in his or her favour, the judgment debtor is usually afforded the opportunity of satisfying the judgment.[4]

In practice the judgment debtor often makes arrangements at this stage with the attorney representing the judgment creditor for the payment of the judgment debt and costs. In this event a warrant of execution is not normally issued.[5] Payment is made in accordance with the arrangement reached between the parties until such time as the court order in favour of the plaintiff has been complied with in full.

In cases in which no satisfactory arrangement for the satisfaction of the judgment can be made, the plaintiff has a warrant of execution issued against the property belonging to the judgment debtor.

The judgment creditor may sue out the warrant of execution but may withdraw or suspend it by written notice to the sheriff, or the judgment creditor may merely defer execution for up to a month. Such deferral does not amount to a suspension.[6]

The warrant may be sued out by any person in whose favour judgment has been given.[7]

---

[4] The discussion here pertains to cases in which judgment has been granted at the conclusion of a trial. Where judgment by consent or default judgment has been obtained, the warrant of execution is usually filed with the registrar or clerk of the court together with the request for judgment. If the warrant is issued after the grant of default judgment, execution takes place in the same way as in the case where judgment has been granted at the conclusion of a trial.

[5] Section 66(1)(*a*) provides that where the court gives judgment for the payment of money, the amount may be recovered immediately or at the times and in the manner ordered by the court by means of execution against movable property. The fact that a warrant of execution has not been issued against a judgment debtor who has made arrangements with the judgment creditor for the payment of the judgment debt is therefore no more than a gesture of courtesy. Rule 36(7) provides that except where judgment has been entered by consent or default, a warrant of execution shall not be issued before the day following that on which judgment is given unless leave of the court to issue the warrant earlier has been applied for and obtained at the time judgment was granted.

[6] Rule 36(3).

[7] Rule 36(2).

The warrant is issued and signed by the registrar or clerk of the court and delivered to the sheriff.[8] The registrar or clerk of the court must initial any alterations effected to the warrant,[9] reissue the warrant,[10] and, if the court has given the necessary authorisation, issue a second or further warrant if the first warrant has been lost or mislaid.[11] In the latter case, the party who applies to court for the issue of another warrant must give at least five days' notice of his or her intention to do so,[12] and the second or further warrant must be appropriately endorsed[13] and a note made on the record of the case to the effect that a fresh warrant has been issued.[14]

Any court which has jurisdiction to try an action likewise has jurisdiction to issue against any party to the action any form of process in execution of its judgment.[15]

A court other than the one by which judgment was granted (referred to as a 'second court') may on good cause shown stay or set aside any warrant of execution or arrest issued by another court against a party who is subject to the jurisdiction of the second court.[16] A court may also, on good cause shown, stay or set aside any warrant of execution or arrest issued by itself, including an order in terms of s 72(1) for the attachment of a debt then or in future due to the judgment debtor or accruing to him or her (a 'garnishee order').[17] The warrant will be invalid if a wrong person is named in the warrant as a party, but no process will be invalid merely by reason of the misspelling of any name mentioned in the warrant, or any error as to date.[18]

3 ATTACHMENT

3.1 Provisions relating to execution against specific property

Certain property belonging to the judgment debtor is expressly exempted from attachment in execution. Section 67 provides that the following property may not be attached or sold in execution in terms of a warrant of execution issued out of any court:[19]

---

[8] Rule 36(1).

[9] Rule 36(4). Non-compliance with this provision will not, however, per se render the process invalid (*Edwards v Beneke* 1970 (2) SA 437 (T) at 441–2). However, if the alteration is material, for instance allowing execution against immovable and not only movable property, the rule must be followed: *Lambton Service Station v Van Aswegen* 1993 (2) SA 637 (T).

[10] Rule 36(5).

[11] Rule 37(1).

[12] Rule 37(2).

[13] Rule 37(3). The original warrant must be cancelled if it subsequently becomes available (rule 37(4)).

[14] Rule 37(5).

[15] Section 62(1).

[16] Section 62(2).

[17] Section 62(3).

[18] Rule 36(6).

[19] The amounts mentioned in this section are determined from time to time by the minister by notice in the *Gazette*. The present amounts are determined by GN R385 of 1 March 1994, effective from that date.

(a) the necessary beds, bedding and wearing apparel of the execution debtor and of his family;

(b) the necessary furniture (other than beds) and household utensils in so far as they do not exceed in value the sum of R2 000;

(c) stock, tools and agricultural implements of a farmer in so far as they do not exceed in value the sum of R2 000;

(d) the supply of food and drink in the house sufficient for the needs of such debtor and of his family during one month;

(e) tools and implements of trade, in so far as they do not exceed in value the sum of R2 000;

(f) professional books, documents or instruments necessarily used by such debtor in his profession, in so far as they do not exceed in value the sum of R2 000;

(g) such arms and ammunition as such debtor is required by law, regulation or disciplinary order to have in his possession as part of his equipment:

provided that the court shall have a discretion in exceptional circumstances and on such conditions as it may determine to increase the sums referred to in paragraphs *(b)*, *(c)*, *(e)* and *(f)*.

Section 68 stipulates what property is executable. For the sake of completeness, this section is set out in full:[20]

(1) The sheriff executing any process of execution against movable property may, by virtue of such process, also seize and take any money or banknotes, and may seize, take and sell in execution cheques, bills of exchange, promissory notes, bonds, or securities for money belonging to the execution debtor.

(2) The sheriff may also hold any cheques, bills of exchange, promissory notes, bonds or securities for money which have been seized or taken, as security for the benefit of the execution creditor for the amount directed to be levied by the execution so far as it is still unsatisfied; and the execution creditor may, when the time of payment has arrived, sue in the name of the execution debtor, or in the name of any person in whose name the execution debtor might have sued, for the recovery of the sum secured or made payable thereby.

(3) The sheriff may also under any process of execution against movable property attach and sell in execution the interest of the execution debtor in any movable property belonging to him and pledged or sold under a suspensive condition to a third person, and may also sell the interest of the execution debtor in property movable or immovable leased to the execution debtor or sold to him or her under any hire-purchase contract or under a suspensive condition.

(4) Whenever, if the sale had not been in execution, it would have been necessary for the execution debtor to endorse a document or to execute a cession in order to pass the property to a purchaser, the sheriff may so endorse the document or execute the cession, as to any property sold by him or her in execution.

---

[20] The actual text still refers to the 'messenger'.

(5) The sheriff may also, as to immovable property sold by him or her in execution, do anything necessary to effect registration of transfer. Anything done by the sheriff under this subsection (ie sub-s 5) or sub-s (4) shall be as valid and effectual as if he or she were the execution debtor.

(6) Where judgment is given against a member of a partnership or syndicate in an action in which he individually was plaintiff or defendant, his or her interest in the partnership or syndicate may be attached and sold in execution.

3.2 The procedure for attachment of movable property

Once the warrant has been issued and handed to the sheriff for execution, the sheriff must, as soon as circumstances permit, go to the residence, place of employment or place of business of the judgment debtor, or to another place pointed out by the execution creditor, and attach the property situated there.[21]

Where the sheriff is in doubt as to the validity of any attachment or contemplated attachment, he or she may require the party suing out the process in execution to give security to indemnify him or her.[22]

According to Annexure 1 Form 37, the security must read as follows:

No. 37
Security under Rule 38

* For use in the District Court

In the Magistrate's Court for the District of ....

held at ....

Case No .... of 20......

In the matter between

.... Execution Creditor

and

.... Execution Debtor

Whereas the said execution creditor obtained judgment in this court against the said execution debtor on the .... day of ...., 20 .... in the sum of R .... together with the sum of R .... for costs;

And whereas under the said judgment execution has been issued and property/a debt/emoluments has/have been attached;

Now therefore the said execution creditor binds himself or herself to the sheriff of the aforesaid court that if the attachment be hereafter set aside, he or she will satisfy any lawful claim against him or her by the said execution debtor for damages suffered by the said execution debtor by reason of the said attachment;

And .... of .... binds himself or herself as surety and co-principal debtor in a sum not exceeding R.................for the due fulfilment by the said execution creditor of the obligation undertaken by him or her.

Signed and dated at .... this .... day of ...., 20......

....

Execution Creditor

---

[21] Rule 41(1)(*a*).
[22] Rule 38(1).

Witnesses:

1. ....

Signature and address

....

Surety and co-principal debtor

2. ....

Signature and address

....

NOTE: Where the security is for the repayment of moneys attached by a garnishee order, a similar form should be used, the words 'refund the gross amount paid by the garnishee' being substituted for the words 'satisfy any lawful claim against him or her by the said execution debtor for damages suffered by the said execution debtor by reason of the said attachment'.

When he or she arrives at the residence or place of business of the judgment debtor, the sheriff must demand payment of the judgment debt and costs. The sheriff must exhibit the original warrant of execution and hand a copy of the warrant to the execution debtor or leave it on the premises.[23]

If the execution debtor pays the judgment debt and costs (or part thereof), the sheriff must forthwith endorse the amount paid and the date of payment on the warrant, and the endorsement must be signed by the sheriff and the execution debtor or his or her representative.[24] If the execution debtor is unable to pay the judgment debt and costs, then the sheriff must require that movable property sufficient, in his or her view, to satisfy the warrant be pointed out to him or her.[25]

The sheriff then makes an inventory and a valuation of this property. Even if the property pointed out to him or her is insufficient to satisfy the warrant, the sheriff must proceed to draw up an inventory and a valuation of so much property as has been pointed out in partial execution of the warrant.[26]

If the execution debtor does not point out any property, the sheriff nevertheless has the power to make an immediate inventory and valuation of the movable property sufficient to satisfy the warrant in whole or in part.[27]

If the debtor declares that he or she has no or insufficient movable property and the sheriff is unable to find sufficient movable property to satisfy the warrant, the sheriff must request the execution debtor to declare whether he or she has immovable property which is executable and enter the reply in his or her return of service endorsed on the warrant.[28]

A copy of the inventory signed by the sheriff must be handed to the execution debtor or left on the premises. The inventory must have subjoined to it a notice of attachment.[29]

---

[23] Rule 41(3).

[24] Rule 41(1)*(d)*.

[25] Rule 41(1)*(a)*.

[26] Rule 41(1)*(b)*. Cf *Sandton Finance (Pty) Ltd v Clerk of Magistrate's Court, Johannesburg, & others* 1992 (1) SA 509 (W).

[27] Rule 41(1)*(c)*.

[28] Section 66(8).

[29] Rule 41(5).

According to Annexure 1 Form 33, the notice of attachment reads as follows:

No. 33
Notice of Attachment in Execution
[Form 33 substituted by GN R1272 of 17 November 2017 (wef 22 December 2017).]

*For use in the District Court

In the Magistrate's Court for the District of ....

held at ....

Case No .... of 20......

In the matter between

.... Execution Creditor

and

.... Judgment Debtor

To: .... Judgment Debtor

Take notice that I have this day laid under judicial attachment the property in the attached inventory in pursuance of a warrant directed to me by the clerk of the court for the district of ...., whereby I am required to cause to be raised of your property in this district or region the sum of R.......... and R .... costs recovered against you by the judgment of the said court in this action together with my charges in respect of the said warrant.

Your attention is drawn to the provisions of rule 43(8)*(a)*(iii) of the rules of the above Honourable Court which reads:

'(iii) Not less than 25 days prior to the date of sale, any interested party may submit to the sheriff, in writing, further or amended conditions of sale.'

The conditions of sale upon which the attached property is to be sold by public auction will be prepared by the execution creditor.

Dated at .... this .... day of ...., 20......

....

Sheriff

If the debtor is not present on the premises or refuses to open the premises or a piece of furniture, the sheriff may open the door to the premises or a piece of furniture, and may use force if necessary to do so.[30]

It often happens that a sheriff comes across money or documents locked away in a piece of furniture. If he or she attaches this, the nature of the document and the amount of money attached must be specified in the inventory. The money or documents must be sealed and taken at once to the sheriff's office for safekeeping.[31]

As soon as the inventory has been drawn up by the sheriff, the property specified in it is deemed to be judicially attached.[32]

Even though property has been attached in execution, the warrant may at any time be withdrawn or suspended by the party at whose instance it was issued.[33]

---

[30] Rule 41(2).
[31] Rule 41(6).
[32] Rule 41(4).
[33] Rule 36(3).

The withdrawal of the warrant is effected by means of a note made by the sheriff on the warrant and the giving by him or her of written notice of the withdrawal to all interested parties.[34]

After the sheriff has attached the property, there is, of course, still the danger that the property may disappear from the premises of the judgment debtor, or that the property may be damaged to such an extent that there is nothing of value left to sell in order to satisfy the judgment granted in favour of the judgment creditor.

For this reason, the execution creditor or his or her attorney must advise the sheriff, after receiving notification of the attachment, whether the property must be removed to a place of security or left on the premises in charge of the judgment debtor or of some other person.[35]

If the execution creditor considers it desirable that the property be removed immediately once attachment is made, he or she may request the registrar or clerk of the court to approve the immediate removal of the property in question and to endorse the warrant of execution to that effect.[36]

In the absence of such a request, the sheriff must leave the movable property on the premises and in the possession of the person in whose possession the said movable property is attached.[37] Pending the removal of the property, the sheriff may leave it in the charge of some person exercising custody of the goods on his or her behalf.[38] That person may not use, let or lend the property or do anything which will decrease its value.[39] If he or she defaults in his or her duty, the custodian of the property will not be entitled to recover any remuneration for keeping the goods in his or her custody.[40]

Where the property attached in execution is a lease or a bill of exchange, promissory note, bond or other security for the payment of money, the sheriff must take possession of the instrument in question, notify the lessor, lessee or person liable on the bill of exchange or other security and, in the case of a registered lease or bond, notify the appropriate registrar of deeds.[41] The attachment is not valid until the sheriff has carried out these duties.[42]

Where the property sought to be attached by the sheriff is merely the interest of the execution debtor in property already pledged, let or sold under a suspensive condition to or by a third person, the attachment is effected by service by the sheriff of a copy of the warrant of execution upon the execution debtor and upon the third person. The service may be effected in the same way as service of a summons. Upon exhibiting the original of the warrant of execution to the pledgee,

---

[34] Rule 39(3).
[35] Rule 41(7)(*a*).
[36] Ibid. Cf *Letsoho Developers (Pty) Ltd v Messenger of the Magistrate's Court, Alberton, & another* 1993 (2) SA 634 (W).
[37] Rule 41(7)(*b*).
[38] Rule 41(7)(*c*).
[39] Rule 41(7)(*d*).
[40] Rule 41(7)(*e*).
[41] Rule 42(1)(*a*) and (*b*).
[42] Ibid.

lessor, lessee, purchaser or seller, the sheriff may enter upon the premises where the property is situated and make an inventory and a valuation of it.[43]

If the attachment takes place without the prescribed formalities being performed, that attachment will be null and void and any sale in execution which follows will likewise be void.[44] The proper procedure for an owner to follow should his property be wrongfully attached is to institute a *rei vindicatio*.

It sometimes happens that a third person claims property attached or about to be attached as being his or her own. It may also happen that a third party lays claim to the proceeds of property attached and sold in execution. The sheriff must, in such cases, immediately notify the execution creditor of the receipt of the third party's claim.[45]

In these instances, so-called *interpleader proceedings* may have to be instituted.[46]

The sheriff must nevertheless attach the property in question and keep it under attachment pending the outcome of interpleader proceedings, unless it is released from attachment earlier in terms of an order of court.[47]

Property attached by the sheriff remains under attachment for a maximum of four months unless a court order has been granted requiring him or her to detain the property for a further period or unless a sale of the property is pending. If the order in terms of which the attachment was made was obtained on application *ex parte,* the four-month period may not be extended.[48]

If an appeal is brought against the judgment of the court or if an application is made to correct, vary or rescind the judgment, the court may direct either that the judgment be executed or that execution be suspended pending the decision on appeal or on application. The court may order the giving of security in such cases.[49]

If execution is suspended pending appeal, the required security must read, according to Annexure 1 Form 28, as follows:

No. 28
Security when Execution is Stayed Pending Appeal
* For use in the District Court

In the Magistrate's Court for the District of ....

held at ....

Case No .... of 20......

In the matter between

.... Judgment Creditor

and

---

[43] Rule 42(2)*(a)* and *(b).*
[44] *Joosub v JI Case SA (Pty) Ltd (now known as Construction & Special Equipment Co (Pty) Ltd) & others* 1992 (2) SA 659 (N).
[45] Rule 39(4).
[46] Cf the discussion of interpleader proceedings at p 27 *et seq* above and at para 7 *et seq* below.
[47] Rule 39(5).
[48] Rule 41(7)*(f).*
[49] Section 78.

.... Judgment Debtor

Whereas the said .... on the .... day of ...., 20 .... obtained judgment in this court against the said ....for the sum of R................ together with a sum of R.................. for costs;

And whereas the said .... has applied to the court for a stay of execution pending appeal/review proceedings and the court has directed that execution be stayed accordingly subject to the said ....giving security within ....days;

Now, therefore, the said .... and .... of .... as surety and co-principal debtor for the said .... hereby bind themselves jointly and severally to satisfy the said judgment and any further liability which may arise by way of damages or otherwise by reason of such suspension, so far as such judgment may not be reversed or varied on appeal/review; and further severally..................... (insert any further terms required).

Signed at .... this .... day of ....,20......

....

Judgment Debtor
Witnesses:

1. ....

Signature and address

....

....

Surety and co-principal debtor

2. ....

Signature and address

....

....

If execution is allowed pending appeal, the security reads, according to Annexure 1 Form 29, as follows:

No. 29
Security when Execution is Allowed Pending Appeal

* For use in the Regional Court

In the Regional Court for the Regional Division of ....

held at ....

Case No .... of 20......

In the matter between

.... Judgment Creditor

and

.... Judgment Debtor

Whereas the said .... on the .... day of ...., 20 .... obtained judgment in this court against the said ....for the sum of R................ together with a sum of R.................. for costs;

And whereas the said court, notwithstanding that the said .... has noted an appeal against the judgment, has directed the judgment to be carried into execution upon security being given for restitution;

Now, therefore, the said .... and .... of .... as surety and co-principal debtor for the said .... hereby bind themselves jointly and severally to refund the above sums of R........................ and R........................ should the judgment of the said court be reversed and further severally (insert any further terms required).

Dated at .... this .... day of ...., 20......

Judgment Debtor

Witnesses:

1. ....

Signature and address

....

....

Surety and co-principal debtor

2. ....

Signature and address

....

....

If property in the custody of the sheriff is released from attachment or attachment is suspended and the owner or the person from whose possession the property has been removed cannot be traced, the sheriff may not retain possession of the property indefinitely. For this reason, the Act authorises him or her to sell the property by public auction after he or she has published a notice of his or her intention to do so in one English and one Afrikaans newspaper circulating in the district where the debtor's last-known address is situated. The proceeds of the sale are paid into the Consolidated Revenue Fund.[50]

The money paid into the Consolidated Revenue Fund may be refunded to any person who satisfies a judicial officer of the district in which the sale took place that he or she would have been entitled to receive the property after the withdrawal of the attachment.[51]

3.3 The procedure for attachment of immovable property

Section 66(1)(a) reads:

'Whenever a court gives judgment for the payment of money or makes an order for the payment of money in instalments, such judgment, in case of failure to pay such money forthwith, or such order in case of failure to pay an instalment at the time and in the manner ordered by the court, shall be enforceable by execution against the movable property and, if there is not found sufficient movable property to satisfy the judgment or order, or the court, on good cause shown, so orders, then against the immovable property of the party against whom such judgment has been given or such order has been made.'

Prior to the order of the Constitutional Court in *Jaftha v Schoeman & others; Van Rooyen v Stoltz & others*,[52] the practice was that the execution creditor who had unsatisfactorily proceeded only against movables would apply to the clerk for

---

[50] Section 71A(1) and (2).

[51] Section 71A(3).

[52] 2005 (2) SA 140 (CC).

a writ against immovables. In *Jaftha* the Constitutional Court held that this procedure was not constitutional and that the words 'a court, after consideration of all relevant circumstances, may order execution' be read into the section before the words 'against the immovable property of the party'. It was therefore found to be unconstitutional to the extent that it permitted sales in execution in unjustifiable circumstances without judicial intervention. The result is that an application now has to be made to court for the issuing of a writ against immovable property. The relevant circumstances to be considered by the court will include: the size and origin of the debt, the value of the immovable property, the availability of other means of recovery of the debt.[53]

In *Gundwana v Steko Development & others*,[54] the Constitutional Court held that further judicial oversight of the execution process is necessary where execution is sought against the homes of indigent debtors who run the risk of losing their security of tenure. However, the court held that it may be that execution cannot be avoided if there are no other proportionate means to obtain the same end.

Execution is usually made against movable property belonging to the judgment debtor. If, however, there is insufficient movable property to satisfy the judgment debt, then execution may be made against the immovable property of the judgment debtor.[55] The magistrate's court may also order that the judgment be enforced by immediate execution against the immovable property of the judgment debtor on good cause shown.[56]

When the execution debtor declares to the sheriff, at the time attachment is made, that he or she has no movable property or insufficient movable property to satisfy the warrant of execution and the sheriff is unable to find sufficient movable property to do so, the sheriff must ask the execution debtor to declare whether he or she has immovable property which is executable and enter the execution debtor's reply in the return of service endorsed on the warrant.[57]

The magistrate's court also has the power, on application by any interested party, to review and confirm, modify or settle the conditions of sale in respect of any immovable property to be sold in execution of any judgment of a division of the High Court of South Africa.[58]

On 17 November 2017, new rules 43 and 43A were introduced into the Rules Regulating the Conduct of the Proceedings of the Magistrates' Courts of South

---

[53] See also *Menqa & another v Markom & others* 2008 (2) SA 120 (SCA) where the court confirmed that, where a warrant had been issued by the clerk of the court without judicial oversight, sales in execution (and subsequent sales) of immovable property were invalid. This is because it infringed upon a party's s 26(1) constitutional rights, even if the infringement occurred prior to the *Jaftha* case.

[54] 2011 (3) SA 608 (CC).

[55] Section 66(1)(a). Cf *Sandton Finance (Pty) Ltd v Clerk of Magistrate's Court, Johannesburg, & others* 1992 (1) SA 509 (W).

[56] Ibid. In the normal course of events, therefore, movable property will always be attached first, and immovables thereafter. *Nedcor Bank Ltd v Kindo & another* 2002 (3) SA 185 (C).

[57] Section 66(8).

[58] Section 75*bis*.

Africa.[59] Rules 43 and 43A apply to execution against immovable property. The result of the amendments is that the procedures to execute against immovable property in the High Court and the magistrates' courts are aligned.

Rule 43 deals with execution against immovable property other than the residential immovable property of a judgment debtor. According to rule 43(1), a warrant of execution against the immovable property of any judgment debtor may not be issued unless he or she has insufficient movable property to satisfy the warrant or such immovable property has been declared to be specially executable by the court.[60]

A warrant of execution against immovable property must contain a full description of the nature, magisterial district and physical address of the immovable property to enable it to be traced and identified by the sheriff, and sufficient information to enable the sheriff to serve a notice of attachment on the immovable property owner.[61] The attachment of the immovable property must be made by any sheriff of the district in which the property is situated, upon a warrant of execution corresponding substantially with Form 32 of Annexure 1.[62] The notice of attachment must correspond substantially with Form 33 of Annexure 1.[63] After attachment, the sale in execution must take place in the district in which the attached immovable property is situated and must be conducted by the sheriff of such district who first attached the property. However, in certain circumstances the sheriff in the first instance may authorise such sale to be conducted elsewhere and by another sheriff.[64]

Rule 43A applies whenever an execution creditor seeks to execute against the residential immovable property of a judgment debtor.[65] A court considering an application under rule 43A must establish whether the immovable property which the execution creditor intends to execute against is the primary residence of the judgment debtor. The court must also consider alternative means by the judgment debtor of satisfying the judgment debt, other than execution against the judgment debtor's primary residence.[66] A court may not authorise execution against immovable property which is the primary residence of a judgment debtor unless the court, having considered all relevant factors, considers that execution against such property is warranted.[67] The registrar or clerk of the court may not issue a warrant of execution against the residential immovable property of any judgment debtor unless a court has ordered execution against such property.[68]

An application to declare residential immovable property executable must be substantially in accordance with Form 1B of Annexure 1. The application must be on notice to the judgment debtor and to any other party who may be affected by the

---

[59] GN R1272 in *GG* 41257 of 17 November 2017 (with effect from 22 December 2017).
[60] Rule 43(1)*(a)*.
[61] Rule 43(1)*(b)*.
[62] Rule 43(2).
[63] Rule 43(3).
[64] Rule 43(4)*(b)*.
[65] Rule 43A(1).
[66] Rule 43A(2)*(a)*.
[67] Rule 43A(2)*(b)*.
[68] Rule 43A(2)*(c)*.

sale in execution, and must be supported by an affidavit setting out the reasons for the application and the grounds on which it is based. The sheriff must serve the application on the judgment debtor personally.[69]

The notice of application must indicate the date on which the application is to be heard and inform every respondent that, if the respondent intends to oppose the application or make submissions to the court, the respondent must do so on affidavit within 10 days of service of the application and appear in court on the date on which the application is to be heard. The notice must also appoint a physical address, which must be within 15 kilometres of the courthouse at which the applicant will accept service of all documents in the proceedings. Finally, the application must indicate the applicant's postal, facsimile or electronic mail address where available. The application may not be set down for hearing on a date less than five days after expiry of the 10-day period referred to above.[70]

The application to declare residential immovable property executable must be supported by documents which evidences, inter alia, the following information:
(1) the market value of the immovable property;
(2) the local authority valuation of the immovable property;
(3) the amounts owing on mortgage bonds registered over the immovable property;
(4) the amount owing to the local authority as rates and other dues; and
(5) the amounts owing to a body corporate as levies.[71]

A respondent has various options once served with the above application. A respondent may oppose the application; oppose the application and make submissions which are relevant to the making of an appropriate order by the court; or, without opposing the application, make submissions which are relevant to the making of an appropriate order by the court.[72] The respondent that chooses to oppose must admit or deny the allegations made by the applicant in the applicant's founding affidavit and set out the reasons, on affidavit, for opposing the application and the grounds on which the application is opposed.[73] Every opposition or submission referred to in paragraphs *(a)* and *(b)* of rule 43A(6) must be set out in an affidavit, which affidavit must be delivered within 10 days of service of the application and must contain a physical address within 15 kilometres of the courthouse at which documents may be served upon such respondent. It must also state the respondent's postal, facsimile or electronic mail address where available.[74]

The registrar or clerk of the court shall place the matter on the roll for hearing by the court on the date stated in the notice of application.[75]

A court considering an application to declare residential immovable property executable has various decision-making powers. For example, the court may set a

---

[69] Rule 43A(3).
[70] Rule 43A(4).
[71] Rule 43A(5).
[72] Rule 43A(6)*(a)*.
[73] Rule 43A(6)*(b)* and *(c)*.
[74] Rule 43A(6)*(d)*.
[75] Rule 43A(7).

reserve price,[76] it may postpone the application on such terms as it may consider appropriate,[77] it may refuse the application if it has no merit, and it may make an appropriate order as to costs,[78] including a punitive order against a party who delays the finalisation of the application.[79]

In every application brought in terms of rule 43A, the court must consider whether a reserve price should be set. When deciding whether to set a reserve price and the amount at which the reserve is to be set, the court must take various factors into account, including the market value of the immovable property, the amount owing as rates or levies and registered mortgage bonds, and whether the immovable property is occupied, the persons occupying the property and the circumstances of such occupation.[80]

3.3.1 *Procedure*

A warrant of execution against immovable property must contain a full and complete description of the nature, situation and address of the property to enable it to be traced and identified by the sheriff, and must be accompanied by sufficient information to enable the sheriff to give proper notice of the attachment to all interested parties.[81]

When the immovable property is situated in a district other than the one in which the judgment was given, the warrant of execution must be forwarded to the sheriff of the district in which the immovable property is situated.[82] A sheriff is not precluded from attaching immovable property by the mere absence of the execution debtor from the residential or business premises being attached if he or she is able to discharge his or her duty to attach the property.[83]

The attachment of immovable property is effected by the sheriff's serving a notice of attachment, accompanied by the warrant of execution, in the same way in which a summons would be served.[84] The notice is served upon the appropriate registrar of deeds, owner and possible occupiers of the land.[85]

The sheriff may by notice, served in the same way as a summons, require the execution debtor to immediately deliver to him or her all documents in his or her possession or under his or her control relating in any way to his or her title to the property.[86]

After attachment, the sheriff must ascertain and record whether the property

---

[76] Rule 43A(8)*(e)*.
[77] Rule 43A(8)*(f)*.
[78] Rule 43A(8)*(g)*.
[79] Rule 43A(8)*(e)*.
[80] See rule 43A(9) for the complete list of factors.
[81] Rule 43(1).
[82] Rule 43(2).
[83] Section 66(7).
[84] Rule 43(3)*(a)*.
[85] Ibid.
[86] Rule 43(6).

attached is subject to any claim preferent to that of the execution creditor. If so, he or she must notify the execution creditor of the existence of any such claim.[87]

When the execution creditor is informed of the preferent claim, he or she must notify the preferent creditor personally in writing of the proposed sale in execution or apply to the magistrate of the district in which the property is situated for an order directing the steps to be taken to bring the intended sale to the notice of the preferent creditor.[88]

It is important to note that s 66(2) provides:

'No immovable property which is subject to any claim preferent to that of the judgment creditor shall be sold in execution unless—

(a)	the judgment creditor has caused such notice in writing of the intended sale in execution to be served personally upon the preferent creditor as may be prescribed by the rules; or

(b)	the magistrate or an additional or assistant magistrate of the district in which the property is situate has upon the application of the judgment creditor and after enquiry into the circumstances of the case, directed what steps shall be taken to bring the intended sale to the notice of the preferent creditor, and those steps have been carried out, and unless

(c)	the proceeds of the sale are sufficient to satisfy the claim of such preferent creditor, in full; or

(d)	the preferent creditor confirms the sale in writing, in which event he shall be deemed to have agreed to accept such proceeds in full settlement of his claim.'

The notice to the preferent creditor reads, in terms of Annexure 1 Form 34, as follows:

No. 34
Notice in terms of Rule 43(5)(a)
[Form 34 substituted by GN R1272 of 17 November 2017 (wef 22 December 2017).]
* For use in the District Court

In the Magistrate's Court for the District of ....

held at ....

Case No .... of 20......

In the matter between

.... Execution Creditor

and

.... Judgment Debtor

To: .... (Preferent Creditor/Local authority/Body Corporate)

Whereas the undermentioned immovable property was laid under judicial attachment by the Sheriff on the .... day of ...., 20 .... you are hereby notified that it will be sold in execution at .... (place) on the .... day of............................, 20...... at ....(time)

Short description of property and its situation:

....

....

---

[87] Rule 43(4)(c). The ranking of preferent claims falls outside the scope of this work, but see *First Rand Bank v Body Corporate of Geovy Villa* 2004 (3) SA 362 (SCA).

[88] Rule 43(5) and s 66(2)(a) and (b).

> You are hereby called upon to stipulate within 10 days of .... (insert date) a
> reasonable reserve price or to agree in writing to a sale without reserve.[89]
>
> Dated at .... this .... day of ...., 20......
>
> ....
>
> Execution creditor/Attorney for execution creditor
>
> Address: ....
>
> ....
>
> ....

The sheriff appoints a date and place for the sale of the property.[90] The sale may not take place less than 45 days after service of the notice of attachment.[91]

The execution creditor, after consultation with the sheriff, prepares a notice of sale containing a short description of the property and its improvements, magisterial district and physical address, the time and place of the sale, and the fact that the conditions may be inspected at the sheriff's office.[92]

The execution creditor must publish the notice once in a newspaper circulating daily or weekly in the district in which the attached immovable property is situated and in the *Gazette* not less than five days and not more than 15 days before the date of the sale.[93] At least 10 days prior to the date of the sale, the sheriff conducting the sale must forward a copy of the notice of sale to every execution creditor who had caused the immovable property to be attached and to every mortgagee thereof whose address is known and must simultaneously furnish a copy of the notice of sale to all other sheriffs appointed in that district.[94] The execution creditor must furnish the sheriff with proof of publication.[95]

At least 35 days prior to the date of the sale, the execution creditor must prepare the conditions of sale, which must correspond substantially with Form 33A of Annexure 1. Furthermore, at least 25 days prior to the date of the sale, any interested party may submit further or amended conditions of sale to the sheriff in writing. The sheriff must then settle the conditions of sale not less than 20 days before the date of the sale.[96]

---

[89] In *Absa Bank Limited v Mokebe and 3 related matters* [2018] 4 All SA 306 (GJ), it was held that, unless exceptional circumstances exist, a reserve price should be set by a court in all matters where execution is granted against immovable property, which is the primary residence of a debtor, where the facts disclosed justify such an order.

[90] Rule 43(7)*(a)*.

[91] Ibid.

[92] Rule 43(7)*(b)*. In terms of rule 43(8)*(a)* the conditions of sale must be prepared by the execution creditor.

[93] Rule 43(7)*(c)*.

[94] Rule 43(7)*(d)*.

[95] Rule 43(6)*(c)*.

[96] Rule 43(8).

No. 33A

Conditions of Sale in Execution of Immovable Property

[Form 33A inserted by GN R1272 of 17 November 2017 (wef 22 December 2017).]

* For use in the District Court

In re:

.... Execution Creditor

and

.... Judgment Debtor

The immovable property (hereinafter referred to as the 'property') which will be put up for auction on the .... day of .... 20......, consists of:

....

The sale shall be conducted on the following conditions:

1   The sale shall be conducted in accordance with the provisions of rule 43 of the Magistrates' Courts Rules and all other applicable law.

2   The property shall be sold by the sheriff of .... or .... XYZ Auctioneers of .... at .... to the highest bidder without reserve/subject to a reserve price of ....[97]

3   The sale shall be for rands, and no bid for less than one thousand rands shall be accepted.

4   If any dispute arises about any bid, the property may again be put up for auction.

5   (a)   If the sheriff/auctioneer makes any mistake in selling, such mistake shall not be binding on any of the parties, but may be rectified.

        (b)   If the sheriff/auctioneer suspects that a bidder is unable to pay either the deposit referred to in condition 7 or the balance of the purchase price, the sheriff/auctioneer may refuse to accept the bid of such bidder, or accept it provisionally until the bidder satisfies the sheriff/auctioneer that such bidder is able to pay the deposit and the balance of the purchase price.

        (c)   On the refusal of a bid under circumstances referred to in paragraph *(b)*, the property may immediately be put up for auction again.

6   (a)   The purchaser shall, as soon as possible after the sale and immediately on being requested by the sheriff/auctioneer, sign these conditions.

        (b)   If the purchaser purchases in a representative capacity, the purchaser shall disclose the name of the principal or person on whose behalf the property is being purchased.

7   (a)   The purchaser shall pay to the sheriff a deposit of 10 per cent of the purchase price in cash or by bank guaranteed cheque on the day of the sale.

        (b)   The balance shall be paid against transfer and shall be secured by a guarantee issued by a financial institution approved by the execution creditor or his or her attorney, and shall be furnished to the sheriff within .... days after the date of sale.

8   (a)   If the purchaser fails to carry out any obligation due by the purchaser under the conditions of sale, the sale may be cancelled by a magistrate summarily on the report of the sheriff after due notice to the purchaser, and the property may again be put up for sale.

        (b)   In the event of the circumstances in paragraph *(a)* occurring, the purchaser shall be responsible for any loss sustained by reason of such default, which loss may, on the application of any aggrieved creditor whose name appears on the sheriff's distribution account, be recovered from the purchaser under judgment of a magistrate pronounced on a written report by the sheriff, after such purchaser has been given notice in writing that such report will be laid before the magistrate for such purpose.

---

[97] In *Absa Bank Limited v Mokebe* (supra), it was held that, unless exceptional circumstances exist, a reserve price should be set by a court in all matters where execution is granted against immovable property, which is the primary residence of a debtor, where the facts disclosed justify such an order.

   (c) If the purchaser is already in possession of the property, the sheriff may, on notice to affected parties, apply to a magistrate for an order evicting the purchaser or any person claiming to occupy the property through the purchaser or otherwise occupying the property.

9 *(a)* The purchaser shall immediately on demand pay the sheriff's commission/auctioneer's fees and expenses calculated as follows:

     ....;

   (b) The purchaser shall be liable for and pay, within 10 days of being requested to do so by the appointed conveyancer, the following:

     (i) All amounts due to the municipality servicing the property, in terms of the Local Government: Municipal Systems Act, 2000 (Act 32 of 2000), for municipal service fees, surcharges on fees, property rates and other municipal taxes, levies and duties that may be due to a municipality; and where applicable.

     (ii) All levies due to a body corporate in terms of the Sectional Titles Act, 1986 (Act 95 of 1986) or amounts due to a home owners or other association which renders services to the property.

     (iii) The costs of transfer, including conveyance fees, transfer duty and any other amount necessary for the passing of transfer to the purchaser.

10 *(a)* The property may be taken possession of after signature of the conditions of sale, payment of the deposit and upon the balance of the purchase price being secured in terms of condition 7*(b)*.

   (b) Should the purchaser receive possession of the property, the purchaser shall be liable for occupational rental at the rate of R................ per month from .... to date of transfer.

   (c) Upon the purchaser taking possession, the property shall be at the risk and profit of the purchaser.

   (d) The execution creditor and the sheriff/auctioneer give no warranty that the purchaser shall be able to obtain personal and/or vacant occupation of the property or that the property is not occupied.

11 *(a)* The purchaser shall be entitled to obtain transfer forthwith upon payment of the whole purchase price and compliance with condition 9, alternatively, transfer shall be passed only after the purchaser has complied with the provisions of conditions 7 and 9 hereof.

   (b) If the transfer is delayed by the purchaser, the purchaser shall be liable for interest at the rate of .... per cent per annum on the purchase price.

12 *(a)* The sheriff may demand that any improvements to the property sold shall be immediately insured by the purchaser for their full value, proof of insurance given to the sheriff and such insurance policy kept in force until transfer is registered.

   (b) Should the purchaser fail to comply with the obligations in paragraph *(a)*, the sheriff may effect the necessary insurance, the cost of which insurance shall be for the purchaser's account.

13 *(a)* The property is sold as represented by the title deeds and diagram or sectional plan, subject to all servitudes and conditions of establishment, whichever applies to the property.

   (b) The sheriff/auctioneer shall not be liable for any deficiency that may be found to exist in the property.

14 The execution creditor shall appoint the conveyancer to effect transfer of the property to the purchaser: Provided that the sheriff shall be entitled to appoint a new conveyancer should the conveyancer appointed by the execution creditor not proceed timeously or satisfactorily with the transfer.

Signed at .... this .... day of ...., 20......

I certify hereby that today the .... in my presence the hereinbeforementioned property was sold for .... to

....   Sheriff/Auctioneer   I, the undersigned ...., residing at .... in the district of   .... do hereby bind myself as the purchaser of the hereinbeforementioned   property to pay the purchase price and to perform all and singular the conditions mentioned   above.   ....   Purchaser

In the attachment and execution process the sheriff does not act as agent of either judgment creditor or debtor, but he or she acts under statutory authority. However, the sheriff does assume the duties set out in the conditions of sale, such as to give *vacua possessio* to the purchaser.[98]

4 EXECUTION

4.1 The procedure for sales in execution of movable property

After attachment, the attached property is sold in execution.

The sheriff appoints a date for the sale, which is not less than 15 days after the attachment, except in the case where perishable goods are to be sold, where the execution debtor consents to an earlier date or where the court orders otherwise.[99]

The execution creditor, after consultation with the sheriff, prepares a notice of sale. Copies of this notice are put up at the courthouse and at the place where the sale is to be held. The notice must be published not later than 10 days prior to the sale.[100]

If the sheriff is of the opinion, however, that the value of the goods attached exceeds R5 000, the notice must in addition be published in a newspaper circulating in the district at least 10 days before the date on which the sale is to be held, and the execution creditor must furnish the sheriff not later than the day preceding the sale with a copy of the edition of the paper in which the notice appeared.[101]

On the date appointed for the sale, the property is sold publicly and for cash by the sheriff or, with the approval of the magistrate, by an auctioneer or some other person to the highest bidder.[102] The sale usually takes place at the place where the property was attached or to which the property has been removed.[103] Neither the sheriff nor any person on his or her behalf may purchase any of the property offered for sale at a sale in execution either for himself or herself or for any other person.[104]

---

[98] *Sedibe & another v United Building Society & another* 1993 (3) SA 671 (T) at 676A–D.
[99] Rule 41(9).
[100] Rule 41(8)*(b)*.
[101] Rule 41(8)*(c)*.
[102] Rule 41(8)*(a)*.
[103] Ibid.
[104] Rule 39(7).

The costs and expenses of issuing a warrant and levying execution rank as a first charge upon the proceeds of the property sold in execution.[105] Subject to any hypothec existing prior to the attachment, all warrants of execution lodged with the sheriff on or before the day immediately preceding the date of the sale in execution rank pro rata in the distribution of the proceeds of the goods sold in execution.[106]

The right of ownership of a person who purchases property sold in execution may not be impeached by any person after delivery of the property as long as the purchaser was in good faith and was ignorant of any defect in title to the property.[107]

The sheriff must stop the sale in execution as soon as sufficient money has been raised to satisfy the warrant or warrants and the costs of the sale itself.[108] If any balance be left in hand, it must be paid to the execution debtor or, if he or she cannot be found, it must be paid into court.[109] The surplus may, however, itself be attached in the hands of the sheriff to meet any other unsatisfied judgment debts.[110]

On completion of the sale, the sheriff draws up a vendue roll showing details of the property sold, the prices realised and, where known, the names and addresses of the purchasers, as well as an account of the distribution of the proceeds.[111]

4.2 The procedure for sales in execution of immovable property

It is not always necessary that immovable property be sold by the sheriff himself or herself. The execution creditor or any person having an interest in the due and proper realisation of the property may, by notice given to the sheriff within 15 days after the attachment, require that the property be sold by an auctioneer in the ordinary course of business, and may in such notice nominate the auctioneer to be employed.[112] Where a person other than the execution creditor requires that the property be sold by an auctioneer, he or she must also send a deposit of a sufficient sum to cover the additional expense of sale by an auctioneer.[113] If more than one notice is given requiring a sale by auctioneer, the first takes preference.[114]

The sale is held in the court of the district or, for good cause shown, at some other place determined by the magistrate[115] by public auction subject to the conditions of sale.[116]

---

[105] Rule 39(1).
[106] Rule 39(2).
[107] Section 70. Cf *Joosub & Jones & others v Trust Bank of Africa Ltd & others* 1993 (4) SA 415 (C) at 419G ff. The sale in execution must, however, be a valid sale. If it is not, the whole process may be impugned.
[108] Rule 41(10).
[109] Rule 41(11). In terms of rule 41(11), monies paid into court and not paid out within three years must be paid into the State Revenue Fund after three months' notice has been given to the parties concerned.
[110] Section 71.
[111] Rule 39(6).
[112] Rule 43(10)*(a)* and *(b)*.
[113] Rule 43(10)*(c)*.
[114] Rule 43(10)*(d)*.
[115] Rule 43(4)*(b)*.
[116] Rule 43(10) and (11).

For all practical purposes, the sheriff is placed in the same legal position as the owner of the immovable property and he or she may, for the purpose of effecting registration of transfer of the property, do anything that the owner could have done.[117]

The execution creditor has normally by this time appointed a conveyancer to draw up the deed of transfer[118] and all necessary documents will have to be signed by the sheriff and by the purchaser. All monies in respect of the purchase price must be paid by the purchaser to the sheriff, who retains the money in his or her trust account until transfer has been effected.[119] The money remains in the control of the sheriff and is not paid out until transfer has been given to the purchaser.[120]

Within 10 days after registration of the transfer, the sheriff prepares a plan of distribution, indicating how he or she intends to divide the proceeds of the sale (the purchase price) among the interested parties, ie the bondholders and the execution creditor.[121] This plan of distribution (a copy of which is sent to the registrar or clerk of the court) lies for inspection for 15 days in the sheriff's office unless all interested persons inform the sheriff in writing that they have no objection to the plan.[122]

Should any interested party wish to object to the plan of distribution, he or she must, within the 15-day period referred to above, give notice in writing of his or her objection to the sheriff, the registrar or clerk of the court and all other persons having an interest in the distribution. The matter may be brought before the court for review if the grounds of the objection are not removed within 10 days of the expiration of the 10-day waiting period.[123]

The review takes place on 10 days' notice to all interested parties.[124] The court may hear and determine the matter in dispute in a summary manner and thereafter amend or confirm the plan of distribution or make such order, including an order as to costs, as may be appropriate.[125]

If no objection has been lodged to the plan, if the interested parties signify their concurrence with the plan or if the plan has been confirmed or amended on review, then the sheriff must, on production of evidence that transfer has been given to the purchaser, pay out in accordance with the plan of distribution.[126]

---

[117] Rule 43(13). Cf *Sedibe v United Building Society* (supra) and 1991 (4) SA 65 (W).

[118] Rule 43(9).

[119] Rule 43(13)*(a)*.

[120] Ibid.

[121] Rule 43(14)*(b)*. The order of preference according to which the sheriff is obliged to draw up the plan of distribution is set out in rule 43(14)*(c)* as follows: 'After deduction from the proceeds of the costs of execution, the following shall be the order of preference:

  (i) Claims of preferent creditors ranking in priority in their legal order of preference; and thereafter

  (ii) Claims of other creditors whose warrants have been lodged with the sheriff in the order of preference appearing from sections 96 and 98A to 103 (inclusive) of the Insolvency Act, 1936 (Act 24 of 1936).'

[122] Rule 43(14)*(b)*.

[123] Rule 43(14)*(d)*.

[124] Ibid.

[125] Rule 43(14)*(e)*.

[126] Rule 43(14)*(f)*.

4.3 Execution against partnerships

Rule 40(1), (2) and (3) applies to execution against a partnership and provides that, where a judgment debtor is a partner in a firm and the judgment is against him or her for a separate debt, the court may, after notice to the judgment debtor and to his or her firm, appoint the sheriff as receiver to receive any monies payable to the judgment debtor in respect of his or her interests in the partnership. This appointment operates as an attachment of the interests of the judgment debtor in the partnership assets until the judgment debt has been satisfied. Where the judgment is against a firm, the partnership property, so far as it is known to the judgment creditor, must be exhausted first, before the judgment is executed against the separate property of the partners.

5   GIVING OF SECURITY BY THE JUDGMENT CREDITOR

The execution debtor in certain instances enjoys a measure of protection, especially where the possibility exists that he or she has not been advised of the judgment against him or her (which may occur in the case of a default judgment).

Unless the summons instituting action has been served upon the defendant personally or he or she has entered appearance to defend or notice of attachment has been given to him or her personally, the execution creditor must, at least 10 days before the sale of the attached property, give security to the satisfaction of the sheriff for the payment of any sum which the execution debtor may be legally entitled to recover from the creditor for damage suffered by reason of the attachment or consequent proceedings. If security is not given, the attachment ceases to have effect.[127] Monies received by the sheriff under any form of execution other than the proceeds of a sale in execution against property in respect of which security has been given are not paid to the execution creditor until he or she has given security for the restitution of the full amount received by the sheriff should the attachment subsequently be set aside.[128]

The execution debtor may waive the requirement to furnish security by endorsement on the warrant of execution or by writing over his or her signature.[129]

The prescribed fee for security given in terms of rule 38 is recoverable without taxation as part of the costs of execution.[130] The execution debtor may sue upon any surety bond or other document of security given in terms of rule 38 without formal transfer of the document to him or her.[131]

A minister, deputy minister or an administrator in his or her official capacity, the State or a provincial administration are exempt from the obligation to furnish security where they act as execution creditors.[132]

---

[127] Rule 38(2)*(a)*.
[128] Rule 38(2)*(b)*.
[129] Rule 38(2)*(a)* and *(b)*.
[130] Rule 38(3).
[131] Rule 38(4).
[132] Rule 38(5).

6 GARNISHEE ORDERS

6.1 General

Apart from attempting to procure the satisfaction of the judgment debt by means of the attachment and sale in execution of movable or immovable property belonging to the judgment debtor, the judgment creditor may also try to attach a money debt due to the judgment debtor by a third person.

Suppose that the creditor obtains judgment against an artisan. It is clear that the artisan possesses no movable or immovable assets that may be attached in satisfaction of the judgment debt. A third person, however, owes the artisan a substantial amount for work done by the artisan. The judgment creditor may now obtain an order attaching the money due in terms of that debt (a 'garnishee order').

In this example, the artisan is the person known as the 'judgment debtor', and the third person who owes him money is referred to as the 'garnishee'.[133]

6.2 The procedure for obtaining a garnishee order

The general procedure is set out by s 72 and rule 47.

The judgment creditor must bring an *ex parte* application for a garnishee order or act in terms of s 65E(1)*(b)* for the attachment of a debt. The order attaching the debt will direct the garnishee to pay the judgment creditor or his or her attorney at the address of the judgment creditor or his or her attorney, so much of the debt as may be sufficient to satisfy the judgment and costs.[134] A judgment creditor may not apply for a garnishee order against the State.[135]

The application must be supported by an affidavit (or affirmation) by the creditor or by a certificate by his or her attorney stating, in terms of rule 47(1):

'*(a)* a court—
    (i) has granted judgment to the judgment creditor; or
    (ii) has ordered the payment of a debt referred to in section 55[136] of the Act and costs in specific instalments;
(b) the judgment or order referred to in subrule (1)*(a)* is still unsatisfied, stating the amounts still payable thereunder;
(c) the garnishee resides, carries on business or is employed within the district, with mention of the address of the garnishee; and
(d) a debt is at present or in future owing or accruing by or from the garnishee to the judgment debtor and the amount thereof.'

The application must furnish the identity number, work number or date of birth of the judgment debtor so as to enable the garnishee to identify the judgment debtor.[137]

---

[133] Cf in general s 72(1).
[134] Section 72(1)
[135] Ibid.
[136] ie a liquidated sum of money due.
[137] Rule 47(3).

If the application is made to a court other than the one which granted the judgment or order, a certified copy of the judgment or order against the judgment debtor must accompany the affidavit, affirmation or certificate.[138]

When the court hears the *ex parte* application, it may call for such further evidence as it deems fit.[139]

Once the court is satisfied as to the merits of the application, a garnishee order will be issued. This order is a rule *nisi*, and the court will order that the debt be attached and that the garnishee is to pay to the judgment creditor or to his attorney as much of the debt attached as is necessary to satisfy the judgment debt and costs. If he or she fails or refuses to pay the debt, the garnishee must appear in court on a day named in the order to show cause why he or she should not pay the debt.[140]

According to Annexure 1 Form 39, the garnishee order reads as follows:

No. 39

Garnishee Order—Section 72 of the Magistrates' Courts Act, 1944 (Act 32 of 1944)

* For use in the District Court

In the Magistrate's Court for the District of ....

held at ....

Case No .... of 20......

In the matter between

.... Judgment Creditor

and

.... Judgment Debtor

Particulars for the identification of the judgment debtor inclusive of his/her identity or work number or date of birth and address

.... Garnishee.

.... Address of garnishee.

Whereas it has been made to appear to the above-mentioned Court that a debt is at present or in future owing or accruing to the judgment debtor by or from the garnishee;

It is ordered—

(1) that the said debt be attached;

(2) that the garnishee pay to the judgment creditor or judgment creditor's attorney so much of the debt as may be sufficient to satisfy a judgment or order obtained against the judgment debtor by the judgment creditor in the .... Court at .... on the .... day of .... 20...... for the amount of R............ (on which judgment or order the amount of R................ remains due and unpaid) and the costs of the proceedings of attachment amounting to R............ as well as R............ Sheriff's fees.

If the garnishee fails to pay the judgment creditor or his or her attorney as aforesaid, he shall appear before this Court on the .... day of .... 20...... at .... (time) to show cause why he or she should not pay the same.

Dated at .... this .... day of ...., 20......

By Order of the Court,

....

---

[138] Rule 47(2).
[139] Rule 47(4).
[140] Rule 47(5).

Clerk of the Court

....

Judgment Creditor/Attorney for Judgment Creditor

....

.... (Address)

The registrar or clerk of the court notes upon the order the date on which it was made[141] and serves it upon the garnishee and the judgment debtor. The debt is then attached in the hands of the garnishee.[142]

If they wish to show cause why the debt ought not to be attached, the judgment debtor and the garnishee may appear in court on the day fixed for the hearing of the application for the garnishee order, but they may not question the correctness of the judgment upon which the application is based.[143]

The garnishee may seek to aver, for instance, that he or she cannot pay the debt to the judgment debtor, that he or she has a set-off against the judgment debtor, that the debt is due to someone other than the judgment debtor, or that the debt has already been attached.

If the judgment debtor appears and objects to the attachment on the ground that the judgment has been satisfied, that the garnishee is not indebted to him or her or that the judgment is for some reason not operative against him or her, the court may try the issue summarily.[144]

If, however, the garnishee does not show cause why he or she should not have to pay the amount in question to the judgment creditor or his attorney, or the court does not accept his protestations of non-liability, he or she is obliged to act in accordance with the garnishee order and pay the debt to the judgment creditor. If he or she fails to do so, a warrant of execution in the amount ordered to be paid to the judgment creditor may be issued against the garnishee, and he or she will, in that event, be liable for the costs of execution.[145]

When the garnishee shows cause why a garnishee order should not be issued, the court may investigate the matter in full and order him or her to state his defence orally or in writing and on oath. The court may try the dispute in a summary manner and:

(1) The court may order that the matters in issue be tried under the ordinary procedure of the court.

(2) It may order that, for purposes of such trial, the judgment creditor is to act as plaintiff and the garnishee as defendant, or *vice versa*.[146]

---

[141] Rule 47(6).

[142] Rule 47(7).

[143] Rule 47(8). The rule provides that the judgment debtor and the garnishee *may* appear on that day. There is thus no *obligation* on them to appear.

[144] Rule 47(12).

[145] Rule 47(9). Execution in terms of this rule takes place in the same manner as execution against the judgment debtor.

[146] Rule 47(10)*(a)* and *(b)* and s 75(1). In terms of s 75(2), the court has no jurisdiction if it is proved that a third person has a *prima facie* claim to the debt, but that he or she does not reside, does not carry on business and is not employed within the Republic.

(3) It may extend the return day if the garnishee avers that the debt belongs to some other person or is subject to a claim by another person. There is then a dispute as to the entitlement to the debt, and the court may order that this dispute be resolved in the same way as a dispute which is the subject of interpleader proceedings between the judgment creditor and such other person.[147]

On the return day, the court, after hearing the parties who appear before it, may make any of the following final orders:[148]

(1) order payment by the garnishee in terms of the garnishee order;
(2) declare the claim of any person to the debt attached to be barred;
(3) dismiss the application for the garnishee order; or
(4) make such other order as may deem fit.

The court has an unfettered discretion in regard to the order that it wishes to make. The court may, for example, set aside or vary the garnishee order if the judgment debtor can prove that, after satisfaction of the order, he or she will not be left with sufficient means to maintain himself or herself and his or her dependants.[149]

In addition, the court may at any time suspend, vary or rescind a garnishee order.[150]

If it appears that there are unsatisfied claims due to other creditors, the court may postpone the application to enable the judgment debtor to apply for an administration order.[151]

7 INTERPLEADER PROCEEDINGS

7.1 General

Interpleader proceedings are dealt with as part of the present chapter on execution. The reason for this is that interpleader proceedings are almost always instituted in the context of attachment in execution.

In this chapter, reference has already been made to the sheriff's power to attach movable and immovable property belonging to a judgment debtor, as well as a debt accruing to him or her. At the time of attachment, however, it is possible that property is attached which belongs to someone other than the judgment debtor but which happens to be in the possession of the judgment debtor at the time. Examples may be property lent to the judgment debtor, property that he or she is looking after or storing for some third person, or goods purchased by the judgment debtor on instalment but of which he or she has not yet acquired ownership.

It is necessary for the law to protect the owner[152] in order to avert prejudice to innocent parties in consequence of the attachment of their property to satisfy a judgment debt.

This protection is afforded by the procedure pertaining to interpleader claims.[153]

---

[147] Rule 47(11).
[148] Rule 47(13).
[149] Section 72(2).
[150] Section 72(3).
[151] Section 72(4). Cf in regard to administration orders chapter 20 below.
[152] Such an owner is referred to as a 'claimant'.
[153] Section 28(1)*(e)* regulates the jurisdiction of the court in relation to parties to interpleader proceedings. Cf chapter 4 above.

Section 69 of the Act provides expressly for the institution of interpleader proceedings in two situations: first, a person other than the judgment debtor may make a claim to property attached or about to be attached, or to the proceeds of property sold in execution;[154] secondly, two or more persons may make competing claims to property in the custody or possession of a third party.[155] The procedure that is followed in these two situations is discussed below.

7.2 The procedure followed where a third party lays claim to attached property or to the proceeds of its sale in execution

If the claimant wishes to object to the attachment of certain property, the claimant must notify the sheriff immediately that he or she lays claim to the property and that he or she therefore objects to its attachment or proposed attachment, and the sheriff must forthwith notify the execution creditor of the claim.[156] The sheriff must nevertheless proceed with the attachment, and the property attached remains under attachment pending the outcome of interpleader proceedings or until it is released from attachment.[157]

If the third party's claim to the property is not admitted by the execution creditor, the sheriff must draw up and sue out an interpleader summons.[158] In this summons the execution creditor and the claimant are called upon to appear in court on the date specified in the summons to have the claim adjudicated upon.[159] The interpleader summons reads as follows:

No. 35
Interpleader Summons
[Section 69(1) of Act 32 of 1994]
* For use in the District Court

In the Magistrate's Court for the District of ....

held at ....

                                                                          Case No .... of 20......

In the matter between

.... Execution Creditor

and

.... Execution Debtor

To: .... (Execution Creditor)

....

and: .... (Claimant)

....

---

[154] Section 69(1)*(a)* and rule 39(4). This person is referred to in rule 44(2)*(a)* as the 'claimant'. In rule 39(4) the person is called a 'third party'.
[155] Section 69(2).
[156] Rule 39(4).
[157] Rule 39(5).
[158] Section 69(1)*(a)* and rule 44(2).
[159] Cf the example contained in Annexure 1 Form 35.

> You are hereby summoned to appear before this court on the .... day of ...., 20...... at .... (time), to have it determined and declared whether certain movable property, namely ...., attached on the .... day of ...., 20 .... by the sheriff by virtue of a warrant of execution issued by this court on the .... day of ...., 20 ...., in the action in which you, ... the said execution creditor, obtained judgment for the sum of R .... against .... of .... (execution debtor) and which said property is claimed by you, ... the said claimant, as being your property, is or is not your property or to appear to have the claim by you, ... the said claimant, [............................. (claimant)] to the proceeds of property, namely .... attached on the .... day of ...., 20...... by the sheriff by virtue of a warrant of execution issued out of this court on the................ day of ...., 20......, in the action in which the execution creditor obtained judgment for the sum of R............. against .... of......................... (execution debtor) and which property was sold in execution on the .... day of ...., 20......, adjudicated upon.
>
> Dated at .... this .... day of ...., 20......
>
> ....
>
> Clerk of the Court

Upon the issue of an interpleader summons, any action which may have been brought in respect of the property in dispute is stayed pending the outcome of the interpleader proceedings.[160]

The claimant is obliged, at least 10 days before the date of hearing specified in the interpleader summons, to lodge with the sheriff an affidavit in triplicate, setting forth the grounds upon which his or her claim is based.[161] The sheriff forwards one copy of the affidavit to the execution creditor and one copy to the execution debtor.[162]

In interpleader proceedings, therefore, a summons is issued and affidavits are filed. The affidavits play a similar role in these proceedings to that of the particulars of claim in a trial action.

On the date specified in the summons, the parties appear in court for a hearing to determine the merits of the third party's claim to the attached property.

7.3 The procedure where two or more persons make competing claims to property in the possession of a third party

It may happen that a third party (usually the sheriff) finds himself or herself in a position in which two or more persons make competing claims to property in his or her possession. The third party is thus placed in the uncomfortable situation of not knowing which of the rival claimants is entitled to the property (or its proceeds).

In such a case, only one course of action is open to the applicant (as the third party is called in rule 44): that is to issue an interpleader summons, calling upon the rival claimants to appear in court and there to state the nature and particulars of

---

[160] Section 69(1)*(b)*.
[161] Rule 44(2)*(a)*.
[162] Rule 44(2)*(b)*.

their claims and have their claims adjudicated upon.[163] The summons takes the following form:[164]

No. 36
Interpleader Summons
[Section 69(2) of Act 32 of 1944.]

* For use in the District Court

In the Magistrate's Court for the District of ....

held at ....

Case No .... of 20......

To the Sheriff of the Court.

Whereas .... of .... has interpleaded in this court as to .... (state subject matter) which is adversely claimed by .... of .... and .... of .... hereinafter called the claimants;

Summon the said claimants that they appear before the above-mentioned court on the .... day of ...., 20...... at .... (time), and that they do then severally state the nature and particulars of their several claims and whether they will maintain or relinquish the same.

Dated at .... this .... day of ...., 20......

....

Clerk of the Court

If the property in dispute consists of money, the applicant must, when suing out the summons, pay the amount in question into court.[165]

The applicant annexes to the summons an affidavit in which he or she states that:

(1) he or she claims no interest in the subject-matter in dispute other than for charges or costs;

(2) he or she is not in collusion with any of the claimants; and

(3) in the case of property other than money paid into court, he or she is willing to deal with the property as the court may direct.[166]

7.4 The hearing of interpleader proceedings

If any of the claimants fail to appear in court, to file an affidavit or to comply with any order made by the court, the court may make an order declaring such person and all persons claiming under him or her barred from making any claim against the applicant or the sheriff in respect of the property in question.[167]

Upon the appearance of the parties, the court may:

(1) order any claimant to state orally or in writing under oath or otherwise the nature and particulars of his or her claim;

---

[163] Section 69(2) and rule 44(1)*(a)*.
[164] Annexure 1 Form 36.
[165] Rule 44(1)*(b)*.
[166] Rule 44(1)*(c)*.
[167] Rule 44(4).

(2) order that the matters in issue are to be tried on a day appointed for that purpose, and order which of the claimants is to be the plaintiff and which is to be the defendant for the purpose of the trial; or

(3) try the matters in dispute in a summary manner.[168]

The court may also make such order as to the costs of execution as it may deem fit.[169]

At the trial of an interpleader claim, the normal rules that pertain to the hearing of a trial action apply.[170]

---

[168] Rule 44(5)*(a)*, *(b)* and *(c)*.
[169] Rule 44(7).
[170] Rule 44(6).

Chapter 18

APPEALS AND REVIEWS

1 INTRODUCTION

Appeals and reviews are procedures that may be adopted in order to challenge decisions of the lower courts and, if necessary, have them corrected.

Although aimed at similar results, appeals and reviews are different procedures and each is appropriate only in certain circumstances.

In determining which procedure is appropriate, one should begin by enquiring what one's grounds of complaint are. The decision handed down by a magistrate may be erroneous either because the presiding officer has misconstrued the facts of the matter before him or her or because he or she has misinterpreted the law or applied it incorrectly. Alternatively, the decision may be impeachable because of some procedural irregularity that occurred during the conduct of the case. In general, if one complains of the *reasoning* employed by the court in coming to a decision, one will proceed by way of appeal. But if one complains about the *process* which led to the decision of the magistrate, one will proceed by way of review.[1]

Thus, an appeal is in reality a re-evaluation of the record of proceedings in the magistrate's court. The grounds of review, however, are laid down by statute, in s 22 of the Superior Courts Act 10 of 2013, namely:

(a) absence of jurisdiction on the part of the court;

(b) interest in the cause, bias, malice or corruption on the part of the presiding judicial officer;

(c) gross irregularity in the proceedings; and

(d) the admission of inadmissible or incompetent evidence or the rejection of admissible or competent evidence.

In *Johannesburg Consolidated Investment Co v Johannesburg Town Council*[2] Innes CJ described review as 'the process by which ... the proceedings of inferior Courts of Justice, both Civil and Criminal, are brought before this Court [i.e. the reviewing superior court] in respect of grave irregularities or illegalities occurring during the course of such proceedings'.

Although these differences are fundamental and a legal practitioner must bear them in mind when deciding upon the method by which he or she will attempt to have the decision of the magistrate's court upset, there are nevertheless instances in which both the review procedure and the appeal procedure may be used.

Suppose that a magistrate admits inadmissible or incompetent evidence. In such a case the proceedings may be taken on review in terms of s 22(1)*(d)* of the Superior Courts Act. But it would also be correct procedure to appeal should inadmissible evidence on the record be apparent.[3]

Suppose further that the trial court lacked jurisdiction to try the case and that an objection based upon lack of jurisdiction has been dismissed. In such a case, the aggrieved party may apply for review in terms of s 22(1)*(a)* of the Superior Courts Act. It would, however, also be quite in order to bring an appeal in such a case.[4]

Because an appeal is a reassessment of the evidence and proceedings of the lower court, the ambit of the appeal is the record of such proceedings. Reviews, however, may require extensive evidence which is not apparent from the record. This difference results in very different procedures.

The difference is apparent from the treatment of the record. An appeal is heard and decided on the record of the lower court. In *R v Bates & Reidy*[5] Innes CJ said:

---

[1] *Visser v Estate Collins* 1952 (2) SA 546 (C) at 551; *Primich v Additional Magistrate, Johannesburg, & another* 1967 (3) SA 661 (T) at 671–2.

[2] 1903 TS 111 at 114.

[3] *Retief Bros v Estate Du Plessis* 1928 CPD 387.

[4] *King's Transport v Viljoen* 1954 (1) SA 133 (C).

[5] 1902 TS 199 at 200; cf also *R v Parmanand* 1954 (3) SA 833 (A).

'The difference between appeal and review is that an appeal is based upon the matters contained in the record, while in review the appellant may travel beyond the record in order to rely on certain grounds, such as gross irregularity and the admission of incompetent evidence. If the appellant desires to appeal, but is not satisfied with the record as it stands, he may proceed to apply for leave to amend it.'

Appeals are instituted by means of a notice of appeal (in terms of magistrate's court rule 51(4)) and reviews by means of the application procedure (in terms of High Court rule 53).

Appeals and reviews also differ in relation to the period of time within which each must be brought. Appeals must be noted and prosecuted within statutorily prescribed time limits. Reviews need be applied for only within a reasonable time.[6]

Appeals and reviews are each discussed separately below.

2 APPEALS

2.1 General

There are two instances in which the magistrate's court can itself become a court of appeal.

First, where objection is made to the valuation by a local authority of immovable property, s 15 of the Local Authorities Rating Ordinance 20 of 1933 (T) provides for an appeal to the magistrate's court. The procedure for this appeal is set out in rule 50.

Secondly, in terms of s 12(4) of the Black Administration Act 38 of 1927 an appeal lies from the decision of a chief, headman or chief's deputy to the magistrate's court which would have had jurisdiction over the dispute in the first instance. The quantum of the dispute must exceed R10. Section 29A of the Magistrates' Courts Act provides that in such an appeal the court may confirm, alter or set aside the judgment after hearing such evidence as may be tendered by the parties to the dispute, or as may be deemed desirable by the court. The result is that this particular kind of appeal constitutes a virtual rehearing of the case. Regulations regarding procedure for such appeals is provided for in terms of s 12(6) of the Black Administration Act.[7]

All other appeals are from the magistrate's court to the High Court.[8] Section 21(1) of the Superior Courts Act provides that the High Court has the power to hear and determine appeals from all magistrates' courts within its area of jurisdiction.[9]

A party to any civil suit or proceeding in a magistrate's court may appeal against the decision of the magistrate to a main or local division of the High Court that possesses appeal jurisdiction.[10]

---

[6] *Harnaker v Minister of the Interior* 1965 (1) SA 372 (C).

[7] Section 12(6) is repealed by s 1(3) of Act 28 of 2005 on 30 December 2009 or such date as national legislation to further regulate the matters dealt with in s 12(6) is implemented, whichever occurs first.

[8] The divisions of the High Court of South Africa are set out in s 6(1) of the Superior Courts Act.

[9] Section 21(1)*(b)*.

[10] Section 83 of the Magistrates' Courts Act 32 of 1944.

To this general power of appeal there exist two exceptions. First, the parties may, before commencement of the hearing, lodge with the court a written agreement that the decision of the court shall be final and that they undertake not to appeal against the court's decision.[11] In terms of Annexure 1 Form 54 this agreement must read as follows:

No. 54
Agreement Not to Appeal

* For use in the District Court

In the Magistrate's Court for the District of ....

held at ....

Case No .... of 20......

In the matter between

.... Plaintiff

and

.... Defendant

We, ..., of ...., and

...., of ...., the above-named plaintiff and defendant, respectively, do hereby agree, in terms of section 82 of the Magistrates' Courts Act, 1944 (Act 32 of 1944), that the decision of the Court in the abovementioned action shall be final.

Signed and dated at .... this .... day of ...., 20......

....

Plaintiff

Witnesses:

1. ....

Signature and address

....

Defendant

2. ....

Signature and address

....

Secondly, a party may by notice in writing abandon the whole or part of a judgment in his or her favour.[12] An abandonment of this kind would be made where the winning party in the magistrate's court realises that the court has erred, and is prepared to abandon the judgment granted in his or her favour. In this way an 'unnecessary' appeal to the High Court may be obviated.

Where the party so abandoning was the plaintiff or applicant, judgment in respect of the part abandoned is entered for the defendant or respondent with costs.[13] Where the party so abandoning was the defendant or respondent, judgment in respect of the part abandoned is entered for the plaintiff or applicant in terms of

---

[11] Section 82.

[12] Section 86(1).

[13] Section 86(2). See *Vaal Investment & Trust Co (Pty) Ltd v DG Ladegaard (Pty) Ltd* 1973 (2) SA 799 (T).

the claim in the summons or the application.[14] A judgment so entered has the same effect in all respects as if it were the judgment originally pronounced by the court in the action or matter.[15]

Should a party abandon a judgment given in his or her favour because the judgment debt, the interest thereon at the rate granted in the judgment and the costs have been paid, no judgment referred to in s 86(2) or (3) shall be entered in favour of the other party.[16]

In terms of the provisions of High Court rule 39(22) a matter may be transferred from the High Court to a magistrate's court.[17] That rule provides that by consent the parties to a trial are entitled, at any time before trial and on written application to a judge through the registrar, to have the cause transferred to the magistrate's court provided that the matter is one within the jurisdiction of the magistrate's court, whether by way of consent or otherwise.

The summons or other initial document issued in a case transferred to a court in terms of High Court rule 39(22) stands as a summons commencing an action in the court to which the case has been transferred and is deemed, subject to any right the defendant may have to except to it, to be a valid summons issued in terms of the rules. Any matter done or order given in the court from which the case has been transferred is deemed to have been done or given in the court to which the case has been transferred, and the case thereupon proceeds from the appropriate stage following that at which it was terminated before the transfer.[18]

Costs incurred in the case before transfer are costs in the cause, unless the court otherwise directs.[19]

A party does not forfeit his or her right to appeal against a judgment by satisfying or offering to satisfy it in whole or in part, or by accepting any benefit under the judgment or order.[20]

At common law, however, a party may well forfeit his or her right to appeal by satisfying the judgment of the court *a quo* provided that the inference may be drawn from his or her conduct in doing so that he or she does not wish to appeal.[21]

---

[14] Section 86(3).

[15] Section 86(4).

[16] Section 86(5).

[17] In *Nedbank Ltd v Thobejane and Similar Matters* 2019 (1) SA 594 (GP), the Full Bench of the Gauteng Division held that, with effect from 2 February 2019, where the monetary value of a civil action and/or application falls within the monetary jurisdiction of the magistrate's court, it should be instituted in such court unless the High Court has granted leave to hear the matter. In other words, all civil matters falling within the monetary jurisdiction of the magistrate's court may not be enrolled in the High Court, unless the High Court has granted leave to hear such matter. The decision is aimed at promoting access to justice. The court further held that the High Court may transfer a matter *mero motu* to a magistrate's court with jurisdiction if it is in the interests of justice to do so. The decision is currently pending appeal before the Supreme Court of Appeal and therefore, in terms of s 18(1) of the Superior Courts Act 10 of 2013, execution of the decision is suspended.

[18] Rule 50(9).

[19] Rule 50(10).

[20] Section 85.

[21] *Dabner v SAR & H* 1920 AD 583 at 594.

What is required is that the conduct of the losing party is such that it indicates a clear acquiescence in the judgment of the court.[22]

Section 83, which confers upon parties the power to appeal, alludes to an appeal in 'any civil suit or proceeding'. From this one may clearly infer that an appeal may be noted against both a decision arrived at in a trial action and a decision on application.[23]

2.2 Decisions against which appeals may be brought

The Act provides in s 83 that appeals may be brought against three types of decisions:

(1) any judgment described in s 48;
(2) any rule or order having the effect of final judgment, including an order relating to execution in terms of Chapter IX of the Act and an order as to costs; and
(3) in certain circumstances, any decision overruling an exception.

The first category of decisions (those given in terms of s 48) consists of the decisions that a court may hand down at the trial of a case. These are decisions arising out of the court's judgment on the merits of the case.

The second category pertains to orders that may be issued by the court in the course of any action or motion proceedings. These are decisions dealing with preliminary and procedural matters and not with the merits of the case.

The third category of decisions relates to the case where the parties consent to an appeal against a decision overruling an exception before proceeding further in the action, where the decision on exception is appealed against in conjunction with the principal case or where the decision includes an order as to costs.

These three categories of decision are discussed in greater detail below.

2.2.1 *Against a judgment in terms of s 48 of the Act*

Section 48 provides that a court may grant the orders mentioned below when delivering judgment in a trial action. A party may thus appeal against these orders:

- an order granting judgment for the plaintiff;
- an order granting judgment for the defendant;
- an order of absolution from the instance;
- an order as to costs (including costs as between attorney and client);
- an order, subject to such conditions as the court thinks fit, against the party in whose favour judgment has been given suspending wholly or in part the taking of further proceedings upon the judgment for a specified period pending arrangements by the other party for the satisfaction of the judgment;
- an order against a party for payment of an amount of money for which judgment has been granted in specified instalment or otherwise, including an order contemplated by s 65(J) or 73.

---

[22] See also *Maclean v Haasbroek NO & others* 1956 (4) SA 677 (A) at 686G–H; *Blou v Lampert & Chipkin NNO & others* 1970 (2) SA 185 (T) at 199B–C.

[23] *E Castignani (Pty) Ltd v Claude Neon Lights (SA) Ltd* 1969 (4) SA 462 (O); *Myers v Benoni Municipality* 1913 TPD 632.

Although s 48 refers to orders granted in a judgment on 'the trial of an action', appeal may be brought in addition against an order granted in motion proceedings. The question is simply whether the court granted its order after an investigation into the merits of the dispute between the parties. The decision is thus based upon a finding on the merits in respect of the claim for relief sought by the parties.[24] Consequently, it follows that the parties to the dispute envisaged in s 48 may appeal after the court has decided the matter on the basis of evidence on the merits of the case.

The order granted by the court must finally resolve the dispute between the parties. A provisional finding by the magistrate does not constitute a judgment against which a party may appeal. Where, therefore, the parties agree that the court will first determine whether the defendant is liable and, if so, the court will thereafter determine the amount in which he or she is liable, the defendant may not appeal against the finding of liability in principle. He or she must wait until the court grants judgment in favour of the plaintiff in a specified amount.[25]

If a magistrate refuses to grant an order of absolution from the instance at the close of the plaintiff's case, the refusal is not subject to appeal.[26] The refusal is merely a provisional finding. The court has merely found that there is a *prima facie* case against the defendant, but there is as yet no final decision on the merits. On the other hand, if the court is able to grant absolution from the instance at the close of the plaintiff's case, there is indeed an appealable finding upon the merits in favour of the defendant, viz that the plaintiff has not been able to prove his or her case. The court in that event will thus either grant judgment in favour of the defendant or absolution from the instance.[27]

Where the defendant consents to judgment, he or she may not appeal against the judgment, since in that case the court has not made a finding as to the merits of the dispute. The order granted by the court is not a judgment against which a party may appeal: it is merely a record of the agreement between the parties.[28]

2.2.2 *Against a rule or order having the effect of a final judgment*
In the course of a suit, a court may issue a rule or order during the pleadings stage or at the hearing which, although it does not amount to a finding on the merits of the case, nevertheless finally determines the matter.

Suppose, for example, that a court refuses to order the attachment of a peregrine defendant's property in order to found jurisdiction. Although this ruling does not deal with the merits of the case, the effect of it is nevertheless to dispose finally of the matter. Because the order is not granted, the plaintiff will not be able to issue summons and therefore will not be able to obtain the relief he or she desires.

---

[24] *Collett v Priest* 1931 AD 290; *Ramano v Johannesburg City Council; Ngobise v Johannesburg City Council* 1966 (2) SA 527 (W).

[25] This is the view expressed, albeit *obiter,* by Scott JA in *Durban's Water Wonderland (Pty) Ltd v Botha & another* 1999 (1) SA 982 (A) at 992G–I; see also *Santam Bpk v Van Niekerk* 1998 (2) 342 SA (C); *Keet v De Klerk* 2000 (1) SA 927 (T) and *Edie Pieters Eiendomme CC v South Cape Brick CC* 2000 (4) SA 704 (C).

[26] *Caro v Tulley* 1910 TPD 1026.

[27] *Botha v AA Mutual Insurance Association Ltd & another* 1968 (4) SA 485 (A).

[28] *Thambi v Stralka NO & another* 1946 TPD 297.

Suppose further that a court upholds an exception raised by a defendant to the effect that the plaintiff's particulars of claim fail to disclose a cause of action; or the court upholds the special defence that it lacks jurisdiction. In both instances, this spells the end of the case for the plaintiff. He or she may not proceed with the matter—in spite of the fact that the court has not arrived at a finding on the merits.

Since a rule made or order granted during the course of a matter may thus mean the end of the road for a litigant, it is only fair that he or she should be in a position to appeal against that rule or order. Just as he or she has a right of appeal against orders made at the conclusion of a hearing on the merits, so he or she has a right of appeal against rules or orders having the effect of a final judgment.

Only if the effect of a rule or order is final, ie it entails the end of the matter for one of the litigants, may he or she appeal against it. The grant of a purely interim order does not mean that a litigant has finally lost the case, and thus he or she may not appeal against a provisional or interim order.

For years it was a moot point when an order had the effect of a final judgment and when it was merely provisional in nature.

In 1948, this matter was dealt with by the Appellate Division in the leading case of *Pretoria Garrison Institutes v Danish Variety Products (Pty) Ltd*.[29] Schreiner JA, with whom Greenberg JA concurred, referred with approval to the view previously adopted by the Appellate Division in *Globe & Phoenix Gold Mining Co Ltd v Rhodesian Corporation Ltd*.[30] Referring to that case, Schreiner JA stated the position as follows:[31]

> '[T]he principle emerges that a preparatory or procedural order is a simple interlocutory order and therefore not appealable unless it is such as to "dispose of any issue or any portion of the issue in the main action or suit", or, which amounts, I think, to the same thing, unless it "irreparably anticipates or precludes some of the relief which would or might be given at the hearing".'

From the above quotation it is clear that the decisive question is invariably whether the rule or order (which is usually granted in connection with procedural matters) has a final effect upon the principal case.[32] One must examine what legal relief has been sought by the litigant. Should the rule or order relating to some procedural matter affect the legal relief sought in such a way that the party seeking relief is finally precluded from proceeding with the case, the rule or order is appealable.[33] The interests of justice is a key consideration when deciding whether a judgment is appealable.[34]

Similar considerations apply when determining which orders made in the High Court are appealable, although in this instance there has been some relaxation in

---

[29] 1948 (1) SA 839 (A).
[30] Ibid.
[31] Ibid at 870.
[32] See also *National Director of Public Prosecutions v King* 2010 (2) SACR 146 (SCA).
[33] *De Vos v Cooper & Ferreira* 1999 (4) SA 1290 (SCA).
[34] *Khumalo & others v Holomisa* 2002 (5) SA 401 (CC) para 8.

that an order which disposes of a substantial portion of the relief claimed may be appealable.[35]

Where merits and quantum have been separated, a finding on the merits is not itself appealable.[36]

The following may serve as examples of rules or orders having the effect of a final judgment:

(1) A refusal on the part of the court to rescind a default judgment.[37]

(2) The granting or refusal of a final interdict. In the nature of things, a party aggrieved by the granting of a final interdict against him or her will have a right of appeal. But the party who feels aggrieved by the court's refusal to grant a final interdict will likewise have a right of appeal.

What may a party do if the court refuses to grant him or her an interdict? In his or her application for an interdict, his or her case is precisely that damages will not constitute an adequate remedy, hence the claim for an interdict. When an interim interdict is refused, the applicant is in the same position as a person to whom a final interdict has been refused. Although the interim interdict has been refused and it is always possible for a different decision to be handed down as to the grant of a final interdict, the *effect* of the refusal is the same as a final order. The applicant wishes to obtain an interdict. The fact that he or she has been refused one for the time being may place him or her in a position in which the subsequent granting of the interdict in a final form, should such occur, will be of no use to him or her.[38] The granting of an interim interdict is not, however, appealable.[39]

(3) The upholding of an exception to particulars of claim which prevents the case from proceeding further.[40]

(4) The upholding of an exception to a plea on the basis that it discloses no defence. The success of such an exception results in the falling away of the defence pleaded and the defendant is thus placed in the same position as though judgment had been granted in favour of the plaintiff.[41]

(5) The grant of summary judgment, which also prevents the defendant from proceeding with his or her defence and affords the plaintiff a judgment in his or her favour.[42]

---

[35] See *Van Streepen & Germs (Pty) Ltd v Transvaal Provincial Administration* 1987 (4) SA 569 (A); *SA Eagle Versekeringsmaatskappy Bpk v Harford* 1992 (2) SA 786 (A); and definitively *Zweni v Minister of Law and Order* 1993 (1) SA 523 (A).

[36] *Jordan v Bloemfontein Transitional Local Authority & another* 2004 (3) SA 371 (SCA); *Steenkamp v South African Broadcasting Corporation* 2002 (1) SA 625 (SCA).

[37] *Olivier v Fourie* 1966 (3) SA 401 (C); *Mertsch v Autovend Investments (Pty) Ltd* 1971 (3) SA 663 (SWA); *Thornhill v Gerhardt* 1979 (2) SA 1092 (T).

[38] *Setlogelo v Setlogelo* 1914 AD 221 at 226; *Davis v Press & Co* 1944 CPD 108 at 113.

[39] *Steytler NO v Fitzgerald* 1911 AD 295 at 325; *Loggenberg v Beare* 1930 TPD 714.

[40] *Liquidators, Myburgh, Krone & Co Ltd v Standard Bank of SA Ltd & another* 1924 AD 226.

[41] *Gericke v Mangold Bros Ltd* 1961 (3) SA 901 (T).

[42] *Astra Furnishers (Pty) Ltd v Arend & another* 1973 (1) SA 446 (C); *Van Wyngaardt NO v Knox* 1977 (2) SA 636 (T).

(6) The upholding of a special plea that the court lacks jurisdiction.[43]
(7) The upholding of a defence of prescription.[44]
(8) The upholding of a defence of lack of *locus standi* on the part of one of the litigants.[45]
(9) The refusal to grant a postponement, which leads either to a default judgment or absolution from the instance.[46]

Section 83*(b)* provides expressly that appeals may be brought against orders relating to process in execution or relating to the collection of judgment debts. All orders made by a magistrate in the course of these two procedures are thus subject to appeal.

Section 83 also renders appealable any order as to costs.

It is important to note, however, that an appeal against an order as to costs that accompanies a rule or order which is not itself subject to appeal may be treated on a different basis from that rule or order; in other words, even though the remainder of the rule or order is not appealable, an appeal may be lodged against the order as to costs.

In *Pretoria Garrison Institutes v Danish Variety Products (Pty) Ltd*[47] Watermeyer CJ stated: '[T]he merits of the dispute in the Court below must be investigated in order to decide whether the order as to costs made in that dispute was properly made or not.' The court of appeal may thus uphold the appeal as to costs because it is of the opinion that the decision forming the basis of the order as to costs was incorrect, even though the court of appeal does not correct the decision itself because that decision does not have the effect of a final judgment and is thus not subject to appeal.

2.2.3 *In certain circumstances, against a decision or an order overruling an exception*

If an exception is dismissed, it means that the excipient has failed to truncate the proceedings. His or her exception is not upheld and the case must therefore proceed to a hearing on the merits. The dismissal of the exception does not, therefore, terminate the litigation and consequently the order overruling the exception is not a final order against which an appeal may be brought.[48] In accordance with the principles set out above, the excipient whose exception is dismissed may not, therefore, appeal against the dismissal.

Section 83*(c)* provides, however, that in three instances an appeal may be brought against the dismissal of the exception.

First, the parties may agree that an appeal may be brought against the dismissal

---

[43] *Steytler NO v Fitzgerald* (supra); *Tuckers Land & Development Corporation (Pty) Ltd v Perpellief* 1978 (2) SA 11 (T). There is, however, no appeal from an order dismissing such a plea: *Robbetze en 'n ander v Garden Route Resort Services BK* 2004 (4) SA 406 (C).

[44] *Smit v Oosthuizen* 1979 (3) SA 1079 (A).

[45] *Olivier v Lombard* 1933 EDL 176.

[46] *Momentum Life Assurers Ltd v Thirion* [2002] 2 All SA 62 (C).

[47] Supra.

[48] An order upholding an exception is, however, a final order and is therefore subject to appeal: *Liquidators, Myburgh, Krone & Co v Standard Bank of SA* (supra).

of the exception before proceeding further with the action. The parties thus consent to the prior hearing of an appeal against the dismissal of the exception, since, if the appeal succeeds (and the court of appeal therefore finds that the exception ought to have been upheld), the proceedings in the magistrate's court are terminated, no preparation for trial is necessary and evidence need not be led.

Secondly, an appeal may be brought against the dismissal of the exception when an appeal is noted against the eventual result of the trial. In this event the appellant appeals against the finding on the merits, and as one of his or her grounds of appeal he or she avers that the court erred in dismissing the exception. The appellant thus alleges that the eventual judgment of the court was incorrect due to the fact that the exception taken at the start of the case ought to have been upheld.

Thirdly, an appeal may be directed against the dismissal of the exception if the order overruling the exception is accompanied by an order as to costs.[49] As soon as the unsuccessful excipient is ordered to pay the costs of the exception, therefore, he or she may appeal against the dismissal of the exception. Even if the magistrate orders each party to pay his or her own costs, that order as to costs is sufficient to render the dismissal of the exception subject to appeal.[50] Likewise, where the magistrate expressly states that 'there will no order as to costs', this order is tantamount to an order that the costs of the exception are to be costs in the action and an appeal against the costs order—and the order dismissing the exception— may consequently be brought.[51]

The *ratio* is that an order as to costs is a final judgment. Whatever the court may subsequently decide in regard to the case, the order as to the costs of the exception stands. Consequently, an appeal may be brought against the order as to costs and the exception.

Only where the magistrate, in dismissing the exception, orders that the question of costs will be held over for decision at a later stage has he or she not made a final order as to the costs occasioned by the unsuccessful exception. Only in such a case will no appeal lie against the dismissal of the exception.

The question is always whether the magistrate has already made an order as to costs in relation to the dismissal of the exception and is thus *functus officio,* or whether he or she will at some later stage have the opportunity of reaching a decision as to the costs of the exception.[52] Only if he or she has already made an order as to these costs may there be an appeal against the dismissal of the exception.

2.3 The period within which appeal must be noted

It often happens that the magistrate does not deliver his or her full reasons for judgment when the order or judgment is made. If the magistrate does not give

---

[49] *Katz & Co v Harries & Co* 1929 SWA 54; *Lubbe v Bosman* 1948 (3) SA 909 (O).

[50] *Funck v Rothe & Hagen* 1922 SWA 27.

[51] Rule 33(2) provides that if no order is made as to costs, such costs shall be costs in the action. Cf also *Dhlamini v Jooste* 1925 OPD 223.

[52] *L & G Cantamessa v Reef Plumbers; L & G Cantamessa (Pty) Ltd v Reef Plumbers* 1935 TPD 56 at 61–2.

reasons, a litigant may request such reasons within 10 days.[53] The magistrate must deliver his or her reasons within 15 days. An appeal may be noted within 20 days after the date of the judgment appealed against or within 20 days after the registrar or clerk of the court has supplied a copy of the written judgment to a party who has applied for it.[54]

A cross-appeal must be lodged within 10 days after the delivery of the notice of appeal.[55]

2.4 The application for condonation of the late noting of an appeal

If the appellant fails to note an appeal within the prescribed period, he or she must ask the court of appeal to condone the late noting of the appeal. The magistrate's court does not have the power to extend the period allowed for the noting of an appeal.[56]

Although it has been held that a single judge of the main division of the High Court to which the appeal is made may hear the application for condonation,[57] the present practice is that applications for condonation of the late noting of an appeal are heard by a full court. The reason is that the decision whether or not to allow the appellant to proceed with his or her appeal is an extremely important one; it is one that may be taken only in the light of the merits of the appeal. It is therefore preferable in principle for the Full Bench of a division of the High Court to decide on the matter rather than a single judge. Usually the application for condonation of late noting of the appeal is heard together with the arguments on the merits of the appeal.[58]

The applicant who seeks condonation must persuade the court that he or she is entitled to condonation. The court has a discretion as to whether to condone the late noting of an appeal.[59]

The following factors play a role in the exercise of the court's discretion:

2.4.1 *The reason for the non-compliance with the rules relating to the noting of the appeal*

The following factors may play a role: lack of funds;[60] negligence on the part of the attorney where the appellant himself or herself was unaware as to the

---

[53] Rule 51(1).

[54] Rule 51(3).

[55] Rule 51(6).

[56] Rule 60(5).

[57] *Motsamai v Read & another* 1961 (1) SA 173 (O); *De Sousa v Cappy's Stall* 1975 (4) SA 959 (T); *Lipschitz NO v Saambou-Nasionale Bouvereniging* 1979 (1) SA 527 (T); *Multilaterale Motorvoertuig-ongelukke Fonds v Pretorius* 1994 (1) SA 914 (O).

[58] *Meyer v Dowson & Dobson Ltd* 1961 (4) SA 628 (T); *Motsamai v Read* (supra); also *SA Allied Workers' Union (In liquidation) v De Klerk NO & another* 1992 (3) SA 1 (A).

[59] *Fortman v SAR & H (2)* 1947 (3) SA 505 (N); *Palmer v Goldberg* 1961 (3) SA 692 (N); *United Plant Hire (Pty) Ltd v Hills & others* 1976 (1) SA 717 (A) at 720E–F.

[60] *Michaels v Wells NO* 1967 (1) SA 46 (C); *Melane v Santam Insurance Co Ltd* 1962 (4) SA 531 (A).

requirements for the exercise of his or her right of appeal;[61] impossibility of proceeding with the appeal earlier due to illness[62] or any other reason;[63] and lack of knowledge of the court procedure and of the consequences of the court's judgment.[64]

2.4.2 *The prospects of success on the merits*
If it appears to the court that in any event the appeal has no or an extremely slim chance of succeeding on the merits, then the court will not condone the late noting of an appeal.[65] In such a case, it would serve no purpose to allow the noting of the appeal, only to dismiss it after argument has been heard on the merits.

2.4.3 *The importance of the case*
The fact that the case involves large amounts of money or raises an important legal principle may render the court of appeal more amenable to condone the late noting of an appeal.[66]

2.4.4 *The absence of prejudice to the respondent*
The court must determine whether the respondent will suffer substantial prejudice if the late noting of an appeal is allowed. The prejudice to the respondent must be weighed against the prejudice to the appellant if the court refuses him or her permission to appeal.[67]

The party seeking condonation of the late noting of an appeal must apply to the High Court for condonation. The application is brought on notice of motion supported by an affidavit in which the applicant sets out all of the relevant facts as to why he or she failed to note an appeal timeously.[68]

Notice of the application must be given to all interested parties. As already shown, there must not be substantial prejudice to the respondent if the appeal is noted out of time. The respondent must therefore be given the opportunity to inform the court of appeal as to the prejudice that he or she might suffer if the applicant is permitted to note a late appeal.

The court of appeal may strike a late appeal from the roll if no prior application was brought for condonation of the late noting of appeal. In this event, the appellant may bring a proper application for condonation and request the court to

---

[61] *Reinecke v Incorporated General Insurances Ltd* 1974 (2) SA 84 (A); but see *Saloojee & another v Minister of Community Development* 1965 (2) SA 135 (A) at 141C–E for the limits beyond which the court will not condone the negligence of an attorney. *Darries v Sheriff, Magistrate's Court, Wynberg, & another* 1998 (3) SA 34 (SCA).

[62] *Wagenaar v Thomas* 1930 AD 436.

[63] *Wessels v Bosman* 1918 TPD 351; *Beaumont v Anderson* 1949 (3) SA 562 (N).

[64] *Melane v Santam Insurance Co Ltd* (supra).

[65] Ibid; *Federated Employers Fire & General Insurance Co Ltd & another v McKenzie* 1969 (3) SA 360 (A).

[66] *Federated Employers Fire & General Insurance v McKenzie* (supra); *Hall v Van Tonder & another* 1980 (1) SA 908 (C) at 916D.

[67] *Saloojee & another NNO v Ministry of Community Development* (supra) at 142–3; *Transvaal & Orange Free State Chamber of Mines v General Electric Co* 1965 (4) SA 349 (T).

[68] *Nankan v H Lewis & Co (Natal) Ltd* 1959 (1) SA 157 (N); *Boland Konstruksie Maatskappy (Edms) Bpk v Petlen Properties (Edms) Bpk* 1974 (4) SA 291 (C); *Read v Freer* 1920 CPD 250; *Massey-Harris (SA) Ltd v Eksteen* 1932 OPD 29.

permit him or her to bring another appeal. The striking of the appeal from the roll is not a decision that renders the matter *res judicata* and prevents the appeal from being heard again. The striking off, in other words, does not have the same effect as the dismissal of the appeal.[69]

2.5 The procedure on appeal

2.5.1 *General*

In terms of s 83 of the Magistrates' Courts Act, no leave to appeal to the High Court is required. The appeal will be adjudicated by two High Court judges. However, in the event of the judges hearing such appeal not being in agreement, the Judge President—or in the absence of both the Judge President and the Deputy Judge President, the senior available judge—may, at any time before a judgment is handed down in such appeal, direct that a third judge be added to hear that appeal.[70] Both the main and local seats of the relevant division of the High Court have jurisdiction to hear the appeal.[71]

An appellant may either note an appeal in person or instruct his or her legal representative to do so on his or her behalf. The legal representative must be authorised by the appellant to note the appeal. If the legal representative appeals without the necessary authority from his or her client, his or her conduct in doing so may not be ratified by the client after the expiry of the period during which the appeal ought to have been noted.[72]

Although the attorney noting the appeal must be authorised by his or her client so to act, it is not necessary for the attorney to procure a written power of attorney. The noting of an appeal is a procedure that takes place in the magistrate's court, and in accordance with general principles it is not necessary for a legal representative to produce written authority from his or her client to act on the client's behalf in the magistrate's court.[73] Only where the appeal is prosecuted in the High Court must a written power of attorney be filed, since the prosecution of an appeal is a High Court procedure. High Court rule 7(2) provides that the registrar shall not set down any appeal at the instance of an attorney unless the attorney has filed with the registrar a power of attorney authorising him or her to appeal. The power of attorney is filed together with the application for a date of hearing.

2.5.2 *The request for reasons for the decision*

In terms of rule 51(1) the prospective appellant must within 10 days after judgment in writing request the judicial officer against whose judgment he or she wishes to appeal to hand to the registrar or clerk of the court a written judgment, which becomes part of the record in the case. In his or her written judgment the judicial officer must state:

---

[69] *Boland Konstruksie Maatskappy (Edms) Bpk v Petlen Properties (Edms) Bpk (2)* 1974 (4) SA 980 (C).
[70] Section 14(3) of the Superior Courts Act 10 of 2013.
[71] Section 6(4).
[72] *Johannesburg City Council v Elesander Investments (Pty) Ltd & others* 1979 (3) SA 1273 (T).
[73] Rule 52(2).

(1)   the facts he or she found to be proved; and
(2)   his or her reasons for judgment.

The following may serve as an example of the written request:

* For use in the District Court In the Magistrate's Court for the District of .... held at .... Case No .... of 20...... In the matter between .... Plaintiff and .... Defendant
REQUEST FOR REASONS FOR JUDGMENT
TAKE NOTICE that the Plaintiff in the abovementioned case hereby requests that Honourable Magistrate .... within fifteen days of the date hereof hands to the clerk of the court a written judgment in the abovementioned case forming part of the record showing: *(a)*   the facts he or she found to be proved; and *(b)*   his or her reasons for judgment. Dated at .... this .... day of ...., 20...... .... Plaintiff's Attorney Address .... To: The Clerk of the Court ....

The judicial officer provides the written reasons within 15 days of the request to the registrar or clerk of the court.

As soon as the registrar or clerk of the court has received the written reasons for judgment from the judicial officer, he or she must furnish a copy of the reasons to the party who applied for them and endorse on the original minutes of record the date on which the copy of the record was supplied.[74]

After receiving the written reasons for judgment, the prospective appellant must be given an opportunity to decide whether he or she wishes to proceed to note an appeal or to acquiesce in the judgment of the court.

He or she must note his or her appeal within 20 days after he or she receives the written reasons for judgment from the registrar or clerk of the court.[75]

A party may, if he or she wishes, appeal without first requesting written reasons for judgment. In this event the appellant must note his or her appeal within 20 days of the date of the judgment appealed against. He or she may not appeal after the expiry of a period of 20 days if he or she has not first requested written reasons for judgment.[76]

---

[74] Rule 51(2).
[75] Rule 51(3).
[76] *Bell's Butchery v Cape Meat Supply* 1939 TPD 258; *Murray & Daddy (Pty) Ltd v Floros* 1959 (4) SA 137 (N).

2.5.3 *The noting of an appeal*

The appellant notes an appeal by delivering a written notice of appeal to the registrar or clerk of the court and to the respondent. Alternatively, the notice of appeal may be delivered to the respondent's attorney.

Unless the court of appeal orders otherwise, the appellant must give security to the amount of R1 000 for the respondent's costs of appeal. No security shall, however, be required of the State or, unless the court of appeal otherwise orders, of a person to whom legal aid is rendered by a statutorily established legal aid board.[77]

The appellant gives security either by paying the amount of R1 000 to the registrar or clerk of the court or by handing the registrar or clerk of the court, or having someone furnish on his or her behalf, a security bond in that amount.[78]

Security need not be furnished at the same time as the notice of appeal is delivered. The procedure for noting an appeal consists of two parts: the delivery of notice of appeal and the giving of security. An appeal has not been properly noted until both steps have been taken.[79]

The giving of security ensures that the appellant is serious in bringing an appeal and that he or she does not appeal merely in order to embarrass the respondent financially by compelling him or her to oppose the appeal.

Monies paid into court and not disposed of within three years may be paid into the State Revenue Fund after three months' written notice of intention to do so has been given to the parties concerned. The interested parties may thereafter apply for a refund of the amount paid into the Fund.[80]

In his or her notice of appeal (or cross-appeal) the appellant must state:

* whether the whole or part only of the judgment is appealed against, and if part only, then what part;
* the grounds of appeal, specifying the findings of fact or rulings of law appealed against.[81]

It is mandatory for these particulars to appear in the notice of appeal. A notice of appeal may not subsequently be amended by the court.[82]

The appellant is thus obliged to stipulate whether he or she appeals against a finding of fact made by the court, a ruling of law or both. The appellant must also indicate precisely the facts and the ruling of law against which he or she appeals, and the reasons for his or her appeal.[83] The court hearing the appeal will not permit the appellant to argue a point on appeal of which no mention has been made in the notice of appeal, unless the court of appeal especially grants him or her consent to

---

[77] Rule 51(4).

[78] Rule 2(1)*(b)*, meaning of 'give security'.

[79] *Campbell v McDonald* 1920 OPD 255; *Ruebner v Van der Merwe* 1931 SWA 69 at 71.

[80] Rule 51(5).

[81] Rule 51(7).

[82] *Harvey v Brown* 1964 (3) SA 381 (E); *Ex parte Simoes: In re Hasewinkel & another v Simoes* 1970 (2) SA 302 (T); *Kilian v Geregsbode, Uitenhage* 1980 (1) SA 808 (A) at 815D–E; *Songono v Minister of Law and Order* 1996 (4) SA 384 (E).

[83] *Himunchol v Moharom* 1947 (4) SA 778 (N) at 780; *Harvey v Brown* (supra) at 383E–F.

do so.[84] On the other hand, the court of appeal may indeed permit the appellant to put forward at the hearing of the appeal a legal argument of which no mention is made in the notice of appeal. If this were not possible, it would mean that the court of appeal would be bound to decide the matter on the basis of the legal arguments adopted by the appellant rather than on objective legal principles. That cannot be the position; a court of law is obliged to determine the law and to apply it.[85] The court of appeal may, in the event of principles of law having been overlooked by the appellant, penalise him or her by means of an adverse order of costs.

If the appellant appeals against a finding of fact, he or she must indicate as precisely as possible against which finding he or she appeals.[86] It is not sufficient for the appellant to aver merely that the 'findings of fact arrived at by the Honourable Magistrate are not supported by the evidence'.

A notice of appeal may be worded as follows:

NOTICE AND GROUNDS OF APPEAL

TAKE NOTICE that the Appellant (Plaintiff in the abovementioned case) hereby gives notice of appeal against the entire judgment of the Magistrate delivered on .... 20...... in case no .... of 20 .... held in the magistrate's court for the district of .... at ...., in which he or she dismissed the Plaintiff's claim for damages in the amount of R .... with costs.

The grounds of appeal are as follows:

(1) The Honourable Magistrate incorrectly decided that the Plaintiff failed to discharge the onus of proof resting upon him or her.

(2) The Honourable Magistrate erred in law in finding that, in order for the Plaintiff to succeed in his or her claim for damages based upon defamation, he or she is required to prove patrimonial damage.

(3) The Honourable Magistrate erred in law in deciding that the Plaintiff failed to prove his or her claim for damages in the light of the admission by the Defendant that he or she did not dispute the amount of the claim but merely disputed that he or she uttered the allegedly defamatory words.

(4) The Honourable Magistrate erred in making the following findings of law:
   (i) in deciding that in a defamation case the defamatory matter must have been published to at least two persons;
   (ii) in deciding that the Plaintiff was not entitled in support of his or her claim for damages to lead evidence to the effect that he or she enjoys a high social standing in the community.

(5) The Honourable Magistrate erred in making the following findings of fact:
   (i) in calling the Plaintiff a witness unworthy of belief;
   (ii) in regarding the evidence of an impartial witness, to wit ...., as unworthy of belief.

---

[84] *Botes v Grobbelaar* 1924 OPD 90.

[85] *Argus Printing & Publishing Co Ltd v Die Perskorporasie van SA Bpk; Argus Printing & Publishing Co Ltd v Rapport Uitgewers (Edms) Bpk* 1975 (4) SA 814 (A); *Paddock Motors (Pty) Ltd v Igesund* 1976 (3) SA 16 (A) at 23–4; *Road Accident Fund v Mothupi* 2000 (4) SA 38 (SCA).

[86] *R v Nicholson* 1949 (2) SA 585 (N); *Hendricks v Wilcox* 1962 (1) SA 304 (C); *S v Horne* 1971 (1) SA 630 (C); *S v Swanepoel* 1971 (3) SA 299 (E).

2.5.4 *The reasons for judgment after the noting of an appeal*

Within 15 days after delivery of the notice of appeal, the judicial officer must hand to the registrar or clerk of the court a statement in writing showing (so far as may be necessary, having regard to any written judgment already handed in by him or her):

(1) the facts he or she found to be proved;
(2) the grounds upon which he or she arrived at any finding of fact specified in the notice of appeal as appealed against; and
(3) his or her reasons for any ruling of law or for the admission or rejection of any evidence so specified as appealed against.[87]

This statement becomes part of the record.[88]

The same procedure applies to the noting of a cross-appeal.[89]

There is no obligation on the part of the magistrate to furnish additional reasons for his or her judgment after he or she has received notice of appeal. He or she may choose to abide by the reasons for judgment already furnished by him or her.[90]

2.5.5 *Prosecuting the appeal*

The prosecution of the appeal is a matter regulated by the procedure of the High Court. It occurs when the appellant, on notice to all concerned parties, requests the registrar of the court to allocate a date for the hearing of the appeal.[91]

The appellant must, within 40 days of noting the appeal, apply to the registrar of the High Court on notice to the respondent for a hearing date. He or she must also provide a full address.[92] Prosecution of the appeal must be completed within 60 days after the noting of the appeal.[93]

If the party who has noted an appeal or cross-appeal fails to prosecute his or her appeal within the time prescribed by the rules, the appeal or cross-appeal is deemed to have lapsed, unless the court of appeal sees fit to make an order to the contrary.[94]

Within 15 days after receiving notice that an appeal has been set down for hearing, the registrar or clerk of the court must transmit to the registrar of the court of appeal the record in the action, duly certified.[95]

A respondent who desires to abandon the whole or any part of a judgment appealed against may do so by the delivery of a notice in writing stating whether he or she abandons the whole or part only of the judgment, and if part only, what part.[96] Every such notice of abandonment becomes part of the record.[97]

---

[87] Rule 51(8)(*a*).
[88] Rule 51(8)(*b*).
[89] Rule 51(8)(*c*).
[90] *R v Bezuidenhout* 1954 (3) SA 188 (A) at 222D–E; *S v M* 1978 (1) SA 571 (N).
[91] Uniform Court Rule 50.
[92] Rule 50(4)(*a*).
[93] Rule 50(1).
[94] Magistrates' courts rule 51(9).
[95] Rule 51(10).
[96] Rule 51(11)(*a*).
[97] Rule 51(11)(*b*).

2.5.6 *Suspension of execution pending appeal*

The common law provides that a notice of appeal suspends the operation of the judgment.[98] In *Nel v Le Roux NO & others*,[99] the court stated that '[a]s far as appeals are concerned the execution of a judgment is automatically suspended upon the noting of an appeal in terms of a substantive rule of the common law ... and not in terms of s 78'.

Section 78 provides that where an appeal has been noted or an application to rescind, correct or vary a judgment has been made, the court may direct either that the judgment be carried into execution or that the execution of the judgment be suspended pending the decision upon appeal or application. The court grants such an order upon such terms as to security as it may deem necessary for the due performance of any judgment which may be given upon the appeal or application. The section does not refer to the common law, but, it is submitted, must be interpreted as not varying the common law.[100] Thus, the onus is on the successful party, now seeking to execute, to approach the court for an order allowing execution despite the noting of the appeal.

Section 18 of the Superior Courts Act now provides that, unless the court under exceptional circumstances orders otherwise, the operation and execution of a decision which is the subject of an application for leave to appeal or of an appeal is suspended pending the decision of the application or appeal. This is not the case with an interlocutory order not having the effect of a final judgment. The court may 'order otherwise' if the party who applied to court proves on a balance of probabilities that he or she will suffer irreparable harm if the court does not so order and that the other party will not suffer irreparable harm if the court so orders. Where a court so orders otherwise, it must immediately record its reasons for doing so. The aggrieved party will then also have an automatic right of appeal to the next highest court and the court hearing such an appeal must deal with it as a matter of extreme urgency. Such an order will be automatically suspended, pending the outcome of such appeal.

2.6 The powers of the court on appeal

There are two provisions that regulate the powers of a court of appeal: s 19 of the Superior Courts Act and s 87 of the Magistrates' Courts Act. These two statutory provisions apparently exist side by side.

In terms of s 19 of the Superior Courts Act, the Supreme Court of Appeal or a division of the High Court exercising appeal jurisdiction may:

(1) dispose of an appeal without the hearing of oral argument;
(2) receive further evidence;
(3) remit the case to the court of first instance, or to the court whose decision is the subject of the appeal, for further hearing; or

---

[98] *Reid & another v Godart & another* 1938 AD 511; *South Cape Corporation (Pty) Ltd v Engineering Management Services (Pty) Ltd* 1977 (3) SA 534 (A). Where an interim order has been discharged, it is not revived by the noting of an appeal; *MV Snow Delta: Serva Ship Ltd v Discount Tonnage Ltd* 2000 (4) SA 746 (SCA) at 751G–J.

[99] 2006 (3) SA 56 (SE) at 59F.

[100] *Ludwig v Holden & another* 1939 CPD 235 at 241.

(4) confirm, amend or set aside the decision which is the subject of the appeal and render any decision which the circumstances may require.

In terms of s 87 of the Magistrates' Courts Act, the court of appeal may:

(1) confirm, vary or reverse the judgment appealed from;
(2) if the record does not furnish sufficient evidence or information for the determination of the appeal, remit the matter to the court from which the appeal is brought, with instructions in regard to the taking of further evidence or the setting out of further information;
(3) order the parties or either of them to produce at some convenient time in the court of appeal such further proof as the court may deem necessary or desirable; or
(4) take any other course which may lead to the just, speedy and, as much as may be, inexpensive disposal of the case; and
(5) make such order as to costs as justice may require.

The judgment of the court of appeal is recorded in the court appealed from, and may be enforced as though it had been given in the latter court.[101]

3 REVIEWS

3.1 Grounds of review

Every division of the High Court has the power to review the proceedings of all lower courts within its area of jurisdiction.[102]

The grounds for review are set out in s 22(1) of the Superior Courts Act. The following grounds are mentioned:

(1) absence of jurisdiction on the part of the court;
(2) interest in the cause, bias, malice or corruption on the part of the presiding judicial officer;
(3) gross irregularity in the proceedings; and
(4) the admission of inadmissible or incompetent evidence or the rejection of admissible or competent evidence.

With the exception of 'gross irregularity in the proceedings', the grounds are very clearly stated and require little comment.

There are, however, a number of matters that may fall within the ambit of 'gross irregularity in the proceedings'. '[G]ross irregularity' encompasses not only incidents occurring within the court itself, but includes considerably more. It amounts to any irregularity pertaining to a matter and resulting in prejudice to one of the litigants.

A necessary precondition for review is that the litigant seeking review must have been prejudiced by the gross irregularity. If no prejudice was suffered, the court of review will not interfere with the finding of the lower court.[103]

---

[101] Section 88.

[102] The same courts which have appellate jurisdiction may hear reviews. In this regard, see s 21(1)*(b)* of the Superior Courts Act 10 of 2013 and *Nedbank Ltd v Norris & others* 2016 (3) SA 568 (ECP) paras 17 and 18.

[103] *Rowe v Assistant Magistrate, Pretoria, & another* 1925 TPD 361; *Berg v Regional Magistrate Southern Transvaal & another* 1956 (2) SA 676 (T); *Geidel v Bosman NO & another* 1963 (4) SA 253 (T); *Building Improvements Finance Co (Pty) Ltd v Additional Magistrate, Johannesburg, & another* 1978 (4) SA 790 (T).

The following may be regarded as instances of 'gross irregularity':

Disregard of the audi et alteram partem *rule*

This rule is one of the cornerstones of our law. If, therefore, a court makes an order against a party without affording him or her the opportunity of presenting his or her case, the disregard of the rule will amount to a gross irregularity.[104]

Irregularities pertaining to evidence

A gross irregularity may occur on account of the manner in which the court has dealt with the evidence. In terms of s 22(1)*(d)* of the Superior Courts Act, the admission of inadmissible or incompetent evidence or the rejection of admissible or competent evidence is stipulated as a ground of review. Where, however, a court holds an inspection *in loco* in the absence of the parties, the conduct of the court will amount to a gross irregularity even though it is unconnected with inadmissible or incompetent evidence.[105] Likewise, where the magistrate refuses to permit one of the parties to inspect attached property, the refusal constitutes a gross irregularity in respect of evidence.[106]

In the same way, a magistrate may not use his or her personal knowledge of the facts to the detriment of one of the parties where those facts have not been adduced before the court in the proper manner during the course of the proceedings.[107]

Exceeding authority

Under this heading falls any conduct of an unauthorised nature on the part of a judicial officer. As already stated, the magistrate's court is a 'creature of statute', and the court may make only such orders as the Magistrates' Courts Act empowers it to make.[108]

3.2 The review procedure

The review of the proceedings of a lower court takes place on application in accordance with the provisions of High Court rule 53.

The party seeking review directs a notice of motion to the magistrate and to all of the parties affected by the contemplated review proceedings.[109]

In his notice of motion, the applicant calls upon the magistrate:

(1) to show cause why the decision or proceedings ought not to be reviewed and corrected or set aside; and

(2) to dispatch within 15 days after receipt of the notice of motion to the registrar the record of proceedings sought to be reviewed, together with such reasons as he or she is by law required, or such reasons as he or she desires, to give or make and to notify the applicant that he or she has done so.[110]

---

[104] *Pandela v Dlokweni* 1919 CPD 53; *Serfontein v Bosch* 1930 OPD 75; *O'Connell v Attorney-General & Magistrate, Pretoria* 1930 TPD 9; *SA Motor Acceptance Corporation (Pty) Ltd v Venter* 1963 (1) SA 214 (O).

[105] *Hansen v R* (1924) 45 NLR 318.

[106] *Norwitz v The Magistrate of Fauresmith & Bane* 1928 OPD 109.

[107] *R v Steenkamp* 1947 (1) SA 714 (SWA); *S v Bailey & others* 1962 (4) SA 514 (E).

[108] *Visser v Van den Heever & another* 1934 CPD 315; *Ludwig v Holden & another* 1939 CPD 235.

[109] Uniform Rule 53(1).

[110] Rule 53(1)*(a)* and *(b)*.

The notice of motion must set out the decision or proceedings sought to be reviewed and must be supported by an affidavit setting out the grounds and the facts and circumstances upon which the applicant relies to have the decision or proceedings set aside or corrected.[111]

The content of the notice reads as follows:

NOTICE OF REVIEW

TAKE NOTICE that the Applicant (the Defendant in the abovementioned case) hereby calls upon Honourable Magistrate to show cause why the proceedings in the matter between .... (Plaintiff) and .... (Defendant) heard under case number .... of 20...... in the magistrate's court for the district of .... held at .... should not be reviewed and corrected.

TAKE NOTICE FURTHER that Honourable Magistrate .... is called upon to dispatch, within fifteen days after receipt of this notice, to the registrar of the abovementioned Honourable Court the record of the proceedings in the abovementioned case together with such reasons as he or she is by law required or desires to give or make, and to notify the Applicant that he or she has done so.

TAKE NOTICE FURTHER that the Applicant applies for review on the basis that during the trial of the abovementioned matter and before the Applicant had called all of his or her witnesses and closed his or her case, the Honourable Magistrate indicated to .... that he or she would grant judgment against the Applicant and that the said conduct of the Honourable Magistrate constitutes a gross irregularity.

TAKE NOTICE FURTHER that the affidavit of .... attached hereto will be used in support of the application.

The registrar makes the record available to the applicant on such conditions as he or she thinks appropriate to ensure its safety. The applicant must then have copies made of such portions of the record as may be necessary for purposes of the review. He or she must then furnish the registrar with two copies of the record, and the other parties with one copy each. The applicant must certify the copies as true. The costs of transcription, if any, are borne by the applicant and are costs in the cause.[112]

The rule does not stipulate a time period within which the applicant must make the record available to the other parties, but it must be a reasonable time before the hearing of the application for review.[113]

The applicant may within 10 days after the registrar has made the record available to him or her, by delivery of a notice and accompanying affidavit, amend or add to the terms of his or her notice of motion and supplement the supporting affidavit.[114]

Should the presiding officer or any party affected desire to oppose the grant of the order prayed in the notice of motion, he or she must:

(1) within 15 days after receipt by him or her of the notice of motion or any amendment to it, deliver notice to the applicant that he or she intends to

---

[111] Rule 53(2).

[112] Rule 53(3).

[113] *Car-to-Let (Pty) Ltd v Addisionele Landdros, Bloemfontein, en andere* 1973 (2) SA 99 (O).

[114] Rule 53(4); *Pieters v Administrateur, Suidwes-Afrika en 'n ander* 1972 (2) SA 220 (SWA).

oppose the application for review, and in the notice he or she must appoint an address within 15 kilometres of the office of the registrar at which he or she will accept notice and service of all process in the proceedings;

(2) within 30 days after the applicant has, by means of a notice and accompanying affidavit, added to the terms of his or her notice of motion or supplemented his or her supporting affidavit, deliver any affidavits he or she may desire in answer to the allegations made by the applicant.[115]

The applicant has the same rights and obligations in regard to the filing of a replying affidavit as he or she has in terms of the High Court rules pertaining to an ordinary opposed application.[116]

The normal rules relating to the set-down of applications in the High Court apply also to the set-down of review proceedings.[117]

---

[115] Rule 53(5).
[116] Rule 53(6).
[117] Rule 53(7).

DEBT-COLLECTING PROCEDURE

1 GENERAL

The decision of *Coetzee v Government of the Republic of South Africa; Matosi & others v Commanding Officer, Port Elizabeth Prison, & others*[1] declared the imprisonment provisions in s 65 of the Magistrates' Courts Act to be unconstitutional with effect from 22 September 1995.

The Act provides for several means whereby a creditor can exact payment of his or her debt. The process of execution after gaining a judgment has already been dealt with (see chapter 17 above). But the process of gaining a judgment is costly and time-consuming. Because the majority of cases involve the payment of accounts for goods provided, or for services rendered, and for which the defendant has no valid defence, the Act provides in ss 55–60 a procedure whereby judgment can be obtained in this kind of instance without first issuing a summons and following the full summons procedure. These provisions are dealt with in detail below.

The Act also provides in s 65 for a procedure by which debtors could be summonsed before the court to face an inquiry into their failure to pay the debt.

---

[1] 1995 (4) SA 631 (CC).

Following such an inquiry, the court may issue various orders, namely, an order to pay the debt in whole or in instalments, a writ of execution, or an emoluments attachment order.

Prior to the decision of *Coetzee*, the sanction for non-compliance on the part of the debtor was imprisonment, which was described as imprisonment for contempt of court. Sachs J in his judgment in *Coetzee* described this as a misnomer, and held that this form of imprisonment, when it related to failure to pay or the inability to pay debts, to be nothing more than a disguised extension of civil imprisonment for debt, which had been abolished by the Abolition of Civil Imprisonment Act 2 of 1977.[2] Didcott J commented, *obiter*, that he could see circumstances in which imprisonment for failure to pay a debt could be defended.[3] The decision explicitly does not impugn other provisions which do allow imprisonment for failure to pay debts of certain categories, such as maintenance orders.[4]

The decision abolished the committal procedure of s 65 as being contrary to the right to freedom of person. It found particularly that the procedure could not be defended as a justifiable limitation on that right, because the provisions were unreasonable on the grounds of 'overbreadth'. The court held that the committal procedure was separable from the remainder of the section, and that therefore only references to the committal procedure were excised from the section.

The result of *Coetzee* is that the procedure of s 65 has had its teeth drawn. What remains is the inquiry into the financial status of the debtor and the possibility of orders being made as a result of that inquiry. But a creditor will no longer be able to obtain a writ of imprisonment on failure of the debtor to attend such an inquiry. Where a debtor deliberately refuses to co-operate with the courts regarding his or her refusal to pay a debt, therefore, even a proper judgment debt, the creditor who finds that the normal process of execution yields no dividends will have to resort to an administration order in terms of s 74, or to full-scale sequestration.

As correctly noted by Sachs J in *Coetzee*, the small debtor without means will no longer be faced with imprisonment from which he or she can only be rescued by family or friends. Further, creditors will no longer be able to extend credit on the basis that the debt can be exacted through fear of imprisonment. Credit should be extended only to those who are creditworthy and to those who provide proper security.[5]

This chapter deals, first, with the provisions of Chapter VIII of the Act, and then with s 65 as amended by *Coetzee*.

2 RECOVERY OF DEBTS IN TERMS OF CHAPTER VIII OF THE ACT

The chapter provides a procedure whereby a creditor may obtain judgment without the issue of a summons. If the debtor admits liability, the creditor may proceed to gain an order against the debtor.

If the creditor proceeded by way of summons and the debtor consents to judgment, certain provisions also provide for obtaining an appropriate judgment.

---

[2] At 664I–666F.

[3] At 646F–647E.

[4] At 658D and n 51 and n 52.

[5] See the National Credit Act 34 of 2005. Section 80, for example, deals with reckless credit.

Section 56 provides that a registered letter of demand may be sent by the attorney acting for a creditor to a debtor who is liable for the payment of the debt (defined in s 55 to mean 'any liquidated sum of money due') claimed in the letter.

Section 56 further provides that should the debtor pay the debt upon receipt of the letter, the creditor shall be entitled to recover the fees and costs prescribed in the rules for a registered letter of demand provided that the amount of such fees and costs was stated in the letter of demand.[6]

No specific format is prescribed for the letter of demand, unlike the position in regard to a summons.

In terms of s 56 the letter of demand must be sent by registered post by an attorney to the debtor. In terms of rule 4(1)(a) the letter must contain particulars of the nature and amount of the claim.[7]

Section 57 provides that the defendant may admit his or her liability to the plaintiff, that he or she may offer to pay the debt in instalments, and that he or she may agree to allow the plaintiff to apply for judgment against him or her and for a court order in accordance with his or her offer without notice to the defendant in the event of his or her failure to comply with his or her offer to pay the amount due by him or her in instalments.

In contrast, s 58 provides for an unconditional consent to judgment coupled with a consent to an order of court for the payment of the debt in instalments.

In both cases, viz:

(1)   where a defendant admits liability in terms of s 57 and undertakes to pay the debt in instalments or otherwise; or

(2)   where a defendant in terms of s 58 consents to judgment or to judgment and an order for the payment of the judgment debt in instalments,

the defendant may take the steps set out above after he or she has been summonsed or after he or she has received a letter of demand in terms of s 56.

2.1   The procedure where the defendant admits liability and offers to pay in instalments (s 57)

After receipt of the summons or the letter of demand, the defendant may, in terms of s 57, in writing:

•   admit liability for the amount claimed or for any other amount;[8]

•   offer to pay the amount of the debt and costs for which he or she admits liability in instalments or otherwise;[9]

•   undertake to pay collection fees.[10]

The defendant may also agree that in the event of his or her failure to carry out the terms of his or her offer, the plaintiff shall be entitled to apply for judgment for the amount of the outstanding balance of the debt for which liability was admitted

---

[6] The costs of the registered letter of demand are set out in Item 1 of Part II of Table A of Annexure 2 to the rules.

[7] See also rule 4(1)(b) regarding the content of a letter of demand where the original cause of action is a credit agreement under the National Credit Act.

[8] Section 57(1)(a).

[9] Section 57(1)(b).

[10] Section 57(1)(c).

and for an order of court for the payment of instalments in accordance with his or her offer.[11]

If the plaintiff accepts this offer, he or she must advise the defendant accordingly by registered letter.[12]

If the plaintiff accepts the defendant's written offer to pay in instalments and advises the defendant of his or her acceptance by registered post in terms of s 57(1), an agreement comes into existence in accordance with the rules governing contracts concluded by post.[13]

The defendant thereafter proceeds to pay off the debt in instalments. This arrangement may suit both the plaintiff and the defendant. It suits the plaintiff because, with relatively little effort, he or she has obtained an undertaking to pay off the debt coupled with the power, without further ado, to obtain judgment against the defendant should the latter fail to pay an instalment. The procedure suits the defendant because he or she obtains the opportunity to extinguish the debt in instalments without a judgment being granted against him or her.

The offer must set out full particulars of the defendant's monthly or weekly income and expenditure, supported where reasonably possible by the most recent proof in the possession of the defendant and other court orders or agreements, if any, with other creditors for payment of a debt and costs in instalments. It must also indicate the amount of the offered instalment.[14]

Should the defendant fail to perform in accordance with his or her offer, the plaintiff may in terms of s 57(2) request the court to enter judgment against the defendant and to order him or her to pay the judgment debt and costs in specified instalments or otherwise in accordance with his or her offer, and such order is deemed to be an order mentioned in s 65A(1).

The request must be accompanied by:

(1) the summons or, if no summons has been issued, a copy of the letter of demand;
(2) the defendant's written acknowledgment of liability and offer;
(3) the particulars and documentary evidence referred to in sub-s (1A), in order for the court to be apprised of the defendant's financial position at the time the offer was made and accepted;
(4) a copy of the plaintiff's or his or her attorney's written acceptance of the offer and proof of postage thereof to the defendant; and
(5) an affidavit or affirmation by the plaintiff or a certificate by his or her attorney stating in which respects the defendant has failed to carry out the terms of his or her offer and, if the defendant has made any payments since the date of the letter of demand or summons, showing how the balance claimed is arrived at.[15]

---

[11] Section 57(1)(*d*).
[12] Section 57(1).
[13] *Cape Explosives Works v South African Oil & Fat Industries Ltd; Cape Explosives Works Ltd v Lever Brothers (SA) Ltd* 1921 CPD 244; *Kergeulen Sealing & Whaling Co Ltd v CIR* 1939 AD 487; *A to Z Bazaars (Pty) Ltd v Minister of Agriculture* 1974 (4) SA 392 (C), 1975 (3) SA 468 (A).
[14] Section 57(1A).
[15] Section 57(2A).

According to s 57(2B), the court:

(1) may request any relevant information from the plaintiff or his or her attorney in order for the court to be apprised of the defendant's financial position at the time judgment is requested;

(2) must act in terms of the provisions of the National Credit Act 34 of 2005 (NCA) and the regulations thereunder dealing with over-indebtedness, reckless credit and affordability assessment, when considering a request for judgment in terms of this section, based on a credit agreement under the NCA;

(3) may, if the defendant is employed, and after satisfying itself that it is just and equitable that an emoluments attachment order be issued and that the amount is appropriate, authorise an emoluments attachment order referred to in s 65J; and

(4) may, notwithstanding the defendant's consent to pay any scale of costs, make a costs order as it deems fit.

If no summons has been issued against the defendant, then this written request constitutes the first document filed in the action, and it must contain the particulars prescribed in the rules.[16]

In the written request the plaintiff may ask the registrar or clerk of the court to grant judgment for the following:[17]

•   court fees if the request for judgment is the first document in the action;[18]
•   the outstanding balance of the debt;[19]
•   collection fees for which the plaintiff is liable to his or her attorney in the normal course when the attorney recovers the debt on the plaintiff's behalf;[20]
•   interest for which the defendant is liable;
•   the costs of the summons if the defendant admits liability to the plaintiff in terms of s 57(1) after he or she is summonsed;
•   sheriff's fees;
•   costs of the affidavit or affirmation by the plaintiff or the costs of the certificate by his or her attorney stating in what respects the defendant has failed to carry out the terms of his or her offer and, if the defendant has made any payments since the date of the letter of demand or summons, showing how the balance claimed is arrived at;[21]
•   the costs of the registered letter, if the defendant has admitted liability in terms of s 57(1) after receipt of a registered letter;
•   in cases where parties are summonsed in their capacity as partners, judgment may also be requested for the costs of the notice in which the plaintiff, in terms of rule 54(1), called for a statement of the names and places of residence of the persons who were partners at the time when the cause of action accrued.

---

[16] Section 59.
[17] Cf Annexure 1 Form 5A.
[18] Section 59.
[19] Section 57(2).
[20] Section 57(1).
[21] Section 57(2).

If the written request is satisfactory, the court may enter judgment and make an order for the payment of the debt in instalments.[22]

After judgment has been entered and an order for payment in instalments has been made, the debtor must again be notified forthwith by the plaintiff or his or her attorney by registered letter of the provisions of the judgment. If, however, the debtor was present or represented in court at the time when the order was made, it is apparently unnecessary to give him or her such notice.[23]

A judgment entered against the defendant in this way has the effect of a default judgment.[24]

Section 57 applies subject to the relevant provisions of the NCA where the request for judgment is based on a credit agreement under the NCA.[25]

2.2 The procedure where the defendant consents to judgment and offers to pay in instalments (s 58)

In terms of the provisions of s 58(1), the defendant may consent *unconditionally* to judgment and this consent *may* be accompanied by a consent to the granting of an order for the payment of the judgment debt in instalments. The defendant may consent and offer to pay in instalments after he or she has been summonsed or after a written demand in terms of s 56 has been made against him or her. Should the defendant consent to judgment after receipt of the summons or of the letter of demand, the plaintiff may request the court in writing to enter judgment in his or her favour in accordance with the consent. This request is accompanied by:

(1)   the summons or, if no summons was issued, a copy of the letter of demand;
(2)   the defendant's written consent to judgment; and
(3)   if the defendant consents to an order of court for payment in specified instalments, the written consent and full particulars and documentary evidence in order for the court to be apprised of the defendant's financial position at the time the defendant consented to judgment.[26]

If it appears from the defendant's consent that he or she has also consented to an order of court for the payment of the judgment debt in instalments, the court may order the defendant to pay the judgment debt and costs in specified instalments or otherwise in accordance with his or her consent, and such order is deemed to be an order of court mentioned in s 65A(1).[27]

If the defendant consents to an order of court for payment in specified instalments, the consent must:

(1)   set out full particulars of his or her monthly or weekly income and expenditure, supported where reasonably possible by the most recent proof in the possession of the defendant and other court orders or agreements, if any, with other creditors for payment of a debt and costs in instalments; and

---

[22] Section 57(2) is not mandatory.
[23] Section 57(3).
[24] Section 57(4).
[25] Section 57(5).
[26] Section 58(1B).
[27] Section 58(1)(*a*) and (*b*).

(2)   indicate the amount of the offered instalment.[28]

According to s 58(1B), the court:

(1)   may request any relevant information from the plaintiff or his or her attorney in order for the court to be apprised of the defendant's financial position at the time judgment is requested;

(2)   must act in terms of the provisions of the NCA and the regulations thereunder dealing with over-indebtedness, reckless credit and affordability assessment, when considering a request for judgment in terms of this section, based on a credit agreement under the NCA;

(3)   may, if the defendant is employed, and after satisfying itself that it is just and equitable that an emoluments attachment order be issued and that the amount is appropriate, authorise an emoluments attachment order referred to in s 65J; and

(4)   may, notwithstanding the defendant's consent to pay any scale of costs, make a costs order as it deems fit.

Section 58 applies subject to the relevant provisions of the NCA where the request for judgment is based on a credit agreement under the NCA.[29]

The judgment entered in terms of s 58(1) is likewise deemed to have the effect of a default judgment.[30]

If the judgment debtor was not present or represented before the court at the time when the judgment was noted and the order given, then the judgment creditor or his or her attorney must forthwith after the grant of the order notify the judgment debtor by registered post of the order and the consequences of his or her failure to satisfy it.[31]

It may be remarked at this point that the procedure by which an order is obtained in terms of s 58 is simpler than the procedure in terms of s 57. First, the consent of the defendant in terms of s 58 is unconditional—he or she consents to judgment—and, secondly, the defendant need not be notified of the acceptance of his or her offer prior to the plaintiff's application for judgment.

The following procedure would therefore appear to be followed frequently in practice: the plaintiff's attorney and the defendant stipulate that the defendant consents in terms of s 58 to judgment and that, in addition, he or she offers to pay the debt[32] in instalments. The plaintiff's attorney undertakes to make use of the consent and obtain judgment against the defendant only if the latter fails to carry out his or her agreement to pay the debt due by him or her in instalments.

---

[28] Section 58(1A).

[29] Section 58(3).

[30] Section 58(2) read with s 57(4).

[31] Section 58(2) read with s 57(3).

[32] The question arises whether the defendant will also be liable for the costs apart from the debt itself and whether he or she may also pay the costs in instalments. It would appear that costs (including collection fees) may indeed be included in the offer. Section 57(1)*(c)* provides expressly that the defendant may undertake to pay collection fees. Sections 57(1)*(a)* and 58(1) further provide that the defendant may admit liability or consent to judgment *'for any other amount'* (my italics). Cf also s 58(1)*(b),* where express provision is made for the debtor to consent to pay costs. Viewed as a whole, it would therefore seem that there may indeed be a consent or an offer encompassing the debt and all of the costs incurred.

3 THE S 65 PROCEDURE

Where there has been judgment for the payment of a sum of money and the judgment debtor has made a written offer to pay in instalments and such offer is accepted by the judgment creditor or his or her attorney, the judgment creditor or his or her attorney may apply to the court for an order that the debtor pay such amount in accordance with the offer.[33] Such an order is deemed to be an order for the purpose of launching the other procedures laid down in the section.[34]

The offer must be supported, where reasonably possible, by the most recent proof in the possession of the debtor relating to his or her income and expenditure, other court orders or agreements with other creditors for payment of a debt in instalments, and assets and liabilities as prescribed by the rules.[35]

According to s 65(3), the court:

(1) may request any relevant information from the judgment creditor or his or her attorney in order for the court to be apprised of the judgment debtor's financial position at the time the written request—for an order to pay the judgment debt in specified instalments or otherwise—is made;

(2) must act in terms of the provisions of the NCA and the regulations thereunder dealing with over-indebtedness, reckless credit and affordability assessment when considering a request for an order in terms of this section, if the judgment is based on a credit agreement under the NCA;

(3) may, if the debtor is employed, and after satisfying itself that it is just and equitable that an emoluments attachment order be issued and that the amount is appropriate, authorise an emoluments attachment order referred to in s 65J.

3.1 The notice to summon the debtor to appear before the court

The debtor[36] may be summoned to appear before the court if the judgment or order has not been complied with for a period of 10 days from:

---

[33] Section 65. Rule 45(7) provides:
'The written offer referred to in section 65 of the Act shall be on affidavit setting out the following particulars pertaining to the judgment debtor—
(*a*) the full names of the judgment debtor, his or her identity number or passport number, residential and business address;
(*b*) the name and address of his or her employer and his or her employee number;
(*c*) his or her marital status;
(*d*) the number of his or her dependants, their age and their relationship to him or her;
(*e*) his or her assets and liabilities, substantiated where reasonably possible with the most recent proof thereof and attached as annexures;
(*f*) his or her gross weekly or monthly income (including that of his or her spouse and dependants) and expenses substantiated by the most recent proof in the possession of the debtor relating to his or her income and expenditure;
(*g*) the details of agreements with other creditors for payment of a debt in instalments, and of emoluments attachment orders or other court orders against him or her and the total amount payable thereunder, substantiated by copies thereof and attached as annexures; and
(*h*) his or her offer and the dates of the proposed instalments.'
[34] Section 65(4).
[35] Section 65(2).
[36] Section 65A(1). For the sake of brevity, the word 'debtor' is frequently used in this chapter instead of 'judgment debtor', as in the Act. The judgment debtor may also be a juristic person, in which event the person summonsed to appear before the court as its representative and in his or her

(1)   the date on which it was given; or

(2)   the date on which an instalment became payable; or

(3)   the expiry of a period of suspension ordered in terms of s 48*(e)*.

The notice calling upon the debtor to appear before the court in chambers must be in a printed form and indicate the date of the judgment or order as well as the amount of the judgment and the balance of the capital, interest, costs and collection fees which the defendant has undertaken to pay in terms of s 57(1)*(c)* and which remains due on the date of the issue or reissue of the notice.[37]

In terms of Annexure 1 Form 40, the notice reads as follows:

No. 40

**Notice to Appear in Court in terms of Section 65A(1) of the Magistrates' Courts Act, 1944
(Act 32 of 1944)**

* For use in the District Court

In the Magistrate's Court for the District of ....

held at ....

Case No .... of 20......

In the matter between

.... Judgment Creditor

and

.... Judgment Debtor

To ....

.... (If the judgment debtor is a juristic person it must be indicated that the responsible person is summoned in his or her personal capacity and in his or her capacity as the representative of the juristic person.)

You are hereby required to appear before above mentioned court on .... 20...... at .... (time) to enable the court to inquire into your/the juristic person's financial position and to make such order as the court may deem just and equitable, as you/the juristic person failed to satisfy—

(a)   the judgment of the said court of .... given against you/the juristic person on .... 20 .... for the payment of the amount of R .... and R .... costs; or

(b)   the order of the said court of .... 20 ..... that you/the juristic person shall pay in instalments the amount of R .... and R .... costs within 10 days of the date on which the judgment was given or ....

The balance of the debt at present amounts to R .... and the balance of the costs to R ....

You are further required to submit a full statement to the said court—

(a)   of your/the juristic person's assets and liabilities;

(b)   of your monthly/weekly income and expenditure, supported by documentary proof inclusive of a statement by your employer giving full particulars of your emoluments and, in the case of a juristic person, the latest financial statements;

(c)   and the following:

....

---

personal capacity will be a director or officer of the juristic person. The debtor may not be the State. *Lombard v Minister van Verdediging* 2002 (3) SA 242 (T).

[37] Rule 45(1). Cf Annexure 1 Form 40 for the format of the notice.

Notice:

(1) If the court is satisfied on the ground of sufficient proof or otherwise—

(a) that you have knowledge of a notice referred to in section 65A(1) of the Act and that you have failed to appear before the court on the date and at the time specified in the notice; or

(b) that you, where the proceedings were postponed in your presence to a date and time determined by the court, have failed to appear before the court on that date and at that time; or

(c) that you have failed to remain in attendance at the proceedings or at the proceedings so postponed,

the court may, at the request of the judgment creditor or his or her attorney, authorise the issue of a warrant directing a sheriff to arrest you and to bring you before a competent court to enable that court to conduct a financial inquiry. [Section 65A(6) of the Act]

(2) Any person who—

(a) is called upon to appear before a court under a notice in terms of section 65A(1) or (8)*(b)* of the Act (where the sheriff, in lieu of arresting a person, hands to that person a notice in writing to appear before the court) and who wilfully fails to appear before the court on the date and at the time specified in the notice;

(b) where the proceedings were postponed in his or her presence to a date and time determined by a court, wilfully fails to appear before the court on that date and at that time; or

(c) wilfully fails to remain in attendance at the proceedings or at the proceedings so postponed,

is guilty of an offence and liable on conviction to a fine or to imprisonment for a period not exceeding three months [Section 65 A(9) of the Act]

Dated at .... this .... day of ...., 20......

....

Judgment Creditor/Attorney for Judgment Creditor

....

Clerk of the Court

This notice is supported by an affidavit (or affirmation) by the judgment creditor or a certificate by his or her attorney in which the following averments are made:[38]

(1) the date of the judgment or the date of the expiry of the period of suspension under s 48*(e)* of the Act, as the case may be;

(2) that the judgment or order has remained unsatisfied for a period of 10 days from the date on which it was given or became payable or from the expiry of the period of suspension in terms of s 48*(e)* of the Act;

(3) in what respect the judgment debtor has failed to comply with the judgment or order referred to in s 65A(1) of the Act, the amount in arrears and outstanding balance on the date upon which the notice is issued; and

(4) that the judgment debtor has been advised by registered letter of the terms of the judgment or of the expiry of the period of suspension under s 48*(e)* of the Act, as the case may be, and of the consequences of his or her failure to satisfy the judgment, and that a period of 10 days has elapsed since the date on which the said letter was posted.

The notice must specify the consequences of failure to appear in court on the date determined for the enquiry.[39]

---

[38] Rule 45(1)*(a)–(d)*.
[39] Rule 45(2).

When the original judgment or order for payment of the judgment debt referred to in s 65A(1) has been given in any court other than the court of the district in which the inquiry is held, the clerk of the court may not issue the notice calling upon the debtor to appear before the court until a certified copy of the judgment or order has been lodged with him or her.[40]

Any alterations in the notice to the debtor must be initialed by the judgment creditor or his or her attorney and by the clerk of the court before issue or reissue.[41]

The clerk may not issue the s 65A notice until it is shown from the minutes of the proceedings that the debtor was present or represented when judgment was given or a warrant of execution was served on the debtor personally, unless the judgment creditor or his or her attorney demonstrates that the debtor has been notified by registered letter of the terms of the judgment or of the expiry of the period of suspension ordered under s 48(e) and a period of 10 days has elapsed since the posting of the letter.[42]

Section 65A(6) provides that where the court is satisfied that the debtor has knowledge of the notice in s 65A(1) and he or she has failed to appear, or the debtor fails to appear on a postponement date, or he or she has failed to remain in attendance, the court may issue a warrant of arrest to bring the debtor before a competent court to conduct an inquiry in terms of s 65A(1).

Section 65A(8) provides that a person so arrested should as soon as reasonably possible be brought before the court within the district in which that person was arrested. He or she may be detained at a police station pending the court appearance.

If the creditor consents, and instead of arresting the debtor, the debtor may be handed a notice by the sheriff calling upon the debtor to attend court.[43]

A wilful refusal or failure to appear in terms of a notice in terms of s 65A(1) or (8) constitutes an offence, making the debtor liable to a fine or to imprisonment for a period not exceeding three months.[44] Section 65A(10) provides details of the procedure to be followed when the court inquires into the failure of a debtor to attend.

Section 65A throughout makes provision for the summonsing of a juristic person, represented by a director or officer.

3.2 The procedure when the debtor appears before the court *in camera*

When the debtor appears before the court *in camera* on the return day mentioned in the notice, he or she gives evidence under oath or affirmation as to his or her financial position. The court permits examination or cross-examination of the judgment debtor in relation to all matters affecting his or her financial position and his or her ability to pay the judgment debt and costs, and also his or her failure to do so. The court hears such further evidence as may be adduced orally or by

---

[40] Rule 45(4).
[41] Rule 45(3).
[42] Section 65A(2).
[43] Section 65A(8)(b).
[44] Section 65A(9).

affidavit or in such other manner as the court may deem just and as is material to the determination of the judgment debtor's financial position, his or her ability to pay the judgment debt and his or her failure to do so. Witnesses may be summonsed for the purpose of giving such evidence.[45]

The Act prescribes the factors which the court must take into consideration in determining the ability of the debtor to pay the debt due. These factors are:[46]

(1) the nature of his or her income;

(2) the amounts needed by the debtor for his or her necessary expenses and those of the persons dependent upon him or her;[47] and

(3) the amount of periodical payments that he or she is obliged to make in terms of an order of court, agreement or otherwise in respect of his or her other commitments.

The court may, in its discretion, refuse to take account of periodical payments that a judgment debtor has undertaken to make in terms of a credit agreement as defined in s 1 of the NCA for the purchase of goods which have not been exempted from seizure in terms of s 67[48] or which cannot, in the opinion of the court, be regarded as household requirements.[49]

If at the hearing the court is satisfied that the judgment debtor has movable or immovable property which may be attached and sold in order to satisfy the judgment debt or part of it, the court may:

(1) authorise the issuing of a warrant of execution against such movable or immovable property or such part of it as the court may deem fit;[50] or

(2) authorise the issuing of such a warrant together with an order for the payment of the judgment debt in periodical instalments in terms of s 73.[51]

If it appears to the court that there is a debt due to the judgment debtor which may be attached in terms of s 72, the court may authorise the attachment of that debt in terms of that section.[52]

If it is apparent from the evidence that, after receipt of the notice to appear in court in terms of s 65A(1), the judgment debtor made a written offer to pay the judgment debt in instalments or otherwise, or that the debtor is able to pay the debt in reasonable instalments, then the court may order him or her to pay the judgment debt and costs in specified instalments and may also authorise the issuing of an emoluments attachment order.[53]

The further hearing of the matter is thereupon postponed.[54] The proceedings may again be placed on the roll by the judgment creditor or his or her attorney by

---

[45] Cf in general s 65D(1).

[46] Section 65D(4)(*a*).

[47] In the case of a juristic person the court takes into account the amounts required by the juristic person to meet its necessary administrative expenses and for the making of obligatory payments in terms of an order of court or agreement (s 65D(4)(*b*)).

[48] Property exempt from execution.

[49] Section 65D(5).

[50] Section 65E(1)(*a*)(i). This authority serves also as an interdict prohibiting alienation of the property pending execution against it (s 65E(2)).

[51] Section 65E(1)(*a*)(ii).

[52] Section 65E(1)(*b*).

[53] Section 65E(1)(*c*). Cf the discussion of the emoluments attachment order below at para 3.4 *et seq.*

[54] Section 65E(1).

notice delivered or posted at least 10 days before the day appointed in such notice for the hearing.[55]

In terms of Annexure 1 Form 41, the notice reads as follows:

No. 41

Notice of Set-down of Postponed Proceedings under Section 65E(3) of the Magistrates' Courts Act, 1944 (Act 32 of 1944)

* For use in the District Court

In the Magistrate's Court for the District of ....

held at ....

Case No .... of 20......

In the matter between

.... Judgment Creditor

and

.... Judgment Debtor

By hand/By registered post

To: (1)   .... (Judgment Debtor)

....

(2)   Clerk of the Court ....

Take notice that the proceedings against you, the above-mentioned Judgment Debtor, which were postponed on the .... day of .... 20......, in terms of section 65E(1) of the Magistrates' Courts Act, 1944, have again been placed on the roll of the above-mentioned Court. You are, therefore, hereby, in terms of section 65E(3) of the said Act, directed to appear before the above-mentioned Court on the .... day of .... 20...... at .... (time).

Notice:

(1) If the court is satisfied on the ground of sufficient proof or otherwise—

(a)   that you have knowledge of a notice referred to in section 65E(3) of the Act and that you have failed to appear before the court on the date and at the time specified in the notice; or

(b)   that you, where the proceedings were postponed in your presence to a date and time determined by the court, have failed to appear before the court on that date and at that time; or

(c)   that you have failed to remain in attendance at the proceedings or at the proceedings so postponed,

The provisions of section 65A(6) of the Act shall *mutatis mutandis* apply, and the court may, at the request of the judgment creditor or his or her attorney, authorise the issue of a warrant directing a sheriff to arrest you and to bring you before a competent court to enable that court to conduct a financial inquiry.

Dated at .... this .... day of ...., 20......

....

Judgment Creditor/Attorney for Judgment Creditor

Address of Judgment Creditor/Attorney for Judgment Creditor

....

The court may in any event postpone the proceedings at any time in the presence of the judgment debtor or, in the case of a juristic person, in the presence of the director or officer of the debtor, to such date as the court may determine.[56]

When postponing the proceedings, the court informs the judgment debtor or the director or officer in question of the provisions of s 65E(1)(c) and may order the judgment debtor, director or officer to produce such documents as the court may specify at the hearing on the date determined by the court. The court may, in addition, stipulate such conditions as it deems fit.[57]

As far as the costs of the appearance at the hearing in chambers are concerned, the rule applies that the judgment debtor will be ordered to pay the costs unless it appears at the hearing that the judgment debtor has made an offer to settle the judgment debt in instalments that the court considers reasonable or that he or she has notified the judgment creditor that he or she was not able to make an offer and the court finds this to be true.[58] If it emerges that the judgment creditor refused the offer, the court may order the judgment creditor to pay those costs, including the loss of wages suffered by the judgment debtor through having to appear in court in connection with the proceedings.[59]

The court may suspend, amend or rescind its order.[60] If the debtor or his or her representative was not present in court at the time when the order was made, the judgment creditor or his or her attorney is obliged to advise him or her forthwith by registered post of the terms of the order.[61]

3.3 The s 65 procedure and administration orders

The court may postpone the hearing in terms of s 65A(1) if the judgment debtor lodges with the court an application for an administration order[62] prior to or at the time of the hearing.[63]

If a judgment debtor has not lodged an application for an administration order with the court before or at the time of the hearing of the s 65 proceedings and it appears at the hearing that the judgment debtor has other debts also, the court considers whether all of the judgment debtor's debts should be treated collectively. If the court is of the opinion that they should be so treated, it may, with a view to granting an administration order, postpone further hearing of the proceedings to a date determined by the court and order the judgment debtor to submit to the court a full statement of his or her affairs and to cause a copy of the statement to be delivered to each of his or her creditors at least three days before the date appointed for the further hearing.[64]

---

[56] Section 65D(2).

[57] Section 65D(3)(a)–(c).

[58] Although general rules have been laid down, they do not derogate from the power of the court to make such order as to costs as it may deem just (s 65K(3)).

[59] Section 65K(1).

[60] Section 65E(5).

[61] Section 65E(6).

[62] Administration orders are dealt with in chapter 20 below.

[63] Section 65I(1).

[64] Section 65I(2).

If it appears that the judgment debtor's total debts do not exceed R50 000, the court may grant an administration order in respect of his or her estate[65] and stay further proceedings, but may grant the judgment creditor the costs already incurred in connection with such proceedings.[66]

3.4 Emoluments attachment orders

A distinction must be drawn between a garnishee order and an emoluments attachment order. A garnishee order is a method used to attach a debt due to the judgment debtor.[67]

An emoluments attachment order is regarded as part of the procedure for the collection of debt. In this instance, the court orders the judgment debtor's employer to make regular monthly deductions from the debtor's salary and to pay them to the judgment creditor.

A judgment creditor may cause an emoluments attachment order to be issued from the court of the district in which the judgment debtor resides, carries on business or is employed.[68]

An emoluments attachment order must:

(1) attach the emoluments at present or in future owing or accruing to the judgment debtor by or from his or her employer to the amount necessary to cover the judgment and the costs of the attachment, whether that judgment was obtained in the court concerned or in any other court; and

(2) oblige the garnishee to pay to the judgment creditor or his or her attorney specific amounts out of the emoluments of the judgment debtor in accordance with the order of court laying down the specific instalments payable by the judgment debtor, until the relevant judgment debt and costs have been paid in full.[69]

The amount of the instalment payable, or the total amount of instalments payable where there is more than one emoluments attachment order payable by the judgment debtor, may not exceed 25 per cent of the judgment debtor's basic salary. The section defines 'basic salary' as the annual gross salary a judgment debtor is employed on divided by 12 and excludes additional remuneration for overtime or other allowances.[70]

When a court considers authorising an emoluments attachment order after having considered all submissions before the court and after having called for and considered all further available documents, and if the court is satisfied that other emoluments attachment orders exist against the judgment debtor, the court must postpone the further consideration of the authorisation and set the matter down for hearing. The party applying for the authorisation of an emoluments attachment

---

[65] Section 65I(3). The maximum amount of the total debt is determined by the minister from time to time by notice in the *Government Gazette*. The amount of the present determination is R50 000.

[66] Section 65I(4).

[67] Garnishee orders are dealt with in chapter 17 above as part of the procedure in execution of a judgment.

[68] Section 65J(1)*(a)*.

[69] Section 65J(1)*(b)*.

[70] Section 65J(1A).

order must serve notice of the date of the hearing on the other creditors or their attorneys, and on the judgment debtor, if he or she was not present or represented when the consideration of the authorisation of an emoluments attachment order was postponed. The court may, after hearing all parties at the hearing, make an order regarding the division of the amount available to be committed to each of the emoluments attachment orders, after satisfying itself that each order is just and equitable and the sum of the total amount of the emoluments attachment orders is appropriate and does not exceed 25 per cent of the judgment debtor's basic salary.[71]

In *University of Stellenbosch Legal Aid Clinic & others v Minister of Justice and Correctional Services & others*,[72] the Constitutional Court declared that no emoluments attachment order may be issued unless the court has authorised the issuing of such order after satisfying itself that it is just and equitable and that the amount is appropriate. Section 65J(2)*(a)* and *(b)* were declared unconstitutional and invalid.[73] This case accordingly had a significant impact on the South African emoluments attachment landscape.[74]

An emoluments attachment order will therefore only be granted if the court has so authorised after satisfying itself that it is just an equitable that an emoluments attachment order be issued and that the amount is appropriate and such authorisation has not been suspended.[75]

A judgment creditor or his or her attorney must serve, on the judgment debtor and on his or her employer, a notice, which corresponds substantially with the form prescribed in the rules, of the intention to have an emoluments attachment order issued against the judgment debtor.[76] The notice must inform the judgment debtor and his or her employer of the judgment creditor's intention to have an emoluments attachment order issued against the judgment debtor and of the full amount of the capital debt, interest and costs outstanding, substantiated by a statement of account. It must also inform the judgment debtor that, unless he or she or his or her employer files a notice of intention to oppose the issuing of the emoluments attachment order within 10 days after service of the notice on them, an emoluments attachment order will be sought.[77]

Various grounds exist on which there may be opposition to the issuing of the order. Section 65J lists that such grounds include, but are not limited to, that the amounts claimed are erroneous or not in accordance with the law, or that 25 per cent of the judgment debtor's basic salary is already committed to other

---

[71] Section 65J(1A)*(c)*.

[72] 2016 (6) SA 596 (CC).

[73] Recent amendments to the provision were effected through the introduction of the Courts of Law Amendment Act 7 of 2017.

[74] The following articles by S van der Merwe are also worth considering: 'Failure to discharge. A discussion of the insufficient legal recourse afforded to judgment debtors in the South African context.' 2008 *Journal for Juridical Science Special Issue* 71–86 and 'Traversing the South African emolument attachment order legal landscape post 2016: Quo vadis?' – Accepted for publication in the 2019:1 Special Edition of the *Stellenbosch Law Review*.

[75] Section 65J(2).

[76] Section 65J(2A).

[77] Section 65J(2B).

emoluments attachment orders and that the debtor will not have sufficient means left for his or her own maintenance or that of his or her dependants.[78] The notice of intention to oppose must be accompanied by various particulars.[79]

If a notice of intention to oppose is filed and the judgment creditor or his or her attorney does not accept the reasons for the opposition, he or she or his or her attorney may set the matter down for hearing.[80] At the hearing, the court may give an order that is just and equitable, which includes rescinding the emoluments attachment order or amending it in such a way that it will affect only the balance of the emoluments of the judgment debtor over and above the sufficient means necessary for his or her maintenance and that of his or her dependants. It may also make any order, including an order regarding the division of the amount available to be committed to all the emoluments attachment orders, after satisfying itself that the amount is appropriate and does not exceed 25 per cent of the judgment debtor's basic salary and an order as to costs.[81]

The creditor or his or her attorney must prepare and sign the emoluments attachment order and the clerk must ensure that the court has authorised it and possesses the necessary jurisdiction.[82] The emoluments attachment order must be served on the employer of the judgment debtor, and if the judgment debtor was not present or represented when the emoluments attachment order was authorised, also on the judgment debtor, by the sheriff in the manner prescribed by the rules for the service of process.[83]

Rule 46 provides that, when an emoluments attachment order has been authorised by the court, an application to issue that order must be made on a form corresponding substantially with Form 38A of Annexure 1. An emoluments attachment order must be issued on a form corresponding substantially with Form 38 of Annexure 1, and must contain sufficient information to enable the garnishee to identify the judgment debtor, including the date of birth, identity number or passport number and employee number of the judgment debtor.

Forms 38A and 38 read as follows:

No. 38A

Notice of Intention to Issue an Emoluments Attachment Order—Section 65J(2A) of the Magistrates' Courts Act 1944 (Act 32 of 1944)

[Form 38A inserted by GN R632 of 22 June 2018 (wef 1 August 2018).]

* Only for use in the District Court

In the Magistrate's Court for the District of ....

held at ....

Case No .... of 20......

In the matter between

.... Judgment Creditor

---

[78] Section 65J(2C)*(b)*.
[79] Section 65J(2C)*(c)*.
[80] Section 65J(2D).
[81] Section 65J(2E).
[82] Section 65J(3).
[83] Section 65J(3)*(c)*.

and

.... Judgment Debtor

Particulars of the judgment debtor (where available):

Identity number/date of birth /Passport number:..

Employee number: ....

Address: ....

Particulars of the Garnishee:

.... Garnishee

Address: ....

TO: THE ABOVE-MENTIONED JUDGMENT DEBTOR AND HIS OR HER EMPLOYER (HEREIN REFERRED TO AS THE 'GARNISHEE'):

WHEREAS on the .... (date) the Court authorised the attachment of the judgment debtor's emoluments and that the garnishee must pay the judgment creditor or his or her attorney R .... of the emoluments of the said judgment debtor on the .... day of each and every month/week with effect from ..... (date) until a sufficient amount has been paid to satisfy a judgment or order obtained against the judgment debtor by the judgment creditor in the .... Court at .... on the .... day of .... for the amount of R .... (on which judgment or order the amount of R .... remains unpaid) with costs amounting to R .... and the costs of attachment amounting to R .... as well as R .... sheriff's fees.

KINDLY TAKE NOTICE that the judgment creditor intends to apply for the issuing of the aforesaid emoluments attachment order.

TAKE FURTHER NOTICE that the full amount of the capital debt, interest and costs outstanding is the sum of R ...., substantiated by the statement of account attached hereto.

TAKE FURTHER NOTICE that unless the judgment debtor or his or her employer (cited herein as the Garnishee) files a notice of intention to oppose the issuing of the emoluments attachment order within 10 court days after service of this Form 38A notice, the judgment creditor will apply to court to issue an emoluments attachment order. The notice of intention to oppose, if any, must be delivered by—

(a) serving a copy thereof on the judgment creditor or his or her attorney; and

(b) filing the original thereof with the clerk of this Court.

TAKE FURTHER NOTICE that—

(i) in your notice of intention to oppose you are required to give your full physical, residential or business address, postal address and where available, facsimile and electronic mail address; and indicate the preferred address for service upon you of all documents in this matter, and service thereof at the address so given shall be valid and effectual, except where personal service is required by an order of the court; and

(ii) if a physical address is given by you in your notice of intention to oppose and is referred to as your preferred address for the purpose of service, that address shall, in places where there are three or more attorneys or firms of attorneys practising independently of one another, be within 15 kilometres of the courthouse.

TAKE FURTHER NOTICE that—

(1) The contemplated notice of intention to oppose must state the grounds upon which the judgment debtor or employer wishes to oppose the issuing of the emoluments attachment order;

(2) The grounds which may be used to oppose the issuing of the emoluments attachment order include, but are not limited to, the following—

(a) that the amounts claimed are erroneous or not in accordance with the law; or

(b) that 25 per cent of the judgment debtor's basic salary* is already committed to other emoluments attachment orders and that the debtor will not have sufficient means left for his or her own maintenance or that of his or her dependants;

(3) The notice of intention to oppose must be accompanied by—

    (a) a certificate by the employer of the judgment debtor setting out particulars of—

        (i) all existing court orders against the judgment debtor or agreements with other creditors for payment of a debt and costs in instalments; and

        (ii) when reasonably attainable, the amounts needed by the debtor for necessary expenses and those of the persons dependent on him or her and for the making of periodical payments which he or she is obliged to make in terms of an agreement or otherwise in respect of his or her other commitments;

    (b) the contact details of all the relevant judgment creditors or their attorneys; and

    (c) the latest salary advice of the judgment debtor.

TAKE FURTHER NOTICE that if this matter is opposed, it may be set down for hearing on 10 court days' notice.

TAKE FURTHER NOTICE that should you not oppose this matter, application will be made to court on the............ day of .... at 09h00 or as soon thereafter as this matter may be heard for the issuing of an emoluments attachment order.

TAKE FURTHER NOTICE that you have a right to be assisted by a legal representative (a lawyer) of your own choice. IF YOU CANNOT AFFORD THE SERVICES OF A LEGAL REPRESENTATIVE, YOU ARE ENTITLED TO APPLY FOR LEGAL AID IN ORDER TO BE ALLOCATED A LAWYER IF YOU QUALIFY.

Dated at .... this .... day of ...., 20......

....

Judgment Creditor/Judgment Creditor's attorney

Physical address (within 15 kilometres of the courthouse): ....

....

....

Postal address: ....

Electronic mail address: ....

Facsimile: ....

Indicate the preferred address for service: ....

....

* See section 65J(1A)(a) and (b) of the Magistrates' Courts Act, 1944, which reads as follows:

'(a) The amount of the instalment payable or the total amount of instalments payable where there is more than one emoluments attachment order payable by the judgment debtor, may not exceed 25 per cent of the judgment debtor's basic salary.

(b) For purposes of this section, "basic salary" means the annual gross salary a judgment debtor is employed on divided by 12 and excludes additional remuneration for overtime or other allowances.'

No. 38

Emoluments Attachment Order—Section 65J of the Magistrates' Courts Act 1944 (Act 32 of 1944)

[Form 38 substituted by GN R632 of 22 June 2018 (wef 1 August 2018).]

In the Magistrate's Court for the District of ....

held at ....

Case No .... of 20......

In the matter between

.... Judgment Creditor

and

.... Judgment Debtor

Particulars of the judgment debtor (where available):

Identity number/date of birth/Passport number: ....

Employee number: ....

Address: ....

Particulars of the Garnishee:

.... Garnishee

Address: ....

Whereas it has been made to appear to the above-mentioned Court that emoluments are at present or in future owing or accruing to the judgment debtor by or from the garnishee and that after satisfaction of the following order sufficient means will be left to the judgment debtor to maintain himself or herself and those dependent upon him or her;

It is ordered:

(1) That the said emoluments are attached;

(2) That the garnishee pay to the judgment creditor or his or her attorney on the .... day of each and every month/week after this order has been granted the sum of R .... of the emoluments of the said judgment debtor until a sufficient amount has been paid to satisfy a judgment or order obtained against the judgment debtor by the judgment creditor in the .... Court at .... on the .... day of .... for the amount of R .... (on which judgment or order the amount of R .... remains unpaid) with costs amounting to R .... and the costs of attachment amounting to R .... as well as R .... sheriff's fees.

Dated at .... this .... day of ...., 20......

By Order of the Court

....

Clerk of the Court

....

Judgment Creditor/Attorney for Judgment Creditor

Address of Judgment Creditor/Attorney for Judgment Creditor

....

YOUR ATTENTION IS DIRECTED to section 65J(6) of the Magistrates' Courts Act, 1944, which provides as follows:

(a) If, after the service of such an emoluments attachment order on the garnishee, the garnishee believes or becomes aware or it is otherwise shown that the—

(i) judgment debtor, after satisfaction of the emoluments attachment order, will not have sufficient means for his or her own maintenance or that of his or her dependants; or

(ii) amounts claimed are erroneous or not in accordance with the law, the garnishee, judgment debtor or any other interested party must without delay and in writing notify the judgment creditor or his or her attorney accordingly.

(b) The written notification referred to in paragraph (a) must set out the reasons for believing or knowing that the judgment debtor will not have sufficient means for his or her own maintenance or that of his or her dependants or that the amounts claimed are erroneous or not in accordance with the law.

(c) The judgment creditor or his or her attorney must, after receiving the notice contemplated in paragraph *(a)*, without delay indicate whether he or she accepts the reasons given in that notification and if not, set the matter down for hearing in court with notice to the garnishee, judgment debtor or any other interested party referred to in paragraph *(a)*.

(d) The court may, after hearing all parties and after satisfying itself that the order is just and equitable—

    (i) rescind the emoluments attachment order or amend it in such a way that it will affect only the balance of the emoluments of the judgment debtor over and above the sufficient means necessary for his or her maintenance and that of his or her dependants; or

    (ii) make any order including an order regarding the division of the amount available to be committed to all the emoluments attachment orders, after satisfying itself that the amount is appropriate and does not exceed 25 per cent of the judgment debtor's basic salary and an order as to costs

YOUR ATTENTION IS FURTHER DIRECTED to the provisions of subsection 65J(10)*(a)* and *(b)* of the Magistrates' Courts Act, 1944, which read as follows:

    '*(a)* Any garnishee may, in respect of the services rendered by him or her in terms of an emoluments attachment order, recover from the judgment creditor a commission of up to 5 per cent of all amounts deducted by him or her from the judgment debtor's emoluments by deducting such commission from the amount payable to the judgment creditor.

    (b) A garnishee who—

        (i) unreasonably fails to timeously deduct the amount of the emoluments attachment order provided for in subsection (4)*(a)*; or

        (ii) unreasonably fails to timeously stop the deductions when the judgment debt and costs have been paid in full,

    is liable to repay to the judgment debtor any additional costs and interest which have accrued or any amount deducted from the salary of the judgment debtor after the judgment debt and costs have been paid in full as a result of such failure.'

IMPORTANT NOTICE:

YOUR ATTENTION IS DIRECTED to section 65J(3) of the Magistrates' Courts Act, 1944 (read with section 3(1) of the Sheriffs Act, 1986), which provides that only a sheriff may serve this order on a garnishee and, where applicable, on the judgment debtor in the manner prescribed by rule 9 of the Magistrates' Courts Rules. Service of this order by a person who is not a sheriff appointed in terms of section 2 of the Sheriffs Act, 1986, constitutes a criminal offence in terms of section 60(1)*(g*A*)* of the Sheriffs Act, 1986, and renders such service invalid and of no effect. A person who is convicted of an offence in terms of section 60(1)*(g*A*)* of the Sheriffs Act, 1986, shall be liable to a fine or to imprisonment for a period not exceeding three years or both such fine and such imprisonment.

The judgment creditor or his or her attorney must furnish the garnishee and the judgment debtor, free of charge, with a quarterly statement containing particulars of the payments received up to the date concerned and the balance owing.[84]

An emoluments attachment order may be executed against the garnishee as if it were a court judgment, subject to the right of the judgment debtor, the garnishee or any other interested party to dispute the existence or validity of the order or the correctness of the balance claimed.[85]

If the emoluments attachment order has been served and the garnishee believes or becomes aware or it is otherwise shown that the judgment debtor, after

---

[84] Section 65J(4).
[85] Section 65J(5).

satisfaction of the emoluments attachment order, will not have sufficient means for his or her own maintenance or that of his or her dependants, or amounts claimed are erroneous or not in accordance with the law, the garnishee, judgment debtor or any other interested party must without delay and in writing notify the judgment creditor or his or her attorney accordingly. The court may conduct a hearing and make an order that is just and equitable, including rescinding the emoluments attachment order or amending it in such a way that it will affect only the balance of the emoluments of the judgment debtor over and above the sufficient means necessary for his or her maintenance and that of his or her dependants. The court can also make any order, including an order regarding the division of the amount available to be committed to all the emoluments attachment orders, after satisfying itself that the amount is appropriate and does not exceed 25 per cent of the judgment debtor's basic salary, and an order as to costs.[86]

It is possible, on good cause shown, to suspend, amend or rescind an emoluments attachment order, and when suspending any such order the court may impose such conditions as it may deem just and reasonable.[87]

When a judgment debtor to whom an emoluments attachment order relates leaves the service of a garnishee before the judgment debt has been paid in full, such judgment debtor must forthwith advise the judgment creditor or his or her attorney in writing of the name and address of his or her new employer. The judgment creditor or his or her attorney may cause a certified copy of such emoluments attachment order to be served on the said new employer, together with an affidavit or affirmation by him or her or a certificate by his or her attorney specifying the payments received by him or her since such order was issued, the costs, if any, incurred since the date on which that order was issued and the balance outstanding. The new employer is bound thereby and is deemed to have been substituted for the original garnishee, subject to the right of the judgment debtor, the garnishee or any other interested party to dispute the existence or validity of the order and the correctness of the balance claimed.[88]

Any garnishee may, in respect of the services rendered by him or her in terms of an emoluments attachment order, recover from the judgment creditor a commission of up to 5 per cent of all amounts deducted by him or her from the judgment debtor's emoluments by deducting such commission from the amount payable to the judgment creditor.[89]

The recently inserted s 106C provides that any person who requires the applicant to consent to a judgment or any instalment order or emoluments attachment order prior to the granting of the loan is guilty of an offence and on conviction liable to a fine or to imprisonment not exceeding three years. Furthermore, any person who fraudulently obtains or issues a judgment, or any instalment order or emoluments attachment order in terms of this Act, is guilty of an offence and on conviction liable to a fine or to imprisonment not exceeding three years.

---

[86] Section 65J(6).
[87] Section 65J(7).
[88] Section 65J(8).
[89] Section 65J(10).

3.5 The debt-collecting procedure in regard to certain classes of debtor

3.5.1 *Debtors against whom judgment has been granted in the High Court*

Section 65M provides that where judgment for the payment of money has been given by a division of the High Court or a court for a regional division, the judgment creditor may file with the clerk of the court a certified copy of that judgment and an affidavit or affirmation specifying the amount still owing and how it has been arrived at. The judgment creditor's attorney may alternatively file a certificate to the latter effect. The judgment then has all the effects of a judgment of that magistrate's court, even though the amount of the judgment may exceed the jurisdiction of the court. The procedure generally followed for the collection of debts in the magistrates' courts is thereafter followed in collecting that amount. In terms of s 65M, the judgment debtor is entitled to dispute the correctness of the amount specified in the affidavit, affirmation or certificate.

3.5.2 *Juristic persons*

Section 65A(1) provides that where a judgment debtor is a juristic person, a director or officer of the juristic person may be called upon as representative of the juristic person and in his or her personal capacity to appear before the court to show cause why he or she should not be ordered to pay the judgment debt in instalments.

It should be noted that wherever the legislation alludes to a 'judgment debtor', it refers also to the 'director' or 'officer of the juristic person' and, for all practical purposes, the juristic person is placed in the same position with regard to s 65 proceedings as a debtor who is a natural person.

The court may, at any stage of the proceedings, if the director or officer ceases to be a director or officer of the juristic person or absconds, at the request of the judgment debtor replace the director or officer by any other person who at the time of the replacement is a director or officer of the juristic person, and the proceedings then continue as though there has been no replacement.[90]

---

[90] Section 65A(3).

Chapter 20

ADMINISTRATION ORDERS

1 INTRODUCTION

Administration orders may be regarded as a form of insolvency proceeding in which the estate of the debtor is not sequestrated but an administrator is appointed to take charge of his or her affairs and to satisfy the claims due to his or her creditors.[1]

The underlying idea is that the court comes to the assistance of a debtor who is unable to discharge his or her financial obligations, without sequestrating his or her estate. This procedure is especially useful where the debtor is in receipt of a regular salary, his or her business transactions are not large or complex and his or her burden of debt is reasonably small. Where, however, the debtor's financial affairs are in an extremely untidy state, with the result that an extensive investigation into them is necessary, the sequestration procedure provided by the law of insolvency should generally be followed.

The administration procedure is statutorily regulated in considerable detail by s 74 of the Magistrates' Courts Act.[2] It is applied in the following instances:

(1) where a judgment debtor is unable immediately to satisfy a judgment obtained against him or her in court;[3]

(2) where no judgment has yet been obtained against a debtor but the debtor has insufficient cash on hand to meet his or her financial obligations and, in addition, lacks sufficient realisable assets capable of satisfying his or her debts;[4] or

(3) where a judgment debtor is brought before the court in terms of s 65 for an investigation into his or her financial position[5] and at such investigation applies for an order placing his or her estate under administration.

From the provisions of s 74 it is apparent that the amount owed by the debtor must be relatively small in order for his or her estate to be placed under administration. Section 74(1)(b) provides that the total amount of all his or her debts must not exceed the amount determined by the minister from time to time by notice in the *Gazette*. This amount is at present R50 000, as determined in GN 217 in *GG* 37477 of 27 March 2014. An administration order, however, will not be invalid only because at any time the total amount of the debtor's indebtedness may be found to exceed R50 000. In that event, however, the court may, if it deems fit, rescind the order.[6]

Should the debtor's circumstances bring him or her within any of the three categories mentioned above and his or her total indebtedness does not exceed R50 000, the court granting judgment against him or her or the court of the district in which the debtor resides, carries on business or is employed may, upon

---

[1] *Madari v Cassim* 1950 (2) SA 35 (D) at 38; *Ex parte Van den Berg* 1950 (1) SA 816 (W) at 817; *Cape Town Municipality v Dunne* 1964 (1) SA 741 (C) at 744. The debt must be 'due' and not merely payable in the future. *Du Mata v Firstrand Bank Ltd* 2002 (6) SA 506 (W). Also *Fortuin & others v Various Creditors* 2004 (2) SA 570 (C); *Ex parte August* 2004 (3) SA 268 (W). The debtor has to disclose debts which will become payable in the future and these play a role in whether the order is granted. *Mnisi v Magistrate, Middelburg & others* [2004] 3 All SA 734 (T).

[2] It is submitted that s 74 is outdated and requires urgent revision, especially in view of prevalent abuse of the current administration order regime.

[3] Section 74(1)(a).

[4] Ibid.

[5] Cf chapter 19 above.

[6] Section 74(2).

application by the debtor or under s 65I, subject to such conditions as the court may deem fit with regard to security, preservation or disposal of assets, realisation of movables subject to hypothec or otherwise, make an administration order providing for the administration of his or her estate and the payment of his or her debts in instalments or otherwise.[7]

An administration order is therefore an order made by the court when the debtor, as it were, comes to court and says: 'I am unable to solve my own financial problems; please help me by appointing an administrator to take charge of my estate.'

2   THE PROCEDURE FOR OBTAINING AN ADMINISTRATION ORDER

The procedure for bringing the application is a simple one: by drafting a document in accordance with the format prescribed in Annexure 1 Form 44:

No. 44

Application for an Administration Order—Section 74(1) of the Magistrates' Courts Act, 1944 (Act 32 of 1944)

* For use in the District Court

In the Magistrate's Court for the District of ....

held at ....

Case No .... of 20......

In the matter between

APPLICATION FOR AN ADMINISTRATION ORDER BY

.... (Full names and surname)

1   The Clerk of the Court at ....

2   ....

Take notice that I shall apply to the above-mentioned Court on the .... day of .... 20 ...., at .... (time) ...., to make an order providing for the administration of my estate under the provisions of section 74 of the Magistrates' Courts Act, 1944.

A full statement of my affairs confirmed by an affidavit in support of this application is attached.

Dated at .... this .... day of ...., 20......

....

Applicant

Full address ....

....

NOTE: Section 74A(5) of the Magistrates' Courts Act, 1944, provides that the applicant shall deliver to each of his or her creditors at least 3 days before the date appointed for the hearing, personally or by registered post a copy of this application and statement of affairs (Form 45) on which shall appear the case number under which this application was filed.

Together with this application, the debtor is required to submit a full statement of his or her affairs.[8] Section 74A(2) stipulates in detail all of the particulars that must be placed before the court together with the application for the administra-

---

[7] Section 74(1).
[8] Section 74A(1).

tion order. For the sake of convenience, Form 45 may be used to furnish the details of the debtor's affairs as required by the Act.

No. 45

Statement of Affairs of Debtor in an Application for an Administration Order—Section 65I(2) or 74A of the Magistrates' Courts Act, 1944 (Act 32 of 1944)

* Only for use in the District Court

Case No .... of 20......

In the application for an Administration Order of .... (herein-after referred to as the Applicant)

1. Surname of Applicant ....First names ....
    Date of birth .... Identity number ....

2. Residential address ....
    ....

3. Marital status .... If married, state whether
    in or out of community of property ....
    Full names of spouse ....
    Date of birth .... Identity number ....
    If Applicant and spouse are living apart, state from what date ....

4. Dependants:

Full names	*Age*	*Relationship*
....	....	....
....	....	....
....	....	....

5. Name and business address of employer:
    Applicant: Spouse:
    ....
    ....
    ....

6. If not employed furnish reasons:
    Applicant: ....   Spouse: ....
    ....
    ....
    ....

7. Occupation:
    Applicant: ....   Spouse: ....

8. Gross income:
    Applicant .... per week/month   Spouse .... per week/ month.

9. Full particulars of all deductions from income (by way of stop order or otherwise) supported as far as possible by written statements of employer:
    Applicant: Spouse:

Particulars	*Amount* R	*Particulars*	*Amount* R
....	....	....	....
....	....	....	....
....	....	....	....
Total		Total	

10. Detailed particulars of essential weekly or monthly expenses, including transport expenses:
    Applicant: Spouse:

Particulars	*Amount*	*Particulars*	*Amount*
	R		R
....	....	....	....
....	....	....	....
....	....	....	....
Total		Total	

11. Full particulars, supported by statements and copies of the agreements, of goods purchased under hire-purchase agreements in terms of the Hire-Purchase Act 1942 (Act 36 of 1942), or credit agreements in terms of the Credit Agreements Act 1980 (Act 75 of 1980) or the National Credit Act 2005 (Act 34 of 2005) and not paid for in full:

Particulars (purchase price must be stated)	Balance R	Instalments R	Payable weekly/ monthly	Date when will be paid for in full	Reason why provision should be made for remaining Instalment
....	....	....	....	....	....
....	....	....	....	....	....
....	....	....	....	....	....

12. Full particulars of assets purchased under a written agreement (excluding an agreement referred to in item 11) which are not paid for in full.

Particulars	Balance R	Instalments R	Payable weekly/ monthly	Date when will be paid for in full	Reasons why the Administra-tion Order should provide for the payment thereof
....	....	....	....	....	....
....	....	....	....	....	....
....	....	....	....	....	....

13. Full particulars and estimated value of security which creditors have in respect of debt which the Applicant or applicant's spouse is liable for (the name and address of any other person who, in addition to the debtor, is liable for the debt must also be stated):

    ....
    ....
    ....
    ....
    ....

14. Full particulars of immovable property of the Applicant or spouse which is mortgaged:
    Mortgage ....
    Address ....

Description	Market value R	Balance of the bond(s) thereon R	Date when will be paid for in full	Instalments payable	Reasons why the Administration Order should provide for the payment thereof
....	....	....	....	....	....
....	....	....	....	....	....
....	....	....	....	....	....
....	....	....	....	....	....
....	....	....	....	....	....

15. Full particulars of movable property of applicant or spouse:

Description	*Estimated value* R
....	....
....	....
....	....
....	....

16. Full particulars of outstanding claims, bills, investments, bonds or other securities in favour of Applicant investing monies in a savings or other account with a bank or elsewhere:

Name and address of debtor or institution	*Particulars*	*Amount* R
....	....	....
....	....	....
....	....	....
....	....	....
....	....	....
....	....	....

17. All movable property not already stated, including goods pawned, mortgaged, subject to retention or attached for the execution of a judgment:

Description	Estimated value R	Nature of encumbrance if any	Amount of debt encumbered for R	Name and address of creditor in favour of whom encumbered
....	....	....	....	....
....	....	....	....	....
....	....	....	....	....
....	....	....	....	....
....	....	....	....	....

18. If an Administration Order was at any time granted in respect of Applicant's estate, state:

Date of expiry ....

Date when set aside ....

Reasons ....

....

19. If an Administration Order is granted, state the amount of the weekly, monthly or other instalments wh ich the Applicant offers to pay towards settlement of the debts mentioned in the list of creditors in the annexure to this statement:

R .... with effect from .... and weekly/ monthly thereafter, or ....

.... from I

...., from ....

declare under oath:

(1) I am the Applicant.

(2) A judgment /judgments has/have been obtained against me and I am unable forthwith to pay the amount(s), or to meet my financial obligations.

(3) I have no sufficient assets capable of attachment to satisfy such judgment(s) or obligations.

(4) The total amount of all my debts due does not exceed R50 000.

(5) All particulars contained in this statement and in the list of creditors in the Annexure to this statement, as well as the amounts due to them separately, are, to the best of my knowledge, true and correct and that the statement contains all particulars, assets, income and debts of me and my spouse, including my obligations.

....

Signature

1. I certify that before administering the prescribed oath I asked the Deponent the following questions and wrote down his/her answers in his/her presence:

(a) Do you know and understand the contents of the above declaration? ....

(b) Do you have any objection to taking the prescribed oath? ....

(c) Do you consider the prescribed oath to be binding on your conscience? ....

2. I certify that the Deponent has acknowledged that he/she knows and understands the contents of this declaration which was sworn to before me and the Deponent's signature was placed thereon in my presence.

....

Commissioner of Oaths

....

Area

....

Designation if appointment is held ex *officio*

ANNEXURE TO STATEMENT OF AFFAIRS (FORM 45)—LIST OF CREDITORS									
Full name and address of creditor	Nature of claim and balance due	Date payable	Amount payable in instalments	Weekly/ Monthly	Court	Case number	If court order is granted i.r.o. claim, full particulars about order, including particulars of emoluments attachment order or garnishee order	Balance R	Date on Which obligations terminate
....	....	....	....	....	....	....	....	....	....
....	....	....	....	....	....	....	....	....	....
....	....	....	....	....	....	....	....	....	....
....	....	....	....	....	....	....	....	....	....

Attention is directed to the provisions of section 74A(2)*(e)* of the Magistrates' Courts Act, 1944. All the Applicant's creditors and their addresses must be stated in the list in which a clear distinction shall be made between –

(i) debts, the whole amount of which is owning, including judgment debts payable in instalments in terms of a Court Order, an Emoluments Attachment Order or a Garnishee Order; and

(ii) obligations which are payable in future in periodical payments or otherwise or which will become payable under a maintenance order, agreement, stop order or otherwise, and in which the nature of such periodical payments is specified in each case or when the obligations will be payable and how they are then to be paid, the balance owing in each case and when, in each case, the obligation will terminate.

From this example it is clear that the debtor must affirm under oath that to the best of his or her knowledge, the names of all of his or her creditors and the amounts owed by him or her to each of them severally are set forth in the statement and that the declarations made in the statement are true.[9]

If the debtor is illiterate, the clerk of the court assists the debtor to complete the statement on payment of the fee prescribed in the rules.[10]

Once the application is completed, the debtor lodges it with the clerk of the court and delivers it personally or by registered post to each of his or her creditors, at least three days before the date appointed for the hearing, a copy of the application and statement containing the case number under which the original application was filed.[11]

3 THE HEARING OF THE APPLICATION FOR ADMINISTRATION

The application is heard by a magistrate. The debtor either appears in person before the court or is represented by his or her legal adviser. The hearing usually takes place in the s 65 court. Only the parties concerned, ie the debtor and any possible creditors and their legal representatives, are present at the hearing of the application.[12]

The court investigates all of the circumstances having a bearing upon the envisaged administration order.

---

[9] Section 74A(3).

[10] Section 74A(4).

[11] Section 74A(5).

[12] Section 74B(1)*(a)* provides that a creditor, whether or not he or she has received notice in terms of s 74A(5), may attend the hearing. He or she may provide proof of the claim due to him or her and object to any debt listed by the debtor in the statement of his or her affairs referred to in s 74A(1).

The magistrate is assisted in arriving at a decision by the provisions of the Act relating to the onus of proof. The Act stipulates that every debt listed by the debtor in the statement completed by him or her is deemed to be proved subject to any amendments made to the statement by the court, unless any creditor raises some objection to the debt or the court rejects it or requires it to be substantiated by evidence.[13]

On the other hand, any creditor to whose claim an objection is raised by the debtor or by any other creditor or who is required by the court to substantiate his or her debt with evidence must provide proof of the debt allegedly due to him or her.[14]

The court has the power at the hearing to defer proof of debt and postpone consideration of the application for an administration order or to proceed to deal with the application and, if an administration order is granted, the debt when subsequently proved is added to the debts listed.[15]

The following persons may examine the debtor:[16]

(1) the court;
(2) any creditor whose claim has been acknowledged or proved; or
(3) by leave of the court, any creditor the proof of whose claim has been deferred. The legal representatives of the creditors may also conduct the examination.

The debtor may, however, be examined only in regard to the following four points:

(1) his or her assets and liabilities;
(2) his or her present and future income and that of his or her spouse living with him or her;
(3) his or her standard of living and the possibility of economising; and
(4) any other matter that the court may deem relevant.[17]

If at the hearing it appears to the court that any debt other than a debt on the ground of or arising from a judgment debt is a matter of contention between the debtor and the creditor or between the creditor and any other creditor of the debtor, the court may, upon enquiry into the objection, allow or reject the debt or a part of it.[18] The creditor whose debt has been rejected may, notwithstanding the fact that legal proceedings against the debtor are normally restricted by s 74P, institute proceedings or proceed with an action already instituted in respect of such debt.[19] Should the creditor obtain judgment, the debt is added to the list of proven debts.[20]

If it is proved that any administration order has been rescinded within the preceding period of six months because of the debtor's non-compliance with the

---

[13] Section 74B(1)*(b)*.
[14] Section 74B(1)*(c)*.
[15] Section 74B(1)*(d)*.
[16] Section 74B(1)*(e)*.
[17] Ibid. Cf also *Els v Els* 1967 (3) SA 207 (T) at 210E–F, where it was stated that the interrogation of the debtor must be strictly confined to these four points.
[18] Section 74B(2).
[19] Section 74B(3).
[20] Section 74B(4).

terms of the order, no administration order is granted unless the debtor is able to prove to the satisfaction of the court that his or her non-compliance with the order was not wilful.[21]

4 THE ADMINISTRATION ORDER

If the court grants an administration order, the order must take the prescribed form. The content of the order is regulated by s 74C and its form by Annexure 1 Form 51. The form of the administration order is as follows:

No. 51

Application Order—Section 74(1) of the Magistrates' Courts Act, 1944 (Act 32 of 1944)

* For use in the District Court

In the Magistrate's Court for the District of .... held at

.... this .... day of .... 20......

Case No .... of 20......

In the application of

.... (hereinafter referred to as the applicant):

1   It is ordered—

   (a)   that the estate of the applicant be placed under administration in terms of section 74 of the Magistrates' Courts Act, 1944;

   (b)   that .... from .... be appointed Administrator of the Applicant's estate in terms of section 74E on condition that he or she gives the following security for the due and prompt payment by him or her to all the parties entitled thereto of all the moneys which come into his or her possession by virtue of this appointment

      ....

   (c)   that the Applicant pays the amount of R............ weekly/monthly to the Administrator for distribution among the creditors. The first payment is to be made on or before the .... day of .... 20...... and weekly/ monthly thereafter on or before every ..../the .... of each month;

   (d)

      ....

   (e)

      ....

2   Authority is granted—

   (a)   for the issue of an Emoluments Attachment Order under section 65J of the Magistrates' Courts Act, 1944, against the Applicant's employer for payment to the Administrator of the said amount on or before the said times until the costs of administration and the creditors have been paid in full. This authority is suspended on condition that ....

   (b)   for the issue of a garnishee order under section 72 of the Magistrates' Courts Act, 1944, against .... from .... This authority is suspended on condition that ....

   (c)   for the realisation and distribution of the proceeds of the following assets among the creditors:

      (i)   ....

---

[21] Section 74B(5).

    (ii) ....

    (iii) ....

    (iv) of the following assets that are the subject of an agreement in terms of the Hire-Purchase Act, 1942 (Act 36 of 1942) or the Credit Agreements Act, 1980 (Act 75 of 1980) or the National Credit Act, 2005 (Act 34 of 2005), with the written permission of the seller:

        (aa) ....

        (bb) ....

  (d) for the return of the following assets to the seller in terms of the Hire-Purchase Act, 1942 or section 17 of the Credit Agreements Act, 1980 or provisions of the National Credit Act, 2005:

    (i) ....

    (ii) ....

  (e) other (give details) ....;

Dated at .... this .... day of ...., 20......

....

Magistrate

NOTE: In terms of section 74F(1) of the Magistrates' Courts Act, 1944, the Clerk of the Court shall hand or send by registered post a copy of this order to the debtor and in terms of section 74F(2) the Administrator shall forward a copy hereof by registered post to each creditor whose name is mentioned in the Debtor's statement of affairs (Form 45) or who has given proof of a debt.

The content of the administration order that may be made by the court appears from this form.

First, the court orders that the debtor's estate be placed under administration. Secondly, the administrator is nominated and appointed. Thirdly, the amount that the debtor is obliged to pay to the administrator is stipulated. This amount is determined in accordance with the method described in s 74C(2).

It is important to note in particular that s 74C(2)*(b)* makes provision for the court to issue an administration order in terms of which the debtor is allowed an unencumbered residue sufficient to discharge the monthly payments that the debtor is obliged to make under a credit agreement as defined in s 1 of the National Credit Act 34 of 2005 (NCA). The court has a discretion to take such payments into account and in this respect, will be guided by whether the goods in issue are luxury items or necessities, whether the debtor is able to earn income through his or her use of such goods and the size of the amount already paid off on them.[22]

The same discretion is likewise afforded the court by s 74C(2)*(d)* in relation to a mortgage bond or any other written agreement for the purchase of an asset in terms of which the liabilities under it are payable in instalments. The court issues an administration order leaving a sufficient unencumbered residue of his or her income available to the debtor if the court is of the opinion in all the circumstances that the instalments payable are reasonable in view of the judgment debtor's income and the amounts due by him or her to other creditors, or that it is desirable to safeguard the mortgaged property or the asset to which the written agreement relates.

---

[22] *Carletonville Huishoudelike Voorsieners (Edms) Bpk v Van Vuuren en 'n ander* 1962 (2) SA 296 (T) at 301D–E.

The court may take into account the income of the debtor's spouse who lives with him or her in determining the amount reasonably required by the debtor for his or her necessary expenses and those of his or her dependants where the debtor is married in community of property.[23]

As part of the administration order, the court may also authorise the issuing of an emoluments attachment order or a garnishee order.[24]

Where an administration order provides for the payment of instalments out of future emoluments or income, the court authorises the issuing of an emoluments attachment order in terms of s 65J in order to attach emoluments at present or in future owing or accruing to the debtor by or from his or her employer or the issue of a garnishee order under s 72 in order to attach any debt at present or in future owing or accruing to the debtor by or from any other person (excluding the State). The court may suspend such authorisation on whatever conditions the court deems just and reasonable.[25]

5   THE APPOINTMENT OF THE ADMINISTRATOR

When the court nominates and appoints a person as administrator, the appointment becomes effective only after a copy of the administration order has been handed to him or her or sent to him or her by registered post. In the event of him or her being required as administrator to give security, the appointment comes into effect only after he or she has done so.[26]

Security is required of an administrator who is not an officer of the court or a practitioner. Before a copy of the administration order is handed to him or her or sent to him or her by registered post, he or she gives security to the satisfaction of the court and thereafter as required by the court for the due and prompt payment by him or her to the parties entitled to it of all monies which come into his or her possession by virtue of his or her appointment as an administrator.[27]

In cases where the administrator gives or has given security to the satisfaction of the court for the proper performance of his or her duties, he or she is not obliged to give further security in respect of his or her appointment as administrator of the estate of a *particular* debtor.[28] An administrator may thus give security in general for the proper discharge of his or her obligations in respect of every estate for which he or she may be appointed.

---

[23] Section 74C(3).

[24] Emoluments attachment orders are dealt with in chapter 19 above, while garnishee orders are dealt with in chapter 17 above.

[25] Section 74D.

[26] Section 74E(1). As to the discretion of the Court in appointing the administrator, see *Oosthuizen v Landdros, Senekal, en andere* 2003 (4) SA 450 (O).

[27] Section 74E(3).

[28] Section 74E(4).

6 NOTICE OF GRANTING THE ADMINISTRATION ORDER AND OBJECTIONS TO IT

As soon as an administration order is granted, the clerk of the court hands a copy of the order to the administrator or sends it to him or her by registered post.[29]

The administrator in turn forwards a copy of the administration order by registered post to every creditor whose name is mentioned by the debtor in the statement of his or her affairs or who has given proof of a debt.[30]

A creditor who has not received notice of the application for an administration order may object to any debt listed with the order or to the manner in which the order directs payment to be made.[31] Within 20 days after the granting of the administration order has come to his or her attention,[32] the creditor seeking to object must give notice of his or her objection and the grounds for it to the clerk of the court, the debtor and the administrator and, if he or she objects to the inclusion of any debt, also to the creditor concerned.[33]

The court may consider the objection raised by the creditor and:
(1) uphold it;
(2) refuse it; or
(3) postpone consideration of it for hearing after notice given to the persons concerned and on such conditions as to costs or otherwise as the court may deem fit.[34]

7 THE LIST OF CREDITORS AND DEBTS AND ADDITIONS TO IT

As soon as possible, the administrator draws up a complete list on which appears the case number under which the application for an administration order has been filed, and which contains the names of the creditors and the amounts owing to them severally as at the date on which the administration order was granted. This list is lodged with the clerk of the court.[35] The list contains also the names of creditors added to the list in terms of ss 74B(2), 74F and 74G(2)–(6). These are the names of all creditors accepted by the debtor.[36]

This list of creditors is open to inspection by the creditors or their attorneys at the office of the clerk of the court and the office of the administrator at any time during office hours.[37]

A creditor may object to any debt included in the list of creditors.[38]

The creditor who wishes to object must do so within 15 days after he or she has received a copy of the administration order.[39] He or she notifies the administrator of his or her objection in writing, setting out the ground on which the objection is based.

---

[29] Section 74F(1).
[30] Section 74F(2).
[31] Section 74F(3).
[32] Rule 48(1).
[33] Section 74F(3).
[34] Section 74F(4).
[35] Section 74G(1).
[36] *Doyle v Bradfied & another* 1964 (2) SA 430 (T) at 433H.
[37] Section 74G(10)*(a)*.
[38] Section 74G(10)*(b)*.
[39] Rule 48(2).

When an objection is raised, the administrator obtains from the clerk of the court a suitable day and time for the hearing of the objection by the court and thereupon notifies in writing the objecting creditor, the debtor and any other creditors involved of the day and time set aside for the hearing.[40]

It may happen that a creditor wishes to provide proof of a debt owing before the making of an administration order and not listed in the order. He or she lodges his or her claim in writing with the administrator, who thereupon gives the debtor notice of the claim.[41]

The administrator notifies the debtor of this additional claim using the following form:[42]

No. 47

Notice to Debtor that an Additional Creditor has Lodged a Claim Against Him for a Debt Owing Before the Making of the Administration Order—Section 74G(2) of the Magistrates' Courts Act, 1944 (Act 32 of 1944)

* For use in the District Court

In the Magistrate's Court for the District of ....

held at ....

Case No .... of 20......

To: ....(Debtor)

....(Address)

....

....

Take notice that—

....

....

(name and address of creditor) lodged a claim in terms of section 74G(2) of the Magistrates' Courts Act, 1944, for the amount of R............... in respect of .... (particulars of claim) which is not listed in the administration order made against you on the ....
day of .... 20...... in the Magistrate's Court at ....

Kindly notify me in writing whether you admit or dispute this claim on or before the ....
day of .... 20...... Please note that if you admit the claim or no reply is received from you on or before the said date, this claim shall be deemed to be proved, subject to the right of any other creditor who has not received notice of the claim to object to the debt, and shall be added to the list of names of your creditors who share *pro rata* in the payments made by you in terms of the Administration Order.

Dated at .... this .... day of ...., 20......

....

Administrator

If the debtor admits the claim or does not dispute it, the claim is deemed proven, subject to the right of any other creditor who has not received notice of the claim

---

[40] Rule 48(3).
[41] Section 74G(2).
[42] Annexure 1 Form 47.

to object to the debt. The administrator lodges with the clerk of the court a notice adding to the list the name of the creditor and the amount of the debt due to him or her.[43]

The notice lodged by the administrator with the clerk of the court reads as follows:[44]

No. 49

Notice to Add an Additional Creditor to the List of Creditors of a Person Under Administration—Section 74G(3) and 74H(2) of the Magistrates' Courts Act, 1944 (Act 32 of 1944)

* For use in the District Court

In the Magistrate's Court for the District of ....

held at ....

Case No .... of 20......

To: The Clerk of the Court

....

....

Administration Order against ....

Kindly add the name of .... from

.... as a creditor to the

list of creditors sharing *pro rata* in the payments in terms of the Administration Order for the

amount of R...........in respect of.................................

Dated at .... this .... day of ...., 20......

....

Administrator

The administrator thereupon also notifies the new creditor in terms of s 74G(3) that his or her name and the debt due to him or her have been added to the list of creditors of the person whose estate has been placed under administration. This is done using the following form:[45]

No. 50

Notice to Creditor that His or Her Name has been Added to the List of Creditors of a Person under Administration—Section 74G(3) and 74H(2) of the Magistrates' Courts Act, 1944 (Act 32 of 1944)

* For use in the District Court

In the Magistrate's Court for the District of ....

held at ....

Case No .... of 20......

To ....

....

....

Administration Order against ....

---

[43] Section 74G(3).
[44] Annexure 1 Form 49.
[45] Annexure 1 Form 50.

> The above-mentioned Debtor admitted or did not dispute your claim against him/her for the amount of R................................ and your name and the amount due to you have been added to the list of creditors sharing *pro rata* in payments in terms of the Administration Order. Kindly note that other creditors may still object against the debt so listed. In this event, you will be notified.
>
> A copy of the Administration Order issued against the debtor on the .... day of .... 20 in the Magistrate's Court at .... is attached/has already been received by you.
>
> Date at .... this .... day of ...., 20......
>
> ....
>
> Administrator

It may, of course, happen that the debtor does not admit the claim lodged by the creditor but disputes it. If that is the case, the debtor must give notice in writing to his or her administrator that he or she disputes the creditor's claim. The administrator notifies the creditor that his or her claim is being disputed and the creditor may request the clerk of the court to appoint a day and time for the hearing of the objection by the court. The creditor is then required to notify the debtor in writing of the day and time of the hearing.[46]

At the hearing of the objection raised by the debtor to the creditor's claim, the court may:
(1)   refuse the claim as a whole;
(2)   allow the claim as a whole or in part;
(3)   require that the claim be supported by evidence; or
(4)   postpone the hearing on such conditions as it may deem fit.[47]

If the court allows a claim as a whole or in part, the debt, to the extent to which it has been allowed, is added to the list of creditors and debts.[48]

If, before an administration order was granted, any person sold goods to the debtor under a credit agreement defined in s 1 of the NCA, he or she is entitled to demand, because of the debtor's failure to comply with the agreement, immediate payment of the sum of the purchase price still owing and the credit grantor advises the administrator of his election in writing, the following occurs:

The agreement is deemed to create a hypothec on the goods in favour of the supplier by which the amount still owing to him or her in terms of the agreement is secured. Any term of the agreement with regard to the credit grantor's right, in consequence of the debtor's non-compliance with any term of the agreement, to dissolve or terminate the agreement or with regard to the credit grantor's right to the return of the goods to which the agreement relates is not enforceable, notwithstanding anything to the contrary contained in any law.[49]

In this way, the debtor remains in possession of the goods and the claim of the creditor remains secured. This provision must be viewed together with that of s 74C(2)(*b*), that the court making an administration order may allow the debtor a

---

[46] Section 74G(4).
[47] Section 74G(5).
[48] Section 74G(6).
[49] Section 74G(7).

sufficient unencumbered residue to permit him or her to meet his or her financial obligations under a credit agreement.

On the other hand, the court may also, in view of the particular circumstances of the case, authorise the credit grantor to take possession of the goods and to sell them by public auction by an auctioneer nominated by the court after he or she has given written notice to the administrator and to all of the creditors of the time and place of the sale and, if the court has so ordered, after publishing the notice in one or more newspapers designated by the court. The court may also direct, if the credit grantor, credit receiver and administrator so agree, that the goods be sold by private treaty.[50]

Where the credit grantor has sold the goods in terms of a court order and the sale was by public auction, he or she forthwith lodges the auction list with the administrator and pays to the administrator the amount of the proceeds of the sale in excess of the amount of his or her claim and the costs connected with the sale. If the net proceeds are insufficient to pay his or her debt in full, he or she may lodge a claim with the administrator in respect of the balance of the purchase price owing to him or her for inclusion in the list of creditors entitled to share in the pro rata distribution of funds received by the administrator.[51]

8 INCLUSION OF A CREDITOR IN THE LIST AFTER THE GRANTING OF THE ADMINISTRATION ORDER

Reference has already been made to the fact that a person who was a creditor of the debtor *prior to* the grant of the administration order may lodge his or her claim in writing with the administrator after the administration order has come to his or her attention.

If, however, a person becomes a creditor of the debtor *after* the grant of the administration order and he or she desires to provide proof of his or her debt, he or she lodges his or her claim in writing with the administrator, who thereupon advises the debtor of the claim.[52]

One must bear in mind that s 74S(1) provides that it is an offence for a person who is subject to an administration order to incur a debt without disclosing that he or she is subject to an administration order.

The administrator uses the following form to notify the debtor under an administration order that such a creditor has lodged a claim:[53]

---

[50] Section 74G(8).
[51] Section 74G(9).
[52] Section 74H(1).
[53] Annexure 1 Form 48.

No. 48

Notice to Debtor that a Creditor has Lodged a Claim for a Debt Owing after Granting of the Administration Order—Section 74H(1) of the Magistrates' Courts Act, 1944 (Act 32 of 1944)

* For use in the District Court

In the Magistrate's Court for the District of ....

held at ....

Case No .... of 20......

To: .... (Debtor)

.... (Address)

....

....

Take notice that—

....

(name and address of Creditor) lodged a claim for the amount of R.............. in respect of .... (particulars of claim) as a result of which he or she allegedly became your creditor after the Administration Order was issued against you on the day of .... 20...... in the Magistrate's Court at ....

Kindly notify me in writing on or before the .... day of .... 20 .... whether you admit or dispute this claim. Please note that if you admit the claim or no reply is received from you on or before the said date, this claim shall be deemed to be proved, subject to the right of any other creditor who has not received notice of the claim to object to the debt, and shall be added to the list of names of your creditors who share *pro rata* in the payments made by you in terms of the Administration Order.

Dated at .... this .... day of ...., 20......

....

Administrator

If the debtor admits the claim or does not dispute it within the time allowed in the notice, the claim is deemed proven and the administrator adds the claim to the list of claims owing by the debtor by means of a notice lodged with the clerk of the court, in which is set out the name of the creditor and the amount of the debt owing to him or her. The administrator thereupon notifies the creditor that his or her name and the debt owing to him or her have been added to the list. The creditor is not, however, entitled to a dividend in terms of the administration order until the persons who were creditors at the time when the administration order was granted have been paid in full.[54]

If, however, the debtor disputes the claim within the period allowed in the notice, the steps discussed above must again be followed in order to allow the court to decide upon the validity of the claim.[55]

If the court allows the claim as a whole or in part, the creditor is again not entitled to a dividend in terms of the administration order until the persons who

---

[54] Section 74H(2).
[55] Section 74H(3).

were creditors at the time when the administration order was granted have been paid in full.[56]

In the case where the credit grantor in terms of a credit agreement as defined in s 1 of the NCA sells and delivers goods to the debtor after the granting of an administration order and desires to provide proof of debt, precisely the same procedure is followed as that described above.[57]

9   PAYMENTS IN TERMS OF THE ADMINISTRATION ORDER

The debtor pays the administrator the amounts of the weekly or monthly or other payments that he or she is required to make in terms of the administration order.[58]

If the debtor fails to make the payments due by him or her in terms of the administration order, the same procedure applies as that following upon a judgment debtor's failure to pay a judgment debt in instalments after he or she has been ordered by the court to do so. That procedure, broadly speaking, consists of an investigation by the court into the debtor's failure to make the payments due by him or her at a hearing to which the debtor has been summoned. The s 65 procedure discussed in the previous chapter may then be applied.[59]

If, in addition to the administration order, the court has authorised the issuing of an emoluments attachment order or a garnishee order[60] and has suspended its authorisation conditionally and the debtor fails to comply with the conditions of suspension, the administrator may lodge a certificate to this effect with the clerk of the court. The clerk of the court thereupon issues the emoluments attachment order or garnishee order, as the case may be.[61]

An emoluments attachment order or garnishee order is prepared by the administrator or his or her attorney and signed by the administrator or his or her attorney and by the clerk of the court. The order is served on the garnishee by the sheriff by registered post.[62]

After an emoluments attachment order or garnishee order has been served upon the garnishee, he or she is obliged to pay to the administrator the amounts concerned as provided by the order and such payments constitute a first preference against the debtor's income.[63]

The provisions of s 65J(4) to (8) and (10) apply *mutatis mutandis* to the emoluments attachment order issued in addition to the administration order.[64]

10   THE DUTIES OF THE ADMINISTRATOR

An administrator is obliged to collect the payments to be made in terms of the administration order concerned and keep up to date a list (which must be available

---

[56] Ibid.
[57] Section 74H(4).
[58] Section 74I(1).
[59] Section 74I(2).
[60] Emoluments attachment orders are discussed in chapter 19 and garnishee orders in chapter 17 above.
[61] Section 74I(3).
[62] Section 74I(4).
[63] Section 74I(5)*(a)*.
[64] Section 74I(5)*(b)*.

for inspection, free of charge, by the debtor and creditors or their attorneys during office hours) of all payments and other funds received by him or her from or on behalf of the debtor, indicating the amount and date of each payment. He or she distributes these payments pro rata among the creditors at least once every three months, unless the creditors otherwise agree or the court orders otherwise in any particular case.[65]

If any debt or the balance of a debt is less than R10, the administrator may in his or her discretion pay the debt in full if that will facilitate the distribution of funds in his or her possession.[66]

The administrator must pay out claims that would enjoy preference under the laws relating to insolvency in the order prescribed by those laws.[67]

An administrator may, out of the monies which he or she controls, pay any urgent or extraordinary medical, dental or hospital expenses incurred by the debtor after the date of the administration order.[68]

Every distribution account in respect of the periodical payments and other funds received by an administrator is numbered consecutively and bears the case number under which the administration order has been filed. The account must be in the form prescribed by the rules, signed by the administrator and lodged at the office of the clerk of the court, where it may be inspected free of charge by the debtor and the creditors or their attorneys during office hours.[69]

The distribution account reads as follows:[70]

No. 52
Distribution Account in terms of Section 74J(5) of the Magistrates' Courts Act, 1944
(Act 32 of 1944)

* For use in the District Court

Distribution Account No ....

To: The Clerk of the Court

....

....

Case No .... of 20......

Administration Order against ....

Distribution account for the period .... to ....

		A	B	C
A	(1) Amount payable to creditors in terms of the administration order/outstanding amount carried forward from previous statement		-	-
	(2) Total amount due to additional creditors listed after granting of administration order/since lodging of previous statement		-	-

---

[65] Section 74J(1). For a detailed treatment, see now *Weiner NO v Broekhuysen* 2003 (4) SA 301 (SCA).
[66] Section 74J(2).
[67] Section 74J(3).
[68] Section 74J(4).
[69] Section 74J(5).
[70] Annexure 1 Form 52.

				A	B	C
	(3)	Interest			-	-
B	(1)	Administration costs paid for the said period in terms of-section 74L				-
	(2)	Claims paid during the said period that enjoy preference in-terms of section 74J(3)				-
	(3)	Urgent or extraordinary medical, dental or hospital expenses paid during the said period			-	-
	(4)	Other payments during the said period (supply details)		-		-
		Total				
				A	**B**	**C**
		Totals carried forward from previous page				
C		Total amount received by the Administrator during the said period		-	-	-
		Total of C minus total of B		-	-	
		Disposal for *pro rata* distribution				
		Pro rata distribution:				
		....*			-	-
		....*			-	-
		....*			-	-
		Total amount paid during the said period			-	-
		Total of A minus total of B			-	-
		Outstanding amount carried forward to next statement				

Dated at .... this .... day of ...., 20 ....

....
Administrator

* The names of creditors to whom *pro rata* amounts were paid by the Administrator during the said period to be inserted here. (The relevant amounts to be completed in column B.)

The distribution account is subject to review free of charge by any judicial officer at the request of any interested party, and the decision of the judicial officer is final.[71]

An administrator deposits all monies received by him or her from or on behalf of debtors whose estates are under administration:

(1) if he is not a practising attorney, in a separate trust account with any bank in the Republic, and no amount with which any such account is credited shall be deemed to be part of the administrator's assets or, in the event of his death or insolvency, of his deceased or insolvent estate; or

(2) if he is a practising attorney, in the trust account that he keeps in terms of s 33 of the Attorneys, Notaries and Conveyancers Admission Act 23 of 1934.[72]

An administrator who fails to carry out this duty commits an offence and on conviction may be sentenced to a fine not exceeding R500 or in default of payment to imprisonment for a period not exceeding six months.[73]

If, despite having received a registered letter of demand from the administrator, a debtor is at any time 14 days in arrear with the payment of any instalment and an

---

[71] Section 74J(6).

[72] Section 74J(7). Section 86 of the Legal Practice Act 28 of 2014 regulates attorneys' trust accounts. See the brief discussion of the Legal Practice Act in chapter 3.

[73] Section 74W.

emoluments attachment order or a garnishee order cannot be issued or has been applied for unsuccessfully, or if the debtor has disappeared, the administrator must immediately notify the creditors in writing of the fact and request their instructions.[74]

If the majority of the creditors instruct him or her to do so or fail to respond, the administrator must institute legal proceedings against the debtor for his or her committal for contempt of court or take such steps as may be necessary to trace the debtor who has disappeared.[75]

If the majority of the creditors instruct him or her to do so, the administrator must apply to court for the rescission of the administration order.[76]

If an administrator fails to lodge a distribution account with the clerk of the court within one month from the time when his or her obligation to do so commenced, any interested party may apply to the court for an order directing him or her to lodge a distribution account with the clerk of the court within the time laid down in the order or relieving him or her of his or her office as administrator.[77]

If an administrator has lodged a distribution account with the clerk of the court but has failed to pay any amount of money due to any creditor in terms of the account within one month thereafter, the court may upon the application of the creditor, order the administrator to pay the creditor the amount concerned within a fixed period and, furthermore, to pay to the debtor's estate an amount which is double the amount that he or she failed so to pay.[78]

Where the court directs the administrator to lodge the distribution account and/or where the court relieves him or her of his or her office or where the court directs him or her to pay an amount to the creditor, the court may, in addition, order the administrator to pay the costs occasioned by the creditor's application *de bonis propriis*.[79]

If any debt which was due at the time of the granting of an administration order in respect of a debtor's estate is paid in full or in part to the creditor by the debtor after the granting of the order otherwise than by way of payments in terms of the administration order, the payment is invalid. The administrator may recover the amount in question from the creditor unless the creditor proves that the payment was effected without his or her knowledge of the administration order. In addition, the creditor forfeits his or her claim against the estate of the debtor if the payment was effected at the request of the creditor whilst he or she was aware of the administration order.[80]

11 REALISATION OF THE DEBTOR'S ASSETS BY THE ADMINISTRATOR

The court may authorise an administrator to realise an asset of the estate under administration, with the exception of assets subject to a credit agreement as

---

[74] Section 74J(8).
[75] Section 74J(9).
[76] Section 74J(10).
[77] Section 74J(11).
[78] Section 74J(12).
[79] Section 74J(13). Cf chapter 16 above in relation to costs *de bonis propriis*.
[80] Section 74J(14).

defined in s 1 of the NCA,[81] or to return the asset to the credit grantor, and in granting such authorisation, the court may impose such conditions as it may deem fit.[82] If the credit provider as defined in s 1 of the NCA is obliged to pay to the debtor an amount in terms of the Act, that amount shall be paid to the administrator for pro rata distribution among the creditors.[83]

Whenever the court authorises the administrator to realise any asset, the court may amend the payments to be made in terms of the administration order accordingly.[84]

12 THE REMUNERATION AND EXPENSES OF THE ADMINISTRATOR

Before making a distribution, the administrator may:

- deduct from the money collected his or her necessary expenses and a remuneration determined in accordance with a tariff prescribed in Annexure 2 in para 1(*b*) of Part III of Table B;
- retain a portion of the money collected, in the manner and up to an amount prescribed by rule 48(4), to cover the costs that he or she may have to incur if the debtor is in default or disappears.[85]

These expenses and this remuneration may not exceed 12.5 per cent of the amount of collected monies received and such expenses and remuneration are subject to taxation by the clerk of the court and review by any judicial officer upon application by any interested party.[86]

13 THE FURNISHING OF INFORMATION BY THE ADMINISTRATOR

If any creditor applies for information about the progress made in regard to the administration, the administrator is obliged, upon payment of the fees prescribed in the rules, to supply such information as the creditor may desire.[87]

The administrator is obliged, upon payment of the prescribed fees, to supply any other person who applies for it with a copy of the debtor's application and statement of affairs or a list or account containing the names of the creditors and the amounts due to them or containing details of all payments made to creditors.[88]

14 THE FAILURE BY THE ADMINISTRATOR TO PERFORM HIS DUTIES

Should an administrator fail to take proper steps to enforce an administration order, any creditor may, by leave of the court, take those steps and the court may

---

[81] Except with written permission of the credit provider.
[82] Section 74K(1).
[83] Section 74K(3).
[84] Section 74K(4).
[85] Section 74L(1). See *African Bank Ltd v Weiner & others* 2004 (6) SA 570 (C); *Nashua Maritzburg v Groenewald* 2002 (4) SA 356 (W).
[86] Section 74L(2).
[87] Section 74M(*a*).
[88] Section 74M(*b*).

thereupon order the administrator to pay the costs of the creditor *de bonis propriis.*[89]

15 THE COSTS OF THE APPLICATION FOR AN ADMINISTRATION ORDER

Section 74O provides that, unless the court otherwise orders or the Magistrates' Courts Act otherwise provides, no costs in connection with any application for an administration order may be recovered from any person other than the administrator concerned, and then as a first claim against the monies controlled by him or her.

16 THE EFFECT OF AN ADMINISTRATION ORDER UPON OTHER LEGAL REMEDIES

As long as an administration order is of force and effect in respect of the estate of any debtor, no creditor has any remedy against the debtor or his or her property for the collection of money owing, except in regard to:

(1) a mortgage bond;
(2) any debt rejected by the court at the hearing of the application for the administration order; or
(3) by leave of the court and on such conditions as the court may impose.[90]

Any court in which proceedings have been instituted against a debtor in respect of any debt, except:

(1) a debt due under a mortgage bond; or
(2) a debt rejected by the court at the hearing of the application for the administration order

must, upon receiving notice of the administration order, suspend the proceedings but may grant costs already incurred by the creditor, and such costs may be added to the judgment debt.[91]

17 SUSPENSION, AMENDMENT OR RESCISSION OF THE ADMINISTRATION ORDER

The court under whose supervision an administration order is being executed may at any time upon application by the debtor or any interested party reopen the proceedings and call upon the debtor to appear for such further examination as the court may deem necessary. The court may thereupon, on good cause shown, suspend, amend or rescind the administration order, and when it suspends the order it may impose such conditions as it may deem just and reasonable.[92]

The court may at any time, at the request of the administrator in writing and with the written consent of the debtor, amend an administration order.[93]

---

[89] Section 74N. Cf chapter 16 above in regard to costs *de bonis propriis.*
[90] Section 74P(1).
[91] Section 74P(2).
[92] Section 74Q(1).
[93] Section 74Q(2).

Upon application for the rescission of an administration order the court may do one of the following:

(1) rescind the order;

(2) if it appears to the court that the debtor is unable to pay any instalment, suspend the order for such period and on such conditions as it may deem fit or amend the instalments to be paid in terms of the order and make the necessary amendments to any emoluments attachment order or garnishee order issued so as to ensure payment in terms of the administration order, or set aside the emoluments attachment order or garnishee order;

(3) authorise the issue of an emoluments attachment order or a garnishee order to ensure the payments in terms of the administration order; or

(4) set aside or amend an emoluments attachment order or a garnishee order issued so as to ensure payments in terms of the administration order.[94]

The order rescinding an administration order takes the following form:[95]

No. 52A

Rescission of Administration Order—Section 74Q of the Magistrates' Courts Act, 1944 (Act 32 of 1944)

* For use in the District Court

In the Magistrate's Court for the District of ....

held at .... this...day of...........................20......

Case No .... of 20......

Administration Order against .... (hereinafter referred to as the Debtor).

Whereas, after consideration of an application by the Debtor*/an interested party, ie ....*, it appears that good cause exists for the rescission of the Administration Order granted on the .... day of .... 20...... in above-mentioned Court, the said Administration Order is rescinded with effect from the .... day of .... 20......

Dated at .... this .... day of ....,, 20......

....

Magistrate

NOTE: (1) The Clerk of the Court must send a copy of this order by registered post to the Administrator.

(2) The Administrator must deliver personally or send by post a copy of this order to the Debtor and to each creditor and inform the latter of the Debtor's last known address.

* Delete which is not applicable.

A copy of this order is delivered personally or sent by post by the administrator to the debtor and to each creditor, who must also be informed by the administrator of the debtor's last-known address.[96]

When an order of court for the payment of a judgment debt in instalments or an emoluments attachment order or garnishee order has lapsed in consequence of the granting of an administration order, and the judgment debt in question has not been paid in full upon the rescission of the administration order, the court order,

---

[94] Section 74Q(3).

[95] Annexure 1 Form 52A.

[96] Section 74Q(4).

emoluments attachment order or garnishee order revives in respect of the judgment debt, unless the court otherwise orders.[97]

18 ADMINISTRATION ORDERS AND SEQUESTRATION

The granting of an administration order is no bar to the sequestration of the debtor's estate.[98]

As explained at the beginning of this chapter, an administration order constitutes a suitable method of dealing with relatively small debts due by a straightforwardly organised estate. As soon as the financial problems relating to the estate are such that complicated legal and factual issues have to be investigated in order to resolve the financial problems, or the total burden of debt exceeds R50 000, the sequestration of the estate offers a more suitable procedure.[99]

It would therefore seem apposite to weigh up the benefits of an administration order against those of a sequestration order, bearing in mind the particular facts of each case in order to decide which of the two possible procedures ought to be followed. Special attention must be given to the interests of creditors, in order to determine which of the two procedures would be the more suitable.[100]

19 THE INCURRING OF DEBTS BY A PERSON SUBJECT TO AN ADMINISTRATION ORDER

A debtor who is subject to an administration order and who, during the currency of the order, incurs any debt without disclosing that he or she is subject to an administration order, commits an offence for which he or she will be liable on conviction to imprisonment for a period not exceeding 90 days or to periodical imprisonment for a period not exceeding 2 160 hours in accordance with the laws relating to prisons. In addition, the court may, upon application by any interested person, set aside the administration order.[101]

The provisions of s 285 of the Criminal Procedure Act 51 of 1977 with regard to periodical imprisonment apply to periodical imprisonment imposed in accordance with this provision.[102]

---

[97] Section 74Q(5).
[98] Section 74R.
[99] *Cape Town Municipality v Dunne* 1964 (1) SA 741 (C) at 745F–G.
[100] *Madari v Cassim* 1950 (2) SA 35 (D) at 38; *Mamacos v Davids* 1976 (1) SA 19 (C) at 20C–D; *Gardee v Dhanmanta Holdings & others* 1978 (1) SA 1066 (N) at 1070. A contrary view was, however, adopted in *Trust Wholesalers & Woollens (Pty) Ltd v Mackan* 1954 (2) SA 109 (N) at 112, where the opinion was expressed that the court ought not to compare the various methods of dealing with the debtor's estate against each other.
[101] Section 74S(1).
[102] Section 74S(2).

20   THE CHANGE OF ADDRESS BY A DEBTOR SUBJECT TO AN ADMINISTRATION ORDER

A debtor subject to an administration order who changes his place of residence, business or employment must forthwith notify the clerk of the court and the administrator of his or her new place of residence, business or employment.[103]

When a debtor subject to an administration order moves to some other district, the court under whose supervision the administration order is being executed may transfer the proceedings to the court of that district.[104]

21   THE LAPSE OF THE ADMINISTRATION ORDER

As soon as the costs of the administration and the listed creditors have been paid in full, the administrator lodges a certificate to that effect with the clerk of the court and sends copies of the certificate to the creditors (who must also be informed in it of the debtor's last-known address), whereupon the administration order lapses.[105]

22   THE INTERRUPTION OF PRESCRIPTION

In the case of any debt mentioned in the statement of affairs submitted by the debtor in terms of s 74A(1), prescription is interrupted on the date on which the statement is lodged, and in the case a debt not mentioned in the statement, prescription is interrupted on the date on which the claim against the debtor is lodged with the court or the administrator.[106]

If, had it not been for these provisions, the relevant prescriptive period of a debt would have been completed on or before or within one year after the day on which the restriction of legal remedies during the period of operation of the administration order has ceased, the prescriptive period is not completed until a year after that day has elapsed.[107]

---

[103] Section 74T(1).
[104] Section 74T(2).
[105] Section 74U.
[106] Section 74V(1).
[107] Section 74V(2).

GENERAL INDEX